The Virtual Republic

McKenzie Wark lectures in media studies at Macquarie University and is a columnist for the *Australian*. His essays on media and culture have appeared in the *Age, New Statesman, 21C, Meanjin* and other journals.

The Virtual Republic

Australia's culture wars
of the 1990s

McKenzie Wark

ALLEN & UNWIN

This project has been assisted by the
Commonwealth Government through
the Australia Council, its arts funding
and advisory body.

First published in 1997 by
Allen & Unwin
9 Atchison Street
St Leonards NSW 2065
Australia

Phone: (61 2) 9901 4088
Fax: (61 2) 9906 2218
E-mail: frontdesk@allen-unwin.com.au
URL: http://www.allen-unwin.com.au

National Library of Australia
Cataloguing-in-Publication entry:

Wark, McKenzie, 1961– .
The virtual republic: Australia's culture wars of the 1990s.

Includes index.
ISBN 1 86448 520 5.

1. Australia—Civilisation—20th century. 2. Australia—
Intellectual life—20th century. I. Title.

306.0994

Set in 10.5/12 pt Arrus BT by DOCUPRO, Sydney
Printed by Australian Print Group, Maryborough, Vic.

10 9 8 7 6 5 4 3 2 1

Contents

Introducing the virtual republic

*We are never 'at home',
we are always outside ourselves.*

Michel de Montaigne

HAPPENING HITS

I feel like I am a safer driver when I hear something good on
the car radio. If I hear something interesting I can concentrate
on the driving. Without it, my thoughts tend to wander. I'm
one of those people who get caught up in their own thoughts
and can seem a bit vague. Not a good look at parties, and
certainly not while driving. The radio stops me wandering, in
thought and with the wheel.

It puzzles me why I don't get even more distracted with
the radio on than without it. I thought about this—not while
driving, you'll be relieved to know—and I think I have an idea
why. With the radio off, I'm in my own private thoughts. With
the radio on, I'm listening to something public; something
shared by other people. In the back of my mind somewhere,
the other listeners to the radio are also the other drivers on
the road so I'm mindful of them while driving and don't bump
into them.

The flaw with this deal is crap on the radio: bad songs,
loud ads, talkback bigots. Push the button and hear another
conversation. The other flaw is stuff on the radio that is *too*

good. I grew up on pop songs, so every now and then a good pop song will hook me in, and I'm all ears. Strangely, it doesn't seem to hurt the driving, but maybe I just imagine that in the euphoria of the song.

There's a song that made me cry and there's a song that made me want to shout like Johnny O'Keefe. Fortunately there wasn't anyone else in the car at the time. I'm not usually prone to emotional gestures but sometimes something just gets to me.

The song that made me cry was Melbourne songwriter Paul Kelly's 'From Little Things, Big Things Grow'. There's a verse in it about Gough Whitlam pouring dirt through the hands of an elder of the Gurindji Aboriginal people, as a gesture both of returning the land to his people and of expressing the link between the Prime Minister and the Gurindji in their love of the land. I'm getting emotional again just writing about it. I know this gesture is such a small thing, compared to what needs to be done to create for Aboriginal people a real entitlement to land, life, liberty and happiness in this, their ancestral country, but the gesture speaks of the potential to make it so. The song turns that gesture into a story, that people might hear it and remember it in their homes or their cars, over the ether, on the radio.

The song that made me shout with joy was by Yothu Yindi; the dance remix that would become their big hit, 'Treaty'. The part that really got to me is when an Aboriginal voice sings its own language. I have no idea what those words mean. But the power in that voice, the rhythms in the syllables; the sheer confidence in juxtaposing it against the digital rhythms, as if it were the most natural thing in the world. Again, there was a sign of what could be, lurking in this song.

I mention all this by way of introducing the idea of this book. Think of me in my little red Mazda 121, negotiating my way through Sydney traffic, among all the other cars, all listening to the radio. We are the people of Australia, each of us with our own destination. Yet we need to negotiate with each other to get there. There are institutions, like road markings and traffic lights, that make it easy. They channel our urge to get where we want to go into a manageable flow. Yet it all depends on us all keeping our cool, driving with some care—and in Sydney not a little wit—and being aware of and in tune with each other. For me at least, the radio is the image of this—the common world, the public sphere, the virtual republic.

I'll come back in a minute and unpack what 'virtual' and 'republic' might mean. First, an itinerary. *Part 1: Roots* contains two chapters that explain cultural spaces that are meaningful to me, and two chapters where I look at certain cultural traditions, again, ones that I use to explain things to myself. I try to create for you a very broad and long-running picture of how to think about culture and the media and Australia. It's my own personal street map and diary of how I see these things. I don't mean to suggest that everyone has to see things this way. The point is rather that I think everyone ought to share a few thoughts about how they are oriented by their own experience when it comes to thinking about culture and media. So *Part 1* is just an example of something everyone can do: map our collective history as it appears in your history, and vice versa.

Part 1: Roots contains stories about Sydney Libertarians and Glasgow gas engineers, but it also works up some ideas that in *Part 2: Aerials* I put to work trying to make something of recent media events in which cultural issues play a large part. So *Part 2* tries to make something out of what the media made out of writings like Helen Demidenko's book *The Hand That Signed the Paper*, David Williamson's play *Dead White Males*, and attacks on the historian Manning Clark's cold war classic *Meeting Soviet Man*. I look at the debates about the cold war and communism, the Holocaust, literary responsibility, postmodernism and political correctness, multiculturalism and Australian identity. In *Part 2*, the somewhat quirky ideas from *Part 1* meet the terms that the media more commonly uses. In other words, my culture goes out to meet everybody else's.

The Virtual Republic is a bit like radio. I'd suggest reading the chapters in the order in which they are presented, but if a channel gets boring or has wandered off on a tangent you are not interested in, press the button and try the next one. Some chapters, the third for example, start with the particular and move towards the abstract. If that tries your patience, then press on. Each chapter is an essay, and as Friedrich Hugo says, within an essay, 'everything is wavy line, outgrowth, and outgrowth of outgrowth'.[1] Follow a shoot as long as it holds up, and then jump to the next when it bends under the weight.

Another one of my magic car radio moments was the first time I heard gamelan music from Indonesia. The announcer explained that in gamelan, the orchestra divides into two parts, and the instruments in one half are tuned very slightly off pitch to the other half. This is what produced the extraordinary shimmering resonance of gamelan sound. *Part 1* and *Part 2* of this book are meant to resonate with each other, being pitched slightly differently.

THE REPUBLIC

The words virtual and republic also have a resonance, an echo of their rich histories. As the poet Charles Baudelaire wrote in his journal, 'Immense depths of thought in expressions of common speech; holes dug by generations of ants'.[2] I've just dug up the ants' nest of these two words, to see what resonances might echo in them, that might potentially be useful to us today.

The word republic means 'the public thing'. The roots of the word are ancient, connecting us to the world of the Romans—practical people who set about the problem of governing themselves. They did it with considerable success and style, and not a little bloodshed. Their republic didn't last; neither did their empire.

In the English language, the word republic has been with us for four hundred years. It means a state where power derives from the people. Whenever English-speaking peoples took the governing of their collective lives into their own hands, the word republic occupied some space in their minds and hearts, even though its meaning changes from place and time to place and time.

When Australians talk about the republic, they mostly mean constitutional reform to make our head of state an Australian.[3] Our form of government is substantially republican already. Power derives from the people. The people's representatives exercise that power within constitutional limits. The interpretation of the constitution is in the hands of an independent court. These are fine institutions, product of a peculiarly English genius for institutions of government. As Noel Pearson, who once chaired the Cape York Land Council says, 'If there is one thing about the colonial heritage of Australia that indigenous Australians might celebrate along with John Howard with the greatest enthusiasm and pride, it must surely be the fact that upon the shoulders of the English settler or invader—call them what you will—came the common law of England and with it the civilising institution of native title'.[4] While I am sympathetic to the passion for extending the republican aspect of the constitution to the means of choosing the head of state, those remarks of Pearson's make me think that there is more to becoming a republic than that.

This book is not about the constitution of an Australian republic in the legal sense. It is about what I believe is a necessary element of any country in which the people govern themselves. Its concern is the kinds of conversation citizens of our republic can entertain about things and events that are of interest and value to them, individually and collectively. What is the 'public thing' in Australia? It could be anything that has happened, now or in the past, or even the future, that people talk about in ways that express more than private longings.

An example of the 'public thing', in this ongoing conversation the country has with itself is the proposals of the Australian Republican Movement. That conversation waxes and wanes. Paul Keating, while Prime Minister, put the republican tune on high rotation. Since his electoral defeat by John Howard in 1996 it's off the playlist. But it has not gone away. It remains one of the public things that lie about in the 'vinyl closet' of old songs that is culture. The idea of Australia making changes to complete its republican constitution is one of the many things that constitute this other, wider sense of republic; the conversation about things that matter to the public.

I was one of those Australians who felt immensely cheered by the idea of Australia becoming a constitutional republic. I have heard talk of this for many years. Whenever I have heard Donald Horne or Robert Hughes or Malcolm Turnbull talk about it, something in the idea engages me. Here is Helen Irving, from her winning entry in the inaugural Manning Clark essay competition: 'While there is any ambiguity at all about Britain's constitutional powers in respect of Australia, it is hard for Australians to assume an attitude of full determination'.[5] I'm not a lawyer, so while I try to follow these debates about the ramifications of constitutional change I can only listen and decide. What I find so engaging is the idea that these institutions belong to us, that they can be the object of a conversation, that there are mechanisms in the constitution expressly designed to allow us to change it, and most of all, that change is possible: modest, gradual, practical change.

Republic for most people really means finding a way in which Australians can truly govern themselves. Even if the constitution were amended, two serious impediments to self-government would remain. The first is the issue of economic sovereignty. When enlightenment philosophers of the eighteenth century discussed the requirements for perpetual peace among free peoples they came up with many different constitutional ideas, but what both Immanuel Kant and David Hume saw as a great danger was the ceding of economic control to others.[6] For a small country rather heavily integrated into the global economy, this is a very real issue. I sometimes wonder if all the flag waving might not be a distraction from it. This book is not about this issue. Not because it is unimportant, but as with constitutional matters it is not something I know much about.

What this book is about is the other requirement for the self-governance of a free people: cultural autonomy. Without a space and a style of conversation that identifies the things that matter to the Australian people, I'm not sure one can truthfully speak of there being such a thing as an Australian people. It is not as if there is an 'Australian people' that simply exists out there, each one of us an isolated individual in the marketplace. It is because there is a conversation about things that matter to us as Australians that we come to think and act as Australians. This is a conversation that takes place around the dinner table in people's homes, in the classrooms and the boardrooms, on TV and over the back fence. Who are the Australian people? I've puzzled about this question for a long time. The best answer I can give so far is that we are those people who join this conversation about who the Australian people can be.

This might, at first glance, be a formula designed to annoy conservatively minded Australians, particularly those who hold dear fixed images of Australianness. When I was a kid in school, we summed it up in a song: 'football, meat pies, kangaroos and Holden cars'. The football always differed from state to state. To a Sydneysider, football is now owned by Rupert Murdoch. As for meat pies, after *Choice* magazine did their famous survey of what is actually in those little flaps of reconstituted pastry, a lot of people won't go near them. Kangaroos are dog food or road kill. Holden cars are designed and made in Japan or Korea. The Holden part is the badge on the outside. The company that sells them is, and always was, a subsidiary of an American corporation.

This kind of talk depresses a lot of people, so I won't persist. My point is that I don't think it matters what kinds of signs or emblems one thinks of as being truly Australian. They won't always mean the same thing to everyone, and sometimes they pass on by. I don't particularly care what is on the Australian flag or what anthem plays at the Olympics. Dictatorships do an excellent job on banners, tunes, and bunting. What seems to me to be a more usefully conservative way of thinking about Australian culture is to nurture and value and fight to conserve the institutions through which the conversation can take place about all these things. I'll stand for any Australian flag that is chosen by a free people, in conversation with itself—even if it's a pair of Bonds underpants on a stick.

So this is the republic that is the topic of this book: the republic composed of those institutions, from community to culture and education to the media, through which passes the conversation about the things of public concern to the Australian people. I'm not an etymologist, but this seems to me to get to the root of what the word republic means. 'Res' is the 'event' or the 'thing', the source also of the word 'real'. One of the ideas explored in this book is the extent to which it is in the public conversation that we come to know what it is that is real and what is not. No one exists purely as an individual, discovering what is true in the world all by themselves. It's an ongoing, public, collective, social process.

'Publica' is the feminine form of 'publicus', which derives from 'pubes', or adult. The conversation about events and things that one comes to join is something one has to learn to take some responsibility for, by learning to speak in certain ways: in ways suitable for a conversation not restricted to one's own familiars and friends. It's interesting that the word comes from the feminine form, for one of the key issues in the conversation of the republic has been the recognition of the entitlement of women to participate in it, both in the constitutional sense and in the cultural sense.[7] A key problem in Australia in the 1990s is the negotiation of the entitlements and the responsibilities of people in conversation as a public.

THE VIRTUAL

Think virtual and the expression 'virtual reality' comes quickly to mind, describing a technology that creates an immersive, three-dimensional environment within which a 'user' can move and look at things.[8] This is a rather odd use of a very ancient word, which almost by accident brings together three quite different meanings. The 'generations of ants' or, rather, populations of people, worked overtime on this particular expression. Perhaps by reflecting on these uses of the term we can make something of it a little more deliberately.

Virtual has its roots in the word vir, or 'man'. From ancient times it is a word that has come to identify not just a person in general but the best qualities of a person—virtue. And so at various times it has meant valour, righteousness, influence, excellence. It can point to a moral quality, or an aesthetic one. When the eighteenth-century novelist Samuel Richardson speaks of an 'object of virtue', he means a work of art. Virtue has valued different qualities in different times and places as the best of what it is to be human. Virtue has also designated different qualities in men to those it nominates for women. A man of virtue in Nicolo Machiavelli's renaissance Florence was a man of boldness and cunning.[9] A virtuous woman in Richardson's England was chaste and modest. There is no particular quality that is virtue, but virtue is always a quality of people, rather than of institutions. In other words, western culture has for a long time recognised the need for the concept of virtue, even though the particular values attached to the concept change across time and place.

I mention Machiavelli because it was he who first began to inquire as to the qualities of institutions and of people that are required for a republic to last, through good times and bad. He thought a lot about institutions, and influenced a whole line of English language thinkers on the topic. We'll meet some of them later—David Hume, Adam Smith and Adam Ferguson, three of the leading figures of the Scottish enlightenment of the eighteenth century. What are the qualities of a good republican people? Machiavelli had his ideas on that, and the Scots had a few of their own.

The contemporary republic is rather more complicated than that of the renaissance. Machiavelli's republic was a small city-state where people could easily meet in a public place. Ours is a vast continent. Railways and the telegraph made it possible to create a republic of free people across so vast a space. They are the tools by which the conversation moves through the people, and the people move freely through the space of the country. Railway and telegraph were useful tools, just as the explosion of new means of communication in the late twentieth century are useful tools.[10] But the institution of the internet does not in itself make for a conversation of any remarkable quality. It's not just a question of access to it, although that is important. Its usefulness also depends on the qualities of the people who join the conversation, and the institutions which shape those people.[11]

I don't think it is appropriate any more to think about the virtue of a free people as consisting of any one particular quality. We don't all need to meet the same exacting standard of boldness, morality or chastity to embody a virtue of value to the republic. What is troubling in a contemporary republic is how to combine and relate the particular and very widely varied qualities that people have in useful, fair and creative ways. The word virtue can refer to a quality all people are supposed to have, but it is also the root of the word virtuoso, which refers to a special, highly developed quality of a particular kind. In contemporary Australia we are almost all virtuosos at something. Our jobs and the cultures that come with them are far more highly specialised than in the days when the republican idea first entered the heads of people whose passion was to govern themselves.

I'm holding a pen in my hand, a Schwan Stabilo 188—standard government issue from the university. I hold the pen and I look at it. My eyes relay to my brain, via the optic nerve, an image of this pen I can feel in my hand. I hold the pen up before a mirror. I look in the mirror, and I see the pen in my hand. Once again my eyes relay to my brain, via the optic nerve, an image of this same pen. Only it's not quite the same image. It is what is known in optics as a virtual image. By extension, any image I have that comes via a mediating source, not just a mirror but a screen or a speaker, might also be called virtual.

From the same word that means the best quality of a person, we get this word that means a reflected image of a thing. I don't really know why, but it's a happy accident for this book because I want to float the idea of a virtual republic, which combines these senses of the virtual. A republic composed of institutions that produce a conversation, which all Australians are entitled to join, where we come to know ourselves by bringing to it our particular qualities. A republic that can only converse, in these 'postmodern' times, in a virtual space composed of media, rather than in the public square of the old renaissance republics. It is this virtual conversation that produces our sense of the public thing. It is through the virtual that we discuss and confirm what is real to us. Not least the reality of who we are.

THE VIRTUAL REPUBLIC

And so, the virtual republic, the whole point of which is to create a people aware of itself as a people. Not a people bound to any fixed idea of itself, but which knows something of the many pasts from which it descends to the present. A people aware of its potential, of the things it can make of itself, the things it can do and be. This is a third sense of the word virtual, and the hardest to grasp. We oscillate between the euphoria of thinking ourselves absolutely free and capable of anything; and the pessimism of thinking our lives absolutely determined, ground between the wheels of inexorable laws of history or nature. Neither view is justified. Both views trap us into obedience to someone else: those who claim to lead us to a radical remaking of country in the image of their rational schemes; those who claim to be privy to the secret laws that limit all our futures to be pale copies of our past. In contrast to both, the virtual is that world of potential ways of life of which the way things actually are is just an instance.

This is an elusive idea, so I'll leave it at that and come back to it. What I want to signal right away is that it is the foundation for an alternative to both economic rationalism and mindless conservatism. Proponents of the former want to remake the republic in the image of a top down, rational plan; one which nobody really understands, not even its various authors. It is based in the false optimism of enlightenment reason; that it can sweep away 'inefficiencies' without, in the process, harming the other institutions and qualities of life that sustain the country.

It used to be followers of Karl Marx who were most confident that we were more than a swarm of bees, building hives according to patterns innate in our nature. Marxists believed that the worker's party, as an intellectual vanguard, could be the architect of a worker's republic. Now it is followers of a quite different branch of economic theory, which like Marxism claims descent from Adam Smith, that thinks itself qualified to redesign us—the so-called economic rationalists who circulate between the corporations, the economic bureaucracy and 'consultancy'. They may act in the name of a different, and indeed more coherent, theory. They may act for a more powerful, indeed the ruling, class. But there is a striking similarity in the way governance is conceived as either an instrument for imposing a rational plan or as an impediment to it, never as a public thing in its own right.

Conservatives oppose this revolution by stealth—usually on the grounds proposed by Edmund Burke that if institutions last they must be good and if they are good they will last.[12] Just keep everything as it is. A view so deliberately mindless there's not much to say for it.

I want to oppose to both rationalism and conservatism the idea of the virtual—the notion that there is the potential to make things otherwise—not through an abstract plan imposed by experts, but through the conversation that is Australia, that questions and shapes each and every one of its institutions, bit by bit. The virtual republic is one that is slave to neither past habits nor the master plan. This idea has of course had other names, but sometimes one needs to add some new words to the conversation, or fresh dimensions of meaning to its old words.

THE ESSAY

'I am myself the subject of this book.' So wrote Michel de Montaigne to the readers of his *Essays*, a book he began in 1572 and worked on for the rest of his life.[13] What is distinctive about Montaigne is that he eschews writing in a specialised language, and yet he writes of far wider things than mere private confessions of the doings of his own little world. 'Authors communicate themselves to the public by some peculiar mark foreign to themselves; I—the first ever to do so—by my universal being, not as a grammarian, poet or jurist, but as Michel de Montaigne. If all complain that I talk too much about myself, I complain that they never even think about their own selves.'

To 'essay' is to make an attempt. It's a verb, a process; as much as a thing, a product. Essay has the same roots as assay, and the meanings overlap in the sense of weighing up something's current value. *The Virtual Republic* is an essay in Montaigne's sense, and like Montaigne 'I speak as an ignorant, questioning man'. I try to write from my own experience, and from what I can learn from books, about the culture and media that made me and out of which I make myself. It's a sceptical, experimental form, unfortunately much debased by the habit of calling those turgid term papers humanities undergraduates have to hand in 'essays', which usually they are not.

The essay arises out of Montaigne's attempt to use the full range of his own experience and the resources of his unusually well stocked library to enquire after the leading questions of his day, both great and small. He wrote at a time when increasing knowledge of the ancient world and of the new world broke apart the neatly ordered universe of scholastic thought and writing. He wanted to write in a way that would cross the boundaries of specialised, theological knowledge, so that people might get to know him, through his writing, as a 'friend'. Montaigne proposed the idea of the writer, not as a great authority or a great artist, but as a virtual friend. He was a friend, for example, to Shakespeare. Through the popular translations into Elizabethan English by John Florio, Shakespeare came to know this virtual Montaigne, and to make much of Montaigne's world view his own.

I think there is something of value to the virtual republic in this idea of the writer, and writing. Scholarly writing has become even more intensely specialised in the centuries since Montaigne wrote. As the amount of scholarly writing increases, scholarship divides into ever more specialised areas of expertise, ever more distant from each other. This is not a bad thing, to the extent that more accurate, considered and precise studies of each and every particular problem find their way into the archives. The problem is that increasingly, it is only ever other scholars who will retrieve such works from the archives and make use of them. Scholarship breaks up into conversations among specialists, who no longer talk to people outside their speciality and certainly not to anything like a 'public'. Knowledge gets cut up into smaller and smaller units, within each of which scholars can claim to be authorities in their field, knowing all there is that is worth knowing about their field, but where the field itself is a tiny patch.

The essayist is someone who, like Montaigne, cuts across

those specialised fields, trading off authority in one field for a passing acquaintance with several. What the essayist offers the reader is then not the last word on any particular speciality. The essayist makes introductions. That is why the essayist is a 'friend', someone who can make connections among those with whom the essayist is acquainted. The essay attempts a kind of 'hypertext'. The essayist's judgements are always based on incomplete information. They are an invitation to the reader to pursue a connection further. The essayist doesn't pretend to an overview or synthesis of everything. The essay is rather one particular way of negotiating passages through knowledge and experience. Along the way it meets not only scholarship and its specialities but other essayists and their personalities. In the relationships between specialised knowledges that the essay proposes, and in the relationship between the different qualities of acquaintance proposed by different styles of essay, something like a public dimension to writing becomes possible.

I'm sceptical of the 'analysis' of culture and media when its findings remain a thing apart, locked in an internal debate within the academy. Attempts to produce an 'objective' account end up reproducing the cultural prejudices of social scientists. A prejudice for the ring of 'objective' sounding phrases, no matter how much those phrases may leave out on the way to that hollow sound. Attempts to produce 'critical' accounts of media and culture expose less about the ideologies at work in the world they set out to unmask than they do about the ideology of the critics. Criticism wears an ideological mask, too. And in both cases, the result circulates within the academy, where the peculiar rules of proper speaking in the social sciences and the humanities shape the responses that follow as much as the original analysis and critique. The particular qualities of the author are bracketed off, resulting in parades of passive, subjectless sentences, rather like this one.

Which is why in this book I want to write from a particular point of view, but offer this writing to readers not bound by any particular disciplinary or professional constraints. Writing ought to come from somewhere but be prepared to go anywhere. That seems to me to be a key characteristic of our 'postmodern condition'—this time when the old forms, old fables, old boundaries seem shaky and unreal.[14]

We no longer have roots, we have aerials. We no longer have origins, we have terminals. I've repeated those two aphorisms quite a few times over the last ten years, because I keep finding new resonances in what they might mean. I wrote my first book, *Virtual Geography*, to explain them.[15] Ironically, this book might appear to contradict them. It begins in *Part 1* with my particular roots, culturally and intellectually speaking, before tackling in *Part 2* some of the issues in the culture wars to which the media has tuned its aerials in the 1990s. But as we shall see, one's roots these days always seem curiously disturbed by hydroponic immersion in the endless flowing waters of pop media. We make of our culture things made possible by what our culture made of us.

I'm a writer by trade but also by compulsion. So this is a book about how the place of the writer in the public world has mutated and shifted since the culture wars heated up. The focus shifts now and then from what I think has happened to the shape and tempo of the public world to questions about how one ought to intervene there; and on that basis, judgements on what I think about the interventions others have made. Sometimes I've included the interventions I made at the time, and a commentary on them. This means that the writing in this book changes pace and style and genre from time to time. I want to convey a sense of the way public life is composed, not of texts but of events. Public life is composed of chance meetings where the tempos of media and culture clash. A realm in which, as Montaigne says, 'nothing certain can be established about one thing by another, both the judging and the judged being in continual change and motion'.[16]

Both old fashioned literary criticism and new fashioned literary theory make a lot out of the notion that culture is composed of texts.[17] In the process of scrutinising texts, time seems to stop. In this book, things slow down long enough to take a look at texts, but sometimes they speed up to follow the action. I believe the essayist's job is different from the scholar's—it is about depth of perception but it is also about speed of engagement. The essayist is neither an ivory tower expert nor an 'opinion leader' for the masses, but operates in a very curious space and time that I will come in short order to define as the virtual republic.

PART ONE
ROOTS

1

When I hear the word 'culture', I reach for the remote control

Isn't this the answer to the question:
what are we?
We are habits, nothing but habits.
The habit of saying 'I'.

Gilles Deleuze

LINES OF FLIGHT

I'm coming home. The last inflight movie reels to an end. The lights are out and it's almost quiet. The plane hums and murmurs to itself. All who fly in it are one big sleeping body, quietly respirating, dreaming through the night, on autopilot.

I lift the window shade and peer out at the sunless sky and peaceful ocean. I'm as tranquil as that ocean seems—after a few glasses of Australian chardonnay. Very pleasant it is too. Not the least reason to look forward to coming home. To Australia, where even the cheap wines are drinkable.

Not being able to sleep, I'm writing these notes for *The Virtual Republic*. It's a book about the relentless swelling and breaking of sense called the media, and what lurks beneath it; those dark reservoirs and currents of memory called culture; which together make up this dream, that ocean—my country. Perhaps it is your country too. A fuselage of dreams.

Don't mind me, fellow traveller. It's the wine talking. We may be heading for the future in our dreams, but when we wake we will be circling over Sydney. For those straight below, our flight booms loud enough to wake the dead. I might feel a bit groggy when we land, but by the time I get to passport control, I'll be looking the customs officer in the eye while she checks me against my mug shot. I'll be back to my own self, my home self.

Perhaps it is that Qantas ad that screened before the inflight movies that's made me all sentimental. You might have seen it—the one that features all these great Australian singers, each of whom performs a verse of 'I Still Call Australia Home', while the camera whisks over the sublime panorama of desert. What do you make of it? I'm not usually prone to feelings of naive nationalism, but I have had a few, so perhaps I'm just in a gooey mood. I could stop right now and analyse this Qantas ad—I am, after all, a lecturer in media studies. It's what I trained, and what I train others, to do. But these days I'm equally interested in the *feeling* the ad gives me. Rather than critique the ad rationally, peeking beneath its surfaces for its hidden ideologies and agendas, I want to think about what to make of it in a different sense. What is the feeling it generates *good for*?

To what extent do we need this palpable sensation of belonging; that we are all aboard the same flight, buffeted by the same turbulence? We could all just go our separate ways, pursue our private lives, even if, as that great American essayist Henry David Thoreau said, they are mostly lives of 'quiet desperation'.[1] Do we need to be 'we' at all—why not just a collection of I and I and I? Richard White argues convincingly that Australian culture is always something 'constructed', its naturalness and fidelity to place an illusion, and I'm inclined to agree. And yet that illusion seems to make possible what Paul James calls an 'abstract community'.[2] One that we might hope can navigate between global forces and local attachments.

TECHNICS OF THE PUBLIC

For my flight from New York home to Sydney, I bought my ticket and put my life in the hands of the pilots. One can't seriously imagine an aircraft piloted by the democratic argy-bargy of all aboard. Or so I thought, until one thousand other people and I landed a plane together.

Admittedly, it wasn't a real plane, but it was a pretty

amazing experience all the same. I was at *Siggraph 95*, a big computer graphics industry conference and convention. Little paddles were handed out among the audience in the big auditorium. The paddles had a green reflector on one side, red on the other. Different sections of the audience were assigned different aspects of the flight plan to control—height, direction, and speed. Each person turned the little paddle one way or the other, while watching the flight's progress on the big screen. A computer took data from sensors monitoring the paddles, averaged it out and sent our aggregate decisions to the aircraft, which we brought down safely, every time.

Kevin Kelly, the editor of the techno-geek magazine *Wired* and an infectious enthusiast for such things, sees it as an example of the 'hive mind' at work.[3] I was pretty thrilled by it too. But whereas the lesson for Kelly is all about private initiative and its virtues, for me this experience was a simple little demonstration of the lost art of *being a public*. We all did something together, and were aware of doing it together while we did it. We entered the big hall at *Siggraph* as private consumers: buying our tickets and taking our seats. We became, for a moment, public actors: participating in something together without being forced to be other than as we are.

It's a sign of the times that in America today it's usually instances of being a public that employs this kind of gee-whiz technology appear as the cause for celebration. It's a curious thing, but there's a mantra chanted throughout the media to the effect that the media have killed the public. The only media sometimes exempted are new media, which supposedly make up for the failings of the old ones.[4] I suspect that 'publicness' may be alive and well, even in America, in its school boards and city boroughs, on talkback radio and even talk show TV. What is lacking is a language within which to talk about the shifting spaces through which publics form; the changing nature of the things publics talk about; and the variable geometry of media technologies, from the telephone to the internet, that network it together.

RHETORICS OF THE NATION

The public piloting of a virtual plane, or consumers buying tickets for a real one; these are only figures of speech for the way national culture might work. Like all figures of speech, they capture a likeness at the expense of ignoring some attributes of the thing. Unlike a scheduled flight, a country cannot know its future 'destination'. Who knows what events await? But then 'nation' is itself something only graspable as a figure of speech. A nation is never all together in the same place, everyone in plain view of one another, like in a plane, or at the theatre or the marketplace. The people come together in an imaginary space. So it matters which figures of speech we choose to represent that space.

In the 1980s, the market became the dominant figure of speech. When we say 'market', this too is only a way of speaking. To think of society as being like a market is like explaining the term figure of speech by saying that it is like a figure of speech. 'Society' is a rhetorical term, and so is 'market'. There was a time when society was a word that meant one's friends. So when we say society meaning a whole bunch of people sharing a place together, what we are doing is taking a word meaning a relationship of friendship and using it in an extended way as a word meaning a much wider set of relationships, including but not restricted to friendship. Likewise, the word 'market' once meant a particular kind of place where people gathered together and shouted out prices and orders to each other, either in the village square or church yard.[5] When we use the word to refer to a much more dispersed set of transactions, not connected in space and time, once again we are using a figure of speech.

In both cases, that figure of speech is what students of rhetoric call metonymy, or the substitution of a part for a whole. If I say 'ten head of cattle' or 'all hands on deck', head stands for the whole of the cow, hand stands for the whole of the sailor. Likewise, market stands for the whole range of complicated and messy relationships that make a country function. By calling sailors 'hands', I reduce them to one aspect of their being. No doubt ships' captains did this deliberately, to emphasise the relationship of authority. The captain is the head of a ship, sailors are just hands that do what they are told and ought not to think too much for themselves, let alone use any other part of their anatomy too freely. By speaking only about the market, one likewise takes a partial aspect of the kinds of relation that glue us together and puts it in place of the whole. This is particularly dangerous because anything that doesn't look like a market relationship comes to be regarded as some kind of aberration.

What's clear about the 1980s and 1990s is that it is a time when 'market' captured the imaginations of the nation's pilots more than its passengers. In *Making It National*, his excellent book about media and culture in the 1980s, Graeme Turner brackets that period as beginning in 1983, with Australia's win in the America's Cup, and ending in 1988, with the Bicentennial. Within that frame he explores the celebration of business culture, from boom to bust, and its intersections with popular nationalism. Turner's main interest is in the rise of the economy and notions of competition, in business and sport. He laments the replacement of notions of citizenship with those of consumer, and the consequent poverty of ways to 'imagine our commonalities'.[6] By restricting the range of figures of speech through which to imagine Australia, far more limited and limiting ideas about what it might be and can do prevailed than in previous eras, before 'market' became the dominant figure of speech.

If the 1980s began in 1983 and ended in 1988, then the 1990s are also a decade speeding by a little ahead of schedule, particularly after a sharp swerve to the right at the 1996 federal election. If the 1980s were about the market, the 1990s are about culture. My interest in this period is in those intersections of culture and media that tried to fill the lack of the national with stories that brought an 'us' together in the face of threats to our existence—particularly those the media identified as coming from culture itself: political correctness, postmodern scepticism, cultural relativism, sentimental multiculturalism. These are Australia's own imported versions of what the Americans call the 'culture wars'.[7]

In the wake of the reduction of nation to market, to the point where pundits seriously questioned whether one needs a nation at all if one has markets, something seemed missing. The dismal discourse of economics offered, in the end, nothing beyond the path of working, eating, and distracting ourselves until we die—all with the utmost efficiency. What had promised to rationalise those parts of life not worth spending any more time on than necessary, leaving more time for things worthwhile, had promoted itself to the only thing worth anything. What had once been merely the means to the good life touted itself as if it were the ends of the good life itself. Where once we worked to live, now we live to work.

But this fool's philosophy had by the 1990s become enshrined as a state religion. Any questioning of its sacred dogmas quickly brought down the wrath of the new inquisition, who delight in torturing enemies of the faith with their pocket calculators. And so the lack that lurked so palpably, just below the surface of everyday life, was not taken for what it really was—the symptom of a deep public disgust with this confusion of work with life, of efficiency with justice, of price with quality.

As happens in such circumstances, what was wanting was a figure of speech that could describe this lack, this need, this yearning. What the market forgets as a figure of speech could only be remembered in another figure—but which? Neither society nor nation quite managed to claim this lost part of our collective selves. Robert Hughes tried to revive 'nation', speaking on behalf of the Australian Republican Movement at Sydney Town Hall, but it appeared too partisan. Eva Cox tried to revive 'society', speaking in the annual Boyer Lectures on ABC Radio National, in the name of a social democratic vision of the good life, it did not attract partisans enough.[8] And so, in order to name this missing limb of collective life, the figure of speech that came to stand in for what was lacking ended up being 'culture'.

Everything lacking in a world made over in the image of the economy sheeted home to culture, which pundits held at one and the same time to be the source of all our problems, and the remedy. The problem with culture was that postmodernism, political correctness, multiculturalism and crypto closet Marxists had stuffed it up. What was needed was a return to the one true value. How curious that when economic theory offered the aura of a way of conceiving of the whole of life that made it all hinge on something simple, true and eternal, those who wanted to rescue culture sought to make it over in this same theological image. What was needed were 'values'.

Needless to say, a great deal was said in defence of the idea of eternal and absolutely true cultural values. What these God-given sacraments actually are, nobody quite got around to announcing. The tablets were not brought down from Mount Kosciusko.

Having spent time in both the United States and Australia

during the 1990s, what I noticed was a curious playing out of the same conversations in both places, where the figure of speech of the economy was never really questioned, and where 'culture' accumulated all the lost hopes and fears that 'economy' could not answer. The strangest side of it was that people who spend their time imagining, describing and analysing this world of the economy-gone-mad—such as writers, artists, scholars, teachers, thinkers—were being held to blame for the world they—we—tried to invoke. As if to prove once and for all that this really is a postmodern world, the images, descriptions and stories about this world were held to be the cause of its problems, rather than their effects. Opening a newspaper in Sydney or New York, how often did it seem to spit in my face? I had some funny dreams about it, particularly while flying. I get to customs, and the officer checks my passport. Punching my data into the computer, an alarm sounds. I'm wanted by the thought police in two countries for crimes against culture. I'm taken away to an airless room and forced to watch endless videos of Treasurer Peter Costello's budget speeches . . .

MY OWN PRIVATE IDAHO

I wake with a start. Where am I? On a plane. It's OK, it's only a paranoid dream. Perhaps I should have stayed awake and watched the movie. Something set in New York involving men armed with guns and a girl shod in pumps. 'I Still Call Australia Home'—but I have thought about leaving it. I guess a lot of people, when travelling, entertain this fantasy—particularly on long plane flights. I dream about moving to America, becoming an expatriate, pitting myself against the challenge of making it there, in the world's biggest market for the kind of things that I do—writing and reading, speaking and listening, teaching and learning. I'm an optimistic person in some ways, so these fantasies always work out well, in my head at least. I move to New York, struggle along, but in the end, I make it.

I mention this because the kinds of fantasies I feel I can have about being in America seem to me to be a bit different from the ones I feel I can have about being in Australia. My American fantasies are all about *my* fabulous life, *my* brilliant career, *my* wonderful family and small circle of friends. Not because I don't care about other people. I care about other people—even Americans. It's just that I find it hard to have any optimism when I'm in America about what it might be possible to do beyond the individual. It's as if the structures that hold private lives together in some wider framework simply aren't there any more. But when I think about Australia, I can dream about being part of something more than my own private Idaho.

When I think about Australians, I feel a particular kind of *sympathy*. It is as if the sympathy I feel for my family and friends, for people I know and see, somehow extended beyond those little circles, to a wider, abstract circle of people who I do not really know. And yet I wish for these people what I wish for my family and friends—I wish the kind of things silly little greetings and toasts announce. Australians are people I really want to have a good day, a happy anniversary, and a pleasant flight. After a few drinks I think I could even offer a toast to John Howard. After a few more—Kerry Packer.

In America, at least in that wide-screen America of movies and talk shows and newspaper 'think pieces' through which Americans represent their fears and dreams, sympathy feels much more particular. Australians are fellow passengers; Americans are people who just occupy adjacent space. In America, I feel like I am governed by a social contract. I walk around, buy the new issue of the *New Yorker*, ride the subway, read my magazine. It is as if all that connected me to other people was something that kept each of us within a certain limit. The social contract, the myth of America as a society, seems to be that it is a contract that *limits* the passions and actions of people. Those desires always seem like they threaten to break out at any moment. Americans dream of being mugged, bashed, carjacked or serially killed, so Americans grudgingly pay a few taxes to keep the police up to speed in an arms race with gangsters, hoodlums, thugs and punks, and to keep one-and-a-half million former fellow citizens in prison.[9]

It isn't really quite like that, of course. But in their movies and TV, Americans seem on some rarefied level to dream that this is what society is—a contract enforced by the police to keep everyone's raging desires within limits. Once, those desires could escape westward to the frontier, but now they seem all bottled up, ready to go off like a bomb on the subway. The only desires let free aren't those of people any more, they are the desires of money. People are hemmed in on all sides, but money does what it pleases. In America, people dream of *not* losing their jobs, *not* getting mugged, *not* getting sick before they can afford it. There is a poverty in American life. You feel it not just in the way the welfare system has gone freelance and you are solicited for contributions on every other street corner. It's a poverty of the imagination. A poverty of ways of thinking of America other than cash and combat.

INTIMATIONS OF SYMPATHY

I fear it may be getting like that in Australia too. A lot of Australians seem to imagine that our whole way of life is just like the American republic. There is another Australia, the one that makes possible that strange feeling of sympathy I and many other Australians have for each other, as something one just sort of feels without thinking. It's that feeling I had watching that Qantas ad—the feeling of feeling together, with others, the feeling of belonging to a community of sense. As Larry Grossberg argues, feeling is a much underrated quality of what it is that cements people into the wider world.[10] In both analysis and in culture itself, the affections have been relentlessly privatised, pushed back toward the secret worlds of romance, sex and family, but these are really particular instances of a *structure* of feeling: points from which to reimagine the whole of life and create new figures of speech for it.

Let's take just one such affection—sympathy. You feel something, I empathise with the way you feel. We are in sympathy. Some people believe that our feelings of sympathy for those close to us has its roots in biological nature. That may be so, but the feeling one can have for other *Australians* is clearly a cultural thing. It is an extension of those feelings for a small circle of intimates to a wider circle of strangers—by the artificial means of culture.

In the American imagination—the America of the movies—everything begins with the individual, as if we were born, whole and complete, with unlimited passions and desires which can only be tamed and limited by the social contract. The big guy with the gun is a loner, but in the end he always restores *the law*. But as the philosopher and essayist David Hume argued, we are only ever individuals after having been part of some small clump of human life: a family, pack, tribe, gang or clan.[11]

It is in those little containers of familiars that sympathy begins, with sexual 'lust' and love of the—resultant—children. 'Consult common experience', Hume would say, and one finds that even the most cut-throat gangster who will rob you with a switch-blade, or the most rapacious speculator who will rob you with a fountain pen, even they have buddies or family somewhere, for whose benefit they think they are stealing from you.

Perhaps the problem is not so much that the rampant natural passions of individuals have to be forcibly *limited* by a social contract, but that our partial sympathies for those close to us have to be artificially *extended* by a sociable culture. As Hume says in his *Treatise of Human Nature*, '. . . the sense of justice and injustice is not derived from nature, but arises artificially, though necessarily from education, and human convention'. The aims of these forms of artifice are modest: 'experience sufficiently proves, that men, in the ordinary conduct of life, look not so far as the public interest . . . That is a motive too remote and too sublime . . .'. Rather, convention instils such a concern for reputation that people internalise conventions and channel their passions accordingly.

The result: 'By the conjunction of forces, our power is augmented: By the partition of employments, our ability increases: And by mutual succour we are less exposed to fortune and accidents. It is by this additional force, ability and security, that society becomes advantageous'. This from the book that Adam Smith was nearly thrown out of Oxford University for possessing. Smith writes in the *Wealth of Nations* that 'it is not from the benevolence of the butcher, the brewer, or the baker that we expect our dinner, but from their regard to their own self interest'. As with Hume's artifice of justice, Smith's invisible hand of the market has its roots in the passions, in a 'trucking disposition', a desire less to do with having other people than having what they have. As with Hume, it only works for the conjunction of forces when raised to the level of a convention. Consult your own experience: 'nobody ever saw a dog make a fair and deliberate exchange of a bone with another dog'.[12] The market is as much an artifice as any other institution.

Depending on whether one thinks of a social institution as something that limits individual desires or that extends partial sympathies, one can imagine it as either a restraint on the natural energies of the human organism or as a positive means of artificially extending and integrating the kinds of creative and productive ingenuity of our particular little sympathetic worlds—to enable us to fly. In place of plain stealing, the conventions of property; in place of violence, a common world of conversation.

This is one sense I want to give to the idea of a virtual republic: it is that plane upon which people can come to negotiate their particular entitlements, premised on the belief that all members of this virtual republic are equally entitled to have our sympathies extended to them, and from whom we presume a sympathy also extends. Not just because this is a contract that limits parties to its terms, but because this is a culture that negotiates entitlements so that many and varied forms of possible existence may be created.

CONCEPTIONS OF ENLIGHTENMENT

It may be no accident that I find it felicitous to frame these problems using David Hume, one of the key figures of the Scottish enlightenment. The choice that presently faces Australians seems to me not unlike the one that confronted Hume, and his contemporaries Adam Smith and Adam Ferguson. All three were born after Scotland joined the Union and lost her independence in 1707. All three lived through the Jacobite rebellion of 1745, when Prince Charles led a motley army of highlanders that captured Edinburgh and marched on London, only to be beaten at the battle of Culloden. It was the last gasp of the old ways. The lowlands were already mostly for British union. Highland culture was violently suppressed.

'Scotland would never again be a whole world, capable of containing all of her people and meeting their needs', writes Australian poet Les Murray. 'And that is at least an illusion a nation has to create, in order to function as a nation and focus an evolving human distinctiveness. Scottishness was a wounded and partial thing which . . . could never turn enough of her people, at home or in exile, away from what they saw as the economic and social realities of the world.'[13] I think that's a very canny analysis of what the Scots lost, but not of what was gained, a subject I'll pick up again in a later chapter.

The Scottish enlightenment was, among other things, the intellectual accompaniment to the Union tune. Political power had moved south to London, so Hume developed a style of essaying about power, and about the events of the day. Freed from the distraction of governing, Hume, Smith and Ferguson wrote much of the language in which we still speak about it. All three of them saw Scotland's loss of sovereignty adequately compensated by the increase in prosperity. The relationship between the institutions of political sovereignty and economic prosperity became their common theme.[14]

'In the lone houses and very small villages which are scattered about in so desert a country as the Highlands . . .' wrote Smith, 'every farmer must be butcher, baker, and brewer . . .' —and probably does none of these things all that well. Whereas in the towns, the division of labour allows each skill to become a distinct trade: 'the important business of making a pin is, in this manner, divided into about 18 distinct operations'. As also are every other trade and profession, including government, law, letters and art. This worried Adam Ferguson a lot. 'The period is come, when no engagement remaining on the part of the public, private interest, and animal pleasure, become the sovereign objects of care.'[15] A Gaelic speaker and former officer with the Black Watch, a highland regiment formed to serve the Union abroad, Ferguson had a stronger sense of the republican virtues of a sovereign people. Ferguson found himself oscillating, wondering if these were not divergent rather than convergent ideas about the public organisation of private passions.

Hume, Smith and Ferguson all supported the expansion of trade and industry, but were all worried in differing degrees about the consequences. Commercial society does not contain within it the necessary checks against its own corruption. Virtue is a civic value, derived from a certain kind of practice, not of commerce or learning, but of getting on and getting along with one's fellows in what Ferguson was the first to name *civil society*. But virtue is not something innate. It is produced by the intersection of a wide range of social forces. Commerce and culture can contribute to civic virtue, but they can also undermine it. The trick is to develop, to the point where it becomes second nature, a structure of feeling that extends and maintains virtue, by means of the practices it requires of people.

The problem with commerce is that, as Adam Smith so carefully explained, it develops through a division of labour that makes people do very narrow and specific things. Smith saw this division of labour as the driving force of the whole of social change, and Marx would develop a much more thorough insight into this, drawing not only on the productive gains of the division of labour but also those of the development of more and more specialised tools. For Marx, 'second nature' is more than just human organisation, it is the organisation of people with things, machines, and the raw materials of nature itself.[16]

But in developing Smith, Marx set aside the Scottish writer's sceptical queries about whether modern society might not in the end undermine its own conditions of existence; that prosperity and the division of labour might so disorganise the passions that the 'conjuncture of forces' do not join. Ferguson in particular worried about the specialisation not just in the making of things but in the making of culture, government, law and defence. Priests, lawyers, artists and soldiers all come to be specialists who serve others for money. Narrow jobs making narrow people. Nobody acts as a full participant in the whole of civil society. One might have better art, science, law and so on, but a worse civil society. Specialisation makes society as a whole more productive, and this might set people free to engage in civil life—but it doesn't. People just head further and further down the track of specialisation, looking after their own. Nothing extends their passions back out towards engaging with the issues of the whole. Smith's wealth of nations may very well impoverish the virtual republic.

The predicament of these Scots thinkers has an uncanny ring. The lowlanders would give up their sovereignty for prosperity, but wonder all the while about what would become of their culture. The highlands remained impassable redoubts of resistance for some time, but were eventually brought under the sway of economic union. Is this not unlike the union of Australia with the global economy? Do we not hear echoes of Smith and Ferguson, of the language of prosperity and sovereignty? The key term, which seems to me to belong in both vocabularies, is entitlement.

SENSES OF ENTITLEMENT

For Australia to be a virtual republic, all Australians must be entitled to speak, and in speaking define an element of the common world of what is possible. The virtual republic, let us say for now, is the conversation of possibilities, in which people's particular attributes and points of view work out a way of negotiating—and negotiate.

An entitlement is a form of property. That to which one is entitled is that which one may rightly make a claim to have or to share. Not all entitlements are equal. For example, as Bob Connell has pointed out, not everyone appears as entitled to speak via the media. One must at least count as middle class.[17] A road maintenance worker is not likely to be widely reported— unless suspected of murdering hitchhikers.

A further difficulty is not only that not everyone has *as much* property, but that not everyone has the *same kind* of property. The kind of property most Australians understand is the kind for which you mortgage yourself to the bank for the next 25 years—bricks and mortar. All over the land there are families working flat out at two jobs or more to secure it. Families pushed so close to the edge that their sympathies shrink to the smallest circle. Easy prey for unscrupulous politicians who promise to free them from the burden of any wider sympathy—and from having to contribute anything towards a sociable culture beyond all the endless hard work and raising the kids.

All that results is a downward spiral of diminishing possibilities. If one shrinks from sympathy, if one ignores other kinds of entitlement, then one accepts a diminished plane of possibility, where all that one can aspire to is that which one can buy. And so one runs up the credit card, buying one of everything, from a Sony home entertainment centre to a backyard swimming pool. But what happens if you get sick? Who will pay the school fees? What happens when those whose entitlements have been denied become in reality what the theory of the social contract imagines them to be in its limited imagination—rapacious, cut-throat, selfish individuals, entirely without sympathy? Lock all your doors. Don't go out alone or at night. Stay home and watch TV.

Circling in a jumbo jet over Sydney, looking at all the little houses in the morning light, I imagine a nightmare image of Australia, where at night everyone is huddled fearfully by the flickering light of the telly watching videos or pay-per-view in which people very much like these little huddled clumps get picked off in the night by that dark lurking menace of the night known as *crime*.

Cheer up, it's only a movie. Things aren't that bad—yet. Australians still believe in what I call the virtual republic, although it has many other names. To a lot of people it's just the *fair go*. For everyone to have a fair go means that different kinds of entitlement negotiate with each other. There is the entitlement of property, both tangible and intellectual property. There is the entitlement of capital; there is the entitlement of labour. There is a whole bunch of entitlements that come through the tax transfer system. What flat earth economists disparage as 'middle class welfare' is of course nothing of the sort.[18] People pay taxes, and expect to get back a whole range of things beneficial to health and culture and the good life.

Then there are entitlements that are not yet clearly defined. Are homosexuals as entitled to claim sick leave to look after a partner who is ill as straight people who are married or in de facto relationships? Not quite, but perhaps they should be. Isn't that a fair go? Or let's take the biggest issue of them all: what about native title? What is the entitlement now of the descendants whose land was invaded 200 years ago? As Pat Dodson, who chairs the Council for Aboriginal Reconciliation says, 'In a land of relative plenty, there is plenty of Aboriginal poverty, and that poverty has a history. It has a history rooted in dispossession, particularly from access to land but also dispossession from economic, social and political strength'.[19] Entitlement to a share in the common wealth is inseparable from the question of being entitled to speak, and from access to the means to create social and political forms of articulating that right to speak. These things go together. The virtual republic is where they meet.

It is often said that Australia is a very young country. That may be so, but it is also one of the most experienced at the great experiment of the virtual republic. Even if we go no further back than Federation, then we are still talking about nearly a century of conversation that has resulted in the continual expansion of sympathy. It is often remarked that this virtual republic is somewhat lacking in pomp and vision, but I think Hume would have approved of that. A practical conversation, full of folly and delusion to be sure, but not too tied to myths of the glorious past, or dreams of salvation in the future. Ours is what political philosopher Michael Oakeshott calls a sceptical politics, not a politics of faith.[20] Surely this is not unconnected to the remarkable prosperity and peace that characterised Australian history.

Beneath the virtual republic lies entitlement. Because only certain kinds of people have entitlement to speak, only certain kinds of culture find their way into the negotiation of public life. Setting aside the question of entitlement, we come up against this rather gritty and intractable notion of culture. But what is culture? Or rather, what kind of culture makes possible the virtual republic? Let me answer that by recounting an incident that happened to me back in that scariest of American cities, New York.

MEANINGS OF CULTURE

I'm walking down a street in the meat packing district late at night, dressed in a black singlet and jeans. I pass two guys packing a truck, also dressed in dark singlets and jeans. I overhear them discussing options for an evening out. 'You could always go to that faggot club around the corner', the one nearest to me says darkly, pointing in the direction I happen to be heading. 'Take your little a-hole around there. Them faggots will fill it up good.'

Then he looks straight at me.

In the space of a few seconds, the two of us have sized each other up and know one or two things about each other. He is wearing the kind of dark singlet that says 'working-class male on the job'. I am wearing the kind of singlet that says 'faggot going to a nightclub'.

This is the first thing we can say 'culture' is: a wardrobe of *signs* people put out to each other, indicating where we are coming from and what we're about, so other people can size us up and decide what to do next. It is a way of marking out what makes us different.

It's the other guy's move now he and I have made eye contact, and we both know from what he's said that he doesn't like my kind all that much. What does he do? Say, in classic New Yorker style, 'Fuck you!'? Step over and thump me one? No, he stares at me, for one of those moments that seem to cut a hole in time. Then he ignores me completely and I walk on around to the club.

This is the second thing we can say about culture, and the different ways of knowing who we are and who others are through culture. Modern, urban culture is as much about *indifference* as it is about difference, as sociologist Georg Simmel surmised.[21] The man packing the truck and I seem to occupy different kinds of cultural world, but the space where we come across each other belongs, by mutual decision, to neither of us in particular. The space itself in this case is indifferent, and that indifference makes possible the intermingling of different networks of cultural sense.

So culture is a set of signs and rules for their use that signal how we might differ from an other. And it is also a set of signs and rules about rubbing along, or not, depending on the particular cultural convention of that place and time. Some cultures affirm their existence by thumping anyone who breaks their rules. Some cultures are rather more confident about themselves than that, and don't really give a damn.

This is the third thing we can say about culture: there are ethical and political questions at stake as to how open or closed a particular culture is to different behaviours and attitudes, both within the ranks of those it considers 'inside' it, and those it considers 'outside'. The signs and the rules set up these notions of an inside and an outside. There is contestation. There is such a thing as *cultural politics*.

Cultural historian Raymond Williams spent a lot of time trying to come up with a definition of culture. He referred to it as a whole way of life, or a *structure of feeling*.[22] I have always rather liked that expression. It gives you the sense of culture as something you learn, perhaps without really being aware of it, yet it shapes your awareness of everything around you and how you react to things. What I think I respond to in that 'I Still Call Australia Home' video is its appeal, not to signs of nationalism, but to a structure of feeling. The actions of the truck packers and myself in the street are shaped by something we have learned about each other and about getting along in that particular, urban environment. There is a patchwork of such rules, different in place and time, and not always adhered to anyway.

Culture is something one picks up and internalises. It only exists if people act according to the codes and conventions of it. Yet a culture also passes through a set of things external to the members of the group it defines, as artefacts, rituals, texts.

These things should not be confused with culture itself. One learns a culture through these things, but these things only come to have meaning within the networks of actions that people make of them. A simple black singlet becomes a sign.

This is the fourth thing we can say about culture. It uses rituals and artefacts to sustain its coherence across space and time, but it is not reducible to those artefacts and rituals. Understanding culture is not just a matter of reading its 'texts'. One has to follow them around, see what uses or abuses they are subjected to in *everyday life*.[23]

The fifth thing we can say about cultures is that they make sense of time and space for their members. They are a resource for coping with good and bad fortune. In the city where my encounter with the truck packers took place, both the cultures in question are under stress. In New York, gay culture has been hard hit by the AIDS pandemic. Urban working-class culture is struggling because blue collar jobs are drying up. In both cases, the sense of identity provided by the culture is a resource for coping with these bad turns of fortune, but in neither case can culture itself reverse that fortune. That depends on the resources the state and the economy between them put towards health care and employment, in these examples.

Modern living added a whole new dimension to what it is cultures have to manage. Capitalism, as Karl Marx said, is a dynamic force in society, and the modern society it shapes is one where 'all that is solid melts into air, all that is sacred is profaned'.[24] Capitalism accelerated the changes that culture has to try to make intelligible to its members. This is one of the reasons a wide range of people have come to focus on culture, because it appears to be the process at work that lends *continuity* and meaning to lives that otherwise are battered pretty hard by rapid economic and social change.

So the sixth thing we can say about culture is that it has become a focus for attention as capitalism increases the pace and scale of change people have to adapt to. This idea goes back to the Scottish enlightenment, and the idea I've already discussed of the role culture has to play once the division of labour has *fragmented* life and makes of us narrow people.[25]

More radical writers, influenced by Marx, will see the idea of culture as compensation for a fragmented and alienated life as a con. Guy Debord, perhaps the last of the great revolutionary thinkers of Europe, will call it 'the spectacle'. In his view, everything that is alienated from us by the relentless division of labour comes back to haunt us as the media spectacle. You go to work. You make things. You never see those things again. You get paid. With that pay, you are supposed to buy things back again. But the value of the things you made is greater than the value of the stuff you can buy with your pay. The difference is called profit. The people who earn the profit are called capitalists. This way of organising things is called capitalism. As if in compensation for being short-changed of the things one can buy, everything seems to be available as an image.

The images of advertising and TV and cinema and all that present back to the people who made stuff the image of what they made, but no longer possess, appearing as a perfect world of images in all their splendour. As Debord puts it in his own cryptic style, 'all time, all space, becomes foreign to them as their own alienated products accumulate. The spectacle is a map of this new world—a map drawn to the scale of the territory itself'.[26] Debord was always looking forward to the day when workers would give in to the passions the spectacle incites, not just by buying a new dishwasher, but by throwing a brick through the window and taking it. The looting that accompanied the Los Angeles riots is just as much a product of the structure of feeling of capitalism as a Mother's Day shopping spree.

A less apocalyptic view of culture sees it not as false compensation and true revolution, but simply as *resistance*. Cultures are hardy weeds. They tend to make the best of things. They sprout through cracked pavements. Their seeds lie dormant in hard times and hard ground, and flourish in a little light and water. As Michel de Certeau maintains, cultures can be an invisible fibre of little tactics by which people maintain some sense of possibility in lives lived in spaces always under someones's control. For de Certeau, culture resides in the qualities of little everyday actions, always singular, particular, almost unnoticeable. Things that can't ever be entirely plotted on any grid.[27]

So far I have talked about culture as a structure of feeling that everybody within a particular culture more or less shares. There is another notion of culture altogether, which is culture as the best of what was thought and expressed. The English Victorian essayist Matthew Arnold thought of culture this way, and literary and fine art studies still do to this day.[28] They are interested in the question of what constitutes good cultural artefacts. They tend to rest on the belief that the study of particularly good artefacts of culture will make you a refined and gentle human being. So in a sense literary or art intellectuals form a peculiar kind of culture: one that picks out a quite select range of artefacts with which to make a quite rarefied structure of feeling. This kind of critical culture is really just a particular example of the wider process of culture at work.

Learning a particular structure of feeling gives one no special insight into other people's structures of feeling. Indeed, for our present purposes it has to remain an open question whether there is any way at all to get an overview of how structures of feeling, in general, operate. Literary and fine art cultures have no special knowledge of culture in general. The view these cultures hold of other cultures may be even more distorted by prejudice and intolerance of different cultures than, say, working-class Manhattanites.

To sum it up: culture makes use of artefacts and rituals to pass on habits of identity. These resources of identity sustain structures of feeling that organise and make sense of everyday life. Culture has to do so under the extraordinary pressure of the modern division of labour, which fragments people's experience, such that people are always having to negotiate with each other a cultural politics that allows different bits of identity to coexist. Sounds impossible. But it gets even harder when culture finds itself circulated and negotiated not just through media that can simultaneously reach millions.

VECTORS OF MEDIA

For a long time now, cultures had rituals, architecture, writing, art and music to extend their influence across space and into the future, and to record what culture has by way of accumulated resources for getting by and getting along. We don't usually think of, say, an old grave stone as 'media technology', but if by media we refer to the means of getting information from one place to another, or one time to another, then 'media' it surely is. Nor do we usually think of conversation as media technology, or a piano. That these things are around is so much a part of our second nature that they hardly give us pause to consider just exactly how they work.

When something is 'second nature', it means it has become a habit, something taken for granted. It's a useful term, for it implies that, no matter what one's nature may have been to start with, there is a whole bunch of experiences by which it gets made over by culture; made and remade into something else. Culture, then, could be the process by which the jolt of new experiences becomes naturalised into habit—into second nature.

Second nature sometimes means something a bit broader—not just the process by which habits are built, but whole *environments*. People transform nature into second nature. Even Aboriginal cultures did this, if we are to believe writers like Eric Rolls and Tim Flannery about the degree to which 'firestick farming' transformed dense forests into open scrub.[29] Needless to say, since white folks invaded the continent, the transformation of the raw materials of nature into a second nature of roads and buildings has been far more rapid and irreversible.

Aboriginal culture passed on from place to place and from past to future certain kinds of knowledge about how to make second nature. There were—and still are—Aboriginal media technologies. Consider, for example, what Bruce Chatwin described in somewhat lyrical terms as the songlines—the Aboriginal practice of narrating the relations between places in terms of mythic stories which organise a whole knowledge of the land.[30]

In other words, Aboriginal society was an 'information society', just as the society of the white settlers was an 'information society'—and so too is that of the present. This might, at first sight, seem like a strange thing to say. The Labor party politician and visionary Barry Jones introduced Australian readers to the idea of the 'information revolution' in his book *Sleepers Wake!*. I agree with Jones that there are changes going on that 'will raise fundamental questions about the human condition'.[31] But strangely enough, these questions seem to be quite commonplace now. It just isn't the case any more that few are able or willing to talk about the information revolution, as it was once called, or the coming of cyberspace, to put it in the jargon of the 1990s. The idea of a 'new paradigm', far from being new, already seems to be second nature, even before the idea really becomes a reality.

So I want to cut into the figure of speech of the 'information society' another way, and perhaps encourage a little imagination to take off from seeing things otherwise. Let's consider things this way: the information society is not what is new. All societies are information societies. It is something else that is changing. Let's call 'culture' that pattern one recognises in the way a society moves information from place to place, time to time, through which it constructs its second nature. Now, if cultures are the patterns one can see in the way information flies about the place, what if we take a look at the *vectors* that move information around, rather than at the information itself?

A word on this word vector: I've borrowed it from the writings of French urbanist and speculative writer Paul Virilio.[32] It is a term from geometry meaning a line of fixed length and direction but having no fixed position. Virilio employs it to mean any trajectory along which bodies, information or warheads can potentially pass. For example, a flight from New York to Sydney, via Los Angeles, is a vector both me and my baggage might happen to be on. There are certain fixed qualities about this vector. The plane travels at a certain range of speeds, has a certain maximum distance, and so on. But in theory it could fly to any direction from its starting point, and land at any point within a circle, the radius of which is determined by the amount of fuel it can carry. In other words, its flight is of fixed maximum length but potentially in any direction. The virtual dimension to any vector is the range of possible movements of which it is capable.

While flying from New York to Los Angeles, I pick up the telephone and make a call to Sydney, to ask a friend to pick me up at the airport. That call has different properties—it moves faster than the aircraft, obviously, and it moves only information, not bodies and baggage. Virilio's interest is in the way vectors tend to get faster and more flexible, connecting anywhere to anywhere, revealing every last fold of the earth to the observer, and what this might mean for the way power is organised. I'm interested in the way the vectors along which *information* moves separated out from those that move *things*. Information can now almost always get there before you can ship your goods there, or dispatch a division. Second nature starts to appear pretty slow compared to this emerging 'third nature' of communication vectors. Third nature seems increasingly to be in control of second nature. We no longer have roots we have aerials. Or as the Aboriginal writer Mudrooroo says, apropos people like me: 'They love grids, all straight lines, all leading to somewhere'.[33]

This is the other source of anxiety in the 1990s besides the market. The vectors of third nature, from multichannel and satellite TV to the internet, seem always to speed up, proliferate, merge, divide, mutate, and beam in on us from afar. The market seems to be everywhere; the media seem to be everywhere. Market and media merge as endless data-bit-streams, transmitted all the way around the world. They could be stock quotes or soap opera, all rendered purely virtual, instantaneous, ubiquitous, senseless. A perpetual challenge to the imagination, and hence to the very idea of culture, and the very possibility of the virtual republic.

We are not entirely without resources for thinking about such things. The Canadian media studies scholar Harold Innis had the idea that the types of vector people use will not only shape certain kinds of culture, but will offer different possibilities for the shape and durability of society, economy and nation. His famous example, to put it in a very crude way, was to think about the way ancient Egypt built itself out of media with very different properties—stone and papyrus.[34]

Papyrus is what he called a 'space-binding' kind of media. It made possible the transmission of written orders across space, and the return of written reports. It's a useful tool for making empires, and enables the waging of distant military campaigns and colonial administration. On the other hand, stone is 'time-binding'. Through the construction of temples and the pyramids, a priestly caste can sustain their authority from generation to generation. This simplifies Innis' famous essays on these questions a great deal, but the point is that he offers a way of thinking about the potentials that different kinds of media offer.

Innis also argued that it might be important for a society that its culture be based on some kind of 'balance' between space-binding and time-binding media. He was very worried about what he saw as a bias towards space-binding media in his own time, which was why he was very active in the formulation of media policy in the 1950s in his native Canada. I'm less sure about whether one can determine what constitutes bias or balance between different kinds of media, but I think Innis was on to something, nevertheless.

In a remarkable essay on the development of the telegraph, American media studies scholar James Carey picks up where Innis left off.[35] What is distinctive about the telegraph is that it is the first really successful technology for moving information about from one place to another faster than one could move a person or an object. Think about it: Before the telegraph, information had to be moved around by road or rail, but it could not really get there any faster than, say, an army or a wagonload of wheat. But from the telegraph onwards, one vector after another added to this basic ability to move information faster than things. It's not necessarily that there is 'more' information than there ever was before. I'm not even sure how one would measure that. What has changed, since the invention of the telegraph, is the relation between information and other things that society moves around in space—people, goods, and weapons.

These days, cultures may have access to television, radio, mass print media, video, computer networks, and so on. The vectors along which information passes are now many and varied, and not equally available to all cultures. Thinking about culture, questions of power are never far away. From the telegraph onwards, these vectors progressively create a new space of possibilities for organising what happens. After the telegraph came the telephone, the television, telecommunications: a whole series of developments of a certain kind of experience—*telesthesia*, or perception at a distance. They are what made possible the development of Australia as a progressively integrated economy, society and culture. They are the conditions of possibility for the 'abstract community' of nation which can imagine itself, at one and the same time, as diverse and coherent. They are what make possible a virtual republic, where specific cultures bring their interests and passions into an ongoing conversation about what kinds of things might be possible.

Like everything else that sticks around for a while and gets woven into the fabric of everyday life, the experience of telesthesia becomes a habit. I can remember when making an international phone call was a really big deal. Something rare and expensive and requiring special assistance from an operator. Now I just don't think that much about it. Punch in the numbers and there you are, talking to someone on the other side of the world. 'No one's far from anyone, any more', as Telstra ads used to say—as if it were the most natural thing in the world. 'Reach out and touch someone', as another ad puts it. Only you don't touch them. You experience the other person at a distance—telesthesia. How quickly it comes to seem so . . . natural.

While it may feel natural for some to inhabit this media-made world, I suspect there's a fundamental change here that has a lot of people just a bit spooked. It's no longer a case of making second nature out of nature, of building things and getting used to living in the world people build. I think it might be interesting to consider telesthesia to be something fundamentally different. What gets woven out of telegraph, telephone, television, telecommunications is not a second nature, but what I call third nature.

Think back to an image I used right at the start of this book—listening to talkback radio while driving in the car. Here we are in second nature: the traffic, the road rules—what could be more second nature than knowing how to drive? But somehow it still seems remarkable to me that intersecting, overlapping, permeating this whole landscape of buildings and roads and moving vehicles is another, quite different—composed of phone cells and radio waves, via which people have a conversation without being together in the same place.

The matrix of vectors that make up the media also bring with them new problems. The national space of third nature is no longer protected by what historian Geoffrey Blainey called the 'tyranny of distance'.[36] That Qantas ad doesn't just reflect a structure of feeling within Australian culture. It is part of what creates it—the media. How many Australians know those images of the outback desert as something to which cultural sentiments attach because they have seen them on TV, as opposed to having experienced it first-hand? A majority, I suspect, know Australia as an experience of telesthesia. There is another TV ad like the Qantas one, featuring panoramic helicopter shots of the desert. We fly over Uluru, and it turns into a Big Mac, we fly over the Olgas, and they turn into french fries . . . I suspect that some of the anxieties that recur in Australian national culture from time to time may not be unconnected with fresh experiences of the global media vectors reaching deep into Australian everyday life.

Sometimes, even within the national domain, the vectors that make third nature bring together cultures that had formerly been quite separate. Third nature forces negotiations on cultures, whether those cultures want it or not. This I would call the 'tyranny of difference'. A key instance is the role of television in breaking down the distinctions between men's culture and women's culture, which had once had their separate spaces. Watching re-runs of TV sitcoms from the 1950s today, what seems so quaint is what separate worlds the men and the women occupy. He goes to work and hangs with his buddies. She shops and cooks and cleans and dishes the dirt with the girls.[37] But the same television vectors that brought these wholesome images of the divided lives of men and women into those divided lives was also portraying the civil rights movement, the first stirrings of the women's movement, and daily bites of political and social imagery from what had once been a pretty much exclusively male public world. The media pass through all of the neat boundaries of one from the other, forcing fresh negotiations.[38] The debates about feminism and political correctness, which I will take up in later chapters, indicate that this process still has a long way to go.

There has been a vast expansion of vectors that have the ability to traverse *space*, from the telegraph to the internet. But what about *time*? Architecture is also a kind of media, but one designed to communicate across time rather than across space. Think of the Sydney Opera House, as it appears from an aircraft window—a permanent sign of Sydney, still talking to us about its designer's dreams and political folly. Think also of the crude cartoon of its curves held aloft by the dancers at the closing ceremony of the Atlanta Olympic Games. The image of that building—which has existed just a few decades—already the international semaphore for Sydney, recognisable to a TV audience of millions around the world. The image of it is everywhere in space. It is even aboard a Voyager spacecraft, on its way out of the solar system.

Part of the significance of culture lies in its capacity to act as a reservoir of stories and images from which people can draw material that indicates future possibilities. Culture can be a kind of virtual reserve in which the way things could be exceeds the brute and banal facts of the way things are. Have space-binding vectors of telesthesia like the telephone, television and telecommunications overcome the capacity of our time-binding culture to keep up with them? That's something to think about later, when we get on to the anxieties about culture that circulate in the 'culture wars' waged in Australian media.

Seems like since the start of this chapter we've been travelling all over the place. It's a map of this book's horizons. But now it's time to bring it all back home. Please fasten your seat belts. The virtual republic leads a fitful existence. It depends on the extension of sympathy into an abstract community. It depends on the mutual recognition of different kinds of entitlement to participate within it. It depends on the legacy of culture and the reach of the media being rich and expansive enough to sustain it. And then, only then, can one talk about a virtual republic, in which everyone might participate in the trajectory of the nation into the unknown and unknowable future. Even if it comes into being, nothing guarantees that it embodies sufficient wisdom to keep us out of the tail spin of the relentless privatisation of every aspect of everyday life. But I think it's our best hope. The best cure for uncertainty is the harnessing of the thoughts and feelings of all the people in the most productive ways that said assembly can imagine, and in the most imaginative ways that it can produce.

2

Mapping the Antipodes

The only universal history is the history of contingency.

Gilles Deleuze

MAPS

There is quite a particular view of things and the world that comes from being by the sea. I grew up in Newcastle, New South Wales, in what was then an industrial town, about 100 miles up the coast from Sydney. We lived in a white weatherboard house with a flat roof that perched on the edge of a valley. The Pacific Highway ran past the front, and at night the hiss of cars easing around the gentle bend lulled me to sleep.

The house was a sort of antipodean homage to American architect Frank Lloyd Wright, whose prairie houses my father, also an architect, admired.[1] Better living through design. He would show me pictures of them, as we lounged in the lounge room, while fresh sunlight cut with gum tree shadows tipped in through the giant plate glass window. Sometimes birds would crash into that glass and fall to the ground in a stupor. They could see light from the windows opposite and tried to fly right through. It was a house made of weatherboard and light.

From the panoramic window I could look down into the valley and watch the trains go past the quarry and into the tunnel. Down below, the railway; out the front, the Pacific Highway, with the house perched in between. And on the pelmet over the big window, on which the curtains seemed permanently open, sat a model of a ship that my brother had glued together: the *Cutty Sark*, one of the greatest of the clipper ships. It's just a brand of whisky now.

I went to China once. I went to the Shanghai museum. There's not much to see there. But there is a model of the *Cutty Sark*. The clipper ships carried coal from Newcastle, New South Wales to Shanghai, China and tea from China to the ports of England. Steam and Suez put an end to that.[2]

I remember looking at a map of China, in that sunlit room, when I was a child. We had been down at the beach, as usual for a bright summer day, and I was furiously digging a hole in the sand with my little plastic spade. 'Keep digging like that,' my father joked, 'and you'll come out on the other side of the world, in China.' But looking at it on the map at home, China didn't seem to be on the other side of the world. It wasn't very far away at all. And since it was not so far, maybe, one day, I could go there and see for myself.

When I did go to China, I realised that in lots of ways I had learned a conception of the world as the English saw it, building their empire. It's a conception of the world that begins with its oceans. You run your finger across the blue of the map until you find a likely edge. Then you ask what the land beyond that coastal edge is good for: a safe harbour for her majesty's ships, a deep river down which to bring the raw materials, and up which to send the manufactured goods, and the occasional gunboat. Colour the land beyond that edge pink for empire.

In China, I met people to whom the world wasn't about edges. It was about what happened in the middle. China is, after all, the middle kingdom. When I tried to explain that I was from the antipodes, from the globe's 'other foot' or other side, the concept didn't make sense. There may only be one world to map, but there is more than one way to map this world.[3]

We had *The Reader's Digest Great World Atlas* at home in Newcastle, and I liked to look through it. When Bugs Bunny outsmarted the bumbling Elmer Fudd, so that once again he 'took a wrong turn at Albuquerque', I looked it up, so he need never ever get lost again. My home in Newcastle, made of weatherboard and light, was also made of books and television.

I've lost that *Atlas*, but I still know all the words to *The Bugs Bunny Show* theme song.

My father didn't like me watching American TV shows. That was a blind he would rather have kept closed. I was attracted to the light from the other side of the world. And perhaps it was not a bad thing. In Bugs Bunny's world, characters aren't really good and bad, they are just different. When they chase each other, we know nobody will get caught or hurt. It isn't about punishing anyone for being different, as if difference were morally wrong. Rather, the chase is a way of making the differences between the characters into something marvellous. Each character has their own special kind of wit that makes them—in the flux of events, with the heavy weight about to fall on them—bring out the best action that is within their nature. *The Bugs Bunny Show* is an ethic for living in an imperfect world, with others who are different.[4]

Sometimes, bored with television, I would take the *Atlas* down from its special shelf and trace the outlines of strange countries onto tracing paper. Then I would colour in the maps with coloured pencils. First, I would draw all the contours of nature. In green and blue and brown I projected an image of the ocean, the land and the mountains. This was a jaggy mass of impassable terrains, each line uniquely tortuous and torturous. The geography of place. All craggy and squiggly and never the same twice.

Then, with a fat black marker, I drew big black dots where the rivers meet the sea. And then, with a ruler, I drew nice straight lines, joining the dots—cities and highways. The geography of space. The geography of 'second nature'. Everything flattened and straightened and smoothed, like the road and the railway and the flat, plain, pure white walls of our house, in between. The natural barriers and contours of the land overcome, made into the scene and the quarry for a second nature of productive flows.

Next, I took out a red marker and fetched some glasses from the kitchen. Placing the glasses over the cities, I traced red circles of varying sizes. I tried to remember how far out of town the radio faded out on those endless car trips, and which cities seemed to have different television when we went there on holidays. The geography of telesthesia, a new map traced on top of nature and second nature. A third nature connecting and coordinating the movements of people, the making of

goods, the extraction of raw material from nature—and trans-
mitting, all the while, images of life, from Bugs Bunny to James
Dibble reading the ABC news.[5]

The development of second nature—of roads and factories
and mines and cities—these are the images that predominate
in the culture of the modern.[6] Like in my favourite episode of
Bugs Bunny, where Bugs has to fight off developers who want
to put a freeway right through the place where he dug his
burrow. The workmen plant dynamite and blast a huge crater,
but Bugs' burrow remains, like a long tall chimney, persisting
right in the middle of the hole. He is like a little bit of
recalcitrant nature, resisting the concreting of the world.

How is it possible, in such a world, that we are still free?
When the highwaymen came to pour concrete down Bugs
Bunny's burrow—a macabre scene worthy of Edgar Allan Poe—
Bugs stands at the opening and unfurls an umbrella.[7] He sends
great gloops of concrete pouring down the sides of the long
funnel that is all that remains of his home. A quick straight-
ening with a trowel, and Bugs has made for himself a concrete
highrise home, using the new material to preserve his old
habitat. The freeway to Albuquerque will have to detour around
him. Bugs is a rabbit of wit and improvisation. How very
Australian.

SPACES OF FLOWS

I still live by the sea, in Ultimo, Sydney. It's a lively place.
When I first came here in the mid-1980s it was a mix of low
income housing crouching beneath giant warehouses and wool
stores. Historian Geoffrey Bolton writes that 'wool, more than
any other single industry throughout the 1950s and 1960s, was
the great mainstay of Australia's export trade'.[8] By the 1980s,
the wool stores stood empty. Walking around Ultimo in the
1980s was like walking around an empty movie set after the
action stops. No more ships, no more trade, no more machine
shops. Film director George Miller had a lot of pigs here once,
while shooting *Mad Max III*. And the old abandoned powerhouse was also a movie set, before becoming a museum.
Buildings lead such contingent lives these days. Not the lives
for which they were designed at all.

By the mid-1990s, the *Sydney Morning Herald* took to

describing Ultimo and adjoining Pyrmont as 'Sydney's fastest growing suburb'. More than 6500 apartments went up in the first half of the decade. The Foxtel cable TV headquarters, Channel 10 and the Sydney Casino inked themselves onto the map, joining the Census Bureau, the ABC, and the state betting agency, the TAB. The *Sydney Morning Herald* itself fitted out new offices just a short walk away, across Darling Harbour. Where once this part of town was about shipping and manufacturing, in the 1990s it is about tourism and information.

Talking heads for the City West Corporation, responsible for the redevelopment of the peninsula, casually talked of private investment in new building of over a billion dollars. Real estate agents enthused about the trend away from the suburbs, where the real estate market went 'ratshit', and towards cosmopolitan living. Or they went into raptures about 'Asian investors', buying Sydney apartments as holiday homes or for their kids to live in while at university. The old Grace Brothers store on Broadway, very close to Sydney University, was converted into 585 units. They sold out in two months, before the conversion was even finished. Most were sold off the plan in Singapore and Jakarta. In Ultimo, 62 per cent of the population were born overseas, compared with a Sydney average of 33 per cent.[9]

I read all this in the Saturday *Herald*, sitting in the French coffee shop. It's cool here, in the shade of a high-rise block, if not quiet. But I don't mind the sounds of kids playing basketball and shouting in Cantonese that waft from the roof of the community centre. There was no coffee shop until quite recently. And certainly no community centre. I lift my gaze from the newspaper. A ball parabolas into the basket.

'The city is increasingly divided between an international core of Australians and foreigners who look across the globe for their cues, and the outlying suburbs, where the people may have more in common with Adelaide residents than the CBD dwellers', writes *Sydney Morning Herald* journalist Deidre Macken. Through the 1980s, Sydney increased its share of both the poorest and the richest Australians, compared to other cities. The wealthy cluster here in the east and in the north, while the poor head west. Draw a line from Castle Hill to the airport, and east of that you have high concentrations of income and education; to the west, high scores for unemployment and obesity. 'The great suburban sprawl is now the size of Perth and, for all the attention it receives, might as well be in Western Australia.'

Like many people living on the eastern side of that divide, I've heard rumours about the west, and about the 'Westies' who live there, but I've hardly ever been. I'm more likely to catch a plane to Melbourne or Manila than to visit Penrith or Parramatta. And I'm more likely to be getting phone calls or email from people in New York than from Emu Plains. On top of the differences in income and education and health between eastern and western Sydney, there is also a difference in mobility. Some people are getting their information from a widely dispersed range of places, and extracting opportunities from that—and some people aren't.

A new regime of power has taken hold of the byways of the planet. A regime not of sea lanes and ship lore, but of comsats and data flows. We live now, as urban sociologist and planner Manuel Castells says, not in a space of *places* but a space of *flows*:[10] flows of information, flows of money, flows of jobs and livelihoods. Third nature: new patterns of proximity, prosperity . . . and poverty. Here I am, here we all are, living on those maps I drew as a kid. Here we are with new problems for the virtual republic, not necessarily anticipated by the designers and engineers of third nature, and not necessarily solved just by drawing up a community centre. Cities are now conjunctures where the diasporas of space meet the diasporas of time.

INVASION DAY

I didn't much care for the Australian Bicentennial celebrations of 1988. It's not just that I sympathise with Aboriginal people who think of Australia Day as Invasion Day, although it is partly that. I grew up reading books on the highland clearances in Scotland, like John Prebble's popular histories; stories of how southern 'improvers', in league with debt-ridden chiefs, turfed the clansfolk off their hereditary lands to make way for sheep and the new commercial economy. As Karl Marx wrote, 'They conquered the field for capitalist agriculture, incorporated the soil into capital, and created for the urban industries the necessary supplies of free and rightless proletarians'.

Some fought back against the bailiffs and troopers, but in

the end the land belonged to the sheep. The highlanders found their way into the cities, where they languished in pools of dispossessed labour until set in motion again by the wheels of factory work. Others emigrated to the colonies, including Australia. Perhaps some made their money running the sheep that finally put the highland wool business out of business, only to see the sheep walks replaced by theme parks of forest and deer, 'as fat as London Aldermen'.[11]

I always imagined this was my story, but I don't really know. I grew up modern, like my parents, and like their parents. And being modern, the past is a lost country. 'All that is solid melts into air . . .' Forgetting feels like a 'southerly buster' blowing in off the sea on a hot Sydney day. So I have no stories of the clearances other than from books, just as I have no stories of the invasion of Australia, other than from books. It doesn't pay to forget—or to invest the past with the burden of too much memory. It's what one makes of the past that frees one from it.

Some of my mother's people were from the highlands. My father's family were Glaswegian. Here there are documents, and from documents come facts, and from facts, a story. John Newlands Wark, born 1817, educated in Glasgow, where he becomes an engineer. Working for the City and Suburban Gas Co. he acquires a thorough knowledge of the process of gas manufacture, both practical and theoretical. But his wife Margaret suffers from asthma, and her doctor advises moving to a more temperate climate. And so John and Margaret take a chance. They sail aboard the *City of Manchester* to Auckland, New Zealand in 1863. Within two years, the first gas flows to the city of Auckland.

The climate was not much of an improvement on Glasgow, or on Margaret's health. So John applies for a position in Sydney, as engineer to AGL, the Australian Gas Light Co. Here's another part of the story where chance plays its part. John Wark isn't appointed, but the chosen applicant, a Mr T. E. James, drops dead a few months into his new position. At his second go, John gets the job, ahead of 24 applicants, and becomes the company's engineer in 1868.

AGL sack him five years later. They catch him using AGL tools and workmen to remove pipes, which he had bought from the city council, from the streets of Sydney. The pipes are on their way to Bathurst, for what will become the first of an extended family business building and managing gas works for country towns. According to AGL, 'Mr Wark was a very good engineer, but a very difficult gentleman'.

The AGL is long gone, but not its very fine circular showroom, opposite Central Railway Station, a short walk from where I live. My father took me to see it, to show me our ancestor's name carved on the foundation stone as the engineer of the gas storage reservoirs that are still under the building. It's now part of a huge commercial complex. It's protected by the umbrella of 'heritage', yet incorporated into the new. Both the showroom and the reservoir stand empty. The site manager spoke in visions of a flash restaurant and nightclub.

Invasion Day 1988 just left me cold. On the one hand I feel like the accidental issue of another dispossessed people, and that I was dispossessed, in turn, of their stories. I grew up modern. So in place of a lost tradition I found another, in my mother's books, taken down from those functional built-in shelves my father designed for them. Here's John Prebble, from her old orange-jacketed Penguin paperback: 'At Culloden, and during the military occupation of the glens, the British government first defeated a tribal uprising and then destroyed the society that had made it possible. The exploitation of the country during the next hundred years was within the same pattern of colonial development—new economies introduced for the greater wealth of the few, and the unproductive obstacle of a native population removed or reduced'.[12] English colonialism did not take place in the antipodes alone. And in the antipodes, many of its foot soldiers were ragged armies of the dispossessed, dispossessing. Irony is the wet-nurse of history.

A little part of that greater wealth from the new economies accrued to the Warks. John Newlands Wark, at the time he was sacked by AGL, was on 700 pounds per year. I can't help admiring knowledge applied to organising the production of something useful, be it gas for streetlights or an architect's plan. Even if those productions become, in turn, the raw material for new designs—the old gas showroom swallowed whole by an office block. The reason why this patrimony might make me look askance at Invasion Day is a little more obscure. If the legacy of those stories about my mother's distant kin instils a certain 'postcolonial' resentment of the English and their empire, then maybe the gas works story is about being neither for it nor against it, but making something out of the space it created, to create something else in turn: gas, light, heat, wealth—and a story.

So while on Australia Day, 1988, thousands of people crowded into Darling Harbour to look at the tall ships, celebrate the invasion of the continent and the birth of a free-range prison, I eschewed the walk down to the shore and watched the whole thing on television. It was a re-enactment of the white invasion of the Australian continent, performed 200 years later for the cameras. As with the first arrival of the First Fleet, on this second coming the invaders parked their boats and thanked their sponsors. Where the English came and colonised, corporate captains came and coca-colonised.

I mention all this because while I think by now you can see why I responded to the whole thing with a certain cynical indifference, I want to explain why it also struck me as quite wonderful. I'm not talking here about the spectacle of English and local panjandrums hopping on and off boats while the bands play and the flags fly and the crowds cheer—before getting on with the serious business of sunning its multitudinous body and getting on the piss. Nor am I talking about the Aboriginal protest, with which I sympathised. Tiga Bayles told the rally that asking Aboriginal people to celebrate Australia Day was like asking Jewish people to celebrate the Holocaust. I'm talking about the strange feeling I had all year in 1988, of the extraordinary parallel between the technologies that made the whole thing possible the first time around, and the technologies that made it possible to celebrate it two centuries later.

POTENTIAL VECTORS AND VIRTUAL VECTORS

For a long time Australian culture has manifested a desperate attempt to fix a few things in consciousness between two great abstract terrains of movement. The first is the sea. The sea, as the philosopher Hegel says, 'gives us the idea of the indefinite, the unlimited, and infinite: and in feeling his own infinite in that Infinite, man is stimulated and emboldened to stretch beyond the limited: the sea invites man to conquest and to piratical plunder, but also to honest gain and to commerce'.[13] Thus, ambivalently, did this first tentative vector traverse the sea.

This word 'vector' has travelled a bit, from language to

language, discourse to discourse, meaning to meaning. I'm very fond of it.[14] Its roots mingle with those of the word 'way'—the way: the road, the course of movement, the path of life. Also tangled up in there is the sense of 'to carry'. The vectors traced by these old English, Dutch and German senses cross with the Latin 'via', and with the sense of 'to weigh'. From there it's a short path to specialised technical meanings. In geometry a vector is a line of fixed length but no fixed position; in physics, a quantity having direction as well as magnitude; in biology, the means of transmission of an infection. I am unaware of a sense of the term in the engineering of gas works, but no doubt an enterprising engineer could think of one.

The sense I give to the term traces a line through all of those senses. To me, a vector is a technology that moves something from somewhere to somewhere else, at a given speed and cost and under certain specified conditions. They come in two kinds: those that move mostly physical objects about the place, and those that move only information. Transport and communication were once one and the same thing. Now communication moves at a faster rate, and is able to model and coordinate movements of ever more intricate design over great distances.

'Cyberspace', people call it, this emergent terrain of information vectors. The novelist William Gibson popularised the term, and it caught on, spreading over the vector, naming the world the vector makes.[15] Cyber means to steer, from the Greek for the rudder of a ship and the one who steers it. Cyberspace is the second great abstract terrain of movement. It began with the telegraph, but speeds up and proliferates in the late twentieth century. Like the navigation of the sea, it gives us an idea of the unlimited: digital! cyber! hyper! multi! inter! data! space! media! active! Like the sea: plunder and conquest; commerce and honest gain. Immersed in cyberspace, people now experience the three kinds of relation that people once felt about the sea.

Firstly, there are *imaginary relations* to the other. The vector connects one to an elsewhere, but rather than think about this as *relating* formerly separate things together and making of them a third and different thing, people become preoccupied by the difference of the other place, and forget about what relates them. In other words, rather than seeing the relations passing *between* places, one sees only the borders that *separate* them.

Rather than seeing the way different qualities mix and combine into a whole new *type* of space, one sees only what is strange, what is other.

I wonder if there wasn't a little bit of this in the story about Margaret Wark's asthma. Glasgow is dank and damp; but the antipodes are the other of dank and damp, they must be dry and warm. So she follows her passion for the other, for the dry and warm climate, which has what she lacks, suitable air for her troubled respiration. Like all passions based on filling a lack in oneself by fleeing along a vector towards the other, it is not quite what she imagined.

Secondly, there is the world of *potential relations*, lurking within the vector: the world of honest gain and piratical plunder. A vector can connect anywhere to anywhere, within the limits of what is technically feasible at a given time. So it has the potential to make connections of a certain kind, which in turn can form the basis for producing something out of what is related. Along the vector to the antipodes flows tools, skills, machines—and out of them John Wark makes gas plants for lighting and heating. Other engineers build roads and bridges, mines and ports, and eventually what flows back along the same vector are wool and wheat and gold.

But thirdly, there is the *virtual dimension* to the vector. An imaginary relation projects a fantasy of how different the other place is, and forgets about what passes to and fro. It is about hanging on to an old identity, by distinguishing it from that with which it mingles. A potential relation makes a fetish out of what passes to and fro, and deals with differences only in quantities—expenses, wages, quantities of goods and their prices; pounds, shillings and pence. It is about making things, but always making more of the same. A virtual relation is about the differences between places *and* about what passes between them. It is about how places differ without forgetting they are connected, and about how they are connected without forgetting that they differ. The virtual side of a vector is all the things that might happen across the terrain it creates that are singular, unique, unrepeatable events—experiences that exceed all categories.

The historian Don Watson points out that, while noticeably prominent in publishing and the professions, the Scots are one of those immigrant cultures to Australia that tended relatively rapidly to lose their cultural identity. But did they just disappear, leaving nothing but their names, scattered all over the landscape? The poet Les Murray claims that upon doing a rough survey he found the 'proportion of Scots Australians among our poets was freakishly high'.[16] The list might begin with Murray himself, Judith Wright, and Ern Malley. Murray's speculations on the subject have a whimsical cast, 'consciously developed as a personal myth'. But developed not so much to insist on Scottish ethnicity as a resistant otherness within Australian culture, but rather to suggest that while many Scots just got on with getting on, some were doing something different. Neither resisting nor desiring assimilation, but making something else. In moving towards becoming Australian, making 'Australian' something else again.

Something like Judith Wright's writing, and the writer Judith Wright.[17] A writer who writes of the lost country of the past, and for an Australia yet to come. One that no longer wilfully forgets its bloodied past; that might institute a treaty between indigenous and settler selves; that might make a different future. Wright is a writer who could only happen because a matrix of vectors moved her ancestors from one side of the world to the other, making differences collide and harden, but also sometimes making differences productive, making them differentiate further and further, releasing the virtual in new ways of being. How very Australian.

Now that we find ourselves enmeshed in a new net of vectors, those of global communication, all the old anxieties about this vulnerable island continent with its fragile soils and fragile culture come back in one form or another, like the chant of the dead. There's the feeling of being caught up in new potentials. There's the feeling of dread, of loss that goes with this, and the tendency to reach for the comfort of identity, to draw a hard line between what is 'us' and what is foreign. But the coming of global media, of cyberspace, is also the virtual come calling. A challenge to let cultures propagate and proliferate along new lines.

It is precisely because the 1788 invasion *succeeded* that Australians look at every new vector that opens towards these shores with ambivalence. It's not guilt that troubles immigrant Australia's relation to Aboriginals as much as the fear that we'll suffer the same fate. Perhaps this is the underlying anxiety, that sense that Australians lack something, and for want of it, may lose the lot. Like the gamblers down at the Sydney Casino in

Ultimo, or like the state government and the developers who built it, everything is wagered on the potentials of the vector. Should luck run against the lucky country, what remains?

These are times of both incredulity towards heroic stories about the past and of a growing public impatience with stories of victimisation. Stories that are, respectively, what Karl Kraus called 'half truths and one-and-a-half truths'.[18] Neither will quite do the job of making good the wound of the buried country of the past. There is not enough puff left to puff the nation up with pride, and the alternative leads only to resentment—the two singularly most useless emotions for actually changing anything.

What these proud and resentful stories have in common is this: that vectors have the potential to erase a culture. A British naval empire came and colonised. American media imperialism came and coca-colonised. What was not useful in the process was discarded. Yet there is another side to these worlds of movement that, twice in Australian history, have caught the continent in their net. That other side is the virtual. The passion to fly by the nets. The will to move and make things move that has nothing to do with otherness or calculation.

The joy I experienced when I heard Yothu Yindi's 'Treaty' on the radio . . . at the time I couldn't explain it, but now perhaps I can. The arc of a voice, cutting against the grid of the beats. It's the joy of the virtual, of listening in to a moment of creation in which Aboriginal musicians from Arnhem Land take a terrain made possible by certain vectors, certain techniques, certain collaborators, to make something otherwise. Something that is not Aboriginal music, nor is it white music. Something that is not rock or country or dance music. Something that is neither a protest song nor a 'sell-out'. Yothu Yindi also sing about 'living in the mainstream', but in moving through the mainstream, they make the mainstream move somewhere else. Towards the virtual republic.

THE PANOPTICON VERSUS NEW SOUTH WALES

If the past is a matter of contingency rather than destiny, of routes rather than roots, then what can one make of it? The historian of ideas Michel Foucault writes about another kind of relation to the past. A genealogy that records the 'singularity of events outside of any monotonous finality'.[19] There is no pure moment of beginning, and no destiny, he says. There is no essence of the people that one might find, magically arising and persisting throughout events. Nothing is, in the end, revealed: 'Truth is undoubtedly the sort of error that cannot be refuted because it has hardened into an unalterable form in the long baking process of history'. We are to search through the generations of our descent, not for foundations, but for the accidents that result, in the present, in this body. Look for the traces left by the past in its practices and postures. History is not about revealing the hidden meaning or order within events, but the grasping of the rules by which bodies are organised.

Foucault's most famous example of the organisation of bodies is contained in his reading of Jeremy Bentham's plans for the Panopticon—the perfect prison, but also the perfect design for a hospital or school.[20] All of which are what Foucault considers 'disciplinary technologies' for making orderly bodies. Better living through design. From the perspective of the antipodes, or at least from a harbourside flat in Ultimo, one can contrast Foucault's notion of disciplinary technologies with what one might call 'vectoral technologies'. It is not the Panopticon but the British navy that in the Ultimo perspective emerges as a key technological regime for putting into practice the rational ambitions of the eighteenth-century enlightenment. As Robert Hughes recalls, Bentham titled one of his pamphlets *The Panopticon or New South Wales?*[21] While Foucault's writings have, I think quite rightly, influenced a lot of Australian writers, his most famous genealogy of the machinery of power is, to our world, a route not taken. As everyone who goes to school in New South Wales is taught, we are here because the British sent their prisoners, off and away, across the seas, bound for Botany Bay.

Bentham's Panopticon and transportation to Botany Bay have some things in common. They are both techniques for dealing with bodies that get in the way. In the case of both panoptic and vectoral technologies, it's about making space visible by seeing it with an overlaid grid. A city might set aside certain sites and build enclosed, panoptic spaces on them, within which a grid and a timetable organise the movements and activities of the recalcitrant bodies. Or a city might build ships and pack those bodies off across the sea, making the vectors to and from the antipodes a way of ridding itself of bodies, but maybe also making bodies productive, setting up flows of useful goods back from the other side. The world becomes the object of the vector, of the potentiality of movement. Bodies, cargoes, weapons, information: this principally naval technology produced, almost as an afterthought, Botany Bay, Sydney, New South Wales, Australia—one of the many antipodes of empire.

CAPTAIN COOK'S CLOCK

Perceptions enable powers: to perceive something is to make it a possible object of one's will. To order perceptions is to create the possibility of ordering the things perceived. The success of vectoral power depended on the ability to perceive the space of the world, and make the space of the world one in which movements can be ordered. This, quite simply, makes it a new world. A world in which a plan can be drawn on a map, and that possibility can be engineered in actuality, in the world the map perceives.

Maps precede territories: one has to know where a place is before one can find it. When I boarded a plane to China I knew roughly where it was going. I knew from the *Atlas* I scrutinised as a child. Because I knew China was there, I could form the desire to travel to it. Paul Foss argues that when western explorers went in search of the antipodes, they were not sailing into blind nothingness, but into a space already 'mapped' by the ancient philosophers.[22] On the other side of this world, according to the received wisdom, was this world's other, its antipode, its other foot. That what was known on the map was less than half, that this lack might be filled by sailing out to find it—now there is an obscure object of an explorer's passion.

What hampered mapping and moving over the oceans until the eighteenth century was the lack of an accurate way to fix the position of a ship in longitude. Latitude is relatively easy. Nature provides ways of perceiving how far north or south on the spinning earth one happens to be. But how far east or west? If one knew the exact time the sun set at one's home port, and could compare it to the time it set where one happened to be, then from the difference a sailor could compute a position on the spinning globe.

John Harrison engineered a solution, an accurate chronometer that would whirr and tick time in a straight line on a ship tossed every which way by the sea.[23] It binds time to its beat. This exact vector through time would allow navigators like James Cook to know their exact location in space, and map that space accordingly. Harrison's chronometer, put together with the other tools of navigation, was already a potential map of the ocean world. Cook made much of it actual, filling in the wavy lines of coast on the grid. A new time and space is produced—a world of possible movements, connections, creations, and conflicts.[24]

One of the things that made the English such relentlessly effective imperialists was the ability to assemble the various elements of a vectoral technology. It's not just a matter of good ships and chronometers. These things have to be brought together with the idea of there being something out there in the first place, and the desire to go find it. Power is always about assembling such odd combinations of things. Vectoral power requires something else as well—a way of linking the passion to discover, the evidence of what is discovered, and the consequent exploitation of that knowledge.

The passion to discover the other side of the world has its roots in the classical world view bequeathed to the west by Plato. In his metaphysical conception of things, what there is to find in the world are bits of evidence for the pure and eternal forms of which things as we find them are mere copies.[25] If I draw a circle, this is but a poor copy of the pure form or idea of the circle. If I draw the world, or at least those parts of it recorded on the maps of the early modern world, the symmetry of the form of the world requires that it have an other side, with attributes that mirror those of the known hemisphere. Hence the fear, and the passion, to go find it—the desire for the other. Even the sedentary Montaigne could write, 'I am so sick for freedom, that if anyone should forbid me access to some corner of the Indies, I should live distinctly less confortably'.[26] More venal desires may naturally follow in the wake of this abstract idea.

In his remarkable book *European Vision and the South Pacific*, Bernard Smith shows how the rise of British naval imperialism precipitates the fall of this neoclassical representation in the eighteenth century.[27] The neoclassical style pictured landscapes in terms of the Platonic ideal, and this aesthetic was institutionally enshrined in the Royal Academy. What the explorer's pictorial artists were enjoined to perceive were the signs of the pure form underneath the craggy outcrops of rock and imperfect specimens of plants and people. The difficulty was that as explorers discovered and depicted more and more things, the less they seemed to fit into the classical order of forms. So began a revolution in the ordering of perception of the world that would lead first to Joseph Banks and eventually to Charles Darwin. If we think of an order of classification as a map of the potential order of things, then in science as in navigation, maps preceded territories. In science as in navigation, one uses a wrong map in order to find out how to draw a more useful one.

The Royal Academy favoured representations of the *ideal* form of things; the Royal Society preferred an aesthetic based on the representation of the *typical*. This would emerge as a more useful kind of map for the natural order science perceived. Through its connection with scientific naval expeditions to the Pacific, the Royal Society saw to it that these more productive representations of the typical became the technique of recording what explorers like Cook and Banks found. This involves a break with the notion that what one is looking for are the pure forms underneath the rubble. Rather, the evidence is gathered in and used to *create* the appropriate categories. The eighteenth century had no explanation for why things, particularly plants and animals, seemed to occur in these categories—that would have to wait for Charles Darwin.

One might classify this eighteenth-century style of representation as a species of empiricism. The same method developed by David Hume for exploring the archives for evidence about matters past is here applied to exploring the seas for evidence about matters present. These two kinds of knowledge come together in what historian Thomas Richards calls the 'imperial archive'.[28] The officers of empire record the typical features and resources of space as they map and explore, and dutifully dispatch them back in orderly series of documents. The abstract grid of the map fills not only with lines of coast but with lines of textual annotation and pictorial representation.

Passion changes: no longer motivated by the lack of the whole, passion now takes the form of a positive production of something out of the vector, the map, the knowledge of what types of things one may find in various places in the world's antipodes. Or at least, this is one strand of the palpitations of colonial desire. There are no doubt others: fear of rival colonial vectors, for example. But the particular relationship I want to isolate is the assembling together of the map, the archive, the ship. And what ships! As Smith says, they 'combined the values of a fortress and a travelling laboratory'. These combine in turn with the resources at the other end of the world that these things bring within reach. And this, in the end, is what matters—the process of making a world.

This process could result in miscalculation, as it did notoriously in the decision to colonise Botany Bay. The land itself did not live up to its representation.[29] Nevertheless, the pursuit of the vector has also been the endless process of refining and verifying information about the world and hence increasing its openness to development and transformation into second nature. As Smith puts it, 'the European control of the world required a landscape practice that could first survey and describe, then evoke in new settlers an emotional engagement with the land that they had alienated from its Aboriginal inhabitants'.

By the end of the eighteenth century, the English imperial archive knew more about the South Pacific than it did about many parts of neighbouring Europe. Some forbidding bulwarks of the Scottish highlands were still a foreign country. British interests realised the potential space of the map and the archive according to a very uneven rhythm. Meanwhile imperial designs draw Terra Australis into the net of a naval technology able to plot a still wavery black line from one end of the earth's map to the other. Along that line flow first the dispossessed, the convicts, then people like the Warks, uprooting themselves more or less by choice. Back along it, after a while, flows the wool and the wheat and the gold. The places that a vector draws together aren't necessarily those nearest each other. The craggy resistance of the shape of nature, and the passions and doubts of imperial strategy shape a strange new world of nearness and farness.

RUPERT MURDOCH'S COMSAT

Toward the close of the twentieth century, every antipode ends up drawn into a new net—this time of comsats and data

47

flows—along which flow the truck and barter of capital transactions, news bulletins and re-runs of old cartoons. Or in the
case of the *Australia Live* TV show, a four hour montage of
sights, sites and cites from across the continent. I was fascinated
by that show, broadcast as a New Year special for Australia's
Bicentennial year. It performed Australia, 'live', or 'in realtime'.
An Australia made possible by modern broadcasting technology,
which could record and uplink a signal, live, from any point
on the continent and broadcast that signal out across its whole
space, receivable at almost any other point.

In what the show made actual, I glimpsed what is now at
least technically possible: a virtual republic within which any
point can choose to communicate with any other point, anywhere across the continent. Even before the internet made it
the simplest thing in the world, the technical problems vexing
one of the great dreams of the enlightenment had all but gone
away. That anyone could perceive anything they chose to
examine, and communicate what they thought or felt about
that perception to anyone else—that might be one dream of
enlightenment perfected. That is a possible cause for joy. That
this is not the actual state of things is reason enough to ask
if perhaps somebody took a wrong turn at Albuquerque.

But then, irrupting through the pixilated fabric of *Australia
Live*, the face of Ronald Reagan. Here, beamed live via satellite
across the world to me and my friends in Ultimo was a reminder
that this technology enables not only a linking of places within
the country into a space called *Australia Live*, but its seamless
linking to an outside. Reagan spoke of 'values' Australians and
Americans supposedly share, but which I did not share. All I
could see in that craggy face was a bad cartoon of empire. Here
was not the least reminder that in the enlightenment dream it
is only the supposedly universal qualities of mind that vectoral
technologies connect, while in practice it was the typical qualities of bodies that vectoral technologies order and control. We
laughed at Reagan, my New Year's party and me, trying to
shield ourselves with an umbrella of wit. How very Australian.
But some anxiety persisted, in me at least, to this day.

In a marvellous essay on *Australia Live*, Meaghan Morris
says 'it was not a failed portrait of a national identity, nor a
poor dramatisation of an Australian social text. It was a 4-hour
tourist brochure for international, including Australian, consumption. It celebrated Australia as a vast reservoir of exotic

yet familiar (cross culturally accessible) resorts and photo-graphic locations'.[30] Again, a question of the passions. The passion that works here is that same productive, potential desire of the vector. Assemble together the TV image, the brochure, your credit card, and off you go. The images offered 'produced Australia as a space for visiting, investing, cruising, developing. Its basic theme was (capital) mobility. Comprehensive notes on risks—drought, grasshopper plagues, restless natives—were included'. In the age of the comsat, whole continents appear as sites of productive potential.

Maps precede territories: when I think of Ronald Reagan, governor of California at the height of domestic conflict over the Vietnam War, I think of the maps that presaged American involvement in Indochina. Maps marked red for 'Communist' and blue for the 'Free World'. Maps with little lines of domi-noes, falling to the free world's antipode, the big bad communist other, one by one by one. I think of the even more ludicrous map of 'civilisations' proposed for the post-cold war world by Samuel Huntington. I think about how wrong maps can be, how mistaken the whole imperial archive can be. Botany Bay, for example. Or Secretary of Defence Robert McNamara—the Elmer Fudd of American empire—running the Vietnam War 'by the numbers', as if it were a Ford auto plant. One where all the numbers, as it turned out, were dead wrong.[31]

Stop this map! I want to get off! Off both of them: maps in which everything takes an idealised form of otherness, appearing as our antipode; maps in which everything is just a resource to be located, assayed and catalogued for its usefulness in creating more of the modern world. Perhaps it's just my own ambivalence about my own genealogy—resentment of the empire on the one hand, and admiration for engineering on the other. Perhaps it is about inventing a line of descent that opens onto the virtual of another way of being in space, of making the world.

ETHOS AND ETHICS

Anything and anyone can be appraised and catalogued in the imperial archive as something useful, as a resource, or as a hindrance to the extraction of resources, something to be avoided or removed. Gold is a resource, to be assayed and exploited, but a ravine is a hindrance, to be skirted or bridged. 'Tractable' natives are a resource, to be put to work. Uncooperative ones are a nuisance to be marched off the nearest cliff. From the potential realm of possibilities for combining resources from all points of the world, more than one empire has selected dispossession, subjection, slavery, and genocide.

This is what critical theorists Theodor Adorno and Max Horkheimer saw as the dark side of enlightenment.[32] To me the accidents of history that make that diagnosis plausible are right here, in the very fact that I am sitting in Ultimo, Sydney, writing this, right here, right now. Here I am, a stray offspring of instrumental reason and the vector it drew from England to Australia, and the productive flows it desired, imagined, supervised and recorded, from one side of the world to the other. But what lies buried here, underneath my apartment block, the community centre, the AGL showroom? What worlds are lost when new worlds are made? There is quite a particular view of things and the world that comes from being by the sea.

But from where can one acquire an ethical view of this new world? 'Ethic' is a word that goes back to the ancient Greek 'ethos', meaning character or disposition. These days, 'ethos' refers more to the character of the times, the milieu. It's what I've been describing in drawing a parallel between the ethos of the eighteenth century and its naval vectors and the ethos of the twentieth century and its media vectors, both of which overcome barriers, obstacles and partitions, threading space together in ways that make people and things into resources, but which also encourages new passions and new ways of life.

'Ethics' might be the practice of judging how to act in a given ethos. It's not the same thing as morality, which I think of as a more or less fixed set of rules, administered by some authority such as a school teacher or a prison warden, that people either obey or transgress. Ethics is more like a style of judging and acting in the river of time, taking each situation as it comes, drawing on one's memory of similar situations, and on the stories one knows that record other people's encounters with events.

A first ethical point of view for judging events in the ethos of the vector is from the point of view of the responsibility I might have toward another.[33] This begins and ends with listening to what the other has to say. For example, 'Captain Cook' cuts quite a different figure in Aboriginal stories, as agent and harbinger of dispossession.[34] The demand that immigrant Australia make amends for a past, the benefits of which most immigrants inherit, is a just demand. What it lacks, in culture if not in the common law, is a zone of indifference within which such a demand can be heard.

When the demand is made on the basis of identity, in terms of the imaginary relationship of otherness between black and white, it is answered, without being heard, with the retort that identity is just a hindrance to the value creating potential of productive vectors. When the demand is made in terms of vectoral potential, in terms of economic self-determination for Aboriginal people, it is answered in terms of identity. As if this threatened to open up a kind of otherness unacceptable to Australian 'identity'. Or in other words, when black leaders say 'Give us back our culture', the answer is, 'That would hinder our economy'; when black leaders say 'Give us the means to build our own economy', the answer is, 'That is contrary to our culture'.

Always, with the extension of the vector across new ground, this same conflict arises: between the identities it connects and the productivity of the connection. Deirdre Macken writes of Sydney as a city divided, between east and west—and the dividing line is in part whether people are of use to the global economy, or form a surplus population, surviving off the rump of a once protected industrial structure, now steadily in decline. The popular unconscious of the eastern suburbs—namely the *Sydney Morning Herald*—imagines 'Westies' in much the same way as lowlanders once imagined highlanders. But what divides Australians, what divided Scots, only appears as a matter of cultural difference when each side of that divide contemplates the other. 'Westie' is the antipodes for the eastern suburbs, as Australia is for England, or the highlanders were for the lowlanders, or the Eficans are for Peter Carey's Voorstanders.[35]

And in each case, vice versa. Not that these poles are in any sense equivalent in their relation of otherness. How can *different* things be equal? But seen in terms of the calculations that fill the corporate archives of today, all such differences come to matter less and less compared to the relative usefulness of a place or a population to the current phase of constructing the world. In the reckoning of a vectoral geography, everything and everyone is just a potential resource for the conjunction of forces.

In such a world, Australia is not yet that passion that I would name the virtual republic—that zone of indifference that institutes the extension of all of the people's desires into a common world of conversation. A conversation that might have something to say about the ordering of things for people, rather than of people as things. In this sense, we are not yet a free people. For there to be a virtual republic, people and things need to maintain relations with each other that express more than their current market value. People and things need the capacity to form their own kinds of relations, and to choose which relations to entertain with the stormy seas of third nature, swooshing and swirling around the globe.

It would hardly be prudent to develop too much of a passion for a return to economic nationalism, and political sovereignty is always relative, no matter who acts the role of head of state. But *cultural* autonomy, matters of education, art and the spirit; that is something else, as Hume and his contemporaries discovered. Here then is one more way of thinking about what culture is, and why it matters: culture is the virtual lurking in the vectoral. Today's corporate archives record the world according to type, measuring all things by a common standard. They record, as Oscar Wilde said, 'the price of everything and the value of nothing'.[36] But culture, when it manages to free itself from the tyranny of the other, is a resource of a different kind, a virtual memory of the swerve of events, of everything that escapes from the magnetic field of identity, and from the grid of merely productive usefulness.

Every vector has its virtual side. It is always present, down at the community centre, or on the radio or in the passers-by in the street. It can be in art too, when art does something else besides play to a demographic and remind it of its identity. Gerhard Fischer, head of German studies at the University of New South Wales, has a passion for the theatre. At the time of the Bicentennial, he conceived of a perfectly ludicrous plan to perform the great German playwright Heiner Müller's *Der Auftrag* as reinvented by an Aboriginal theatre company. Not many people in Sydney had ever heard of Müller, and there wasn't an Aboriginal theatre company. Whether he knew it or not, Fischer was already thinking virtually. He saw no reason why such a screwball thing might not actually happen.

I saw the production that resulted, at Sydney's Belvoir Street Theatre, in 1991. It was very confusing. I heard Fischer speak about it, together with the Aboriginal writer he enlisted, Mudrooroo. This became even more confusing. I'm still trying to work it out. Mudrooroo spoke of the performance as a 'hybrid', of Müller and Mudrooroo, of Aboriginality and high German seriousness. As a hybrid it wasn't a success, and perhaps wasn't meant to be. Mudrooroo wrote a script in which a group of Aboriginal actors, at their last rehearsal, attempt to perform Müller. They discover a few things along the way, and vote in the end not to perform the play after all.

Mudrooroo called it *The Aboriginal Demonstrators Confront the Declaration of the Australian Republic on 26th January 2001 With a Production of Der Auftrag by Heiner Müller*. As he said of this title, 'it reached beyond and sought for a simple reduction which was never forthcoming'.[37] He could have been talking about the whole event. Mudrooroo created a kind of Müller-machine that tries to combine and contrast the antipodes of Müller and Mudrooroo, but breaks down in the attempt. But in its breaking down, something else appears, a moment when different movements pass by each other, making something different again.

Müller's play is set at the time of the French Revolution, roughly the time the invasion of the Australian continent began. But it is about another empire, even if it was one that plotted along the lines of vectors of much the same nautical kind. Three men are dispatched from France to Jamaica to take the revolution to the antipodes, among the slaves. They fail in their commission, as does a contemporary character, caught in a more Kafkaesque task ordered by some Stalinist bureaucracy, in that other empire that collapsed with the Berlin Wall. In Mudrooroo's version, everything begins with the other: antipode not metropolis, English empire not French, capitalist west not bureaucratic east, black not white. A good deal of resentment pours out of it, like vented steam.

And something else as well. There are so many antipodes in the play, each suggesting its own plane upon which things find their identities in their war of opposites. These planes cut through each other, but there's no synthesis. No history of the world ensues. Rather, something better, a glimpse of the virtual, of a past teeming with contingencies, and a future as well. One sees the curve of a new culture, of different ways of telling a story, of enacting the past in the present: *The Aboriginal Artists and Their Collaborators Take What They Need From Whenever to*

Invent a Republic of Their Own. An ethic that passes, if just for a moment, beyond listening to the other, on to creating, not a synthesis, but something else again.

A COMFORT STOP ON THE NULLARBOR

Another ethical point of view—that of the earth itself. The German philosopher Martin Heidegger worried about the way in which what I would call vectoral technologies of perception produce the world as if it were a series of pictures, *framed* as if they were meant for us, brought into *proximity* as if they were meant to be—just for us. The combination of vectors of mapping and movement produce the earth itself as if it were the most natural thing in the world that it respond to our passions.[38] Of this conceit, the earth complains.

It would take us way beyond the scope of this book to take up that particular point of view. I'll just say I'm sceptical about criticism that tries to unmask the artifice of human institutions in terms of any kind of claim to a more appropriate way of listening to nature, or as Heidegger might say, of 'listening toward being'—a being that for him always eludes us. Heidegger's great merit is to break thought out of its human-centred point of view. But there is too much melancholy longing in his way of thinking.

What ruptured the seductive call of Heidegger for me was reading the singularly outlandish work that the philosopher Gilles Deleuze wrote with the rogue psychiatrist and all-round troublemaker Felix Guattari.[39] They too are interested in thinking about a world in which human activity is not the centre of everything, but they maintain a somewhat more open-ended idea of what the rest of nature might be like, and take more interest in the ethos of the experimental methods through which science produces knowledge of the world. Like Hume, they are not particularly interested in the essence of human nature. They are more interested in what it can become. The artifice of human enterprise reveals the virtual side of things: unexpected, singular, transient, without measure or precedent. That second nature exists is evidence of the possibilities lurking within nature. That third nature exists suggests there are yet more things the world can become. Modern science, inheritor of Banks and Darwin, tells us about the vectors along which nature itself moves. But must we think of nature as laws and limits, or can we think of it as an engine of creation, with which, *respectfully*, to make still other natures, other worlds? Deleuze and Guattari's criticism of the world as it is points not back to some essence we have lost, not to an unwritten law we must all obey, but forward to as yet unactualised instances of the virtual. Who knows what a culture can do? Who knows what a country can become? Who would want to set limits in advance to what Judith Wright called 'the movement of Australian poetic consciousness'?

A moment I'll never forget—climbing down from the bus into the baking hot sun, and stepping onto the clouds of red dust that is the Nullarbor Plain. There's an airline pilot's strike on, and the only way I can get to Perth from Sydney is overland. I'm feeling out of place so far from my beloved east coast, and out of time, travelling at bus tempo. So there I stand, at the roadside truck stop, after days on the bus, suddenly motionless. I stare at the tiny curlicues of dust; I look to the horizon, endlessly still. What snaps me back to the present is the Aboriginal man in the cowboy hat who walks past me, heading for the roadside diner, festooned with the red and white livery of Coca-Cola and the petrified swoosh of the logo, the 'dynamic ribbon device'. I'm a little weary, but I think I see something, or hear something. I'm trying to keep in focus two images of his land: the horizon at infinity and the almost imperceptible dust that he stirred in passing. Perhaps it's the ethos of those Scots engineers, but while I think about the geological time of the land, and the 'eternal now' of the Dreaming, and the historical eye-blink of white settlement, I think not of what's buried in the past, but what might yet be made of it in the future. If ever you cross the continent by road, and I recommend it . . . don't take Heidegger to read on the way.

DYNAMIC RIBBON DEVICE

Somewhere between reading Deleuze and Guattari and that moment on the Nullarbor, I started thinking about a third ethical point of view: not the other subject, not the objectified earth, but the vector itself. Living amid the moving lines of vectors, like living too close to the freeway, is often cause for anxiety. An anxiety I would call antipodality: the feeling of being neither here nor there. But I think there can be a positive side to this feeling too. Where postcolonialism seems to have a passion for diagnosing the symptoms of empire within the colony, antipodality is about what *else* gets produced besides repression and guilt.[40] What is produced is the world, always a new world.

The antipode is always the other pole, the other destination. Other to what? To the other one, of course. Postcolonial writing can get caught up in psychoanalysing the way each pole seems to imply the other; rely on the other. There's no colony without empire, but then there's no empire without colonies either. You can spend a lifetime diagnosing the repressed symptoms of each in the other, finding colony in the scars of empire, finding empire even when the colony thinks it is thinking for itself.[41]

This cultural therapy that postcolonial critics perform has parallels in popular postcolonialism, which prescribes the panacea of the republic. But whether for or against its constitution, it always seems to be about its other. Either Australia ought to cut its symbolic ties with England, or it should maintain its ties with England. Our antipode is thought in relation to the other one, as if its identity depended on their being an other, from which it came or from which it went. Either way, it amounts to the same thing. Both sides of the 'republican debate' talk of Australia as England's other. Both remain in the same imaginary relation. Why talk about imaginary relations when there are vectoral ones that create far more possibilities— and dangers—for this virtual republic?

When antipodes appear, it is because a space exists within which both poles are produced. For me, that space, my history, is the sea. Or rather, that space is what vectoral technologies, when applied to the sea, made possible. What possibilities can be made actual if the resources of the world could be brought into proximity with each other? Many possibilities, only some of which were realised, like the British Empire. One could think of better things to realise out of the virtual world of vector, just as one could think of better things to do for Margaret Wark's asthma than the climate of New Zealand.

Experiencing antipodality is unsettling. There is nothing uniquely Australian about it, although it is a common enough structure of feeling in Australian life.[42] This is a place which is always in a relation to an elsewhere, which is always defined by its relation to a powerful other. Sometimes it's our imaginary friends: the British or the Americans. Sometimes it's spectral threats: the reds, the blacks, the yellow peril. There's the endless temptation to want to identify completely, for or against the powerful other: Washington or Moscow, the British crown or Confucian 'values'.

I think that these days the experience of antipodality is growing ever more common. The globalisation of trade flows and cultural flows made possible by information technology re-opens the old wounds of identity, breaking the skin at unexpected places. The volume and velocity of information in circulation keeps rising. Popular music, cinema and television, the raw materials of popular culture, are increasingly sold into global markets in accordance with transnational financing and marketing plans. Suddenly cultural identity looks like it is in flux. The relations and the flows are more clearly in view than the sources or destinations. Images don't seem to be representations any more, of the ideal or the typical. They seem to just proliferate and differentiate from each other.

Cultural differences are no longer so tied to the experience of the particularities of place. These 'vertical' differences, of locality, ethnicity, nation are doubled by 'horizontal' differences, determined not by being rooted in a particular place but by being plugged into a particular circuit. Both free market liberalism and the feminist movement are instances of contemporary 'horizontal' movements of difference, both now caught up in a crossflow with 'vertical' ones of the nation and ethnicity. We vainly try to hold a shaking umbrella over forms of difference that are rapidly blowing away with the vectoral winds.[43] And then we find that the umbrella of identity has blown away as well.

This new experience of difference is an experience of an active trajectory between places, identities, formations, rather than a drawing of borders, be they of the self or place. This is antipodality. Antipodality is the cultural difference created by the vector. The acceleration of the vectors of transnational communication makes this antipodality more common. With satellite TV beaming into every part of the globe that can afford it, with the internet spreading from west to east, many people are experiencing it. In the overdeveloped world, both the culture of everyday life and the culture of scholarly thinking about the present seem to me to betray traces of unease if not downright paranoia about antipodality. Yet it is the emergent axis of technocultural conflict.

As the tyranny of distance gives way to the tyranny of difference, nations acquire new defensive mechanisms. Let's take as just one example the still-dominant media of television. The integration of the space of the Australian continent into one media market happened quite recently, via satellite technology. At one and the same time broadcasters have integrated the national broadcasting space and hooked it up to the global satellite feeds.[44] Until recently, this integrative tendency was countered at the national level at least by local content rules in television broadcasting. As with local content rules in radio, these were successful in promoting the production of high quality, popular media products, which in turn were successfully marketed overseas. Australian TV programming now has a global audience, and Australia is a successful supplier of recorded music to the world market. In all, these pragmatic policies, fruit of an inventive, sceptical policy process, balanced some degree of autonomy with a cosmopolitan media flow. The combined effect of the influence of rationalist 'free market' beliefs and pressure from American program producers to have services, including cultural ones, included under free trade agreements, promises a steady erosion of autonomous Australian cultural intervention into the global flow.[45]

Pasts leave marks. Perhaps when I think about living in Australian culture, I'm thinking about the culture of the living room where I grew up, in Newcastle. I think of a house perched between great flows of traffic and trade. A house with panoramic windows, through which pours the light of a southern sun, and through the window of television the light of a different day. A house where those rays mingle, Bugs Bunny in the bush—making something different from either. A house equipped with an archive that contains the tools for the job. So when I think about the indefinite, unlimited possibilities of a media-soaked planet of noise, I think about the kinds of structures one might design that might engage with it.

What would things be like if the vector was perfected? What if there were no blinds to keep out the light? Imagine; but imagine carefully. Don't think utopia, the best of all possible worlds. Don't think dystopia, which is just a utopian dream turned upsidedown. Think all the consequences and possibilities at once. Think of the future as a heterotopia, a mix of different kinds of space. 'Perhaps we have not become abstract enough.'[46] What would it mean to become more abstract, ever more abstracted from the boundedness of territory and subjectivity? One can imagine a delirious future, beyond cyberspace. Not the future of Marx's communism: from each according to their abilities, to each according to their needs. Rather the future of the abstract, virtual space of the vector made actual: where third nature is not just a space of resentful imaginings of the other, nor of feverish gambling on potentials that promise only more of the same, but a zone of indifference for free creation. Better living by design. The question to ask is why this is not coming to pass, as advertised.

I feel the need to go looking for roots. A strange thing for me to be saying! 'We no longer have roots, we have aerials', I said.[47] I never said this was a good thing, or a bad thing. Just something to keep thinking about. When one is implicated in a network of vectors, chance cuts across the past, but leaves its traces on the bodies of all those it cuts. There's no past to search for that will reveal a true identity or destiny. But there is a past that might say something about the wit of knowing when to hold up the umbrella and when to sing in the rain.

3

The Libertarian line

But theories are made only to die in the war of time.

Guy Debord

MY CITY OF SYDNEY

To the chauvinistic Sydneysider, the only reason Melbourne exists is so that Sydney might have some characteristics that one may cherish, solely by virtue of the comparison. Melbourne exists, in other words, as an exercise in structuralism.[1] This is the doctrine according to which terms acquire meaning in relation to other terms. Words form a structure known as language, that rather opaque sheet that divides us from things. On the face of that sheet turned towards us we can read the signs that supposedly correspond to the things of this world that language papers over. On this plane of language, terms have relations to each other, and from those relations, language generates meaning about the world on the other side. We know what the spirit of Sydney is to the extent that it is *different* from Melbourne. Germaine Greer said it best: 'Let Sydneysiders welcome tourists with open arms and parted thighs, Melbournians do their best to make them wish they'd never come'.[2]

Is there a distinctive intellectual culture in Sydney? Donald Horne thought there was when he wrote *The Lucky Country*, at least when compared to its Victorian antipode. If Melbourne thinkers stress social improvement, nationalism, and conscience, Sydney is about social difference, cosmopolitanism and the good life. Sydney University teaches 'a destructive analysis of practically everything and the consolation of feeling oneself part of an elect'.[3]

Many would suspect that to be a description of the scourge of civilisation known as postmodernism, but Horne was talking about a much earlier intellectual influence—the philosopher John Anderson. I suspect there is a strange continuity between what Anderson taught when he arrived in Australia in the 1920s and the distinctively Sydney style of intellectual work that I learned in the 1980s and which is alive and well to this day. As the radical jurist and 'Push' alumnus Jim Staples says, 'Anderson's influence runs through this society right up until the present time'.

The line that runs from Anderson to the present is not an unbroken one. It's a series of cracks and gaps, caused by the tension of the present, twisting and buckling received ideas, until they snap into a new pattern. From Anderson's Freethought Society, the Libertarians split off. From the old style Libertarian 'Push', the Kensington 'Futilitarians' break away. Then comes the feminist and liberation movement splinterings of the 1970s, a pattern broken up again by postmodern thought in the 1980s.

A possible title for this story is the one the *Sun Herald* gave it: **HOW A BUNCH OF BOHEMIANS BECAME THE RICH AND FAMOUS**.[4] The occasion was the publication of Anne Coombs' book *Sex and Anarchy: The Life and Death of the Sydney Push*. It followed the less noticed biography of Anderson by Brian Kennedy, *A Passion to Oppose*, and Judy Ogilvy's 'impressionist memoir', *The Push*.[5] The press had a field day with the Coombs book, treating it as a pretext for revisiting the sex life of former Libertarians made good. The whole thing was treated gently, on the comfortable assumption that Libertarianism can safely be placed in a structural box *elsewhere*. Melbourne literary gossip columnist Peter Craven professed incomprehension, and concluded that it must be 'a Sydney thing'. Jill Kitson managed to present the Kennedy book entirely in the light of its indictment of Anderson's private life, not his public legacy, and concluded with a rare airing of the ABC's famous recording of Anderson singing 'Those Sydney

Blues'. All safely contained in the past, not the present, to a private tragedy, not public struggles, to sin city Sydney, not marvellous Melbourne.

The story I want to make here isn't about packing the memory of the Push away in a box, but of showing how the practice of critical thinking—and critical drinking—shapes a kind of ethical practice for living, a 'technique of the self'.[6] As paradoxical as it may sound, it is precisely that people influenced by this tradition made themselves so differently from each other that constitutes it as a tradition. A tradition that embodies a reflection on one's circumstances and the production of one's self as a new relation, a new release of potentials. At the very least, Push people led interesting lives.

A genuine philosophy is about more than books and arguments. It's about recognising the virtual side of one's existence. This has nothing to do with vague romantic spiritualisms. The virtual is a very real thing: a movement happens, a mind thinks, a self expresses, the virtual becomes. Not the self as defined by the institutions of state, family, culture, but the self as it produces itself out of its own forces, as it enacts itself in the contingent events of everyday life. One never goes down to the same river twice, as Heraclitus said.[7] Meaning not only that the river flows, and changes, but that the one that finds itself bathed in it changes, too. Body; river—two changing forces, of different kinds, that change in different ways, at different speeds. So every time they cross paths, the encounter is absolutely singular, an instance of the virtual.

And so, for all their differences, from John Anderson to the Push legends Darcy Waters and Roelof Smilde, to the Libertarian philosophers Jim Baker, Bill Bonney and Ross Poole, or the Push women such as Liz Fell and Germaine Greer, to the 'baby' Push, Wendy Bacon and Frank Moorhouse, there runs a river created out of thinking, drinking, arguing, and making something that places one's self in a creative, productive, original relation to the moment. Perhaps that is a Sydney thing, but it certainly isn't over.

PORTRAIT OF THE PHILOSOPHER

Dobell's painting of John Anderson hangs in Fisher Library, at the University of Sydney, where he held the Challis Chair of

Philosophy from 1927 to 1958. The chair in which Anderson sits, the loose suit and the background all seem made of the same bluey-brown substance, as if to illustrate a key concept of Andersonian thought: that all things that are real are equally real and real in the same way. There are no mysterious forms or spirits animating the Andersonian universe. All is of one substance, cut from the same cloth. Everything that is real is an event in time and space. But one thing does stand out in Dobell's creation: Anderson's intensity of gaze. This is the Anderson of whom a successor in the Challis Chair, David Armstrong, said 'there was not an atom of tender-mindedness in the man. He was remorseless, ab-so-lute-ly re-morse-less'.

Anderson came to Sydney from Edinburgh, shortly after the 1926 general strike, in which he had sided with the workers. He had already worked out most of the framework of his philosophy, a version of the 'realism' then gaining ground in English-speaking universities.[8] What was distinctive about Anderson was his rare commitment to maintaining the *comprehensive* side of philosophy as reflective, rational thought about all aspects of life, rather than as a narrow specialist discipline. Anderson also saw philosophy as a necessarily *oppositional* mode of thinking and way of life, sustaining itself out of its critical distance from the beliefs and dogmas it finds around it, both in everyday life, in politics and culture, and in philosophy itself.

'My opposition to Idealism in philosophy', he wrote, 'is bound up with my opposition to Capitalism.' Idealism made 'mind'—pure rational consciousness—the centre of the universe, a miniature or image of God's self awareness, here on earth. Mind is where the divine or necessary order of the world finds its expression and culmination. Realist philosophies react against this, reinstalling the independent existence of things of this world. 'There are only facts,' Anderson wrote in 1927, 'occurrences in space and time.'[9] The things in the world, like workers in a factory, need no god and no master.

There are many versions of the doctrine of realism, including those pursued by Anderson's academic inheritors.[10] But what is often lost are those qualities of Anderson's thought that connect to his early oppositional practice of philosophy, as a way of life. Anderson opposed notions of mental life and social life as purely rational orders, one mirrored in the other. He was wary of the two-way traffic between authoritarian conceptions of society, in which different things are subordinated to the pure, rational, unified order of reason, and similar conceptions of the mind as also having such a hierarchical structure. He saw this assumption as the origins of a *servile* philosophy, upholder of the present order, or an order to come, in which all is harmonised, where conflict and opposition are irrational residues. There is, he said, a 'close connection between the upholding of a hierarchical doctrine of reality and the maintenance of a social hierarchy'.[11] For Anderson, both mind and society are active, productive, plural fields, full of clashes and creations.

For Anderson, all things are pluralities of conflicting forces in process—not unlike what French philosopher Gilles Deleuze, working from a quite different tradition, will later call 'multiplicities'. The urbane Parisian and the antipodean Scot have one, very ancient philosophical ancestor in common. As Anderson writes, 'We have to reject the distinction between being and becoming, and recognise, with Heraclitus, that whatever is, is in process and whatever is in process, is'. Perhaps it is no coincidence that the philosophies influential in Sydney in the 1930s and the 1990s are both instances of 'a positive and pluralistic logic of events'.[12] But Deleuze goes the furthest in making difference the key concept for a way of thinking, and a way of life.

Deleuze and Anderson are rare among philosophers in that their work appears to be immediately useful for thinking about the time and space of everyday life. Both were not only public figures, but their work was useful to people engaged in all kinds of other things. Perhaps this is because both Anderson and Deleuze fashioned concepts for the flux of time rather than of an ideal grid of space. As Ermanno Benciavenga says in a useful essay on Montaigne, 'one view of knowledge makes it consist of representing the world, another makes it consist of coping with the world'. Both Anderson and Deleuze are certainly appealing to an essayist. As Montaigne said, 'I do not portray being: I portray becoming'.[13] And so essayists might tend to be drawn towards a philosophy of coping with becoming, even thriving on it. Anderson's thought certainly inspired a tradition of Realist philosophers interested in the problem of representing the world, particularly in science, but what is of interest to me is the other side of Anderson, the philosopher of flux. This is an essayist's appreciation of Anderson, not a Realist philosopher's.

Anderson's interest in Karl Marx and Sigmund Freud was not entirely unusual for the times; what he did with their writings was untimely. Anderson saw in both writers a positive process of ripping into the fantasy of society and mind, as ordered, unified and rational. Here were clear, unsentimental exposures of what lay behind those comforting illusions: conflicting social forces, struggling over the produce of labour and industry, fighting it out for political power; conflicting mental forces, struggling it out between desire and convention, a great tangled multiplicity of drives and repressions. What Anderson rejected in both doctrines was what it would take western thought another generation to reject—the new fantasies they fostered of the social or psychic cure for conflict—on the barricades or the couch. In this he prefigures in a curious way the radical rereading of Marx and Freud that Deleuze undertook after the failure of the Parisian revolt of May 1968.

Deleuze and Anderson both assign particular roles to aesthetics in keeping a channel open to the multiplicity of things. Anderson was an early supporter of the writing of James Joyce, at a time when *Ulysses* was effectively banned in Australia. Perhaps Anderson saw the struggles of Stephen Dedalus to find a way out of the maze of repressive church and state and family obligations as something like his own 'refusal to serve'. In his famous 1941 essay on 'Art and Morality', Anderson argues that there is 'an interesting parallel between literary and political censorship'. Or in Anderson's terms, 'censorship "manufactures the evidence" of social solidarity'. It suppresses differences in the name of a moral or national unity that is defined in advance and held above question—precisely by banning the very means of questioning it. 'To speak on behalf of morality . . . is to speak on behalf of the principle of authority.' And presumably vice versa.

As Anderson reads Joyce, Stephen's struggle is against hell on earth, 'the self-alienation of the spirit'. Only through refusal of the consolations of ideal orders can self-alienation be struggled against, if never overcome. No more 'nodding at an image, repenting, letting one thing "stand for" another—the whole system of anti-intellectual pretences'. Anderson is a practitioner of enlightenment, but not of the classical kind—reason cannot make the world over in the philosopher's image. Reason reveals the thinker's compromises with servility and commences the struggle against it, opposing the thinker to the world—permanently. This is the source of the scepticism about utopian designs on the future that can be traced in a faint and crooked line from Anderson to present day Sydney libertarianism.

Anderson attributes the desire to ban Joyce to the way in which he confronts the servile with 'a freedom they have lost', and attacks the 'ceremonial and fetishistic system by which they conceal these things from themselves'. And here he makes what will become one of his most striking and remembered statements: 'freedom in love is the condition of other freedoms'. Anderson attacks the subordination of sexual enjoyment to reproduction, and the association of the pursuit of desire with guilt and sin, for 'without exercising some command over the sexual life of the lower orders, authorities could never keep them docile'.

And then Anderson stops short, in a way Deleuze does not, on the brink of thinking through the connection between social and sexual hierarchy, and their difference from social and sexual multiplicity, not to mention the connection between forms of multiplicity of all kinds. Multiplicity in the production of thought, sexuality, art—and everyday life. Anderson, the free-thinker, the man who would not stand to attention in the university quad when the carillon played God Save the King, produced in thought and writing a most radical doctrine, but one from which he himself would retreat, in an orderly fashion, back to fantasy, hypocrisy, cant.

A FANTASTICAL WAY OF LIFE

It's not hard for me to see the appeal Anderson's thinking once had. I felt it myself when I bought Jim Baker's book on *Anderson's Social Philosophy*, with the Dobell portrait on the cover, from Arthur Warner's bookshop in Hunter Street, Newcastle, when it came out in 1979. It said on the flap that state parliament censured Anderson—twice. That seemed to me an excellent recommendation. Baker presented an Anderson remarkably consonant with the critical thought of the 1970s, or so it seemed to me. When I left Newcastle for the 'Big Smoke' the following year, it surprised me that in the Sydney radical circles I quickly fell in with, Anderson was remembered only as the rabid cold warrior he became in the 1950s. Being rather impressionable, I put Baker's book aside—for 15 years—until Anne Coombs' book on the Push made me think about Anderson again.

Anderson and some of his students formed the Freethought Society in 1930, and for 20 years it functioned as a milieu in which Anderson could exercise a patrician authority over the dissemination of his thought. Horne gives a vivid account of Anderson at work, not with the Freethinkers, but the Literature Society, of which he was also President. Horne writes: 'When he began speaking in an urgent Glaswegian sing-song the room seemed stilled by significance'.[14] It's a tribute to the power of the vector of speech that this man, whose prose was far too astringent to be broadly persuasive, could exercise a lasting influence through lectures and discussions up the pub afterwards.

Anderson trained his freethinkers only too well. An increasingly reactionary Anderson compromised his principles by joining the ranks of those anti-communists who would countenance restricting freedoms at home in the name of the kind of pervasive threat to national unity Anderson had formerly seen as the very root of servile thinking. The break, when it came, was over Menzies' Communist Party Dissolution Bill. Anderson, of all people, caved in to the belief that a free people lack the resolve to fight tyranny, unless they accept a little tyranny of their own.

The Libertarian Society began meeting at the Ironworkers' Hall in lower George Street in the summer of 1950–51. As Roelof Smilde says, 'we wanted to get downtown . . . We saw the university as an enclave, as elitist'.[15] The Libertarians would be very different in style. But something crosses over the break, something of the Socratic maxim that Plato cites in the *Apology*: 'the unreflected life is not worth living'. Or more positively, the philosopher is someone who lives a certain kind of life—one of reflection. The way things appear may not be the way things are. By recourse to reason, false appearances are exposed, false beliefs discarded, and a right course of action might begin.

The mute ambition of philosophy is more often than not that the right action might flow from right thinking, sometimes to the point, as in Plato and Marx, that the world might be made over in its design. Nietzsche wanted to overcome that vain ambition, and produce a philosophy, and philosophers, who acted in accordance with the productive and multiple messiness of the world. There was a little of Nietzsche in Anderson, but perhaps a little more in the Libertarians, in their break from conformity as an act of will.[16]

The Libertarian break was a refusal of the increasingly dogmatic side of Andersonianism, but one which depended for its confidence on precisely the kind of critical unmasking of dogma that the putative Libertarians gleaned from Anderson himself. In particular, they saw a contradiction between the critical force of Andersonian practices of thought and the odd mix of quietism and reaction that presided in Anderson's application of his thought to practice. It relied, also, on the Andersonian power of speech, the practice of a reflective—and argumentative—way of life. The pub became the symposium.

Anne Coombs gives us portraits of Darcy Waters and Roelof Smilde—drinkers, gamblers, all-night arguers. She understands their libertine sexuality, and their relentless, rigid opposition to all authority, but seems puzzled by the anti-careerism. By this one steady abstinence, perversely enough, they became legendary. Darcy Waters' ASIO security file claims he was one of the organisers of The Society for the Promotion of a Fantastic Way of Life. One can't help wondering if this is a joke put over on a hapless informer, or an informer's joke on the secret police they served.

The Libertarians freed themselves from Anderson's patriarchal authority, but perhaps not from the *anxiety* behind Anderson's aggressively masculine style of intellectual life. To some extent, the Libertarian men looked like a reaction, a return to the hard-drinking, hard-gambling stereotype of matey Australia. Men for whom Guy Debord's panegyric to himself seems singularly apt: 'Even though I have read a lot, I have drunk even more. I have written much less than most people who write; but I have drunk much more than most people who drink'.[17]

Judy Ogilvy recalls that 'most of the Push were scholarship students. The smartest girls shoplifted so they could dress well enough to attract the best men, for Push women were dependent on men for society, protection, and freedom of movement—for almost everything the wealthier girls got from their colleges or families'. On the other hand, 'their living allowances, although meagre, gave them more freedom than students who lived in college or in their parents' homes'.

Borrowing from the writings of feral Freudian Wilhelm Reich, the Libertarians started to see an even stronger connection between sexuality and power than Anderson. Reich saw human character as having three layers: an outer shell of civility, enabling people to adapt to their servile role; a second layer of repressed sadistic impulses, the root both of fascism and every-day acts of singular violence; and an 'inner biologic core'.[18] It's rather like Rousseau's invocation of a spontaneous human nature, hemmed in by artifice.[19] This biologic core acquires its two outer shells because of the repression of its drives and instincts, which would otherwise find their expression in a free sexuality and a free and cooperative production of the means of everyday life.

Reich sounds as often as not like a crackpot. But his eccentric rereading of Marx and Freud did lead to the interesting idea of a 'sexual economy'. He thought of this by way of analogy with Marx's idea of a capitalist economy. If in the latter, workers have the products of their working energies alienated from them, then in Reich's sexual economy it is the free expression of sexual energies that is taken from people, and channelled into repressive structures of nation and family. If Anderson saw a parallel between sexual repression and servility, under the influence of Reich the Libertarians saw it as its very basis.

The alternative, a free circulation of sexual energy, is of course exactly what the men of the Push had in mind. From talking to Push women, Coombs concludes that 'a woman gained her status in the Push from whom she was fucking. If you wanted to gain a position within the Push you had to "put together the right sequence of political fucks" . . . A very clever tongue, extravagant behaviour or spectacular promiscuity could ensure a place in the pantheon of Push heroines'. Ogilvy puts it pithily 'the Push had four rules for sex: be skilful, don't be romantic, be spontaneous, think of it as nothing special'. And she has an interesting account of the economy behind such transactions: 'Push women were always conscious of how important it was to graduate. If they didn't seize the few opportunities open to them, if they did not become teachers or librarians, the future offered them no security at all . . . In the meantime they were dependent on their scholarships'. Meanwhile, 'the men in the Push tended to remain there, mateship enduring as a stronger bond than sexual attraction'. And since they could usually pick up casual work—for a while Waters and Smilde worked on the wharves—they could get by.

In the 1960s, other parts of society started to catch up with the Libertarians, particularly as sexuality freed itself from the old patterns and, with the aid of new contraceptive tech-nology, became more fluid. The Push itself expanded like wild weed but thereby becomes a less identifiable presence. Little shoots of it head off in all directions, and tangle up with other instances of Sydney's plural cultural mix.

FUCKED BY GOD'S STEEL PRICK

John Anderson liked to sing, and there is a rare recording of three of his songs. The Joycean 'Ballad of Joking Jesus' had greatly offended the historian Manning Clark with its 'old hat blasphemy'. He concluded that Anderson was 'a man of great gifts who, for some reason I did not understand, devoted the last half of his life to swimming upstream against the great river of life'.[20] A telling example is Anderson's relentless opposition to expanding higher education. Another of Anderson's songs, the 'Philosophical Blues' satirised those who had forsaken the one true university to 'punch the bundy' at the University of New South Wales (UNSW). By the time of his retirement in 1958, the power of speech—exercised in that corner of the Sydney Uni quad where the jacaranda tree sprouts vivid purple every spring— was in its autumn as a source of intellectual force as far as the techniques of the self were concerned.

As intellectual life became more plural in its institutional bases, the power of the old men of the Push faded too. By 1970 Push alumnus Liz Fell was teaching at UNSW, where a young Wendy Bacon was a postgrad student. There were no longer regular meetings in the philosophy rooms at Sydney Uni. Younger Libertarians at Kensington formed their own on-campus group, the Futilitarians, perhaps named after the pessimistic side of the Libertarian structure of feeling, as movingly expressed in the Frank Moorhouse story, 'Futility and other Animals'.[21] Bacon came to be one of the editors of the student newspaper *Tharunka*. A modest enough event, after which, all hell broke loose.

The most famous story about Wendy Bacon involves her appearance at the trial of *Tharunka* editors for obscenity. Bacon, Fell and others turned up in nuns' habits with lines from the offending poem on them. Bacon's read 'I've been fucked by God's steel prick'. After that *Tharunka* became *Thorunka*, an underground publication that, according to one of its editors, Val Hodgson, was a challenge to all 'outmoded puritanical virtues'. While the media scrum focused on the obscenity, the

Futilitarians published articles on the Gurindji people's struggle with the Vestey's meat company, articles on gay liberation by Dennis Altman and women's liberation by Germaine Greer, and Frank Moorhouse's column 'Around the Laundromats'.[22]

By early 1971 there were 41 charges against people connected with it. Bacon represented herself in court. Rather than accept that the publications were obscene and wriggle out of the charges on grounds of 'artistic merit', Bacon wanted to challenge the whole idea of a 'community standard', as it would appear to the 'reasonable man'. In a conflicted, plural society, any such norm must be a fantasy. Bacon wound up spending 8 days in Mulawa women's prison—the first person jailed on censorship charges since 1948.

Bacon did something interesting to the old Andersonian idea of the oppositional self. The old man practiced that idea from behind the bulwarks of the sandstone quad and his suburban North Shore bungalow. The Libertarians practiced their oppositional lives in the zones of indifference of urban life, in pubs and streets from Ultimo in the west to Darlinghurst in the east. But with Bacon, the oppositional self makes appearances where it had previously not drawn attention to itself, in the public court rather than the public bar, and in a new kind of space, in the media. Bacon used the obscenity trials to break through the separation of the spectacle from everyday life.

Older Libertarians weren't necessarily interested or involved. It was in some respects a new movement. Lots of tiny cracks separated the old Libertarian line from the Futilitarian energy. For one thing, where the old Push tended to distance itself from media attention, the Futilitarians set out to exploit it. They seem to have been influenced as much by Guy Debord and the Situationist movement as by the older Libertarians.[23] And they had available to them a tool not in the hands of older radical movements—cheap and quick offset printing. Bacon and others also had a hand in the *Little Red Schoolbook*, a handy compendium of commonsense on sex, drugs, school, parents and other troubling matters for the young and tender minded. I still have the copy I was given by my big sister as a contribution to my education.

Frank Moorhouse contributed stories and essays and organised literary supplements for alternative publications. Cultural historian Tim Rowse gives an interesting account of Moorhouse's essays of the time as presenting 'the view that it is increasingly difficult for intellectuals actively to comprehend Australian society'. Confronted by its multiplicity, 'Intellectuals can do little to lead or manage these refractory and disconnected subcultures'.[24] In the maps of multiplicity that are Moorhouse's 'discontinuous narratives' one finds both an aesthetic and an ethical preference for pluralism, one wary of 'the Americans', but fascinated by the possibility of locating a place where intellectuals might install themselves in an ironic relation to the pullulating whole, comprehend it and embrace it.

In *Conferenceville*, Moorhouse sees the little intellectual world of the conference as itself just another subculture, a temporary community, and plays on the ironic possibilities of both presenting himself as a character conforming to the rules of self-presentation—and preservation—in that world, and commenting on the tiny currents of power and desire coursing through the encounters. Moorhouse's own presentation of a paper appears in the book as an essay of the pluralist position and a sly undercutting of its authority. At a time when Humphrey McQueen was beginning to see the mass media as a monolithic ideological block, Moorhouse looked for the more subtle, pervasive effects of media culture.[25] And he not only presents a new argument, but in a new literary form.

I remember the early Moorhouse stories, another legacy of Arthur Warner's Newcastle bookshop, mostly for their satires of the pretensions of left wing activism. What I and many other readers perhaps perceived less clearly is what Rowse draws attention to—that articulation of an alternative that anticipates both the celebration of difference in postmodern culture and the problem of finding a place in it from which to write. Wrestling with the futility of action that merely strengthens that which it opposes through its recognition of it, Moorhouse settles instead for a way of producing a writing—and himself as a writer—in the space of possibilities that plurality allows. In *Grand Days*, his historical evocation of the culture of the League of Nations, Moorhouse will write his own prehistory to the mature form of his cosmopolitanism.

OUTCASTS, ECCENTRICS, PERVERTS

'Long as a yard of pumpwater, iridescent, opaque'—Beatrice Faust's tribute to fellow feminist pioneer, Germaine Greer.[26]

Greer had left Sydney and the Push by the time *The Female Eunuch* made her famous, but she is nevertheless a distinctly Libertarian voice in 1970s feminism. Her first book is perhaps not held in much regard now, but is still a marvellous example of how to *essay*. As Virginia Woolf wrote in her essay on Montaigne, which she turns into an essay on the essayist's avocation: 'To communicate is our chief business; society and friendship our chief delights; and reading, not to acquire knowledge, not to earn a living, but to extend our intercourse beyond our own time and province'.[27] I think that applies to a number of those singular women who took up the essay as a way of extending a kind of friendship that would become known as feminism.

'The acts of sex are themselves forms of enquiry, as the old euphemism "carnal knowledge" makes clear: it is exactly the element of quest in her sexuality which the female is taught to deny', writes Greer.[28] Unless, of course, she spent some time among Libertarians. From the assaying of sex itself to the assaying of writing, Greer throws herself at the matter with striking confidence. She begins, like Anderson and the Libertarians, from Freud, 'the father of psychoanalysis. It had no mother'. Freud has long posed a problem for feminism, because while acknowledging from the get-go that sexuality is intimately tied up with the experience of gender difference, he sees the roots of sexuality in a relentless masculine way, and bases everything on the private world of the bourgeois family.

Like Reich, Greer connects the form of the family to the form of the whole of society. Her critique of the nuclear family is not made in terms of the 'sexual revolution' of the 1960s, although this is how it was headlined at the time. Greer contrasts the alienated world of the 'nuclear' family of modern everyday life to what she calls the 'stem' family of provincial Italy, a context in which she lived and wrote for some time. Whatever one makes of that particular example, Greer introduced with it a far more subtle understanding of the relations between family, state and economy. The form of domination in one was not simply a reflection of the form of domination in another. For example, she saw the Italian extended family form as well able to 'provide a source of cohesion which is inimical to state control for it is immovable, and its strongest loyalty is to itself'. Rather than a monolithic 'sexual economy', here we strike a rather Andersonian notion of a plurality of institutions that form people in contrary ways, and allow different possibilities for producing the self.

The book is a record of Greer's own production of herself, free from the 'servile fripperies' of the then conventional ways and means of producing one's self as a woman. Some of it sounds a little too much like a Reichian appeal to cast off the outer trappings of character and allow the repressed energies to float free. It opposes 'the ideology of routine' through the 'pleasure principle' and 'spontaneity'. And this is not without its price. 'The abandonment of slavery is also the banishment of the chimera of security. The world will not change overnight, and liberation will not happen unless individual women agree to be outcasts, eccentrics, perverts, and whatever the powers-that-be choose to call them.'

It's cause for both celebration and wonder that 25 years later, Kathy Bail, introducing a collection of writings by do-it-yourself style feminists, will casually note that when she was a girl 'the *Female Eunuch* was on the bookshelf at home next to my father's car racing trophies'.[29] Second wave feminism's early influence may have arisen out of the vector of direct speech. Coombs recounts stormy meetings of Push women, at which they discussed and overturned the Reichian holy of holies—the male orgasm as the universal model of the natural release of sexual energy. (The cartoonist Jenny Coopes didn't go: 'I didn't care about whether dicks gave you orgasms'.) But what's interesting is how what began as speech quickly passed into other vectors of communication, such that Kathy Bail or myself could encounter these various essayings of the ethical life that sprung in part from Libertarianism lying around the place in paperback.

A striking example is the genesis of *The Coming Out Show* on ABC radio—perhaps the first media expression of second wave feminism to become an ongoing institution. Liz Fell and a dedicated group of women fought ABC management, authoritarian production processes, vigorous outside lobby groups and Dame Leonie Kramer to create not only an hour a week of radio for women, by women. They fought to reverse systematic discrimination against women within the national broadcaster and to open a space within the media as a whole for women to communicate. It is all too easy to forget that in the 1970s most women working in the ABC were in the typing pool and the most women broadcasters could expect to aspire to was to become a production assistant. Issues of censorship, representation and 'balance' come up again and again in the discussions of *The Coming Out Show*'s attempts to put shows to air on sexuality, motherhood and women at work.[30]

This part of the story wouldn't be complete without mention of the philosophy strike at Sydney University in 1973.[31] Some Push people, including Liz Fell and newcomer Anne Summers, were involved, but it belongs in this story more for the irony of the return of the repressed to the jacaranda corner of the quad. As the distinguished philosopher Paul Feyerabend put it: 'Sydney has but one opera house, one arts centre, one zoo, one harbour, but two philosophy departments. The reason for this abundance is not any overwhelming demand for philosophy among the antipodes but the fact that philosophy has party lines, that different party lines don't always get on with each other and that in Sydney one has decided to keep the peace by institutional separation'.[32]

The strike did indeed split the department, but the strikers got their way—a course in feminist issues in philosophy, to be taught by Liz Jacka and Jean Curthoys. Challis Professor David Armstrong would henceforth head a department quarantined from futilities such as feminism, which would henceforth take place in the department of General Philosophy. After its Marxist and feminist enthusiasms, 'GP' turned towards recent continental philosophy. Armstrong's 'Trad and Mod' department continued Anderson's legacy in a narrow and specific sense: the teaching of a technically much refined version of Realist philosophy. But the GP department would return to that other legacy: the teaching and the practice of a comprehensive and critical philosophy; philosophy that engages with all aspects of life.

MEDIA STUDIES

After the success of the philosophy strike, Bill Bonney found himself looking for a way out of the General Philosophy department. Bonney was a passionate man, able to perform the kind of withering criticism of any kind of cant or hypocrisy typical of the Push. But he was also an Oxford trained philosopher who believed in the practice of reasoning as something apart from the 'struggle'. When a job came up as Associate Head of the School of Humanities and Social Sciences at what was then the New South Wales Institute of Technology (NSWIT), later to become the University of Technology, Sydney (UTS), he took it.

Taking such a job was a bit of a step down in the hierarchical world of higher education. The vocational emphasis of such colleges would have mortified Anderson. But Bonney could see potential in the idea of a course in 'communication', or what would later be known as media studies.[33] Bonney attracted a group of radical teachers and scholars to the place. As Paul Gillen, who was my thesis supervisor at NSWIT in the 1980s said of the place in the 1970s, 'the faculty rapidly acquired an air of feverish adventurism, and an equally feverish reaction'.[34] By the time I was a postgrad and then a lecturer there in the late 1980s, the temperature had cooled a bit.

I won't go into the politics of the place, other than to say that in my experience, 1970s leftists have a remarkable ability to conform to Moorhouse's caricatures of them. More interesting is the way a recognisably Andersonian understanding of pluralism transmuted itself into a conceptual and practical relation to the media. As Bill Bonney and Helen Wilson wrote in the textbook that summed up a considerable amount of the approach to media studies that came out of NSWIT: 'there is no such thing as the public interest. There are class interests, individual interests, fluctuating group interests. But to suppose that there is such a thing as the public interest is to suppose that there is a single "public"'.[35] I vividly remember reading those words in 1983, while half listening to a debate at a Young Labor conference, in which delegates from the east and the west of Sydney argued over cuts to hospital services in the east and plans to move those services out west. Both groups, of course, had full rhetorical command of the 'public interest'.

At the level of analysis, Bonney wanted to build a media studies that would uncover the economic and political roots of particular kinds of influence, and would also unmask those influences at work in mass media images. At the practical level, the department had a strong commitment to independent media production, particularly community broadcasting. There was some hope that the ABC could be a place where genuinely innovative broadcasting had a place—*The Coming Out Show*, for example. In the main, the emphasis was on a do-it-yourself style of media, which sought to connect particular community interests with the tools and techniques of contemporary media.

But Bonney had 'inadequately exorcised his Libertarian past', according to Macquarie University philosopher and Push alumnus Ross Poole, who argues that 'it is possible to defend a broader and more unitary notion of public broadcasting than he himself allowed'.[36] While Bonney breaks down the notion of public interest into its constituent plurality of interests, the process stops there. These sectional interests appear to have the unity and coherence that public interest as a whole does not. Public interest is false, but community interests appear as somehow more authentically coherent. In theory—but in practice, this first disaggregation invites others. In the process of making independent film or community radio at NSWIT, what a lot of people found was that community interest was no less a fiction than public interest. It too could fragment and fissure into a multiplicity. At any level, the articulation of interest rests on the fiction of an identity, or a habit of saying 'us'.

Much to the distaste of the old radical crowd, the very practice of making media and thinking about it at NSWIT gave rise from time to time to its own special brand of postmodernism, when people who wanted to keep making media started to alter the premise a bit. No longer was it a matter of searching for the authentic communal identity to represent, it was a matter of *making* an identity as an enabling move for producing images that audiences may or may not choose to read with a knowing irony, or embrace as their own. But I'll return to that curious story next chapter.

Poole takes up a more conceptual problem with the whole NSWIT approach, when he points out that it underestimated the importance of access for specific communities to a wider public sphere through the media where their particular interest can join the conversation with others. In Bonney's conception, plurality was a matter of plural interests, each with its own pure channel and way of speaking. Poole opens up another possibility—of a plurality also of voicings, where interests and expressions rub up against each other.

ANDERSON AGAIN

Looking back on it all from the late 1990s, what is interesting about Sydney in the late 1970s and early 1980s was that across the margins of the academy, the arts, and radical politics one could still find the traces of the Libertarians. But it was as if what had happened was a movement away from unreflected practices, of politics or of life, and back towards a critical thinking—one directed in part against an ossified Libertarianism itself. I found elements of that in publications like *Intervention*, the *Gay Liberation Press*, the *Working Papers* collections, particularly *Language, Power and Subversion*, but also the better known *Truth, Power, Strategy*. Perhaps not entirely by accident, the rethinking often passed through Michel Foucault and Gilles Deleuze, who belong to a very different and distinctly Parisian kind of Libertarianism.[37]

The first instinct of a Libertarian-inflected culture looking for a way to reflect critically on its own ossifying roots was a return to the old antagonist, Marxism. But the more enduring one was to look for other routes that bypassed both what Deleuze calls 'state philosophy' and Marxism, which to both Deleuze and Foucault is suspect as the philosophy of the alternative state-in-waiting. The line they pursued might be called the philosophy of the 'outside', or 'nomad thought'. I doubt that they quite had in mind the kind of nomads who trek from oasis to watering hole across the pubs of Sydney, but in a curious way the refreshment of the Libertarian spirit about town came through the confluence of the two streams of antipodean and Parisian free thought. This subterranean past may account for why the percentage of people in the English-speaking world who have worked with or on Deleuzean thought who are or were from Sydney is 'freakishly high'.

Like a series of André Breton's famous 'communicating vessels'—from the Andersonians to the Libertarians to the postmoderns, in spite of all the ruptures and disavowals—something passes from one formation to the next, not in spite of but because of the critical distance each produced in relation to its own prehistory. If there is a genealogy of Sydney Libertarianism, it would perhaps be one of a form of critical difference, one which deserves to be thought as a continuity precisely *because* of its ability always to differentiate itself from past incarnations that lose their reflective and critical edge.

And yet there are uncanny parallels between Anderson's own thought and that of Foucault, Deleuze and the kinds of applied forms of both that characterise Sydney postmodernism. As the Andersonian philosopher Jim Baker wrote of his teacher, 'his position is, above all, one of realism, empiricism and pluralism'. Anderson's pluralism involved seeing the world as a complex of events in space and time that could not be reduced to any single metaphysical principle. On this he often sounds strikingly contemporary.

When Anderson criticised the erection of war memorials as a fetish to a false belief in the sentiment of nationalism, he was already doing 'cultural studies'. But he was really only doing what Socrates did, which was to inquire into the popular culture of the time and expose the irrationality of its beliefs. He was not quite capable of doing something that is more subtly present in some of the Socratic dialogues, which is inquiring into the rhetorical construction of such beliefs, and offering a critical alternative which is itself reflectively aware of its own rhetorical artifice. But that is certainly what happens in, for example, the famous Meaghan Morris essay 'At Henry Parkes Motel'.[38]

Morris is also, in many respects, a remarkable contemporary instance of an intellectual self-making. Some of her earliest essays arise out of contact with some Libertarian inspired and assisted radical movements, but she manages to free the Libertarian commitment to pluralism from its Reichian fantasy of an underlying and all embracing sexual economy. Morris looks rather at particular institutions and the kinds of experience of self they afford. To put it simply, Morris did for the Australian essay what Moorhouse did for the Australian short story. Like his discontinuous narratives, her essays frequently jump from one perspective within a plural world of cultural difference to another. The result, far from being any kind of 'relativism', is a genuine attempt to negotiate between different ways of seeing things and phrasing them—not to make differences go away, but to find the space within which they might have a productive exchange.

If, as Hume thought, conversation is one of the most necessary kinds of artifice for extending sympathy across people's differences, then Morris has for a long time been one of the most clear-sighted members of that avant garde of Australian letters that saw the need to extend and expand the range of places within which dialogues might occur in this most plural of pluralist cultures. One way of seeing what she writes, perhaps not without some irony, is as something John Anderson's thinking both enabled and prevented. Enabled, in his early commitment to pluralism; prevented, in his authoritarian refusal to see that the commitment to pluralism necessarily entails a recognition of a plural world of *experiences* of that pluralism. There may only be one right way of reasoning, but there are very many ways of perceiving the things a public may need to reason about, and very many things different members of a public may think matter.

I think it is wrong to see Anderson and his differential descendants as necessarily elitist practices of the 'elect', although the so-called 'right wing Andersonians' such as Donald Horne seemed caught up in such a mood in their youth.[39] Anderson defended the interests and way of life of intellectuals as a distinct minority. Here one can see an early version of the distinctive lack of interest Sydney intellectuals show for assuming a missionary role to speak on behalf of society as a whole. Anderson also seems to believe that there must be a way for a plural, democratic society to manage conflicts without violence. In an uncanny way he sometimes points towards the problem of multiculturalism as a framework for the democratic resolution of conflicts, and towards a conception of it as a plural, participatory practice that organises itself from the ground up, rather than as an administrative imposition from the top down.

In other respects, Anderson's approach is more limiting. David Armstrong sums up the key tenets of post-Andersonian Realism thus: 'Physical objects or happenings stimulate our sense organs. As a causal result of this, we acquire immediate knowledge of their existence and their properties. By immediate knowledge is meant knowledge which is not inferred from, or suggested by, any further knowledge, or any basis or ground for knowledge. This knowledge is not necessarily verbalised knowledge, but it is always knowledge which it is logically possible to put verbally. It is propositional in form. And although such knowledge is immediate, in the sense just defined, it is not incorrigible knowledge'.[40] Now, it may shock some of my postmodern colleagues, but I agree with Armstrong that we can have immediate knowledge of a thing or an event. The leaf falls. The door opens. The problem is that while there are things of which we can have immediate knowledge, most public things are not of this kind.

For example, Aboriginal deaths in police custody. Those whose experience of this is most direct are dead. Those whose experience of this is almost as direct, lie. The public thing put under scrutiny is not direct knowledge but knowledge inferred from, and suggested by, documents and testimony sought through public hearings. Public life exists to create knowledge of things that can only be known indirectly. The philosophical tools of most relevance deal not with the analysis of things but the analysis of language. So while the 'Trad and Mod' department of philosophy at Sydney University continued Anderson's work on experience in the direction of a Realist philosophy of science, philosophy as a tool for public life drew on other sources.

There were other limits to Anderson's practice of philosophy. He had a one-eyed idea about conflict. There was a plurality of interests in Anderson's conception, but he did not think about a plurality of kinds of conflict. He did not think about the way spaces of conflict are constituted, how economic, cultural and political conflict might be intertwined and yet in some respects also distinct. Hence he did not see, as Ross Poole does, that there may be different kinds of action appropriate to the different zones of conflict. Or as I would put it, that the rise of third nature requires new ways of thinking about the intersections that make up the plurality of the republic.

Anderson commended opposition to servility and a practice of self-constitution, like that of Stephen Dedalus. But his conception of this was limited, not least by his own inability to completely put it into practice. He remained more servile than he knew, to elitist and authoritarian notions of the philosopher-king. The Libertarians were well trained enough in his practice to see the inconsistencies in Anderson and to break with him. They were better students than he knew. They made their break, and in the legendary stories of Smilde and Waters, one has Dedalus in full and honourable refusal of the servile state. But they were characters, not authors, of this idea. They did not find a way to produce a self beyond servility and self-alienation that could appear as such within the wider world. They existed in the gaps and cracks of a servile world.

Moorhouse and Bacon, in their highly singular ways, produced something more than futile refusal. Bacon took opposition out of the margins of Sydney's inner city and into the mainstream media, either through the subversive spectacle of the *Tharunka* trials, or later as a journalist and activist. She ran for election in Sydney's inner west on the No Aircraft Noise platform. Moorhouse went his own subtle way, as an ironist, inserting his slow-burning writings into the literary sphere. Both found new ways to produce tools for self-making beyond the bar room argument.

Bonney and Fell took this in another direction. Beyond making themselves into subtle or spectacular authors of their own image, they found ways to create institutions that extended opposition and self-constitution. *The Coming Out Show* and the UTS Communications course lighted upon the spectacle itself as the particular space of conflict among others where oppositional institutions could have an effect.

But beyond that there is yet another issue, one signalled in Ross Poole's writings. How can one effect something more than a personal act of self-constitution, something more than turning oneself into an exemplar, something more even than constituting an institution that can function as a new space for others to acquire the tools of oppositional self-making? How can one intervene in the shaping of the space of conflict itself? In this case, intervene in the space of the virtual republic; the space of indifference where conflicting modes of making people negotiate. In a way the figure of speech I would want to offer for thinking about Australia is not the 'market' or 'society' or 'community', but the city. Or to take it down a notch to something even more specific, the kind of city street where rednecks and faggots can acknowledge each other's existence and yet pass on by. In Poole's writing, the issue, I think, is one of extending that kind of institution into a kind of larger, more abstract kind of artifice.

Other cities have other traditions, also distinctive and productive. This is just one particular past. Without knowing it at the time, I lived in its shadow. It still casts a shadow, one with as many branches as a jacaranda tree, and with even more tangled and matted roots, unseen. As I want to show in the next chapter, the contemporary world offers a quite different space for culture's techniques of the self. Some of Sydney libertarianism flows into Sydney postmodernism, or rather, two streams of thinking, acting and writing came across each other in the 1980s.

Postmodernism came to town partly because in the 1980s the global media vectors reached ever so subtly into every corner of everyday experience, in a way not really clear in previous decades. We no longer have roots we have aerials. But postmodernism took on a distinctive quality because, in their efforts to grasp and make useful that kind of media experience, the 'postmoderns' had access to techniques of the self and their institutional homes that were the organised expression of libertarianism. Every artist and writer has had to break away, sometimes subtly, sometimes dramatically, from the servile structures of family and state. One no longer has to go looking for the space within which to make such a break in the downtown pubs of Sydney. By the 1980s there was a plurality of institutions within which one might learn a sceptical, even an oppositional way of thinking about institutions. Now there's an ironic story—and it's the story I want to tell in the next chapter.

4

A secret history of Sydney postmodernism

Australia has become a post of infinite posts.

Mudrooroo Narogin

THE POSTMODERN REPUBLIC

What was postmodernism?[1] I think it's an interesting time to ask. Particularly in the light of the speech Don Watson gave at Mieta's in Melbourne, later published in essay form as 'A Toast to the Postmodern Republic'.[2] He was speech writer to Prime Minister Paul Keating at the time. Whatever shape the republic takes, Watson said, there will be 'something unstructured, if not deconstructed about it . . . I'm only just game enough to say it: it might be the first postmodern republic, and I mean that in the nicest possible way. I mean a republic that exalts the nation less than the way of life. Whose principal value is tolerance rather than conformity, difference rather than uniformity'.

He's talking there about what in the early 1980s were pretty marginal concerns, to be found in the little magazines and art gallery catalogues. In the early 1990s they became, for a moment at least, rhetorical options for the nation. Possible grounds for creating notions of Australian culture and identity in the early 1990s. This is not unprecedented. Literary critic A. A. Phillips coined the now popular expression 'cultural cringe' in an essay for the Melbourne quarterly *Meanjin*. Donald Horne, an editor of the Sydney magazines the *Observer* and the *Bulletin*, gave us the 'lucky country'.[3] With Watson, as with Phillips and Horne, critical essay writing became a resource for thinking the nation's creativity, and thinking the nation creatively.

To me there was a sly irony hidden in Watson's creation of a notional 'postmodern republic'. One of the major themes of postmodernism in the 1980s was that creativity results from the appropriation and recombination of existing elements in culture that speak through us rather than as some kind of spontaneous act of romantic genius. Seen in those terms, Watson borrowed and collaged together ideas current from postmodern thought in a thoroughly postmodern fashion. If those postmodern currents had made much of the fragmentation and multiplication of identities, then Watson rose to the challenge of finding a way to make that very plurality the premise of an essentially Australian identity.

Only one cannot appear to bestow tolerance and difference from above, as Watson does in his speech. And that is not just my reading of the kind of theoretical underpinnings Watson offered for Prime Minister Paul Keating's version of the republic. The electorate seemed to think so too. With the victory of John Howard's brand of mindless conservatism in the 1996 federal election, all that returns to the margins from whence it came. With the departure of Keating and Watson, someone else will be writing quite a different prime minister very different speeches. The postmodern republic retired to the Jurassic Park of history.

History is a republic of documents. I've hoarded several milk crates full of papers that are bones of a postmodern life, if there was such a thing. I've always wondered what I would ever actually do with this ossuary. I think now they are perhaps meant for carving an image of a certain cultural moment that had its day and will have to wait now, for another time, to come again. And so—a secret history of my postmodernism. Which is not Don Watson's, although there may be some obscure caledonia where they are cousins.

SECRET HISTORY

Nostalgia is the vice of seeing one's particular past as having universal significance. Like everyone else in their mid-thirties or younger, I've learned this through the repetition of misty remembrances of the 1960s by people who were around then— or claim they were. As the years go by, this increasingly takes the even more than usually tiresome form of a gnashing of (false) teeth about how wrong everyone got it in the 1960s, and how we really need to return to the values of the 1950s instead. As if nothing had been said or done in the 1970s, 1980s and 1990s to make up for the follies of the 1960s.

So it is with some fear and loathing that I shake the dust off my documents from the 1980s. I have an allergic reaction to old paper, for one thing, so I see even my own past through the delirium of a sneezing fit and a handful of antihistamines. That my body wants to expel the dust of the past as quickly as it inhales it seems to me an entirely healthy mechanism.

What emerges from these ossicles is not quite the kind of story I told in the last chapter. That story inevitably simplifies, omits, turns a network of associations into a one-way flow of connections. But with a little bit of distance it's possible to do that. That past seems ready to have some lines extracted from it and preserved. It is also a past that quite a few people are now digging up, so what is lost in one selection may very well turn up in another. The past is a republic of documents in the sense that there is more than one thing that can be made out of the traces left of it.

The particulars of the 1980s I want to recall are those things that seemed to mark for me what was contemporary. The philosopher Jean-Luc Nancy describes a contemporary as 'someone in whom we recognise a voice or a gesture which reaches us from a hitherto unknown but immediately familiar place, something which we discover we have been waiting for, or rather, which has been waiting for us'.[4] So in this chapter, that which I want to recall from the misty world of nostalgia are those writings that seemed, at the time, to me at least, absolutely necessary to describing the experience of the contemporary itself.

This is a bit of personal archaeology of the 'population' of rhetorics and practices that was postmodern life in Sydney in the 1980s. A culture that, if one understands a little about it—about what hopes, what energies it expressed—doesn't appear quite as sinister as it appeared in the culture wars of the 1990s. Nor was postmodernism entirely unprecedented. Far from being just an ignorance about the past, the postmodern condition has a history, and is itself a particular kind of understanding of history. Not that much of this is yet public knowledge. Postmodernism has what American essayist Greil Marcus calls a secret history, '. . . the result of moments that seem to leave nothing behind, nothing but the mystery of spectral connections between people long separated by place and time, but somehow speaking the same language . . .'.[5]

Marcus, a brilliant essayist but a bit of a 1960s kind of guy, tells a story about the 1980s that excavates the punk insurrection, and traces its subterranean connections back to the insurrectionary avant-gardes that periodically burst upon the stage of western history, such as Dada and the Situationists. It's an historical configuration that Marcus sees as embodying the ' . . . demand to live not as an object but as a subject of history—to live as if something actually depended on one's actions'. That insurrectionary moment had its effects in Sydney city culture. Punk subjectivity left its traces, as I recall, and as Vivien Johnson records in her evocative book on legendary band *Radio Birdman*. When they played French's Tavern, it could be an exhilarating, even frightening thing. That moment when, if you are out of it enough, it seems like the noise, the movement, the crowd, the space, everything conspires to wilfully rip culture apart from the insides out.[6]

The moment that interests me seems to come two beats after that, and embodies a different passion. The postmodern moment dwells in the lees of the failure of the project of becoming the subject of history. After the curtain closes on those radical moments comes the inevitable feeling of lost possibility, of despair and soul searching. But after *that* comes a certain scepticism, a certain relief that the true believers, in either their optimistic or pessimistic phase, did not prevail. After revolutionary and activist modernism comes a conservative modernism of devout quietude, and after that comes postmodernism, which as we shall see is something else again.

First come the Angry Penguins, then comes Harold Stewart and James McAuley to play their cruel hoax on the radical pretensions of the Penguins, by inventing a revolutionary proletarian poet for them—Ern Malley. When this cruel poppy-lopping hoax comes into the tabloid light, the Penguins claim that the Malley poems are really inspired genius—let loose from inhibition by the cloak of the phantom Malley, the two cranky anti-radicals were really at their best. One–two, one–two, around and around the parade ground this argument goes. But Malley, the black swan of trespass, remains as his biographer Michael Heyward says, 'an enigma half a century of debate has not solved'.[7] The enigma of writing, of language, of art, of authorship—if you want something to set you thinking about those things then Malley is your man. That's what makes him a postmodern poet.

Or perhaps, against this rhythm of cultural history, the postmodern isn't the third beat, but is something altogether untimely, a way of thinking and acting that always waits in the wings. Like the way Malley waits to be made into something more than a note in the history of Australian letters. Jean-François Lyotard, the man who, probably more than any other, put the idea of the postmodern in circulation in the 1980s, says that postmodern writing is that which 'denies itself the solace of good forms . . . which searches for new presentations, not in order to enjoy them but in order to impart a stronger sense of the unpresentable . . . .'. It 'proceeds at its own pace. Montaigne is the absolute model here. Writing marches to its own beat and it has no debts'.[8]

In other words, for its leading advocate, the postmodern isn't the same thing as the contemporary. It's a particular kind of aesthetic that has happened again and again. This is why I've referred to the contemporary moment in terms of another idea—third nature. Now it's time to bring them together. I think that when people's experience of third nature reaches a certain critical mass, then the postmodern sensibility starts to become far more common than it usually is.

CLASSICAL IRONY

The spirit of Sydney postmodernism is a spirited irony. The most common form of irony with which most people are familiar is sarcasm, where what is said is the opposite of what the speaker means. More generally, irony is any statement or image where there is some kind of dislocation or displacement of one or other element. Between who speaks and who listens, between what is heard and what is said, between the context and the utterance, something is *deliberately* awry. The word comes from a Greek word meaning to dismember, and that is apt, for irony cuts into the flow of language, drawing attention, for those who notice, to the different registers and orders in which things can be said.

In Plato's dialogues, when Socrates speaks, he often pretends to be ignorant about something. What is beauty? What is truth? By feigning ignorance, he goads the authorities of his time into pontificating, and through his deft questions, cuts through the flab of received wisdom, showing its incoherencies and inconsistencies, its tautologies and contradictions. No wonder the Athenians got jack of him. He shows that their most cherished beliefs are hollow abstractions. As the great Danish philosopher Søren Kierkegaard wrote, 'the whole substantial life of Greek culture had lost its validity for him, which meant that to him the established actuality was unactual, not in this or that particular aspect, but in its totality . . .'.[9]

Socrates did not satirise the Athenians, or criticise them. That would presume that he had an alternative 'republic' up his sleeve to propose, and unlike Plato, he did not. In any case, an established order rarely lacks the wit and the power to persuade its beneficiaries that as orders go the present one is preferable to an alternative. A wise regime not only tolerates but encourages a little satire and criticism. But irony, pursued with Socratic rigour, is something else. The ironist simply twists each rule and convention of speech, showing that the accepted rules, far from being necessary, are merely instances of a whole plurality of imaginable rules. The ironist does not attack the legitimacy of the present order in the name of another order. The ironist questions the order of language within which the legitimacy of any order rests. The ironist is not a critic, arguing that there is something lacking in the order of things, in the name of an imaginary other order that might fill the gap. Irony is only critical if it stops short. If it keeps going, it becomes virtual. It illuminates the very grounds upon which *any* order is conceived and made legitimate—language, at work in the world.

When questioned by the wily Socrates, the priest can do no better than to propose that Athenians worship what is holy, and that what is holy is worshipped by Athenians. To the priest, that is the limit to what he can know and imagine. To the Socratic ironist, it is a pattern of conventions in language, of which there could be an infinite number. The displacements of irony set Socrates free. The whole of language, every social convention, all the trappings of belief, are merely arenas in which he can engage his fellow citizens in dialogue and displace himself from their limits. This is the corrosive, liberating wisdom of the first of the first Great Books of the 'western canon'.

MODERN IRONY

'The trouble with great literature is that any asshole can identify with it.' Such is the caustic observation of the German essayist and novelist Peter Handke.[10] Great Books are works around which there is a safe consensus of taste. Adding one's assent to the clamour of cheers for Shakespeare requires no great courage and hardly marks one's own taste as in any way distinguished. Nor does denouncing as 'trash' what the majority happen to think is trash. This is why people who take the assaying of art seriously are always looking for something more challenging upon which to chance their wits.

One way of going about this is to exhume forgotten works from what Greil Marcus calls the 'dustbin of history': take what an age thought ugly and unworthy and reappraise it. Show why something despised as vulgar actually has some beauty about it. For example, in his book *Mystery Train*, Marcus identified great works of popular American song from the blues to rock'n'roll.

A somewhat different technique might be to make an ironic move away from looking at works of art (or literature or music) and asking: 'Is it beautiful?'. One can ask instead: 'Is it art?'. In this ironist's view of taste, the works that have value are not those that conform to certain ideas about taste, nor even those works that deliberately transgress good taste. What matters are the works that question the whole category of what art is.

The most striking example of an ironist of this stamp was Marcel Duchamp, the artist famous for purchasing a urinal from the plumber's shop and displaying it in an art show. Once again there is that Socratic displacement, that questioning of conventions that reveals their conventional nature. Duchamp called such art objects 'readymades', meaning that these works of art already exist, and are simply waiting for the artist to designate them as a work of art by signing them, giving them a title and placing them before a public that expects a work of art. He also suggested reverse-readymades—turn a Rembrandt into an ironing board.[11]

Which brings us to Andy Warhol, who pretty much did exactly that. Rather than look for ironic displacements between things and art objects, between the public space of art and other spaces, Warhol opened up the whole field of contemporary images as a space and time across which he displaced images, from one convention to the next. From magazine to wallpaper, to newspaper to painting to TV interview to film and back again.[12] Through his early ironic gestures in art, Warhol created a space within the mass media to continue his ironic movement right across its vast canvas, although in the end, the infinite jostle of images against images that is contemporary third nature swallowed him whole. A perfectly ironic career.

IRONY NOW

The postmodern sensibility begins with Warhol, although it has a secret history that runs back not only to Duchamp, but to Kierkegaard's reading of Socrates. While irony is part of a great tradition in the west, it is only after Warhol that one realises that irony is not the preserve of a few quick-witted thinkers or artists. The subtle and pervasive weaving of the media vectors of third nature into every and any convention or situation makes irony a fact of everyday life. Irony is everywhere, already. One can't free oneself from convention when irony itself has become the convention, as it surely is when *Frontline* is a hit TV show and Dave Graney is a rock'n'roll star.[13] The trick to pull off in this situation is to make *irony itself* ironic, to double it over onto itself.

As Catharine Lumby writes: 'What if the role of the artist and the status of the art object were so uncertain that there was no longer a status quo to disrupt? Indeed, where would the possibility for ironic gesture lie when irony had become the status quo? In such a situation, irony might be said to have had its revenge—to turn on those who wield it—and collapse into complacency'. What lies at the end of this thought is a certain vertigo: the artist or the writer might be the object, not the subject of the creative act. 'The makers are no longer in control of the ironic possibilities. Rather, it is the objects themselves which mock us for our attempt to fix their aesthetic meaning and value.'[14]

What might have brought about such a situation? The proliferation of media vectors undermines the established orders of representation. Signs just don't stay put where they were supposed to be. Whether celebrating or deploring it, critics to the right and left agree that this makes the old verities of cultural order appear somewhat shaky. Once fixed points of cultural identity and value appear subject to flux. Which led one troubled postmodernist to a somewhat irksome question: 'What if the vector becomes so ubiquitous that every point becomes mobile, and every point becomes interconnected with every other point? *What will become of us?*'.[15]

In such a situation, irony is no longer something that a writer can confidently claim is simply an effect of her or his creative and subjective will. Irony becomes objective, produced by the media's effect on the public sphere, which now undermines itself to the point of disrupting its circuits of meaning, its partitions of good sense and good taste. The allegedly postmodern scepticism about 'values', be they ethical or aesthetic, isn't just impudence. It has its basis in the experience of a world made over into a third nature of images flowing, ceaselessly, seamlessly, across the landscape.

The social world of second nature divided space and assigned activities to separate places. Women were supposed to stay at home, while men went to the pub—unless the women had run away and joined the Libertarians. Third nature means that the vector crosses all the old boundaries, passing through every wall. Where once everything had its place, now everything has its own time slot. The upshot is that the public is no longer distinguished from the private as a distinct place. Private matters work their way along the vector into the public realm—particularly through feminism and its slogan 'the personal is political'.

The political also gets pretty personal, with the rise of the telegenic politician. What Ronald Reagan and Bill Clinton have in common is an ability to be public figures who come across well in the private world of one's lounge room. They appear, via TV, as polite, well mannered, strangely intimate guests in our own home. Once politics was about speechifying in town halls; now it's about a casual chat in a few million lounge rooms. As Lumby quips: 'Do not adjust your set. That black thing in the centre of your screen is the hole the public sphere made on the way out'.[16]

Or as Eric Michaels puts it, in a suitably parodic style: 'Andy Warhol became famous in the 1960s for saying that, in the new electronic age, everybody would be famous for five minutes . . . Never noted for his mathematics, Warhol's prediction may require a recalculation: if you take the number of radio and TV transmitters operating everywhere in the world and multiply this by the number of total broadcast hours each, and then divide by the total world population, the result might indicate that by, say, 1982, everybody, everywhere, had had their five minutes. The precise date when this happened, I submit, marks the beginning of the postmodernist moment. At that point, we were required to come to some new relationship between texts and audiences'.[17]

Given that this is a story about irony, it will come as no surprise that everyone who had anything to do with postmodernism distances themselves from it. Postmodernism is nothing but a crate of empties left over when the party ends. But perhaps it's time to redeem them. One could write a whole essay on what the postmodern isn't, and wasn't. By the mid-1990s, it had become a favourite bogey of the tired old 'new left' and the wearisome old 'new right', who erased their differences and became a culture of reaction precisely in their wilful refusal to understand what the new moment entailed. They got by on a series of artless parodies, to the effect that the postmodern was a mindless 'relativism', a recline into 'nihilism' or a celebration of the 'popular'. In so doing, they proved themselves even less artless victims of the postmodern condition of the public sphere than the self-styled pomo ironists. Their artifice lacked not only substance, but grace. Although in the case of David Williamson's plays and sermons, there was no shortage of force.[18]

And of course they missed the point—that the postmodern, as an aesthetic strategy responding to a condition of the proliferation of signs, was a revaluing of all values; which means overturning the table of assumed and established taste, preferably with a flourish, but not just in the interests of another order of taste, and certainly not in favour of the mere sarcasm of preferring the low to the high. The postmodern is not an inversion of the relationship of high culture to pop, but a series of tactics meant to displace it so that one can begin to evaluate afresh.

IN THE MARGIN OF MARGINS

In a fit of absent mindedness, the Visual Arts Board of the Australia Council funded what will turn out to be the most daring, original and necessary literature of the 1980s. For it was the little art magazines that I now hoard in my milk crates, like *Art & Text*, *On the Beach*, and *Tension*, where Australian sensibility reinvented itself.

The Oscar Wilde of Australian art in the 1980s was without doubt Paul Taylor, founding editor of *Art & Text*, contributor to *Tension*, curator of 'Popism', and all round hustler of what would become the postmodern sensibility. Taylor had the cunning and the wit to see Australian culture as more than a valid site for the production of a truly contemporary art. He imagined it as the *exemplar* of the emerging taste of the 1980s. If this was to be a time when art grew self-consciously subtle and subtly self-conscious about its borrowings and relations with its own past and with popular culture, then Australia's peripheral vision of the global art world was the-postmodern-in-a-can.

The postmodern moment was about the conscious exploitation of one's irredeemable status as an object of history, not least of cultural history. Avant-garde art from dada to punk was about jamming, interrupting, breaking with one's cultural matrix. The postmodern strategies for making culture would instead quite consciously play on memory, citation, pastiche, on the wit of knowingness about the past, not its carnivalesque overturning. It would be what Catharine Lumby called, 'the aesthetics of surrender'.[19] Or as Ted Colless and David Kelly said in their aleatory 'Lost World' essays, published in *Art & Text*, 'No longer the victimised outsider but the continuum of the insider, disillusioned, dispassionate, left alone in a world well lost'.[20]

What for Colless and Kelly demanded a wistful melancholy, Taylor was quick to spot as an opening for a rhetorical gambit with more immediate purchase, more power. Australia, he said, 'can be called a culture of temporary culture because of its enormous and all-pervasive skills in setting up and dismantling its own cultural programs and its metaphors of cultural progress

and aspiration according to their momentary efficacy'.[21] Taylor
had the cheek to talk about our 'multinational culture', a play
on the confluence of corporate capital and the whole way of
life adapted to its stringent contingencies. In place of the
resentment and hysteria about the CIA sacking Whitlam and
the coca-colonisation of Australia, Taylor saw Australian de-
pendency as itself a site for a certain kind of cultural
opportunity. Australia was the original postmodern culture precisely because it had always been derivative. Rather than see
this in terms of a cultural cringe, as a lack of something, Taylor
saw it as an asset.

That Australia borrows even its avant-gardes from elsewhere
is for Taylor just part of the expediency. 'Australian culture
hasn't necessarily "come of age"; rather, it is the beneficiary of
a worldwide loss of confidence and nostalgic yearning for lost
utopias.' Here we have an early version of the argument that
Australian culture is always and already postmodern. Flung out
on the antipodes, always the 'other foot', not able to get on
the good foot—nothing for it but to plunder all the cultures
beaming in via satellite, from James Brown to Roland Barthes,
or preferably both—with a bit of Warhol on the side. Its unique
creation is a culture of appropriation, not of creativity. Australian art is always derivative of elsewhere. But the Australian
style of appropriation is a unique creation. That is the original
irony of Australian culture. In this moment when the dominant,
metropolitan cultures give up the ghost of acting as the subject
in history, the very antipodality of Australian culture comes
into its own, having always been a culture of 'effects' rather
than 'causes'.

Searching for a signal event in both local and global time,
Taylor nominates the 1956 Melbourne Olympics as an emblem
of an era of events in the world doubled by their simulation
on television. If the coming of the Olympics to Australia was
meant to signal our 'modernity', the fact that it was at least
experimentally televised was for Taylor a mark of a
'postmodernity' to come. He speaks to and for and from a
generation that grew up in television's pixilated light, dwelling
in the shadow of its silent majorities, aggregated as consumers
of spectacle but otherwise devoid of consensus.[22] Those of us
born into TV's cool embrace, as something already part of the
landscape, would never see the world the same way again. The

doubling of perception in this relentless flow of images from elsewhere would work its way into our dreams and thoughts.

The role of contemporary art and writing would be to make apparent this doubling of the world in endless flows of images. And beyond that, the cold fact of the endless making of the appearance of the world as relentless images could be teased out. Postmodernism thus had two projects. One was historical, to explain this moment in perception when images proliferate through the media and work their way into the landscape. The other was conceptual: to ask not just 'Is that good art?' but, 'What is art?'. And to ask not just: 'Is that a true perception?' but 'What is perception?'.

Taylor was a brilliant wit with a remarkable eye. And he was fully aware of the way power worked through art and its institutions, as the essays he wrote from New York, published in *Tension*, show.[23] Like Wilde he worked the 'politics' into the wit to the point where the wit was the politics.[24] To champion the aesthetic as something distinct from moralising sermons is of course a moral position in itself. A position that favours the infinite freedom that opens up when images and words reflect on themselves and reveal the sublime beyond the limits of the freedom we think we know.

STYLE AND POWER

'We hear a lot these days about superficial style obsessed postmoderns: but the smart young things about town have very little to teach the Left about the politics of authoritarian control through style. We're the ones, after all, who installed a ruthless surveillance system monitoring every aspect of style . . . the fact that some stylish kid might be striking nihilistic poses in the latest exhibition catalogue is quite frankly the least of my worries.'[25] That was Meaghan Morris, in 1985, on politics then. Morris is a key figure, at the crossroads between Paris and the Push, both of which are places where she studied. By opening up the whole question of the rhetoric of speaking and appearing, Morris was one of the people who opened the door to an even more self-consciously ironic style of writing.

But Morris was always aware of addressing at least two kinds of reader. On the one side she is conducting the libertarian's ongoing war with the authoritarian elements of the left.

These are the readers to whom she has offered the tactical concession about 'nihilism', ten years before it will occur to David Williamson to use it as a term of abuse. On the other hand, she is also addressing those 'superficial style obsessed postmoderns' and reminding us of the way the shimmer of images are still woven from a taut fabric of power.

The particular 'nihilistic poses' referred to might very well have been those of the students of Ted Colless, when he was at the Power Institute. Ted was and remains the critic's critic, the antipodean Walter Pater, if not exactly as widely known as his arch and elegant writings demand.[26] For Colless, the critic invents the very possibility of the aesthetic image and its autonomous being in the world through the struggle to produce it in language. Time and again, Colless conjures up images and concepts of astonishing and lucid beauty, and reminds us that we see and are astonished by the light only because of the impenetrable shadows from which the image and the word are cast.

The Error of My Ways, Colless' collected essays, begins by conjuring up a young Ted watching TV: 'Before the grey, spectral smears of late 1950s television, I sat innocent but expectantly through the Disney Mousketeers' jitterbug-like dance routines. I was waiting for the little pleated dresses to spin out and up above the girls' black knickers. The delight was purely phenomenal: only fleeting impressions of a firmness, fullness of the bottom or hip as the fulcrum for an energy that tipped the world. No thoughts of the origin or destiny of that vitality, let alone the content of such revelations of physique and movement. Later in the evenings, from the same screen luminous flying saucers would loom out of the drear pearl skies over a black and white American town as if they were coagulations of the material energy of television itself'.[27]

From the Museketeers Colless fashions the beginnings of an essay, or a way of writing essays, about perception itself. This has nothing to do with 'relativism', but everything to do with scepticism, in the tradition of Montaigne's judicious, ironic, prudent use of doubt.[28] The issue is perception. Colless is not particularly interested in the question of whether the images he perceives are good or bad copies of the idea of a 'real world'. He is interested in the way TV images differ from that ideal, and in being different, how they are perceived, and what passions might flow from such perceptions.

This postmodernism has nothing to do with a celebration of 'popular culture', as John Docker hopes, and Peter Goodall fears.[29] Both these literary critics have many valuable insights into the relationship between popular culture and high culture and the role of intellectuals in policing the boundaries. But the whole point of the postmodern critique is that these boundaries had become arbitrary, mere marketing devices for the lazy-minded culture consumer. Under the impact of proliferating vectors, whole new cultural landscapes, forms, experiences and modes of judgement spring up. The postmodern vocation was not to abandon 'standards' and embrace the popular, but to abandon *received ideas* about standards and rediscover how to make aesthetic judgements, free from outdated categories and assumptions. What makes Colless contemporary, in a way that Docker is not, is firstly that when he looks at television he perceives *television*, but also that he sees that the experience of television calls into question received ideas of what it means to perceive, and what might constitute good things to look at, as opposed to bad ones.

Like Paul Taylor, Colless writes for the generation of aesthetes for whom television and pop are a necessary landscape of perception. But if the media really have swallowed up the public sphere and turned it, willy-nilly, into a fathomless third nature, then one cannot take for granted that there is a solid place to ground one's speaking position, as an essayist, an intellectual, as anything. One has to begin ironically, by displacing one's self from the certainty of simply writing from some romantic notion of creative inspiration. One has to create a new way of creating, one that begins by taking its distance from any such assumptions. One begins again, from page one. And like the only true and original heretic, one starts from knowing that one knows nothing.

This is what the postmodern writers of the 1980s took from Meaghan Morris—the self-conscious grounding of criticism in its own reflection on itself and its particular speaking position, in the moment. Writing has to provide its own rhetorical platform, rather than simply assume a moral authority or a claim on the real. What writers like Colless, Lumby or Taylor left behind in Morris is the reflexive gesture back to the new left and its aura of moral and political certainties. That is an historical moment consigned, before our time, to the dustbin of history. They had May 1968, we had Countdown.[30] They had the Soledad Brothers, we had the Brady Bunch.

FRESH LANDSCAPES

Paul Taylor hangs his case for an Australian postmodernism across the gap between two canonic films: *On the Beach* and *Mad Max*.[31] Ross Gibson, one of the editors of the little magazine, also called *On the Beach*, wrote one of his finest essays on *Mad Max*—for *Art & Text*. Gibson reads *Mad Max*, and in particular the third film *Beyond Thunderdome*, as a story about a new relationship to landscape. What fascinates Gibson are the images of landscape in this film that aren't the pristine vistas of a sacred nature or an exploitable resource, but are a space littered with the wreckage of past attempts to use it. By setting the film after the apocalypse, director George Miller creates an imaginary time where irony rules. All the old orders of things and signs are busted wrecks in the sand. Max has to begin again, outside the assumed order of things, making a new world up as he goes along.

The film then offers a choice between more or less free ways of ordering culture and nature, past and present, self and environment. Max has to choose between a world based only on the institution of property—Bartertown—or ones based on conversation and storytelling. He bets on storytelling. The movie ends with the storyteller to the tribe, with a rapt audience gathered about her, seated in the burnt out ruins of the old powerhouse in Ultimo. She tells the story of Max himself, the story we have just seen in the movie, only she tells it differently to her audience to the way George Miller told it to us, his cinema audience. The film is a sort of imaginary secret history of the spectral connections that might get made in the conversation between generations, on into the future.

The *Mad Max* trilogy is part of a conversation in Australian culture about landscape. It lies in the wake of the early explorers like Mitchell and their will to dominate the landscape and make it useful. It moves away also from a submission to a landscape that is a curiously empty yet spiritualised other in Patrick White's *Voss*. Gibson sees in *Mad Max* a place where one can 'begin again', assembling fragments of image, sense, memory and self. 'In a culture that is beginning at page one, all available signs and artefacts might be counted temporarily equal.'[32] Like Taylor, Gibson plays with the old image of Australia as a culture of failure. But in the wreckage of received ideas that came to dominate or sublimate the landscape lies a new field of potentials—a democracy of objects. Gibson reads Max as a mythic reincarnation of Sturt, Eyre, Leichhardt and Voss, where the failure of conquest becomes the triumph of conquering the will to conquest. Gibson sees in Max a figure that goes beyond the noble failure of the hero, of the subject in history, of the colonial project of treating the land as a plane of action. Here at last is the image of a figure who will begin again: 'Now Max is simply moving with the continent, reading it a little more cannily, growing from it'.

This idea of a practice of reading the country also appears in the work of Stephen Muecke, particularly his collaboration with the painter Krim Benterrak and Aboriginal storyteller Paddy Roe, *Reading the Country*.[33] Muecke recorded and transcribed Roe's stories about his country, and in the process started to write about them in a new way. Mudrooroo is critical of Muecke's methods, of the way he 'barricades the discourse of Paddy Roe' between slabs of Muecke, in which Roe is 'reduced to discourse as heard through the ears of a European'. There is an absence of 'critical and political comment' and no analysis of 'Aboriginal-being-in-Australia'. Mudrooroo then goes on to contradict all of that by declaring that the 'fringe soul of the Aborigine' does indeed 'peer out' of the book.

What he doesn't say is that the book is structured precisely to accommodate readers who think or feel differently. Mudrooroo can read it through the transcripts of Paddy Roe's storytelling, a reader like me can approach it through Muecke's essay-writing, still another might start by looking at the paintings. Muecke designed his book this way—taking account of the fact that the conversation about reading the country has to start from points of view that as yet don't share a zone of indifference. While Mudrooroo is quite justifiably tired of hearing about it all from the white point of view, the white point of view does not yet know how to hear much else.

Trained as a structuralist, Muecke was well versed in the procedure of extracting the story, turning it into a text, breaking it down into its constituent terms, organising the terms in a grid, and showing the structure within the text that generates the meaning. But in *Reading the Country* he starts to do something different. Rather than separate text from performance—and performer—Muecke looks instead at the connections between a term in the story and a place Roe indicates with his finger. He threads the story back into the land. The story isn't about the land. The land and the story get produced together, out of the network of movements of Aboriginal people across this intricate space of stories.

Borrowing from Gilles Deleuze, Muecke called this new practice of reading the country a 'nomadology'.[34] The idea was that rather than overlay a grid over space so that one can organise movements on it instrumentally, the relation of people to the land will work another way. It's the movements of people that produce the fluid, changing, but seemingly eternal web of stories that constitute Aboriginal knowledge. It's the movements that produce land and people as networks of places, networks of kin and obligation, networks of stories that may be told or not told.

Put Mad Max and Muecke together, and what I think you have is a postmodern rejoinder to the long-running conversation in Australian culture about landscape. It is an alternative to the Bartertown mentality, where land is just something to be valued and traded. It is also another way of reading the country to that vaguely spiritual quest for redemption through going out into the desert and confronting it as some kind of existential other. That way of seeing the land seems originally to have been a way of justifying a white presence in the land, by telling stories about how the white soul faced down the sublime emptiness of the continent and did not blink. Ironically, in the popular imagination, this now seems to have been transferred back onto Aboriginal culture. Aboriginality now has value *only* to the extent that it has this eternal spiritual link to land. The Aboriginal becomes a mediating category, occupying the place once held by explorers and bushmen, through which urban Australians can jindy up to the great otherness of the land.

Ross Gibson makes Max an ironic version of that mediating figure. Stephen Muecke makes Paddy Roe a different figure in the land altogether. He is both a preserver of ancient and sacred stories and a creator of new stories, and through the telling of new stories, he preserves storytelling itself. Muecke records, for example, the story of the good oil company and the bad oil company, the one that engaged in a conversation with

Aboriginal people about land use, the oil company that didn't—
and their respective fates.

YUENDUMU STORY

1 April 1985: daily TV transmission by the Warlpiri Media
Association begins at Yuendumu, 300 kilometres north-west of
Alice Springs on the edge of the Tanami Desert in central
Australia. At the time they commenced, the programs were
unauthorised, unfunded, uncommercial and illegal. The decision
to start broadcasting was taken after 18 months of fruitless
negotiations with the Department of Communications for an
experimental licence. The studio and transmitter were installed
by the community at its own initiative for a cost of $4000.[35]

This wasn't exactly headline news, but the Warlpiri television story did circulate through some constituencies in the
plural world of Australian culture. I found out about it a couple
of years later, when the American anthropologist Eric Michaels
launched his book For A Cultural Future at the Chauvel Cinema
in Paddington, Sydney. An appropriate enough venue, in an
ironic sort of way, for it is named after Charles Chauvel, the
Australian director who made white Australia's cinematic mas-
terpiece about its Aboriginal other—Jedda.[36]

Michaels showed videos from a number of indigenous media
projects, but the most interesting tapes were from Yuendumu.
The edits were a little unstable, the image flickered and rolled,
but I had the distinct impression, watching them, that I was
looking at video that came from quite a different sensibility to
my own, or indeed to any I could name. Like many people in
that audience, I watched the images of a very different kind
of storytelling, one that I would have to learn about if I wanted
to have a conversation with it, or about it. We watch, politely,
but perplexed. The Chauvel Cinema in Paddington became that
space of indifference, where otherwise incompatible formats of
culture somehow found a way to coexist as they passed each
other by.

Michaels was based in Brisbane at the time, I think. When
he moved to Sydney he was already very ill. He died in a
Sydney hospital, watching Dallas on TV. So this isn't really a
Sydney story, other than that it was through publishing and
publicising his work in Sydney that Eric's friend Paul Foss

established his reputation outside the small world of Aboriginal studies, in other, no doubt equally small worlds such as cultural studies, screen studies, the art world and media policy. What Foss recognised was that while Michaels was by training an anthropologist, he was by inclination an essayist. His writing was like a diagonal line inscribed across the neat divisions of scholarship. Like Meaghan Morris, Michaels was working in the midst of the plural flux of culture. Like her, he created his own place from which to speak by displacing himself, ironically, from one position to another. Out of those movements, from one point of view to another, emerges the temporary platform upon which to begin an essay. Michaels, like Morris, took on the difficult problems of finding ways and means to extend the artifice of conversation. He was working on this problem both within Aboriginal communities, and between Aboriginal communities and a postmodern world.

Aboriginal communities quite rightly feared that the introduction of satellite TV would have a detrimental impact on their lives. In setting up their own station, the people of Yuendumu wanted to fight fire with fire. Few remote Aboriginal communities have adequate telephone services, so the prospect of being blasted by an information vector from on high before having a simple set of vectors for people to communicate amongst themselves is certainly disturbing. Can one have an autonomous culture while bathing in the endless waves of telesthesia, of images made by other people, for other reasons, according to other values? Yes you can. But if you have one of the oldest cultural traditions in the world still going on, would you want to?

The Yuendumu community had many years experience of 16 millimetre film and VHS home video. They did not underestimate the dangers or potentials of 'new media'. Film posed particular problems because it meant assembling people together in close proximity. Traditional restrictions on association were difficult to maintain: mothers-in-law would be too close to sons-in-law; 'promised brides' would be too close to amorous and unsuitable suitors. The films were often shown under circumstances controlled by whites in settings such as school or church, where whites would determine the circumstances of discussion and interpretation of the film. The content of even the most innocuous Hollywood films, with their relentlessly romantic morality, come into conflict with a social order which stresses the transactual role of marriage in connecting people together in ways that sustain and develop the memory of the past and relationality in the present.

Home video provides a partial contrast with this situation. At least with home video the vector connects Hollywood to the central desert people in small groups in their own camps, and people have some control over the viewing circumstances. The qualities of this particular vector have some potentially positive effects. People can choose what they want to watch, thus escaping from the paternalism of white authorities. Kung Fu movies were very popular, not least because in them it is mostly whites who are on the receiving end of those gracefully choreographed kicks.

The possible harm or benefit of vectors from without is in part determined by the ability of the local community to control the conditions of reception and interpretation. There is a lesson in this story for all media workers involved in the extension and deepening of third nature: rather than orienting media development to a universal goal, Michaels would commit us to enabling the maintenance and development of autonomous media. Not a universal model of a future productive system, but diverse and self-managed practices. For Michaels, this is what it means to be committed ethically for a cultural future. Irony for all, not just the rich.

The most challenging part of Michaels' work lies in its attempt to map out just how communications in the western desert works. Michaels shows a strong connection between information and the land. The significance of this is how different it is. In the modern western imagination, it is possible to conceive of agriculture or even industry as connected to place. Take a look out of an aeroplane window. Land is something you survey and divide up into squares that people can own. Homes and offices, farms and factories occupy those squares; each squats in its own slot on the grid. But everything else pretty much moves about, particularly information, which seems less and less connected to place. Money, migration, the prevalence of vectors—there are lots of reasons for this. The modern world makes institutions that free people, things and information from place. There are still rules about what information can go where. Some things are public, some things are private. But the distinctions between public and private are pretty abstract. I have a particular place, my flat in Ultimo, and a telephone number, but on one level they are just slots in a grid. Any meaning they may have is personal.

Michaels argues that Warlpiri space works differently. It's not a grid of private property, it's a network of places. Those places correspond to a network of stories. Some are well known stories, some are just anecdotes, but some are sacred stories that only certain people are entitled to know. The network of places and the network of stories hold together, and are held together by, a network of people. Some people inherit stories about places, and rights to go to those places; some people acquire stories and rights by being around those places a lot. Either way, power works through entitlement to the stories, and the places, but it tends to be distributed across a number of people. You negotiate your way across the landscape, dealing with whoever knows the stories that matter at each node along the network. This way of life, in which information is tightly bound to place and restricted to particular people, then comes in contact with third nature, with satellite TV, with information of the most rootless kind. That is the intersection that Michaels thought was so important, and not just for the Warlpiri, but for all of us.

I don't think Michaels saw Warlpiri culture as a model for anyone else. It is rather a particular example of cultural survival, from which one may learn something about how to achieve cultural autonomy otherwise, and from which one might learn to respect other people's paths across the treeless plain of third nature. The problem Michaels poses very directly is that third nature overrides the boundaries communities maintain against flows of information. A community is a group of people who clear a space in the wider flow of information, within which what the members of the community say to each other in some way or another takes priority over what can be heard coming from without. Michaels forces us to confront very serious issues of how much autonomy any community can have, or perhaps ought to have, to determine what information flows across the bounds within which it defines itself.

It's hard to 'see' the culture of one's own community. I know what we like; I know what we don't like. But it's hard to see the whole fabric of it. If I can't see culture as it is, it's even harder to imagine what else it could become. Which is why the stranger come among us, the Mad Max, the Eric Michaels, is of inestimable value.

UTS, FOR EXAMPLE

'Writing', says Stephen Muecke, 'can neither totally invent, nor totally reflect social realities. Writing, being neither purely subjective nor objective, neither internal nor external, aspires to the independent status of the intransitive verb, or the trace, the path to be followed'.[37] Muecke came to Sydney to teach textual theory at the University of Technology, Sydney (UTS), and if there was such a thing as a UTS postmodernism, at least in the writings of people like Sabrina Achilles, Bernard Cohen and Justine Ettler, it was partly a result of students taking advantage of tools Stephen handed them and spaces he opened up.[38] What I recognised in Stephen, and what I think these other younger writers recognised, was that he was a contemporary.

Muecke has an interest in the way stories produce certain kinds of experience of the self. Stories are techniques of the self. Is it necessary for stories to both stimulate and respond to a feeling of *lack* in one's self? One feels rootless, unanchored, fearful of flux. So one reads a story which firstly encourages one's fear of such contingency and then offers to fill this absence with an order. It might be an order in space, a hierarchy, or an order in time, a narrative with a disturbing beginning but a resolution at the end. Attach one's self to this other thing that has order and all will be well in the world: a crime novel, for example; or a history book; or the story of the postmodern republic.

Muecke is wary of stories about the nation that are based on the destabilising assumption that it lacks something. The cultural cringe was such a story. Australia lacks the refinement of London or New York. Australians have to either go get it or be second-rate. The republic is sometimes also such a story. We have to have this new order or the whole place won't make sense. Muecke worries about Aboriginal reconciliation as also being a story about lack, where Aboriginal culture is just something that has to be added to the order of the national culture to fill the disquiet of white Australians.

Muecke's own storytelling, in *Reading the Country* and elsewhere, is about looking for another way of making stories, and making ways of life out of stories. It's something taken up by younger writers. In *Tourism*, Bernard Cohen borrowed the idea of an imaginary travelogue from Italo Calvino, but gave his quirky towns Australian place names and filled the whole thing with his singularly original wit. Where Muecke's project was reading the country, Cohen decided instead to write it. Using a matrix of Australian place names as a structuring device, he filled each place with meaning, in a kind of joke structuralism. Where Muecke wants to excavate another kind of relation to the land, buried under the grid, Cohen shows how the grid and its contents are arbitrary, and could be otherwise. The meaningfulness of second nature as a grid of places is only skin deep.

Tourism wasn't exactly well received. No-one quite knew what to make of it. Cohen won the Vogel Award in 1996 for his second book, *The Blindman's Hat*. I want to quote from it, to give you a feel for Cohen's particular wit:

'Dust is like atmospheric art, temporary drawings on the sky. Dust is how you know where the air is and where the wind is going, even if, on a physical level, you know already, because it has gone into your eyes. Dust sometimes moves with the traffic, stopping at the stoplights and giving way to pedestrians and people on bicycles and purveyors of apples and pears pushing carts of produce. Dust is something you can never catch because once you have caught it, it's no longer dust. It's grime or dirt or feathers. Dust is the roads getting enthusiastic. It is the meaning of "carried away". Dust is always carried away. It is easy to be enthusiastic about dust. Sometimes there are huge pieces of dust which you can catch and they turn out to be cardboard boxes. Tiny pieces hide in nostrils all over the city. We could have a giant dust hunt and everyone would find as much as she or he wanted.'

This brief but gritty little essay on dust is from the mind of Muffy the dog.

Freed from the rather abstract formal device of the map and story, Cohen's second book is instead a layering of the everyday with the ineffable. Rather than organise everyday details into stories of love and lack, Cohen uses them instead to stage a much more multiple network of relationships. He breaks out of the neatly ordered space of the domestic drama, that plague of banality that haunts so much Australian writing. He is alive to the qualities of language—you could substitute 'language' for 'dust' in Muffy's essay on dust, and you would have Cohen's distinctive take on a postmodern aesthetics of language. Or better yet, substitute 'the virtual'. The virtual is something you can never quite catch because once you have caught it, it is no longer virtual. It's grime or dirt or feathers.

In Justine Ettler's *The River Ophelia*, the writing at first sight looks far more artless than in Cohen. The novel reads like the diary of a woman on the verge. But there's a reason for this, and we get to it towards the end.

'Justine followed Juliette over to one of the glass cabinets. Inside, mounted on a wooden stand, was a volume of Sigmund Freud's *On Metapsychology*. The book was open at the first page of the essay, "Beyond the Pleasure Principle". Blood and clotted tissues poured out from the centre of the binding, and spilled over into a tiny stainless steel drain below.

"Incurable texts are of considerable scientific value," Juliette pointed out.

Goose bumps went running up and down Justine's arms. "They're part of an experiment?"'

The experiment is literary rather than scientific. John Anderson made Freud's pleasure principle into an axiom of a realist understanding of the mind as a field of conflicts. The Libertarians made it the slogan for a return to a supposedly natural sexuality. But for Ettler, it is first of all a certain kind of textuality. Not one that lends itself to a structural analysis, but rather to a deliberately obvious pun. She is not going to scrutinise Freud's words and put all his terms into little boxes and show how they work to produce meaning. She makes the incurable language of desire perfectly literal. Neither language nor desire are there to be 'cured', they are virtual worlds out of which to make a writing, a writer, and readers.

Writing can make many other maps of desire, alongside Freud's. Maps of the ocean, anatomies of sensation, of how sense appears and disappears in language. Ettler ironises Freud, taking his grid of the passions and playing it out as a theme with variations. *The River Ophelia* is also an incurable book. Ettler describes it as an 'excursion into uncharted waters of female desire. It deals with self-mutilation, threesomes, abortion and the sordid world of all night bars, drugs and all manner of kinky sex practices'.[39] It affirms that women have sexuality, power, lust, madness, but it refuses to see any such quality as making women the big bad other, and refuses also the now well established reappropriation of the refractory girl as a feminist hero. *The River Ophelia* can carry a reader beyond good and evil, into the virtual dimension of making passions, sensations, relations to the world.

Writing the country, writing language, writing desire—not in terms of a lack that has to be filled, not in terms of a whodunit that has to be solved, not in terms of deciding if the other in the story is the good guy or a bad girl—writing rather that produces the virtual dimension of language itself. That virtual side of language is its endless resources of sensation, of particular qualities it can express, out of its otherwise predictable, structured, grid-like world. Moments when, through the opaque sheet of language, we sense bodies moving, pulsating, mutating, just below the surface. The postmodern moment calls for those qualities of language as the resources necessary for making sense of the peculiarly novel and complex experiences of now, after the revolution has not come.

FERAL CINEMA

It was as if a parody of Donald Horne's generalisations about the differences between Melbourne and Sydney were staged when Adrian Martin came to town in 1986. The showdown took place at a conference on culture, art and politics.[40] The Melbourne boy wanted to talk about 'the big picture', typical Melbourne stuff about the intellectual's responsibilities. Catharine Lumby gave the classic Sydney answer—that the big picture usually looks after itself and pays very little attention to a mere writer, but what concerns the writer is writing and writing's style. She used it as an occasion for one of her Wildean one-liners: 'Perhaps really excellent writers have developed the knack of getting things wrong, flawlessly'.[41] While Lumby's taste and temperament was and is the antipodes of Martin's, they remain in an odd way joined at the hip, as contemporaries. They perceived different sides of the same thing at the same moment.

Where John Anderson talked about pluralism, the postmodern term was difference.[42] Then as now, there's a problem about whether a writer ought to just defend and develop a little corner of that, or should try to speak for and to and about the whole of it. So when Adrian Martin squared off against Catharine Lumby there seemed to be some secret history at work that was and remains a secret even to the participants. All the same, Martin played a key role in defining a postmodern sensibility that was more genuinely populist than could ever arise out of the cloistered halls of the University of Sydney's Power Institute, from which sprang both Colless and Lumby. Martin was a product of screen culture and post-punk do-it-yourself Super–8 film nights at Melbourne's Clifton Hill community centre. He was, and remains, a cinephile.[43] He is that devotee of 'feral cinema' who puts in a charming cameo performance as himself in Emma-Kate Croghan's film *Love and Other Catastrophes*.

The significance of Martin's essaying is that it was the most elegant expression of a practice of beginning again, in a democracy of cultural objects, rather than being merely a theory about it. Martin's writing is like a pop Montaigne, making surreal leaps between Pasolini and Krazy Kat, Walter Benjamin and Arnold Schwarzenegger, Mizoguchi and Clint Eastwood. Even his nuttiest associations have an uncanny knack of seeming right on the money. Here is a sensibility that has trained itself, through the self-discipline of writing, to follow the lineaments of cultural experience, not the arbitrary conventions of 'interdisciplinary' criticism, and certainly not the 'high journalist's' idea of 'high culture', as if this were something self-evident and immutable.

'Surreal' and 'nutty' are favourite Martin adjectives. He looks in culture high and low, and he finds those moments when culture reveals itself as a mass of arbitrary codes, borrowed conventions, hokey narratives that reveal shiny horizons of madness, sex and death in spite of themselves. Like Ross Gibson's essays, Martin's book *Phantasms* reveals a reader of profound wit. Enemy of formalism and moralising, he reconciles the theoretical and the popular in drop-dead prose.

What Lumby objected to was Martin's insistence on framing such a practice, 'Melbourne style', in a grand idea of the intellectual's mission in relation to culture, rather than 'Sydney style', in a preoccupation with the formal problems of the practice of writing itself. Another way of looking at it is that between them they embodied two possible readings of Meaghan Morris, the engaged public intellectual, or the (post) structuralist critic.

The irony is in how it turned out. Ten years later, Martin is in danger of making the 'big picture' into a residual, repetitive sign of itself, disconnected from anything other than the lovingly detailed criticism he practices, particularly in his Radio National voice essays on cinema. On the other hand, Lumby developed her style of critique into a critique of style that works across a wide range of contexts, from journalism to academia to public policy. In her book *Bad Girls: The Media, Sex and Feminism in the 1990s*, she makes the postmodern reflection on styles of speech and writing one of the bases of a feminist critique of the media. It is also a media-savvy Libertarian critique of what feminism owes to what Morris called the 'politics of authoritarian control through style' as practiced by the 1968-inspired radical left.[44]

If there is a fatal irony about 1980s postmodernism, it is that its fate, in the end, was determined by neither of these self-styled and self-styling options. What determined the fate of 1980s postmodernism and consigned its chalky remains to dusty milk crates was something that Meaghan Morris saw coming, if nobody else did—that the temporary culture of little magazines, artspaces and quasi-left wing movements that were its habitat would give way to a more rationally ordered and 'disciplined' cultural life. The institutions of the media, the subsidised art world and the academy absorbed postmodernism into its feature pages, catalogue essays and course lists.

What had been a wilful exercise in producing one's self as a finely tuned mediator of the objects and signs of a world awash with proliferating images became in itself a part of that flow of images, freely appropriated by others for quite other purposes, from Don Watson's celebration of the pomo republic to David Williamson's attack on pomo nihilism. Or perhaps most appropriately, Tony Moore's 1996 documentary for ABC TV, *Bohemian Rhapsody*. A fair fate for a movement that reconsidered creativity as appropriation, that it in its turn is appropriated in such different ways. Baz Luhrmann took it to the world in his brilliant cinematic appropriation of William Shakespeare's *Romeo and Juliet*, a film which clearly shows the influence of the Paul Taylor school of media appropriation aesthetics.[45]

'Postmodernism' is words and images proliferating along the vectors of the media like a virus. This postmodern conception (or 'meme') now also gets about like a virus. In the process, it mutates beyond recognition. Postmodernism began as an idea about how language proliferates, but this idea of language itself began proliferating, mutating and adapting to new host environments. Now there's an irony. By the time people like David Williamson caught it, it was a completely unrecognisable strain. Then it is no longer of any interest what it means, for it no longer means anything. The curious thing is how it reproduces itself, even in the minds of those who think they are its antibodies.

Meanwhile whatever will be *post* postmodernism stirs again, in the little magazines and art catalogues.[46] Or perhaps, also most appropriately, on the World Wide Web: signs without meaning, creation without licence, perception without verification, simulation without sanction—that is the negative image of the future promised by irony, where irony is free, where irony doubles and redoubles itself, where only the displacement of displacement can be perceived at all. All else is the ruin of truth.

REORIENTATION

While Taylor fled, in the end, to New York, others felt the pull of another destination. In one of his rare but remarkably prescient essays, video artist Peter Callas quotes that most quixotic essayist Jean Baudrillard on his travels in America, 'You wonder whether the world (America) itself isn't just here to serve as advertising copy in some other world'. That other world, adds Callas, 'is Japan'.[47] Perhaps it was the cartoons that prepared us: all those hours watching *Astroboy*, *Gigantor*, *Speed Racer*, *Kimba*, and of course *Shintaro* on the ABC, with dubbing so bad it would become a running joke on *The Late Show* in the 1990s. In the 1980s, Japan was cool.[48] Callas knew why.

In something of a departure from the postmodern obsession with the sign and the image, Callas took an interest in the vector. What fascinated him about Japan was firstly, its relation to technology. Rather than reading this through a romantic tradition of opposition to technology in the name of an unsullied nature, Callas saw in Japanese culture an embrace of 'technology as territory'. In Japan, 'the image has for most of this decade been merely the thing that illustrated the hardware'.

Callas cautions against a simplistic notion of 'technological nationalism'. The first public broadcast system might have been built in Nazi Germany in 1935, and might have been used to celebrate the first mass spectacle in the 1936 Berlin Olympics, but the companies and the patents behind the technology were partly British, Swedish and American. For Callas, technology creates territories of its own, only partly captured by national ambitions. To the list of 'horizontal' differences I offered earlier of movements that trouble the 'vertical' partitions of nation, such as feminism and the free market, one could add technology itself.

Working in Tokyo making 'ambient video' for a Japanese department store, Callas was well placed to observe some peculiarities of the media vector from the centre of that centreless metropolis that has done the most to bring together money, media and technology in frighteningly original ways. The way video images poured out of *public* spaces he found particularly fascinating. The screen could be something other than a privatised experience. Tokyo seemed to absorb images from everywhere. Where New York was already beginning to 'function as a museum of itself', Tokyo observed and absorbed the whole of the world, showing CNN in the streets and ambient video of Thai temples in the elevators.

Callas sees this as a kind of virtual imperialism, an ability to capture images from everywhere and display them in captivity, rather like the British Museum's Elgin marbles or the Metropolitan Museum in New York. The images come in to Tokyo, as tribute, while the electronic consumer goods pour out. Callas finds it curious that Japanese electronics has names like Pioneer, Victor and Ricoh's 'Copy Frontier'. 'In peering through these electronic devices, Western innocents are surveying a terrain which no longer belongs directly to them.'

That seems like an appropriate place to end my essay on postmodernism—or perhaps I'll leave off with the last scene of Geoffrey Wright's film *Romper Stomper*, in which three fucked-up Australians in their twenties, pure products of all kinds of forgotten social dysfunction, fight to the death at knifepoint on the beach, somewhere south of Melbourne. Up on the cliff above, Japanese tourists admire the view and record these desperate antics on their state-of-the-art Sony Handycams and Canon Quickshots.

There is a lot in that image that the public conversation about the film simply refused to discuss. The three white kids on the beach are clearly the victims. But there is nothing noble about them. The two boys are racist, neo-Nazi skinheads and all in all right bastards. The girl may be an incest survivor, yet the earlier scene where she gets even with her ever-lovin' daddy hardly portrays her in a redeeming light. There is nothing morally redeeming about being a victim. While racist thugs make a spectacle of themselves fighting on the beach, the cameras record everything from above. A premonition of the way global media vectors would pick up and broadcast Pauline Hanson's victim talk around the world. Those vectors not only reach right in, breaching the bounds of any and every notion of Australian community, they also run in the other direction. Australians no longer have the luxury of a conversation kept within bounds. Also disturbing in this image is the idea that others might control the means of perceiving the fight on the beach of Australian culture. Actually it's the film maker, Geoffrey Wright, who shoots this image. But within his image is the possibility that this local control could be disrupted, just like that of Yuendumu. The problem with becoming Don Watson's postmodern republic is that this appears to dispense with the illusions that make it possible to think that, the vector not withstanding, culture can have an inside and an outside, an us and a them, that is just simply there, the bleached bones of a secure past.

One way of describing the contemporary moment, one that I find in Callas, and find reflected also in the other writers here, is that this new landscape of third nature defines new zones of creativity, but also new worries about how to recreate ideas and practices of community, identity, nation and culture. Here is a place and time where the Libertarian preoccupation with autonomy meets the postmodern fascination with artifice. Here is a moment when the ground of writing can't be taken for granted. Nothing one might attach it to, either for or against, seems stable enough. Everything vaporises on contact. So a writer needed a strategy for producing a place from which to start writing. That place, one way or another, ended up being created out of irony, puns, displacements, shifts and juxtapositions in points of view, carried far enough that the reader starts to see the texture of language itself, and perhaps beyond.

Looking at the surfaces of language, these writers saw something that was not neatly divided into black and white. It was not a transparent instrument for changing the world. Nor was it a mirror, reflecting back the precious soul of the writer, being 'creative'. It was all those things in part, but not on the whole. It was a slippery substance, within the folds and flows of which one could find the qualities with which to write otherwise. To write without resentment, fear, or lack of the other. The postmodern writing of Foss and Taylor, Morris and Michaels, Gibson and Muecke, Martin and Lumby, Ettler, Cohen and Callas avoided those traps. As I want to show in *Part 2*, the postmodern writings of Riemer, Manne and Gaita, Koch, of Garner and Williamson—did not.

PART TWO

—

AERIALS

5

The Demidenko effect

However other nations may rival us in poetry, and excel us in some other agreeable arts, the improvements in reason and philosophy can only be owing to a land of toleration and liberty.

David Hume

If thought does not measure itself by the extremity that eludes the concept, then it is from its inception like the background music the SS played to drown out the screams of its victims.

Theodor Adorno

MEDIA EVENTS

'Dog bites man', isn't a news story. 'Man bites dog'—now that might be. Both the theory and the practice of what gives a story 'news value' is a somewhat occult business.[1] A lot of news editors simply say that a good story is just something they have a gut feeling about. Given that most people would rather not subject these people's colons to a close inspection, it's helpful to remember a few rules of thumb.

The further away something happens, and the less 'like us' the people it happens to happen to be, the less likely it is to be news. If a massacre happens in a far off forest and no Australians were there to get killed, it didn't happen. The more important the person is that does something, the more likely it is to be news. If I get my toenails cut, nobody is interested. It's an event so lacking in news value even *I'm* not interested. If Michael Jackson gets his toenails cut—that's news. Exclusive interview with the manicurist about what colour his little toe was, and so on. Very unexpected things are news, but so too are very expected ones. An aircraft on a scheduled flight blowing up gets coverage, but so too do elections and the Melbourne Cup. A lot of people are waiting to know if they bet on the winner.

'Culture' is rarely newsworthy, in any sense of the word. Big, well promoted events or personalities with packs of publicists working the fax machines on their behalf are of course often news, but they are news because they are well known, not because there is anything in the cultural material involved that matters all that much. Does anyone really care about what Michael Jackson *sings*? Culture is in some respects the antithesis of news. It's about an endless, almost infinite series of little acts of making sense of things, be they books or songs or everyday gestures, through which people learn and practice and sometimes modify the structures of feeling through which they engage with the world. People 'do' culture for all sorts of reasons, for pleasure or distraction or self-improvement or because their parents make them. Regardless of the reason, people do a lot of it. It's a pervasive, elusive thing, which is probably why it's also such an elusive idea to try and hold in the mind as a concept. It's certainly not the sort of hard edged thing from which a keen reporter makes news.

Culture is rarely news. Except in times when culture itself becomes the space where conflict erupts, rather than representative political life. What is striking about the early 1990s is that a series of conflicts popped up through the domains of culture into the news columns. Some new names became household names, and some old familiars regained currency: Helen Demidenko, Helen Garner, David Williamson, even the late Manning Clark. New public things circulated for our inspection: political correctness, postmodernism, Generation X. Some old ones came in for a fresh evaluation, particularly feminism, multiculturalism and Aboriginality.

Taken on their own, each of these things may seem accidental. Taken together, I think they indicate certain tensions in the institutions meant to piece culture and media together. Some issues are to do with Australia's increasingly permeable and pervasive relations to the world, some with specifically Australian problems to do with people's ability to define themselves culturally and map their relations to others and to the world.

What *Part 2* of *The Virtual Republic* sets out to do is explore some of those events, revisiting them to look for what they might tell us about the character of who and what was involved, about the quality of the various parts of the machinery of public life that came to light in the process, and finally, what they might tell us about the virtual republic. These events are actual instances of something elusive, almost inconceivable—instances of what might be.

We can be thankful that, for the most part, politics in Australia is what Oakeshott calls the politics of scepticism.[2] In this post-cold war, supposedly post-ideological world, there are, all the same, some stalwarts of the politics of belief. There's something of a preponderance of economic rationalists keeping the faith in key government departments and media commentary.[3] Perhaps it's because of the ventriloquism of politicians acting as hand puppets for these master thinkers, whose views are then repeated by pundits reading off the same graph, that real reporters and the public turned to culture for some actual debate. In practice, few politicians share the faith of the rationalisers, even if they appear to talk the talk. They tend to do what politicians always do. They take ideas, shop them around, consult their constituencies, hash out a compromise.

The sound of contemporary politics is in stereo. It's as if one's tax accountant is just winding up a long peroration about some very exciting new ideas about depreciation schedules in one ear, while a slightly demented and very drunk football fan gives his considered opinion of the opposite team in the other. Compared to their ancestors Ming and Chiff—leaders of large enough stature to acquire nicknames—Howard and even Keating seem like such *little* men, standing on the shoulders of giants.

Perhaps this is why, starting with the ever inventive former Prime Minister Paul Keating, politicians started borrowing from culture, trying to coopt its languages and signs and celebrities. The trouble is that culture is so damned unpredictable. Statistics are easy, they just go up or down, and one says the usual things about this. Straightforward and as boring as a lecture on the J-curve. Culture, on the other hand, goes every which way but straight. As Paul Keating found out the hard way when he tried to make republican national symbolism, rather than constitutional reform, a political issue. As John Howard found out when by quietly pandering to racist resentments in the electorate his party unwittingly unleashed the teacup tirade that was Liberal party candidate for the seat of Oxley, Pauline Hanson.

So let's look at some of the *strange cultural media events* that seem to contain within them some clues about all this. These chapters all concern things that seem to me to meet the four criteria of that term. They are 'strange' in that they all had a singular quality about them that meant that commentators didn't at first quite know how to pigeon-hole them. They are 'cultural' in the sense that they were about tensions within people's structures of feeling. They are 'media' in the sense that the story broke out of the review pages and engaged more than the usual specialised, professionalised, culturati. They are 'events' in the sense that they took on a life of their own and became self-moving public objects with viable careers, independent of who got the ball rolling and why. The event that carries the name of Helen Demidenko meets all of the requisite requirements.

THE DEMIDENKO EVENT

Gleebooks is more than Australia's best bookseller, it's an institution. Not the least of its vital functions is to operate as a sort of casual place where bookminded people can run into each other and swap gossip. It was at a book launch at Gleebooks that it was first put to me that Helen Demidenko's Vogel Award-winning novel was, in the words of my gossip-swapping fellow writers, 'anti-Semitic'.

I can't for the life of me remember who I was talking to, so you'll have to take my word for it. I tell this vaguely remembered anecdote for two reasons. Firstly to say that while I read the book before it broke as a news story, I read it under the shadow of the 'anti-Semitic' charge. Secondly, as a small bit of counter-evidence that people in the 'literary world' were indeed alive to the political issues all along, and were hardly in need of newspaper columnists to remind them of the significance of the Holocaust.

So I bought the book—I have one of the first printings that still says 'Helen Demidenko' on the cover. When I was in Adelaide for the Association for the Study of Australian Literature conference, I meant to ask her to sign it. She was there to accept another award, the ASAL Gold Medal. By then word was out about the anti-Semitism thing. Several people joked to me as she swept past with her companion of the time that as they were both so strikingly blonde and tall and aloof, they really looked like proper Aryans. It was said in that ironic way that things are said that are not 'politically correct', yet which people can't resist saying anyway. It wasn't much of a joke, and I didn't say anything about it, but the whole thing made me feel uneasy. I was uneasy about the book, about that stupid little joke, but mainly about something else: about what exactly is the responsibility of a writer? What was her responsibility? What was mine?[4]

I write columns for the *Australian* about these sorts of things, but I was holding off on writing about this. Maybe it would blow over. But no, the damn thing just got bigger and bigger, particularly once David Bentley reported on page one of the Brisbane *Courier Mail* that while the author of *The Hand That Signed the Paper* may be Helen Demidenko, the author of Helen Demidenko was one Helen Darville.[5] This complicated things. New issues of authenticity and identity poured into the already volatile concoction of the Demidenko effect. I had to think about this some more.

The following January, I wrote in the *Australian*: 'It's time to declare Helen D's novel *The Hand That Signed The Paper* an unqualified success—for all concerned. This is one controversy where everyone got what they came for. The book's critics from the right such as Gerald Henderson and Robert Manne got to parade their historical learning. Its critics from the left such as Guy Rundle got to flash their superior moral worth. Defenders of the autonomy of the literary sphere such as David Marr got to discourse on the republic of letters. Jewish and Ukrainian spokespeople got to claim they are misrepresented—and to represent themselves for a bit. The publisher got publicity that money can't buy. Journalists got a story to chase—one even won a Walkeley award for it'.[6]

Most of the commentary on all this still centres, now as then, on the book and the author, and the endless interpretation of the intentions and veracity of both. What I wanted to do instead was examine the 'Demidenko effect', and the media event it triggered. What exactly were the causes and contours of the media event around this book and author? If we make the media event the focus of our thinking, rather than seeing it as answerable to an original text and the intentions of its author, then the behaviour of the various parties to the controversy appears in a different—and often far less flatter-ing—light. This is a story of the moral banality of all those who boosted their ethical stakes in the public sphere at Demidenko's expense—myself included. It is a story about the limits of liberalism and the lengths old cold warriors will go to fend off their own obsolescence. In place of that ethic of condemnation popular on the right and the left, we can posit what Ghassan Hage described on ABC radio as an 'ethic of understanding'.[7]

And so, what I propose to do here is look briefly at two of those who got what they came for—Andrew Riemer and Robert Manne. Then I want to talk about Hannah Arendt. Karl Marx once said that 'all the great events and characters of world history occur, so to speak, twice . . . the first time as tragedy, the second time as farce'.[8] Perhaps the media event produced by the Demidenko effect was a gauche antipodean echo of the reception of Arendt's writings about Adolf Eichmann. From a consideration of Arendt I then want to look at the difference between an ethical and a moral way of casting the problem of telling the story of the Holocaust. Finally, some thoughts on eight ways it might be 'phrased'.

RIEMER'S LIBERALISM

Andrew Riemer is well known in Sydney for his book reviews in the *Sydney Morning Herald*. He is a patient explainer and supporter of the qualities of modern literature and some of its postmodern progeny. He is a rather impatient polemicist against anything new in critical philosophy. He is also known for his autobiographical writings, such as *America With Subtitles*, a book about exploring the fraught encounter of his modern if some-what provincial Hungarian parents with exile in New York. It's worth reading together with his *The Demidenko Debate*, since across both one finds the same meditation on what it means to have roots in a secular, modern Jewish culture.[9] I bought both at the Sydney Writer's Festival in January 1996, read them over the weekend, and wrote my column as a review of Riemer's Demidenko book.

Riemer sensibly puts *The Hand* in the context of the diminishing space that contemporary literature has to work within. He talks of the loss of faith in the authorial voice, and the rise of scepticism about the ability of fiction to convey an author's intentions directly to a reader. Seen in this context, Demidenko glimpsed a quite extraordinary strategy for bringing a big theme in 'by the back door'. The book begins like any other small scale, contemporary novel, with an everyday scene. The narrator drives into a petrol station. But within that small frame the most terrible stories will unfold, told with a not quite unflinching but at times perfectly deadly coolness. As Riemer says: 'The novel is distinguished by its engagement with the most controversial of all literary undertakings: the representation of evil'.

The novel works. It opens a space. Others put something into that space, ranging from polemics about the Jews and the Bolsheviks to apologies for the pure land of imaginative writing. In Riemer's case, he makes this book the touchstone for defending a liberal notion of tolerance. This has two aspects. One has to tolerate views with which one does not agree. One also has to tolerate ways of speaking that don't conform to one's own prejudice about speaking. One has to tolerate, for example, the imaginative novel.

Riemer's own tolerance has its limits. It would not extend, it seems, to Justine Ettler's *The River Ophelia*, which is condemned as 'a cynical exploitation of a type of sexuality not far removed from the bestial'. Nor does he extend the same rights of self-invention allowed to the novel to the novelist. Like David Marr, Riemer wants the imaginative novelist to be completely real and prosaic. Imagination is OK, it seems, but only in its place. That place, even among liberals, can be rather narrow.

There is also a limit to how far he seems to want to be troubled by moral uncertainty. Literature may have scaled back its ambitions to proportions suited to its place in the scheme of things today, but for Riemer critical thought has to remain firm on the big questions of right and wrong and resist 'relativism'. The problem is that exactly the same sceptical spirit that hauled in the wider pretences of the novel also affected critical thinking. Not only the novelist, but the essayist also, confronts a world without certainties. That does not mean that one stops looking for ways to make ethical sense.

Demidenko's gesture is insidiously postmodern, it's true. The scandal is that she undermines neat moral fables. There is no absolute evil in her world—and hence no absolute innocence. Her Ukrainian killers are not devils, they are flawed human beings, acting on a mixture of delusion and self-interest. Like Geoffrey Wright's *Romper Stomper*, she opens a crack in the grand fables of the early twentieth century and lets a little late twentieth century scepticism in. What if anti-Semites were people? How would we understand them? What if the great truth about the evil of the Holocaust had thrown a shadow over lots of little stories, no less true, but a good deal more complicated? How can we keep faith with the big story, about a great evil, and yet bring the rest also into the light?

Like everyone else, here I am projecting something into the open space of Demidenko's book that isn't necessarily there. But that is what makes it such a useful book. We can even use it to illuminate something Riemer isn't quite prepared to accept. He wants to use Demidenko's book as a foil to the grand moral or political schemes he sees lurking in the cold war mentalities of critics like Manne or Henderson. For all their appeals to historical 'fact', what they really want to do is preserve a neat moral universe, where only the Nazis and the Communists are ever really the bad guys.

Riemer detects in thinking people of Demidenko's age (or mine) a disbelief in these convenient grand stories. But he wants to stop the train halfway to its next station, where not only the enterprise of imaginative writing, but those of historical interpretation, textual theory and moral thought also start to question their sense of certainty. Riemer is less prone to the hectoring tone of Henderson or quiet certainties of Manne, but I suspect that his alternating tones of tolerance and impatience may also be losing their appeal to all but the ageing newspaper editors, who seem to want to indefinitely extend a public platform to what are really the rhetorical and historical assumptions of a passing era. To question accepted senses of certainty is not the same thing as 'modish relativism'. It is to begin again to ask the hard questions, here in the debris of the world that the eclipse of the cold war—and of the cold warriors—has left us.

ARENDT'S POSTMODERNISM

Robert Manne also wrote a book-length study, *The Culture of Forgetting*.[10] Manne is the editor of the conservative journal *Quadrant*, but is more widely known as a columnist for the *Australian*. Riemer and Manne made an odd couple, slanging it out in the papers with columns that were among the most considered at times, but which both shared a good many assumptions. Both are the children of European Jews forced to flee Nazism. Both are writers shaped by the cold war. Both scan the horizon for symptoms of cultural decline.

Their views on Demidenko turned on different values. Riemer argued firstly that the book is anti-Semitic in a mild and 'acceptable' sense, and secondly that a novelist's obligations are firstly aesthetic. Manne found the book's anti-Semitism far beyond acceptable, and insisted throughout that novelists aren't exempt from moral considerations. But in spite of these differences, what they have in common is a notion of overlapping spheres of public life, of literature, history and the media, each of which has at least some degree of autonomy. The debate turned partly on questions of *degrees* of licence and responsibility.

Robert Manne thinks Demidenko's novel is about radical evil, and describes the behaviour of some of the characters as psychopathic. But this misses the point—if evil is committed by a psychopath then we cannot hold the individual morally responsible. A psychopath, by definition, is someone deficient in some psychological ability. The value of the book is surely its presentation, in a contemporary language, of what Arendt called the banality of evil.

The idea of a banal evil is quite different from the idea of a radical evil, even though we can find both ideas in Arendt. In *The Origins of Totalitarianism*, the notion of radical evil has prominence, although one can also find there the first intimations of Arendt's later and highly controversial theme of banality. Manne, who professes to have been influenced by Arendt's *Origins* book, does not quite seem in his Demidenko essay to grasp what exactly she was groping towards. Like a good many cold warriors, he took *Origins* to be a call to arms to oppose the Soviet Union, but his use of Arendt seems to stop about there. And here it is that this intellectual who complains about 'contemporary Australian university miseducation' reveals something of his own.[11]

It is significant that Manne mentions Arendt's *Origins* book as a signpost on his road to the anticommunist right and not her later work, for while Arendt might have become a leading figure of the cold war right, her work took a far more interesting and problematic direction, and that direction involves the concept of the banality of evil and a corresponding idea of the *political good life* not compatible with an intellectual cold war anti-communism complicit with black lists and witch-hunts. Arendt herself warns in a late footnote to *Origins* of the 'totalitarian tendencies of McCarthyism'.[12]

The scandal of Hannah Arendt is that she came to see evil as a product of the foreclosure of thinking, not as the product of an evil train of thought. She worked out the implications in a modern context of this classical idea. The banality of evil is that of a nice family man like Adolf Eichmann, the kind of bloke who does his job, minds his own business, keeps his nose clean and the files in order. What protects against evil is not just an individual's ability to think, but a politics of thinking—a space in which all kinds of people can bring their *singular* perceptions to bear on a common object or event and talk about it. *This* is the republic—the public thing.

This idea is a scandal on a number of fronts, and this is perhaps why the likes of Robert Manne shy away from the very indecency of it. Arendt is a scandal to the liberals because she denies that popular tenet of liberal thinking that would associate freedom with a realm of private pursuits of endeavour and family life. All that is mere necessity to Arendt—we can be free and good and just and beautiful only in a *public* life, where thoughts meet, where qualities are compared. She is a scandal to contemporary conservatives because she denies any possibility of a 'Higher Law'.[13] There are no moral precepts, only cases; no moral lessons, only memories. She is a scandal to the cold warriors because she refused to accept the foreclosure of a just political realm in the name of resistance to a greater enemy. Rather the state should perish than that justice not be served. She is a scandal to a certain kind of Zionism because she saw a *political* lesson for the Jews in the Holocaust, not a religious or moral one.

More broadly, she is a scandal in relation to a certain kind of humanism that might be seen as underpinning all of the above. Totalitarian power arises out of certain subjective conditions, but it is a transhuman machine, incorporating bodies, buildings, vectors, weapons. What may prevent it is not the moral steadfastness of individuals, but a political practice, the free practice of thought in a virtual republic. This is a way of thinking not well suited to a neat appellation of blame to individual bodies, no matter how much Arendt may have accepted the verdict against Adolf Eichmann. Her book on Eichmann was read as opening a space for the argument that the Jews were complicit in their undoing. But I think her point was not that individual Jews were to blame for a failure to resist or for complicity with the Nazis, but that they were caught up in a systematic foreclosure of a space of thought and action that might have prevented the Nazi machine from assembling its industrial technology of death. The tragedy is that her book did not open a space in the virtual republic for talking about the foreclosure of space in the virtual republic itself.

VALUES AND VECTORS

The Hand That Signed The Paper is in many respects a more than adequate fictional world from the point of view of the banality of evil. What puzzles Fiona Kovalenko in the novel is why it is that her nice uncles could be murderers. But for Arendt it is precisely those who value only the qualities of a private life who are *most* capable of murder. What clearly makes Robert Manne uncomfortable in the novel is its indictment of the private life, and its refusal to treat evil with any piety. Evil is an everyday affair.

The truth content of Demidenko's novel has nothing to do with the facts of history. Manne quite correctly shows that it gets facts wrong. Rather, the book is a proposition about how the nightmare logic of totalitarianism can come to pass. The book is true only to the extent that this proposition is possible. It's a strikingly Arendtian proposition. It begins with the obliteration of a public life among the 'Ukrainian' peasants by the imposition of the Stalinist master plan. The peasants form, and preserve, a fantasy about how this came to pass. They blame it on the Jews. No common world, no public sphere, no virtual republic exists in which such an idea might be tested, and so it persists. When the Nazis come, they subordinate the Ukrainian fantasy to their own. The Ukrainians, without quite realising it, swap obedience to one master for that to another. They give up their freedom to a new master, willingly, because they think the new master will free them from the old one. Twice deprived of a common world in which doubt and dissent might have a place, Demidenko's Ukrainians live a divided life in which they perform their duties ruthlessly and maintain a private life of unconcern. The evil of their acts is largely unremarked, there being no place where it might be remarked upon. Thought is subordinated to the Nazi will, and will directs actions untroubled by thought's doubts.

Regardless of its author's intentions, the book succeeded admirably in presenting this banality of evil before a public that took upon itself the right to judge it from many and varied perspectives. The tragedy of it is that many of those judges felt obliged to judge the author rather than the fictional world the author chose to set before us, or to treat that fictional world only as evidence for or against the evil of its author, or of various imagined contemporary bogeymen. Our old cold warriors cannot resist any temptation to seek out nameless, faceless bogeys—only now it is 'postmodernism and sentimental multiculturalism' rather than the communists and their 'fellow travellers'.

While both the *Quadrant* crowd and the more liberally minded Andrew Riemer chose to see in Demidenko signs of the decline of culture, surely we have here every evidence of the opposite. The public political process as Arendt defines it actually worked quite well. In spite of their manifold differences, a wide range of people confronted a common object, thought about it, and pleaded their case. The pervasiveness of contemporary media made this possible. I think the media did a pretty good job of picking out of literary culture an issue with a wide range of ramifications. No matter how much professional Cassandras might have invested in the idea of decline, the virtual republic seems on any objective evidence to be alive and well, even if at any actual moment it may not always live up to its potential.

But there is no reason to be too self-satisfied. How might the virtual republic work better? How best might individual sensibilities be brought to bear on a common object before a public? For Arendt there are three aspects to the life of the mind: thinking, willing and judging. The original thinker in the western tradition is Socrates. The Socratic method sets thinking in train by asking of a particular object or event what universal category stands behind it. What is courage? What is faith?

For Arendt, this thinking of particulars as examples of universals is a way of life (of the mind) that has passed. We moderns have lost faith in universals—and the danger is that having lost faith we will do things about which we have not thought. And the danger of that is at best a call for a return to lost faith—which is about all that remains of contemporary conservatism. At worst it is Eichmann. God is dead, but so too are what the philosopher Jean-François Lyotard will come to call the 'grand narratives'—the legitimating moral fables of progress.[14] But for Arendt the worry is that our will is answerable only to private concerns and to hell with everybody else. Hell is identity politics.

Conservatives like to believe that without a return to some lost value what remains must be nihilism and relativism. But Arendt did not think so. She was a 'premature postmodernist'. She thought to the contrary that outside the imposition of universal categories on the events and objects that trouble us it was possible for thinking and willing to work otherwise—to work in combination with the practice of judgement.[15]

JUDGEMENT

Now, judgement is not in itself a concept, so much as a practice. As Hume said, ethics is something 'more properly felt than judged'.[16] We judge every day. We decide things without reference to universal rules, by looking at a particular object or event and comparing it to other particular objects or events we have learned about from the media or remember from our own experience. Like Montaigne, we might be sceptical about how far our judgement extends, but we often mean more than a mere subjective preference, if something less than a statement of scientific proof. In any case the judgement emerges out of the relation *between* statements, not from my reason alone.

Judgement is a form of interaction and is not purely private. We require the examples, lessons and testimony of others through which to think about the instance at hand. Which means that our ethical decisions depend on the company we keep as much as vice versa. Ethics depends on ethos; ethos depends on ethics. We cannot judge where all think alike, however. The eccentric view reminds us of the limits of judgement. It prevents a certain form of what is merely a judgement pretending to be a universal rule. Difference is a precondition for the practice of judging, and the impact of excluding a view from the process of judging is not to be taken lightly. And that's the basis for a defence of some of what is currently derided as 'political correctness', to the extent that it is really about opening a space in which to hear other voices, with other kinds of entitlement.

Judging happens in public: ' . . . everything that appears in public can be seen and heard by everybody and has the widest possible publicity. For us appearance—something that is being seen and heard by others as well as by ourselves—constitutes reality'.[17] Public is the world itself, the world outside and between private lives, that gathers us together and separates and relates us. ' . . . the reality of the public realm relies on the simultaneous presence of innumerable perspectives and aspects in which the common world presents itself and for which no common measurement or denominator can ever be devised'.[18]

It is not a common 'human nature' that underpins the virtual republic, nor does it represent the general interest; rather, it is where different attempts to articulate the general interest and to generalise about its basis in common attributes confront each other in conversation. While we may all differ, we come to contemplate the same objects and events. Which is precisely why it matters what objects and events appear to us. This common world ends when objects are no longer seen from many points of view. Or to add a condition Arendt did not foresee—when people no longer contemplate any common objects or events at all.

The coming to its majority of a generation raised on the broadcast media vectors means that a good many people are now exposed pretty much simultaneously to the same event, and have remarkably overlapping memories at least of the recent past. This means that more people than ever before can bring their differing views about an event to bear on it and arrive at a judgement about it. I wonder what happens as we move into the post-broadcast world, where channels proliferate. Will there still be common objects? A thought for another time.

Can we speak, then, of a virtual republic—one that is largely mediated, that produces a common sense of place and time out of the many and varied vectors of the media? Let's be more specific: can a republic be 'virtual', not just in the sense of being made out of third nature, out of mediated experience, but virtual also in a more philosophical sense. The virtual, in this latter sense, is a universe of how else things might appear.[19] The virtual is not just the open horizon of the future; it is also the open horizon of the past. Not in the sense that one can change the past. Rather, that the past can be drawn into many more productive relations with the present than at present appear.

This is a sense of the virtual I want very much to keep alive, even though the public spokesmodels for the dismal science of economics keep telling us that we have no alternative but to tighten the belt another notch, save more, spend less, work harder and stop complaining because we can't afford it. But do we live in order to work or do we work in order to live? And what kind of life is possible? The virtual republic is that place where we can still hope, without limit, even if on the cheap.

One acts by responding to the event as if there were a dialogue one could have, on the basis of this shared event and one's singular experience, with others who do not share your experience but are thinking about the same event. If one acts *as if* there was a virtual republic, and others do too, then there will be. That doesn't mean that there is automatically a common ground upon which to have a debate. People will make all kinds of statements, many of which can't be reconciled with each other and are not even the same kinds of statements. People will use all kinds of entitlement to put statements in circulation and not everyone's entitlement to speak is equal.[20] There are no fixed rules—the rules of debate are also always up for debate. Often the way to prevail in the virtual republic is to act in such a way that one proposes a new rule.

When judging an event, if one acts on the assumption that others will also judge the same event, and judge it also from a particular point of view, then one calls the virtual republic into being. When judging an event, if one acts on the assumption that it might yield a new perspective, allowing you to stand outside of common sense for a moment and see it otherwise, then that I think is the second notion that might be of use. Use it as an opportunity to pluralise yourself, to think outside yourself, from another point of view.

AESTHETICS

This is more of an aesthetic idea than an ethical one. It's a matter of valuing events in culture that open up a hole in the fabric of common sense, through which we can see exactly what common sense is—a fabrication of judgements about representations of events and events of representation. In those terms, a good book is not just one that is well composed according to the formal qualities of good writing that hold at a given time. A good book is something that compels us to think otherwise, because it contains possibilities that we would not otherwise see. Here we meet the 'postmodern' again. Helen Demidenko's book is interesting precisely because it incited people to debate what constitutes a good book.

This aesthetic of judging cultural events in terms of their effects is in a wider sense an ethical choice. One that values the opening up of possibilities, no matter how ragged around the edges, over affirming the same old, same old, same old limited sensibility. It also means that what one is judging is not this book or that song, but the whole process by which a book or a song passes through public and private life. The virtual republic is a space of possibilities that opens up anywhere and everywhere in the whole space of culture, not just in 'literature'. In keeping with the refusal of any Higher Law or pregiven principle of judging, we have to accept that we cannot know in advance where the fine aesthetic moment in culture will come.

And so, the virtual republic, virtual in many senses, republic only in one—the rule of the people, who bring their many and different points of view to bear there on events of common interest that reveal possibilities of hope, courses of action and perhaps also, at the end of the day, some notion of how to reason in and about the world. We have heard judges utter inanities about half the human race. We have seen police officers take bribes on candid camera. We have witnessed business leaders convicted of grand fraud and petty greed. We have noticed newspaper columnists who plagiarise with less guile than the most dimwitted schoolboy. In short, we have no authority left but ourselves, and nothing to judge others against but our own experience. God is dead. Ideologies are just dead boring. The responsibility for the virtual republic is entirely in the hands of those who choose to constitute it.

BURNT WORDS

Two young women look at the exhibits in the Sydney Jewish Museum. One is Jewish, the other, not. The other one points to a picture of Hitler and says, 'Don't you just *hate* that man!' Her Jewish friend, puzzled, replies, 'Don't *you*?'[21]

It's a story Sophie Knox, one of my students, put into a piece she was working on, about a visit to the Museum. It got me thinking. The Jewish woman's question implies that regardless of what culture the other woman claims to come from, she also has a certain responsibility to remember and judge the history of the Holocaust. The question that comes to my mind, is: yes, but is it the *same* responsibility?

In the short but energetic life of the modern world, the Holocaust is a permanent scar on its skin. The facts of what happened are not open to serious dispute. But what those facts may *mean* is another story. It may mean this: the Holocaust happened because of the rise of Nazi totalitarianism. An alliance of world powers defeated the Nazis, but the evil of totalitarianism lives on, in the Soviet Union. Therefore, nothing else matters but that a new alliance oppose this evil. Or it may mean: the Holocaust happened because of an ancient resentment of God's chosen people. Their extermination in Europe was only averted because, for entirely other reasons, an alliance of powers needed to oppose and defeat Germany. Therefore, nothing else matters but that the Jews have their own state so that they might defend themselves.

Both these meanings are actually true—and also not true. Not true to the extent that they exclude other meanings. In remembering only *this* way, they forget other histories, some of which may be just as true. Both meanings are true to the extent that they remember the facts and place those facts in a story that connects the past to the present, as that past affects the present of a particular group of people. Both are not true to the extent that they would deny the complexity of meanings that might arise from the facts. They become moral fables, legitimising certain responsibilities in the present, but forgetting others. Forgetting, for instance, a responsibility for justice for the Palestinian people, or of oppressed people who happened to live in client states of the American alliance throughout the cold war.

Meanwhile, back in the Museum, one would hope that both

women, looking at Hitler's portrait, would respond with a kind of enlightened hatred. But not necessarily of the same kind. It's not that those closest to the event necessarily bear some added responsibility for the story. Some survivors refuse to talk about the Holocaust, and as we shall see there are several things a silence may mean. The therapists might say otherwise, but I think such a silence has to be respected. And yet—someone has to take responsibility for this past, even if no one can assume the responsibility for all of it. It must be shared, and perhaps not evenly. It has to be remembered in different ways. The truth of the matter lies not in any particular story, but in the common world of remembrance of all the stories.

Perhaps even the ones that aren't true. I've seen those neo-Nazi home pages on the World Wide Web, and they make me angry. And yet, I wonder. Attempts to deny the Holocaust are not factually or ethically defensible. There is nothing on that point worth discussing. So the question to ask is, what does the continued existence of this denial, in the face of the facts, tell us? It might tell us that for some the horror is too much. It is an ever present incitement to memory. It tells us also that moral fables don't always work; that by limiting what the past might mean, one limits also the plurality of people who might come to know the facts through the fable. Those of us who want the truth of the Holocaust remembered have to share at least a tiny bit of responsibility for these instances where its truth is denied.

The image of Nazism shadows Australian public life and won't go away. It appears in very different guises, from Demidenko's novel to the film version of Thomas Keneally's book *Schindler's Ark*, retitled *Schindler's List*, and Geoffrey Wright's *Romper Stomper*. The two films make a thought-provoking double bill. The Spielberg version of the Holocaust seems to me to be a version of its moral fable. The Wright film, much condemned on release, is a serious attempt to answer the question of why, in spite of all that is remembered about the Nazi past, it can still articulate such a thing as a neo-Nazi desire. It's a film some would prefer had never been made. Is it right to insist on silence?

I think it was at the launch of *The Australian's Review of Books* that I met the columnist Frank Devine. Standing drinks in hand in the function room of the Intercontinental Hotel, I searched for something convivial to say. No easy task, for I can't imagine a columnist with whom I might have fewer prejudices in common. But this was a public event, and public space and time is for conversation—so we talked about the one point where we do intersect, the question of free speech. And this was when Devine told me this story that still gives me pause for thought.

Devine, who defended Demidenko, recalled that he was asked whether he would give her novel as a present to a friend who was a survivor. Devine *wants* to answer yes, because he thinks his defence rests on this. His questioner thinks his defence fails if he cannot in good faith give it to a survivor. I certainly couldn't make a present of it. And yet I don't see that anything hinges on this. The *rightness* of a certain cultural artefact is not something absolute or universal. It is context bound. But neither fixed are the various contexts within which a cultural artefact might be appropriate. I've already argued that I don't think there is a distinctive 'literary sphere', exempt from ethical judgement. Demidenko's book could be constructed as literary, but was just as readily treated in ethical, historical, polemical registers—even in a legal one when questions of alleged plagiarism were raised, and dismissed.

The facts of the Holocaust are not in question; the stories made from those facts are nothing but questions. The Demidenko event was finally winding down when William Gass and Daniel Goldhagen published new books that, as fiction and history, rephrased it all over again.[22] Romona Koval interviewed William Gass, and asked him about the limericks one of the novel's characters writes.[23] She quoted to him a particularly vile one about 'making Jews into lamps'. Koval then puts this to Gass: 'Other ditties there are about Jews being made into soap. Unfortunately members of my family were made into soap—unfortunately for them, unfortunately for me, and maybe unfortunately for you, because how do you expect me to read this without thinking about what happened to them, and about why you would want to make light of that?'. Gass replies that of course it is not Gass who is making light of these things, but a character in a novel. He claims to have set the novel in Indiana precisely because of the strength of far right organisations in some parts of that state. He claims there is a larger moral purpose behind the aesthetic design of the work.

It's a fascinating interview. What matters, in the end, is not who is right in the debate about the relationships between aesthetic and ethical responsibility, but that there is a conversation about it, in which phrases are added, one after the other, shifting the work from one space to the other—the virtual republic. But there is more: Koval and Gass assume *different* responsibilities in relation to the past, drawing on different kinds of entitlements. Koval feels she has to ask, in the name of the people who were made into soap, and he feels he has to answer, in the name of the tradition of the modern novel. That there are stories in dispute between them keeps the facts alive.

Which is why, in the end, it is not desirable that there be limits to the stories about the facts, or that the facts be reduced to a moral fable. What is then lost is the living presence of the facts as they are called into being in the clash of stories. That there are clashes is in turn what makes many people feel that they are responsible for remembering particular stories, and therewith keeping alive the facts. And I'm reminded by what I hear in this radio interview of what Eric Michaels found in the western desert: the problem of just how particular our ethical responsibilities for phrases happens to be.

One of the things that entitles one to join a conversation of this kind is that one has at least attempted to think seriously about it. Thinking seriously about it means bringing all of one's particular memories (and forgettings), one's intellectual resources (and limitations) to bear on it. The question, then, is: what is *my particular* responsibility to this past? Within the space of which stories do I feel both obligated and entitled to speak of it?

Seen in that light, the difficulty of Helen Demidenko is obvious. She confused two ways of speaking: from imagination and from descent. I think what not even the author had the nerve or the self-knowledge to realise at the time was how strange it was to combine them in such a way. To use imagination, not only to make the work, but to make the author who would then appear to claim the entitlement to speak by descent. She did what we all do, in a somewhat attenuated form. We all make ourselves as we make our pasts, in stories.

That it failed as a conceit, that the facts came out, means we no longer need condemn it, and can instead turn our attention to making something of it. The lengths she had to go to create an entitlement, as a young writer in Australia, are symptomatic of the difficulties for young writers in a time when a limited range of age-cohorts seem to have usurped the whole of the entitlement to speak on anything other than 'youth problems'—but that's a topic for another time. Here I just want to make it emblematic of the range of ways of making the facts of the Holocaust tell a story.

I think it no cause for moralising that writers advance their own position, as entitled participants in the virtual republic, by means of the creation of new stories and new ways of telling stories out of so grave a collection of facts. Hume had a very sober perspective on such situations, and counted it a blessing that the artifice of public life could invent ways to turn passions such as vanity, pride and self-assertion toward a useful end—in this case by creating the desire to tell stories that there is a collective value in having told. Not everyone is motivated to make as much *money* from stories as Steven Spielberg but even that may have its uses.

But then I *would* say that, because it justifies my own attempt to use the facts of the Holocaust as the test for the idea of the virtual republic, as a space where people bring many different stories to bear on the facts publicly known; where it is not necessary that those stories be compatible with each other, only with the facts; where it is not necessary that particular kinds of story stay in their respective spheres; where there need not, and cannot, be only one criterion of judgement, or a hierarchy of criteria of judgement. A story I cannot tell. At least not as an essayist, for the essay is a form that struggles, through language, to speak truthfully about experience.

Like the non-Jewish woman in the Museum, my relation to this story isn't by descent. My experience doesn't alter the facts of the Holocaust, but it does provide me with other resources, and perhaps another kind of responsibility, in telling a story about that event. By way of illustrating such a conception, I want to talk about eight ways of telling stories about the Holocaust. Or in Lyotard's terms, of phrasing it.

A phrase, for Lyotard, is any utterance linked to a previous one, and to which another may yet attach.[24] A phrase may be a sentence, a paragraph, even a whole book, and sometimes just one phrase in the grammatical sense—the actual linguistic unit of speech or writing doesn't matter. What does matter is that for Lyotard the meaning of a previous phrase can be modified by a subsequent one. For example, if you think of Demidenko's book as a phrase, then what followed was a flurry of additional phrases, some of which modified the previous phrase, the book, by reading it as history, while others modified it by reading it as literature. Demidenko even modified the phrase of the book herself with her subsequent phrases in which she claimed it was based on recordings of oral histories from family members. In each case, the genre of the first phrase is determined by the one that follows it. Lyotard takes a pragmatic view of the vexed question of genre. It's not a question of uncovering the secret essence hidden in the book. Everything interesting happens *in between* that first phrase and all the subsequent ones. The true meaning of Demidenko is not hiding in the text or even in the author's intentions. For Lyotard, meaning happens in public. On this point he develops a line of thought not unlike that of Hannah Arendt.

After the phrase of Demidenko came phrases that sought to modify how it was read. Even more striking, along came subsequent phrases that modified those modifying phrases. The 'public thing', in this case, was not so much Demidenko, as this process of phrasing and rephrasing, 'after Demidenko'. That thing, the Holocaust, is a public thing that refuses to be forgotten. But strangely, it refuses to be remembered, to be phrased, in any conclusive way. It is a public thing because of its refusal to be definitively phrased.

The moral of this story, about that story, is that the more universal the significance of the event to be remembered, the more, not the less, different the phrases that need to join the conversation will be. So I want to talk about eight ways a writer might try to phrase such an event.

Silence

A sentence can sentence, but a silence? What can it mean to be silent about the Holocaust? If, when a phrase appears in which the Holocaust is present, and I am silent in the phrase that I append to it, it may mean one of four things. (1) Maybe I am saying: in that phrase about the Holocaust, the one who speaks of it isn't competent to speak and so I do not recognise it. (2) Or maybe I mean: now that the Holocaust has been phrased, I am silent because *I* am not competent to speak of it. (3) Or perhaps: I will be silent because I doubt such a thing happened, or means what you say. (4) Or: that is a thing about which one cannot speak without misrepresenting it.

In the two columns I wrote for the *Australian* that touched on Helen Darville's two creations—*The Hand That Signed The Paper* and its putative author, Helen Demidenko, I talked about the *media event* that followed, and was silent about the Holocaust.[25] I was silent in the first column, very explicitly, to say (1). I doubted the novel's ability to competently phrase the Holocaust. But also, in both columns, to say (2). Who am I to speak of such things? I defer to the authority of the survivor, even if survivors sometimes choose not to speak. Their silence means more than mine. I was haunted throughout by the phrasing of (4). How can I say, without saying it, that perhaps this event cannot be adequately phrased?

None of which would matter, had not Raimond Gaita, Professor of Philosophy at the Australian Catholic University added a phrase of his own, in his phrasing of me in the Jesuit magazine *Eureka St*. In what he adds to what I did not say, he makes my silences out to mean (3). Which means that he takes me to be competent to phrase the Holocaust, precisely because he claims I have not competently done so. But has he? Has anyone? Let's use this as a test case to explore the difference between what I would call a practice of ethical judgement and the idea of a moral order.

As the essayist John Hughes has since reminded us, every remembering is a forgetting, a putting in place of the multiple layers and consequences of such an event—*this* particular story.[26] No matter how right that story is, it is not a transparent window onto the past it remembers, but a palimpsest that shrouds it even as it preserves its traces. And so I ask you: what are the adequate ways of phrasing the Holocaust, other than silence? Let me offer some thoughts on seven other ways.

Compulsory moralism

'The trouble with Darville's book', says Gaita, 'is not that it denies absolute evil. It is that it has no serious sense of the evil it depicts.' Gaita's objection to the book is a moral one. And in the way I would understand the term, clearly a religious one. A 'serious sense' of 'evil' is a religious preoccupation, not a literary one. A serious sense of *form* is that with which literature concerns itself in, say, de Sade, who relentlessly pursues writings' transgression of writing, or Kafka, who writes of the law and the law of writing.[27] Gaita may phrase a moral *after* Demidenko, but must we impose that standard on the practice of writing literature itself?

Must we consider the Holocaust, as Gaita claims, an absolute evil? I have never expressed a view on this. But Gaita *assumes* I would answer in the negative. And so: 'Anyone who wants to go beyond Riemer to assert that even the Jews who perished in the Holocaust were not "absolutely innocent", must have the courage to believe that, to some degree at least, the Jews got what they deserved. Wark, while intending to praise Darville, joins her most severe detractors in attributing to her the thesis that even in the Holocaust, there is no such thing as innocent suffering'. Here we learn something about how a moralist's mind works. I must believe the Jews 'absolutely innocent' and if I do not, then I must believe they 'got what they deserved'. I must get religion on this, or I will necessarily think evil.

Gaita seems unable to accept that someone who thinks differently to him might also be an ethical person. I believe all people who can think are equally entitled to make ethical judgements in public, to correct the views of others and to have their views corrected. That assumes nothing but that we are all flawed human beings.

To me the Holocaust was an unmitigated crime. It culminates a series of Nazi crimes, including the suppression of an ethical public life and of the rule of law itself. The Holocaust was a criminal act, and there are no extenuating circumstances. I accept that there are conceptions of the world in which it means something to talk about the Holocaust as absolute evil. That means nothing to me. I reject the doctrine of 'absolute evil' (as meaningless) and I reject also the view that the Jews 'got what they deserved'—as untrue. I accept Gaita's moral commitment and the difference of his thought. Gaita does not accept my ethical commitment or the difference of my thought. For him there are right-thinking people, and wrong. For me there is the common world of judgement, where all our flawed and partial thoughts might, in their difference, resonate in the flickering light of the truth. The reader can judge which she or he prefers: compulsory moralism or the ethics of difference.

Abject metaphors

Gaita's mode of thought is premised on having a secure grasp on the moral high ground in advance. Only I need be tested on the Holocaust, apparently. But what if we test Gaita's thinking—is his moralism adequate?

What can Gaita mean when he says 'the Jews were murdered in the spirit of ridding the world of vermin'? The first half of this sentence is a fact. The second half is a figure of speech, a metaphor. Like all metaphors, it captures a likeness of an aspect of the thing it represents, but occludes others. The Nazis themselves used this metaphor, and Gaita, like many others, rightly preserves a memory of this. He uses it to remember an aspect of the Nazis, of course. He does not think this of the Jews. But there's the rub—to understand how criminals think, we have to represent criminal thoughts.

Does Demidenko think the unthinkable thoughts of Nazi-inspired Ukrainian criminals to represent what they thought, or because it is what she thinks? Is she obliged, as a writer of a fiction, to know the difference, or merely to do an adequate job of thinking and writing so that we might have the results to judge? Gaita performs the tasks of thinking of the criminal's thought and judging it unambiguously, Demidenko did not. She 'became Ukrainian'. Does it make any difference for thinking the unthinkable and judging it to be performed by one man creating and judging, as opposed to a woman creating and others judging? If one believes that every individual must aspire to embody the whole of what would be God's judgement within themselves, then perhaps so. If one sees us as flawed and different bits to be assembled the best way we can, then perhaps all that matters is that Darville's creations may be *both* freely made *and* freely judged.

But back to Gaita: is it enough to turn this Nazi metaphor against the Nazis? If the Jews were 'vermin' how does one explain the fact that in some cases they were worked to death, that they were made *productive*? Vermin are not given serial numbers. The carpet-bombing of Vietnam by American B–52s seems to me more in the spirit of 'ridding the world of vermin'. The singular horror of the Holocaust is not adequately expressed in this metaphor alone. And so, in using it, perhaps a little more caution; to preserve rather than forget what it leaves unsaid.

Gaita makes this one metaphor the premise of his doctrine of absolute innocence: 'When people are murdered as though they were vermin, nothing they did can diminish the evil done to them'. If *nothing* diminishes, then for Gaita that innocence is absolute. 'Nothing that the Jews or Gypsies had done could *weigh in any scales* against the evil done to them in the Holocaust.' Look at the image I have emphasised here. Another metaphor. One might think of scales of justice. One might think of the judicial process applied by the Israeli court to Adolf Eichmann, for instance. Now, if in moral terms the Holocaust is an absolute evil, then for a court to judge upon it means for that court to dispense absolute justice. What court would be so bold as to claim to represent absolute justice? To represent, in short, the justice of God? The 'scales' in Gaita's metaphor can only belong, in the end, to God.

About God's scales of justice and absolute evil I have nothing to say. I respect Gaita's right to frame stories in such terms. But they are particular terms, not universal ones. They forget too much. They exclude too much, in advance, that may need to be remembered.

Politics of storytelling

How might we add resonance to our understanding of the Holocaust? Gaita has offered the metaphor of 'vermin', which says something true but which partially represents the truth. He offered the metaphor of 'scales', which represents an unequivocal judgement, but in a way that not everyone can find equally meaningful. I have already suggested that we can think of the Holocaust as an unmitigated crime. In the context of the all too human justice that can be dispensed by a war crimes trial, that too is but barely adequate. But there are other ways of writing the Holocaust, besides silence, moralism and metaphor.

It is one thing to say that the Jews, or even 'some Jews' were morally complicit with their fate. It is quite another thing to say that the political strategies pursued by Jewish communities in Europe did not succeed in protecting them. I have never made, and would not make, the first claim. Hannah Arendt makes the second claim, and I find her argument about this has some weight, if on the whole I agree with Lucy

Dawidowicz that the strategies were right but the odds over-whelming.[28] That is a political debate, not a moral one. It is a story about power, strategy and survival.

I read Arendt as providing at least four understandings of the Holocaust. (1) In terms of European anti-Semitism, of which she provides a history. (2) In terms of the calculations of the imperial form of power, which treats subject peoples as just another more or less tractable raw material. (3) In terms of the rise of totalitarian forms of power, quite antithetical to the state, which abandon the prudent management of power in favour of a relentless liquidation of all forms of opposition to its fantasy of historical mission. These three understandings are in her book *The Origins of Totalitarianism*. In *Eichmann in Jerusalem* we strike the beginnings of another understanding. (4) In terms of the 'banality of evil'.[29] This argument hinges on Arendt's valuing of the common world of public judgement. After the Nazi liquidation of that world comes the rise of the 'private man'. Eichmann: a good family man who loves his kids and makes the trains run on time—to the camps.

I think Arendt chose to tell more than one story because the Holocaust is a dark crossroads where several forces at work in the modern world intersect. One of these stories is a specifically Jewish story. 'When you are attacked as a Jew, respond as a Jew', she said. And she did. But the point of her version of the story of European anti-Semitism was to point to the fact that the political strategies adopted by Jews in Europe had not worked, and that in this there were lessons not to be forgotten if the state of Israel is to survive.

But Arendt told other stories, and to other ends—and so: the story of totalitarianism. Arendt distanced herself from the cold warriors who made a career of this term, and warned of 'the totalitarian tendencies of McCarthyism'.[30] All the same, in showing that there are totalitarian features shared by Nazism and Stalinism, I think she was saying something profoundly important—that the Holocaust has not ended. If one can think of the Holocaust as a conjuncture of several histories, then one can accept as more than a provocation Tiga Bayles' remark that asking Aboriginal people to celebrate Australia Day is like asking Jewish people to celebrate the Holocaust. There is a common history within which one can see them as the same event—the conjunction of forces that treats both land and its populations as a resource or an obstacle to the expansion of empire. So long as these forces within modernity are still at work, then barbarism will not vanish from history. Not only is totalitarianism still at work in the world, but so too is imperialism. The identification of 'surplus' populations—highlanders, Aboriginals, Jews, Tibetans, East Timorese—too intractable to be useful, or impeding the expansion of a given state, continues.

Poetry after Auschwitz

Arendt did not want the singular historical moment of the Holocaust to be forgotten in the very act of remembering it. The storyteller's job is not to collapse such an event into the categories and narratives of what is conventionally thinkable, but to show what exceeds them—'the epic side of truth'.[31] Primo Levi is aware that the horror one feels reading of his survival can't be adequate to the horror described, nor is the horror described adequate to that experienced by those who did *not* survive.[32] This is not entirely what Adorno meant when he wrote that 'to write poetry after Auschwitz is barbaric', but it is nevertheless appropriate to pause and reflect on this.[33]

The problem has to do with the adequacy of writing as an accounting for horror. Andrew Riemer argues in *The Demidenko Debate* that modern literature on the whole shrinks from what Gaita calls the 'serious sense' of 'evil'.[34] What Gaita simply refuses to countenance is that this is in itself an ethical practice, and one based on a frank recognition of the powerlessness of writing when confronted with the moment of violence. Certain kinds of writing have no choice but to bide time. Writing's value is in times of peace, when the common world of judgement in public may return. One of the ways writing bides its time is by turning in on itself, concentrating on the 'serious sense' of sense itself. Which perhaps explains Edmond Jabés: 'I say that after Auschwitz we must write poetry, but with wounded words'.[35]

Here in its starkest form is the problem of modern thought. Poetry does not redeem us. Reason does not preserve us. Indeed for Adorno, instrumental reason is part of the problem, extending its master plans from the domination of nature to the engineering of peoples.[36] But the Holocaust must be remembered, not least but not only because there are vicious people who deny it ever happened at all. But how?

'What can Wark mean when he says that we should rethink the Holocaust, free of the illusion that there exists absolute evil and absolute innocence?' I did not say this, because it might lead to misunderstandings. But what might Wark mean, were he to say that: the *fact* of the Holocaust is something we should not stop testing as to its meaning? Nothing less than that we cannot claim to have understood it yet.

Sly ironies

Gaita: 'Wark's words matter even if he is too muddled or too unserious fully to mean them, because the foul claim which they are naturally taken to express was published in Australia's premier quality newspaper'. To whom is it 'natural' that lurking behind what I actually said is a 'foul claim' that I did not say? Robert Manne, for one: ' . . . I am referring here to an article in the *Australian* by its postmodern cultural critic, McKenzie Wark—which suggests that the Holocaust was a neat moral fable due for sceptical deconstruction and which could praise *The Hand That Signed The Paper* for its debunking of the idea of the "absolute evil" of the perpetrators of the Holocaust . . .'[37]

Like most moralists, Manne and Gaita have a cloth ear when it comes to irony. I said that 'it's time to declare Helen Darville's novel . . . an unqualified success—for all concerned. This is one controversy where everyone got what they came for'. I explicitly name Manne as one of the beneficiaries—his moral good sense is here entirely dependent on the fact of Darville's book. 'Deep in my heart I believed that in a truly civilised culture a book like this would not have been published', writes Manne. For all his protestations to the contrary, to blacklist a book is censorious, and not civilised.[38] To the ironist, what is civilised is that the book be published, that Manne phrases a response, and the ironist insinuates the dependence of the good on the bad. How can this be a 'culture of forgetting', when it has *Robert Manne* to remember?

I did not praise the Demidenko book for 'debunking' anything. 'The novel works', I said. 'It opens a space. Others put something into that space . . .'. The perceptive reader might notice that in judging this book I do not use Manne and Gaita's moral sense, but nor do I use Andrew Riemer's formal or literary sense either. I am judging the *effects* of the book. In

Lyotard's terms, I'm interested in what phrases can be attached to the phrase of the book, and in doing so, decide, for the moment, what it will be taken to mean. I am not judging its moral or literary qualities here, but what it makes *possible*. It makes possible this extraordinary and wide ranging proliferation of phrases. What is more important than what is in a certain young woman's novel is what kind of public might judge it.

In the book in which he made the term 'postmodern' famous, Lyotard began exploring the plural nature of the conversation of what I call the virtual republic. He later expanded this into a meditation on Theodor Adorno's indictment of the dark side of enlightenment, and its ability to frame and order the world as a mere resource for the will. Lyotard took as his starting point the phenomena of Holocaust denial, and he took it at its strongest point, the claim that there is a lack of *direct* evidence that Jews died in the gas chambers. The claim has a grotesque validity, in that no-one who entered those chambers came out alive. By taking an absurdly literal view of the 'scientific' procedures of historical evidence, Holocaust deniers such as Faurisson can write: 'I have analysed thousands of documents. I have tirelessly pursued specialists and historians with my questions. I have tried in vain to find a single former deportee capable of proving to me that he had really seen, with his own eyes, a gas chamber'.[39] In the face of such an outrageous demand, one can understand why some survivors might choose silence, and the reasons for that silence.

Lyotard leaves it to the historians to furnish the proof, and pursues another question. It's the question that troubles Adorno, of the instrumentality of reason, of its ability to exclude certain kinds of entitlement. To the extent that the 'sceptical deconstruction' Manne talks about as 'postmodern' begins with Lyotard, then it begins with Lyotard's own questioning of his responsibility in relation to the Holocaust. His answer, like that of Arendt, is to develop a conception of the virtual republic.

For Arendt, the public thing is that which people come out of their private lives to judge through their different ways of seeing and thinking. Lyotard is more interested in exactly how such a conversation can take place if there are different ways in which stories are phrased, and those ways of phrasing are incompatible. He does not seriously consider Faurisson's standards of historical evidence. I find it hard to believe that even by those standards there is not evidence enough. The point is that it is logically possible for a case to exist where an injustice has been done, but the way of telling the story, to make the facts of it a public thing, are not compatible with the prevailing standards of what counts as evidence.

To give a pertinent example: how were Aboriginal people to press their claims for justice in respect to their land while the doctrine of *terra nullius* prevailed, according to which they were not in possession of it to begin with? The tortuous process by which the Mabo and Wik cases found such a thing as 'native title' is an example of an attempt to adjudicate between sstories phrased in different ways.

What follows from this for me is more than an opposition to censorship, whether it be official or of the gatekeeping kind, where publishers and editors keep 'unacceptable' stories from being told. What Lyotard's story about the Holocaust calls me to contemplate is how, in cases such as Demidenko's, one can resist rejecting it out of hand because it breaks rules of good taste or good form, and find a way of speaking that does it some justice, without denying in the process the justice of what is said against it.

This is not a matter of compromise. One can only compromise when stories that make claims about their entitlements have something in common. Rather, it's about what may be an ironic kind of phrasing, which displaces what is said, for and against. With a thing like this, I don't see what's to be gained by wagging the finger. Rather, it's a case of producing something else, another understanding. I don't see what's gained by pointing to what we lack, as if all this were signs of a culture in 'decline'. If there is a sign of that it's the insinuation of guilt by association between 'postmodern scepticism' and 'Holocaust denial'—an insinuation made in apparent ignorance of the sources of that particular scepticism in the first place. The moral fables of the cold war years have left us with very poor standards of public conversation, no matter how polite the utterances may be. Fortunately, with the cold war over, the potential returns for something else.

Becoming Ukrainian

The Hand may be a 'bad' book, aesthetically and morally.[40] That is for its readers to decide and debate among themselves. I will

THE VIRTUAL REPUBLIC: AERIALS

say that it is a book that in Georges Bataille's terms *transgressed* into the realm of the 'unthinkable', and it is only through such transgressions that the virtual republic reaffirms what is unthinkable.[41] Such a transgression illuminates not only a particular aspect of what is 'unthought', but the very processes by which a culture decides on its boundaries of thinking. It is the light in which the thinking of the unthought reveals, renews and affirms itself. Transgression is inseparable from the good.

Transgression is necessarily a form of 'violence', in the sense that its breaking into the unthinkable will offend those most vulnerable to the particular boundary of culture that it crosses. Transgression in art is preferable to transgression in, say, politics. Rather a Helen Demidenko than a Pauline Hanson. There is nothing positive in the latter's transgressions for the Aboriginal people of Ipswich. But there is the possibility of reaffirming the meaningfulness of the Holocaust in the wake of the transgressions of Helen Demidenko. And there is the possibility of affirming the value of a free and diverse common world where all Australians, in all their differences, can in the light of a literary transgression add phrases onto it that decide, in the end, what it will mean.

If Manne was serious in thinking of me as a 'postmodern' critic he would at least have gathered that I am more interested in the author as an effect of the practice of writing than as its supposed origin.[42] What was this becoming, this author-and-book and all that followed?

The thing nobody has yet made much of is why she became a *Ukrainian*. Manne puts it down to 'sentimental multiculturalism'. But that explains nothing about why she became a Ukrainian and not a Tartar or a Basque, or like B. Wongar and Leon Carmen, an 'Aboriginal'. Why become the descendant, not of the Nazi 'hand that signed the paper', or of the innocent victim, but the hand *in between*, that pulled the trigger? The ones who are not really powerful, (following orders) and are really not the victims (killers, with delusions of revenge). Not many people think she really succeeded, it seems, but has anyone asked: why did she try? A mystery, still.

To Gaita it will remain a mystery, since he excludes anything revealing in such cases from consideration within his moral community. There is only an inside to this moral community, and exclusion. Since transgression doesn't figure as part of the practice of thinking *across* the boundaries of community, the bounds themselves cannot really be thought. The only way back from transgression, for Gaita, lies in the transgressor's remorse, 'the terrible discovery of himself and what he did'.[43] Transgressors' lives have an absolute value, but what they think, the way they think, and what they become, is excluded from consideration.

Gaita writes elsewhere that 'To believe that it is arguable whether the Holocaust is a fiction invented and sustained by a Zionist conspiracy is not to reveal the virtue of an open and critical mind: it reveals that defect in judgement, that false semblance of an intelligence wary of dogma which we call gullibility . . .'.[44] I completely agree. A gullibility that scepticism trains the mind against.[45] But something in addition to a moral judgement against such thinking is required. How is it to be understood? Such things must be understood if we are to find ways of preventing anti-Semitism, rather than merely making pronouncements against it when it appears, always moralising after the fact. That understanding has in some sense to be prior to moral judgement. How does Hando, a character in *Romper Stomper*, become a 'neo-Nazi'?

Gaita goes on to write: 'some Jews who are in one way or another, professionally concerned with the Holocaust, with anti-Semitism and their effect on Jewish life, have no sense of how serious it is to make it arguable whether someone is an anti-Semite'. He further accuses Professor Bill Rubenstein of making a criticism of Robert Manne that is 'an expression of a corrupted sense of what the Holocaust has made unthinkable. Some of the Jewish establishment now abuses the awe felt in remembrance of the Holocaust and the legitimate taboos which are inseparable from it'.

It may not matter that Gaita refuses to seriously think about how one becomes an anti-Semite. It may not matter that he has no interest or inkling of what it means to become a writer, to write along a certain line, regardless of consequences. But surely it does matter that he refuses to think how one might become a keeper of the flame of the meaning of the Holocaust, as a story with central meaning to one's community, and which phrases the contemporary significance of one's community in the common world. Gaita's ideal moral community seems composed, in the end, only of people thinking what Gaita thinks they ought to think, and excluding what Gaita thinks ought to be unthinkable. It would be a common world that cannot recognise, in their difference, what it means to become Helen Demidenko *or* Bill Rubenstein. He makes different kinds of judgements against them, in different contexts. But in both cases he negates what they choose to become, in the name of abstract standards of what the common world is and what they, as members of it, ought to be.

Moral fables

Arendt put the Holocaust in the context of totalitarian power, and this legitimated the conversion of the historical understanding of wartime anti-Fascism into that of cold war anti-communism. This is how Manne understands Arendt.[46] As it happens, I think Manne was right to phrase Stalinism as an oppressive regime beyond salvage. Manne has often been a good storyteller. But with the Soviet Union gone I see no need in public life for the continuance of the cold war moral fable with all its forgettings. Yes, the Holocaust means the murder of the Jews. Yes, the Holocaust means the threat of totalitarian power. But it also stands as a mute reminder that the technologies of violence are still at work in other imperial regimes.

That Demidenko issues from what Manne calls a 'culture of forgetting' may well be so. But it is not clear why or how the Holocaust comes to be forgotten. I questioned whether the moral fables of the cold war, and the incredulity that their erasures and omissions provoke, might not be part of the reason. That is at least as plausible as blaming it all on 'postmodernism'. The cold war, and the cold warriors, are as answerable for whatever may be deficient in our common world as anybody else.

Last offering

A good culture both remembers and forgets, and above all doesn't forget that it forgets, when it remembers. A good common world can publish the unthinkable and publish the reminding rejoinder when the unthinkable has just been thought. A good media sphere opens its pores to significant differences when phrases are in dispute, and also provides a little space for commentary on the arc of the event itself, as it passes—which was and remains the goal of my particular contribution. All of these elements, of culture, media, and the common world they make, come together around the public thing or event as the virtual republic.

I write about media events, from the inside. I wrote, for example, about the end of the cold war, and the challenge it poses to the moral fables of conservatism.[47] Cold war conservatism is in trouble, and knows it. Without the Red Menace, nothing prevents its many constituent phrases from unravelling. Conservatives now squabble among each other—as they have done over Demidenko. Hence the fatuous campaign against the new 'common enemy'—the hydra-headed beast that is at once 'postmodern scepticism' and 'political correctness'—something simultaneously too free in its desires and too strict. Hence Manne's elegant reworking of possible common contours for a new conservative consensus.

But the Holocaust is not the property of anyone's moral fable. It is a black hole burnt through the very possibility of the common world itself. No phrase is adequate to it. Not even silence. Every word offered for it burns. It burns the past it recalls, it burns the reader it lights upon, it burns the context in which it is written—it burns *every* writer who writes it. It burns *writing*, and covers the facts with ashes.

'To think the disaster . . . is to have no longer any future in which to think it', writes Maurice Blanchot.[48] And yet he attempts it. Writing: the vector through time; here lie all failed attempts to describe the unthinkable—the virtual. I can only offer eight ways of phrasing the Holocaust, none of them satisfactory. What matters, in the end, is the attempt always to find another. It is in the changes in the chain of phrases that memory stays anchored to a past that exceeds it.

6

Political correctness and the
perils of the pale penis people

Is there still a possibility of public truth?

Elias Canetti

*We have not the strength to follow our reason all
the way.*

La Rochefoucauld

HOW TO INVENT AN ENEMY

'I pity you. You're a young white male at the turn of the 21st
century and your time is past. I wouldn't be you for anything.'
So says the diffident old professorial curmudgeon, just as he is
about to be ousted from the Great Books course at Havenhurst
College by a cabal of politically correct students. But then, and
after wallowing in a stout blend of burgundy, Beethoven and
self-pity, he rallies, he takes them all on. Marching proudly into
his class of surly students, he declares: 'Let the past argue with
the future! That is the process. That has always been the
process. This is all I have to offer'. While a few Blacks, Asians
and women skulk, the rest give him a standing ovation, which
he waves off in favour of a lecture on Rousseau.

A famous feminist reporter returns to her *alma mater* to
receive an honorary doctorate, and takes a film crew with her
to record the event. The thing she looks forward to most is
the chance to record herself sitting in on a women's studies

course. After all, as she reminds everyone more than once, she was one of the people who agitated for its creation in the first place. The class starts late. The earnest, mousy woman who teaches the class explains that punctuality is a kind of 'patriarchal dominance'. It's all downhill from there for the famous journalist—the women in the class all find her loud, rude, abrasive, pushy—patriarchal, in a word. No matter what she does or says, they reject everything about her.

These sound like typical political correctness stories, of the kind that appear and reappear in newspaper editorials. PC, it seems, is everywhere. Wherever you go, some PC fanatic, fresh from a women's studies class at uni will be there to tick you off. It used to be Reds under the bed; these days it's PC in the WC. But the first of these stories is from a now defunct TV drama called *Class of '96*. The second, from the TV sitcom *Murphy Brown*. While the rhetoric of PC is everywhere, actual *documented cases* are surprisingly thin on the ground. I sometimes wonder if PC is more fantasy than fact.

When editorialising about the perils of PC in the *Australian*, the playwright David Williamson only offers one actual instance, and a second-hand one at that. He claims that at a writer's conference in the 1980s someone showed him a checklist issued by New Zealand Broadcasting's drama department detailing 20 ways women are not to be depicted.[1] The accompanying picture shows Williamson as Gulliver, pegged to the ground, presumably by the Lilliput league of PC. And yet, when I tried to write about Williamson's play *Dead White Males* for the *Australian*, my section editor was so concerned about libel that the review was 'legalled' by the paper's solicitor. The changes requested would have so diluted the point of the piece that there was no point in even trying. I was practically the only living Australian writer Williamson actually named in his anti-PC essays, and yet I was denied the chance to reply out of paranoia about Williamson's alleged 'litigiousness'. So much for PC as the leading threat to free speech . . .

Marlene Goldsmith, a Liberal member of the New South Wales state parliament, hangs her witty repartee about PC in the universities on a coat. That's right, a coat. Her thesis supervisor, and the other academics at lunch, had fake Burberry tartan ones. Hers was shiny gold. Therefore, PC.[2] The wealth of sartorial variety one can observe whenever the NSW parliamentary Liberal Party gather, both blue *and* grey, is presumably why Goldsmith prefers the company of this famously freethinking bunch to that of the conformist academy.

'PC' was originally an expression used by tolerant left-of-centre American academics to sum up precisely the sort of attitude they tried to avoid. In Australia, the thing a sensible leftie would usually eschew is being too 'IS', or 'ideologically sound'. Those in Australia who made the 'PC' charge transplanted the American 'PC' rhetoric and ignored the local 'IS' one. All the noise about 'PC' in Australia is an echo of somebody else's axes grinding. What was once an ironic bit of self-criticism among leftists was turned into a stick with which to beat them when PC became the slogan of choice for the reorganisation of right-wing attacks against one of their traditional enemies—the liberal, secular humanities academy.

Allan Bloom might be credited with providing the first bit of intellectual backbone to the anti-PC movement, with his high-toned book *The Closing of the American Mind*. The wilder claims of a left-wing 'McCarthyism' first surfaced in the fringe publications of the American right. A book called *An Illiberal Education* by former 'domestic policy analyst' for the Reagan administration Dinesh D'Souza padded it out.[3] It made headlines. Its claims have not stood up to scrutiny. *New Republic* magazine generously described it as 'an any-weapon-to-hand collection of slightly suspect anecdotes'.

The campaign against PC was initiated by far-right-wing think-tanks with a great deal more money than credibility. Allen Bloom and Dinesh D'Souza both received money from the Olin Foundation. Richard Bernstein, who wrote an infamous *New York Times* beat-up, thanked the Bradley and the Smith-Richardson Foundations 'for making my research possible'. These PC myth makers are not defending free speech, they are practicing bought speech. PC is a remarkable example of the way free-floating public anxiety and resentment can align itself, like iron filings toward a magnet, if there is a fantasy object within range that has enough of a charge—and enough publicity.

Not surprisingly, PC comes out of that dim corner of American public life where right-wing sentiment meets obscure foundation money. It's the most recent example of what political scientist Richard Hofstadter once famously called the paranoid style in American politics.[4] A style of politics expert, above all, in the art of inventing an enemy. At various times in the past this enemy has been Catholics, Blacks, Jews, Egg-heads, Reds and Queers. Now it is Feminism, Multiculturalism, Postmodernism, Political Correctness and Queer Theory. But while there is more linguistic tact in the naming of public enemies, the paranoid style remains essentially the same.

What one might call the late paranoid style has one other difference from its earlier forms—it seems to have acquired an ironic distance from its own history. For example, anti-PC campaigners sometimes turn the tables and accuse their enemies of being the perpetrators of a 'new McCarthyism'. Ironic, because Senator McCarthy was the purest expression of the right-wing paranoid style. The contemporary right now projects onto the contemporary left the stigma of guilt for its own past crimes against tolerance, diversity and free speech.

But like Senator McCarthy's famous lists of communists working for the government that he never quite managed to produce, the evidence for PC is weak. The American Council for Education conducted a survey in 1991 that found 'little evidence of controversy over political correctness' on campus. Perhaps they forgot to survey Havenhurst. In Australia it would be hard to point to any instance where debate has actually been silenced on any social issue by the left. It is hardly in a powerful enough position to do so. But never let the facts stand in the way of a good fantasy.

Fantasies can be dangerous. There never seem to have been quite as many reds under the bed as advertised, but the witch-hunt for them was real enough. Have we have all forgotten what real McCarthyism was like? President Truman's 1947 order authorising the FBI to conduct loyalty checks on federal employees unleashed a witch-hunt from which American intellectual culture never recovered. The attacks on leftist and liberal intellectuals, conducted then as now in terms of a defence of 'free speech', led to the sacking of hundreds of faculty and government employees. Some, like mathematician Chandler Davis, went to prison rather than accept unconscionable attacks on civil liberties. Others, including literature scholar F. O. Mathiessen and historian E. H. Norman were driven to despair and suicide.[5] In Australia, security checks on academics and writers were routine. ASIO spied upon and harassed Australian writers. Security reports on the politics of authors and academics were used against them. Some of Australia's most famous authors were denied financial support on purely political grounds.[6]

VICTIMS

If America's McCarthyite purge of the academy, the arts and the civil service was a genuine tragedy, then PC is a fantasy and a farce. It is difficult to find any comparable evidence of discrimination against conservatives today. Some of the most oft-cited cases involve little more than a questioning of the views of respected teachers by students from minority groups.

The most frequently cited case concerns Harvard historian Stephan Thernstrom and his course 'The Peopling of America'. Some of his students claimed that his teaching of southern plantation life was biased towards slave-owner accounts, and that he was unresponsive to their criticisms. They took their complaint up in the student newspaper. He continued to ignore them. They took it to the Harvard Committee on Race Relations. The Harvard administration, after some argy-bargy, upheld Thernstrom's academic freedom. It was Thernstrom himself who decided to respond to criticisms of his course by simply not teaching it. Far from a threat to 'free speech', what we have here is students exercising that very right. There is no evidence that the students wanted their teacher silenced or his course banned. They simply had a difference of opinion and they felt Thernstrom was not listening to them, so they pursued the matter outside the classroom. Yet if you were to believe what many prominent news sources wrote about it, Thernstrom was a 'victim' of political correctness.

Another frequently cited case involves Nancy Stumhofer, an English professor at Pennsylvania State University, who asked for a reproduction of Goya's painting of the Naked Maja to be removed from her classroom. Aha! Political correctness! So claimed the conservative pundit Paul Johnson. Even the usually astute liberal art critic Robert Hughes fell for this one. He blamed it on 'academic thought police' from feminism's 'repressive fringe'.[7] But did Stumhofer really think the painting was 'sexually harassing' her? According to Stumhofer herself, she wanted the painting moved because when she tried to teach developmental English classes while standing in front of it, she could hear the students laughing and making remarks to each other, while looking past her at something on the wall. Far from having the painting 'censored', she asked for it to be moved to a more public part of the building than her classroom. The issue here really is not censorship, merely the appropriateness of certain contexts for displaying a nude.

Even the relatively trivial cases of PC in action that conservatives—and a few gullible liberals—made so much of often don't stand up to close scrutiny. Meanwhile, conservatives mounted vociferous attacks on free expression in the arts, such as the obscenity charge against Robert Mapplethorpe's photographs and the campaign against the National Endowment for the Arts.[8] Conservative academics and culture workers are certainly not losing their jobs. They are not being silenced or suppressed. They are merely being asked to explain themselves.

When conservative students complained about a Black education professor at the University of Chicago and called for his removal, the national press was not moved. Nor did we hear about the complaint taken up against Stumhofer by a conservative colleague and a maintenance worker when she distributed parts of John Berger's book *Ways of Seeing* that contained reproductions of nudes. Or that Joe Rabinowitz, news director of the Fox network station in Washington wrote a memo to the chair of Fox urging the firing of 'politically correct' employees. These stories don't fit the fantasy of political correctness as conservative cultural activists have crafted it and as the media has come to believe it. They don't jibe with the current alchemy of 'news value'.

These and other well publicised cases of alleged political correctness on American campuses are studied in some detail by John K. Wilson in his useful book, *The Myth of Political Correctness*, published by the reputable academic house of Duke University Press.[9] As Wilson writes, by 1991, '. . . PC went from an obscure phrase spoken by campus conservatives to a nationally recognised sound bite used to attack political dissenters on the left'. An earlier campaign by the right-wing group Accuracy in Academia that was based on spying on left-wing academics failed, being too clearly McCarthyite and in breach of the principles of academic freedom. But with the PC campaign, 'The conservatives gain a major strategic victory when they declared themselves to be the oppressed . . .'.

'Without the support of liberals, the conservatives' attacks would have been dismissed as the same old complaints . . .', writes Wilson. So they dressed up a conservative attack on the left as a campaign for free speech and civil rights. Particularly successful was the appeal to the resentment among journalists and the public of the privileged world of Ivy League education.

What is truly disturbing is that while the news media prides itself on accuracy and fact-checking, a handful of incidents that are open to a range of interpretations were blown up into the PC fantasy. A few instances of alleged left-wing PC have received all of the media attention, while persistent attacks on the left receive practically none. While there may be room for debate about campus sexual conduct codes and the definition of rape, the celebrated examples all come from liberal colleges. On the subject of the draconian standards applied to both faculty and student behaviour at many religious educational institutions across America, conservative pundits are curiously quiet.

UNIVERSITY AND OTHER CATASTROPHES

There are three sources of resentment of the academy. One is that gaggle of old cold warriors, nostalgic for the old days of the clear and present danger, beating up PC as some kind of replacement for the communist menace. A second source is those branches of the culture elites who feel they are losing their authority—particularly the old Whitlam ascendancy of writers and artists who benefited from a previous government's largess in the arts but who are no longer the last word in intellectual sophistication. Compared to the newly expanded academy, however, they have pretty good access to the mainstream media. The third source of resentment is students themselves. In the 1980s, the Hawke government increased the numbers in higher education far more than the funding. Students found themselves crammed into classrooms for what often seemed like a meaningless paperchase.

The academic in David Mamet's play *Oleana* quite rightly talks about higher education as the 'warehousing' of a generation, only he is too full of himself to explain this to his student in a way that doesn't seem patronising or offensive to her.[10] He has his own worries. The tragedy is that they are both having a crisis that neither can explain to the other, and as a consequence, it all ends rather badly.

I saw the play down at the Wharf in Sydney, courtesy of an ABC Radio National program that wanted to host a panel discussion on that play and a rather forgettable film called *Gross Misconduct*. In that movie, an American philosophy professor is hounded around Melbourne University by a totally gorgeous student, who makes him have sex with her, then claims he raped her.[11] In short, a middle-aged male fantasy. In the radio panel discussion, the feminist writer Eva Cox and I squared off against the film's script writer, Lance Peters. It was all very silly—not least because the point of view of students themselves was nowhere represented in any of this. We were all free to say what we liked on the panel—and we did. The host even had the nerve to ask me if I had ever fucked my students. But certain voices weren't heard. At a time when more people than ever before experience university life, those experiencing it were absent from the public conversation.

At least until a charming comedy about university life called *Love and Other Catastrophes* came along. Shot on the same Melbourne University locations as *Gross Misconduct*, it showed that film up as the tacky fantasy it was. It's about the lives and loves of a bunch of university students, made with great wit and style. Adrian Martin makes a cameo appearance as a cultural studies lecturer. It may not be a profound film, but it does work its way up to the most unrepresentable thing in the whole of cinema—joy.

The film makes great sport out of various precious under-graduate manglings of high theory and high-mindedness. Most portrayals of the semi-educated are far more malicious, as if one were better off being a complete fool than half a one. In this film, we feel as if we're all half educated, half fool. At least about anything that matters, like love and other catastrophes. This is a wiser work of art than, for example, David Williamson's *Dead White Males*. When that play tries to be serious it seems just too foolish. When this film fools about, it distils just a little good sense.

But there is an added reason why *Love and Other Catastrophes* was, for me at least, a joy to watch, particularly in the context of some of the more bizarre fantasies about universities. The film is an idea, of sorts, about university life: about what it's for, why it matters. The film reminds me of my own time as an undergraduate, as I'm sure it does for a lot of people. What's more important is that the film reminds me of qualities

I really like in a lot of my own students. And it reminds me of why I really like teaching. It's a film about the serendipity between what gets taught and what gets learned, at least in those university courses that are about things that really matter, like the idea of love, the experience of joy, or the remembrance of loss. There is nothing more important than learning to perceive, to feel, and to think for one's self. Everything else about what happens at a university is entirely secondary.

THE WHITLAM ASCENDANCY GOES BACK TO SCHOOL

Both Williamson's play *Dead White Males* and Helen Garner's book *The First Stone* were pretty popular with my students, these being among the few well promoted reflections on campus life to make their way through the geriatric arteries of the contemporary media sphere.[12] Both appear to be about raising the alarm concerning new movements in the humanities academy such as an excessively moralising feminism. Both see the new breed of academics as cynical and manipulative in their attempt to seize hold of students' minds.

From talking to my own students, many of them took to both the book and the play with enthusiasm but tended to find them both patronising.[13] I don't know about anyone else's students, but mine seem pretty keen and able to think for themselves and filter out the views of their teachers—including me. It didn't take them long and required absolutely no prompting from me for them to ask after Garner and Williamson's own claims to authority, their own appeal for the hearts and minds of the young. They can be a canny lot, this 'Generation X', particularly when it comes to decoding narrative and images.

The publicists working on promoting *Dead White Males* and *The First Stone* did an excellent job of sticking the cattle prod to the media, and got it to jump on the issues both raised about higher education, although at somewhat cross-purposes. To some younger readers and theatregoers, here was some recognition of going through the life-changing experiences of higher education under conditions where, by government decree, the *form* of it is fast becoming a cheaply produced, mass consumer product. To the weary pundits of the newspaper world, on the other hand, it was about how everything had gone wrong with the *content* of education. By some remarkable stroke of fate, education had all gone wrong just after they happened to have left it.

All in all, importing the rhetoric of PC from the right-wing public relations campaigns in the United States did not serve us well as a talking point about education. A case of a public conversation about the wrong public thing. It confused rather than clarified the issues of concern in the rather different Australian higher education system. But hopefully, David Mamet's *Oleana* will be read and performed—it's a far more interesting American text to explore. *Love and Other Catastrophes* is circulating out there on video, and people going through the higher education experience might be lucky enough to chance upon it in the video store, have a good laugh, and use it to reflect on that stage of their lives, or in the case of those of us who chose it as a profession—our chosen lifetimes.

ALMA MATER

In the early 1980s when I was in my twenties, I volunteered for courses in women's studies, taught by Judith Allen, Rose-mary Pringle and Vivien Johnson. At that time, these were separate units in different departments at Macquarie. Later, these and other units became an interdisciplinary program, as happened at quite a few universities.

I was often the only male in class. Judith's classes took place in her office. Maybe nine or ten people, jammed into a tiny room. Rosemary's classes were a bit more relaxed—I think we even sat on lime green bean bags strewn incongruously across the standard government issue brown carpet. It was a very 1970s kind of thing. She was writing about women in the workforce at the time—detailed studies of what actually hap-pens in a whitegoods factory or a bank. I remember Vivien lecturing on the book she had put together about women's refuges—she was involved in the movement to set them up and subsequently wrote a book about it. I'll never forget Vivien, who seemed so small and frail, furiously smoking Marlboros while talking calmly about women turning up bruised and battered, scared to death of their own husbands.[14]

At first I found it a bit intimidating. A lot of the women in the classes were mature age students. They had *kids* my age.

They had come back to university to get the education they missed out on when they chose to raise a family. There were some younger women, often very energetically committed to the cause, as young people sometimes are. I found it prudent to just listen for a while, rather than barge on in as usual. And do you know what? I learned something. Something about other people's perceptions of the world; other people's way of refining and sharpening those perceptions against the stone of sociology, history or philosophy.

I got lower grades for my feminism courses in my final year than for anything else. Outrageous! Discrimination! I thought about lodging appeals. But then I thought about it some more. In the first place, I really wasn't as well read in this stuff as the other students. I was busy reading other things. Nor did I have the first-hand experience of the issues of some of the better students in these classes. Should that matter? Surely university should be a level playing field!

But the problem with that argument is that for some of those women, it wasn't a level playing field at all. Running a household for a husband and raising kids were the things they knew most about. They felt disadvantaged in other courses that dealt with areas of public life from which they had been excluded. There were things they had to read about in books to catch up on. Women's studies offered one or two courses that dealt with *their* experience, its history and its place in the contemporary world. No wonder they did well in such courses. It's easier to grasp detailed research about something if you have some first-hand experience of what is being talked about. If you have had an unwanted pregnancy, or been paid a lower wage than your male colleagues, it's easier to get from that experience to a concept about it than if you haven't. Women's studies was those women's home base in the humanities, the place where they were sure they knew what they were on about, where they got the confidence to tackle other issues. For me, it was the other way around. I was expecting to do well in it because I knew I was pretty up on continental philosophy, or whatever. But I had never changed a nappy and was struggling to care for a potplant.

In my whole time as an undergraduate I never once felt that the moral or political pressure coming from other students or from teachers shut me up for good. There were some pretty strongly held views, among both the staff and the students. It could be pretty intimidating. But then, to some extent it was supposed to be. Among other things, the humanities and some of the social sciences are about transforming one's own experience into something that one can both understand and communicate. So one learns how to argue. How to find relevant facts. How to choose and apply a relevant interpretive framework. What the known weaknesses of other propositions are and how to go after them. I know these are supposed to be 'Mickey Mouse' courses—the kind few people actually fail. But they are also courses in which few people really shine. Perhaps because it's not just about adding some skills to who one already is. That previous sense of self changes in the process. One produces oneself differently, drawing in new resources, adding powers, but also making one's own experience an object of transformation.

I certainly knew a few ideologues as an undergraduate, and very occasionally I get them now in my classes. Such people have always been around. Militants and god-botherers, missionaries and thought police. Read Manning Clark's memoirs of his education, *The Quest for Grace*, and they are there. 'Heart dimmers' and 'life deniers', he called them—both better expressions than that clumsy import PC.

As Clark used to say, real believers don't need to make the world conform to their needs. They are strong enough to endure a world that thinks and acts otherwise. I've had some lively and illuminating conversations with true believers. I supervised a thesis once on the relationship between Moslem faith and enlightenment as both pertained to a practice of broadcasting for a Moslem country. Or another, on how the west use human rights as a propaganda strategy against China, as seen by a very cool and sharp young Chinese apparatchik. We had some interesting arguments, but precisely because of a lack of anxiety about whether the process would challenge anyone's belief.

I've also supervised work that has challenged a student's whole identity. Those can be dangerous. Learning is threatening. It changes you. I've had students come to see me and burst into tears, not just from the ordinary working pressure of getting a thesis finished, but because they really feel in danger of losing a sense of self, of becoming someone else. I see my role as a teacher in such a metamorphosis as supporting the person who wants to grow, intellectually. I still know what this is like, as I still experience it myself.

Sometimes it's hard for students to know how far to use the university as an environment for self making. How seriously to take it, whether to 'go on' or go 'back to the real world'. It's hard advising students about it, too. The honours student who cried in my office surprised us all, even herself, by getting a first, but decided not to go on. She works in advertising now. I get postcards from her from all over the world, full of little adventures and affairs. She seems happy with the decisions she made, the differences she made in herself, of herself, and for herself. Some students, frankly, aren't up to it. A few now resort to chanting a little mantra to keep new ideas from bothering them: PC . . . PC . . . PC . . . PC . . .

Perhaps I'm getting conservative, but I think I agree with John Anderson that the humanities academy isn't for everybody. Everyone ought to have the opportunity, but not everyone has the passion, or the strength, to make themselves the instrument to which the tools of knowledge are to be applied by their own hand. So it doesn't surprise me that there's a paranoid reaction sometimes. While I was writing this, somebody spray painted 'fuck off fuck you' on my office door. Quite a few other doors and walls were daubed too, so maybe it wasn't personal. I got talking to the cleaner when he came, and he was quite expansive on the subject: which parts of the campus, what kinds of slogan, which times of year. This one seemed to have a particular, not quite articulate complaint about the whole higher education system. Incomprehensible slogans about money, power, oppression. I was pretty disturbed by it, but in a way I admired the spirit of the sprayer. Somebody out there somewhere on campus put up a strenuous resistance. To what exactly, not even they seemed to know.

The alma mater and her alumni: nourishing mother and those she nourished. An old Roman title, bestowed upon Cybele, transferred to universities in the seventeenth century. In the context of the rise of women's studies, it's ironic. In the context of the Greek idea of knowledge as a practice for self-transformation, apt. To study in the humanities seriously is to align oneself with a new line of descent. Some of the things attributed to political correctness are really attributes of humanities scholarship in general, at least when it's pursued with some thoroughness.

My own university days certainly changed me. I chose the most radical institutions, courses and teachers available. I came to it a fire-breathing radical, opposed to tradition. I ended up an upholder of a radical tradition. The experience made me more conservative.

It's not surprising that it's *writers* who have a certain friction with the university as an institution. Serious writers have their own memories of self making, their own lines of descent from texts of their own choosing. Usually, there are other institutional spaces—the Pram Factory or the Balmain Push, for example. But writers tend to have a more romantic view. They like to think they are authors, also, of themselves. Real scholars tend to submerge themselves in the institution; real writers submerge the institution in themselves. I have quite a bit of sympathy with the writerly disdain for the group-think of the university crowd. But sometimes it edges over into a quite bizarre fantasy, and a quite interesting choice of words.

Political correctness is 'anathema to true literary creativity', according to David Williamson, because it imposes its ideologies on the writer, making writers construct characters that conform to PC models, and bars writers from constructing characters based on other ideologies; Williamson's example being his own preference for biological determinism. The argument has an odd tension in it, between Williamson's resistance to academic criteria per se, and embrace of particular ones. On one page he decries 'politically correct role models' in writing, on another he is confessing that *Dead White Males* did 'take sides', in favour of an odd amalgam of liberal humanist and evolutionary theories. What I find unsatisfying about that play is not that it satirised things in which I believe. It doesn't satirise anything I even remotely recognise as an interesting or current idea. Rather, it's that it fails to affirm the feisty independence of the practice of imaginative, literary art and reaches instead for props from another department of the alma mater.

Williamson's anxiety about the influence of the academy isn't well served by the fantasy about it that permeates his plays and essays. The plot to this fantasy is that the academic is a threat to good order, and it comes in two flavours—both American imports. Academics are immoral 'postmodern sceptics' doing relativist 'cultural studies', who believe in nothing but power and will do anything to manipulate it to further their own nihilistic ends; academics are moral fanatics who believe in rigid and austere dogmas that deny people free expression and rob them of their enjoyment of harmless every-day bits of fun. The coherence of this anxiety is, as Hume might say, a matter of the passions, not of reason.

The Slovenian philosopher Slavoj Zizek has a diagnosis for this fantasy.[15] This bad 'other', in this case academics, are perceived to be a threat to 'our' way of life, because of their excessively lax or strict relation to 'our' desire. By identifying them as excessive they are separated from us and our way of life. But what is imputed to these imaginary academics is precisely *our own* fantasies about being more correct, or less correct. The tensions internal to Australian culture about codes of behaviour are transferred onto somebody else, in the form of a fantasy. The desire for a strong moral order, in particular, comes back embodied in the fantasy of PC. Just as the desire to be a cynical, amoral libertine comes back in the form of the 'postmodernist' lecher lecturer Dr Swain in *Dead White Males*.

Phantom armies of PC zealots are conjured out of a few dubious anecdotes as a pretext for staging popular resistance to them. We can all feel good about how liberal and liberated we are, battling this invisible enemy of liberty that is really nothing more than our own perverse passion for a repressive order.

Fantasies of nihilistic academics stand as ciphers for hidden desires. Or as one taxi driver remarked to me around the time *Dead White Males* and *The First Stone* made their media run, 'So you teach at a uni? Must be great, surrounded by all that young snatch!'.

CULTURAL STUDIES

If there is a coven in the tea room bubbling up an urn-full of spells to trouble the world's moral order, they certainly haven't invited me to join them for a herbal Darjeeling. What I have noticed going on about the place is a debate about what kinds of protocols of speech might enable free speech to express a wider range of views on a wider range of topics than is currently the case in Australian public life. That project brought together people whose roots were in feminism, multiculturalism, Aboriginal cultural activism and much else besides. It was a vast and amorphous movement, part of which one can identify as Australian cultural studies.[16]

I've been a part of that project, or at least a fellow traveller—I went to its conferences, published in its journals, engaged in some of its debates, publicised it in the *Australian*. Two of its leading practitioners, Meaghan Morris and Stephen Muecke, summed up the cultural studies project in a thoughtful editorial for a journal called *UTS Review*, which is something of a house organ for the alma mater of my graduate degree, the infamous UTS Humanities department.

Cultural studies in the 1980s saw itself as part of a wider public debate, the aim of which was, they said, 'to rethink Australian culture as an open experiment where many histories and cultural inheritances interact . . .'.[17] In such a context, cultural studies itself would draw on 'an evolving, contested form of Esperanto' in the humanities that tries to think about culture in a situated way. It ought not to become 'a moralising genre of "theory"—socially groundless, history free, weighed down by a mass of references to a "world" composed of other theoretical writings—that cannot engage with the cultural differences it endlessly invokes'. But it would draw on the work of professional humanities scholars, on a 'discursive community' that is 'constituted by an effort to find ways to articulate incommensurability as well as inequality, and thus by a capacity, often a commitment, to think the conditions in which community formation becomes possible—for diverse groups of people'. The language is a bit awkward, perhaps. We all have to write now in an academic world dominated by the dialects of American graduate schools. As a firm believer in cooking up one's own pet jargon, I'd say that the project here announced is cultural studies as the creation of an actual little corner of a virtual republic.

Cultural studies had at least three moments. The first was the discovery of just how different the experiences of Australians actually are and always were, for example, the hidden history of women or migrant experience. The second was the criticism of cultural institutions that had ignored or suppressed particular cultural values or aspirations, for example, the forced adoption of Aboriginal children and the imposition of mission religion. The third moment was the positive attempt to imagine how Australian culture could be otherwise—what might free, open, diverse, creative culture be like?

Sometimes cultural studies operated with too narrow an understanding of cultural difference. It left some of the older and deeper cultural currents out of the picture. For example, it assumed there was a strong and central 'dominant' culture of big white blokes that would take care of itself. But there isn't, and increasingly it doesn't. Compared to twenty, even ten years ago, feminism is winning. Fighting about the exclusion of women from the boardroom is progress, compared to fighting about the exclusion of women from *jobs*. And hooray for that. In any case, the object of feminism as a politics was and is mostly structural. It's about changing the rules by which institutions produce and reproduce themselves. It's taking quite a bit of monkey wrenching, but it's working. The fantasy object of the pale penis people, on the other hand, has a quixotic aspect to it. It's probably more true that there were and remain networks of old boys, looking after their own, than to say that there is a PC conspiracy. And yet it's worth looking at the fantasy aspect of this as well. What was projected onto the image of the patriarch was in part a desire that nobody wanted to own up to. The desire to have and to hold—power.

The irony is that an image of the dominant white culture was kept in place by the very attempts to find an alternative to it. The ways of speaking that proliferated in the humanities were more conservative than its adherents knew. They took for granted something that was already fragmenting and increasingly isolated from the drift of the various proposals for the further reform of manners of speaking. And one can't help wondering, in the fantasy about the white patriarchs, how much was actually a desire precisely that such a group *continue* to hold actual power, so as not to diminish the *moral* entitlements of those excluded from the compromising business of authority.

I can vividly remember the arguments that went back and forth between the bean bags in the sociology seminar room when I was an undergrad. There *has* to be a patriarchy, otherwise there can be no feminism. So everything was organised around the fantasy of the patriarchal other and his all embracing power. This particular feminism was organised negatively, around what it didn't have. Not the 'penis envy' of Freud's odd theories, but *power*. Sometimes that power was represented through the image of the 'phallus', and it was assumed that the whole structure of language and social life was imbued with it. Sometimes this fantasy came with elaborate and nuanced detail, but it was more often than not still wedded to this fantasy structure.[18] It was a *useful* fantasy. It motivated a lot of women to go and do something about structural inequalities, in domestic life and in the workplace, for example. But perhaps it concedes too much in advance.

MEDIA STUDIES

Take, as an example, the feminist critique of the media. Sure, one can find racist and sexist stereotypes in the media, and all that. But one can also find quite the opposite. Both feminism and multiculturalism are themselves now part of popular culture.[19] It is no longer possible to treat feminism and pop media as separate boxes. The women who edit women's magazines, by and large, went to university, picked up some feminism, and are trying to apply it in situations that are inevitably difficult and compromised, but apply it they do. They have not abolished their nemeses, and probably never will. Browse through any popular women's magazine and you will find articles with a feminist bent sandwiched in between diet tips. That's the very tasty, tangy, tangible diversity of the virtual republic.

Media studies scholars spent a long time trying to reduce the weird proliferation and diversity of pop media to some underlying essence or ideology. It was a 1960s thing. Media studies folk argued about whether the media were patriarchal, racist, pro-capitalist, or all three. Everything had to be unmasked and exposed as evil—something ordinary people were assumed to be too dumb to do for themselves. Then scholars like Ien Ang started to wise up to how competent ordinary people were at negotiating the meaning of what they see and hear in the media, all by themselves, without the help of media studies scholars.[20] It's like in that Leonard Cohen song—'everybody knows' the media contain this or that prejudice, and people learn how to see through it when it suits them.

While some scholars were off discovering how much diversity there is in the ways people read the media, others were taking a fresh look at the diversity of media images and stories themselves. It's not all reducible to some hidden agenda. Sure, you can go looking for stories in the press or on TV that will bear out your pet theory about the covert ideology of the media—but only if you discard a whole lot of other stuff that doesn't. Mass media are not 'massive' in the sense that it's a great block of sameness, any more than they are massive in that they brainwash everyone into the same evil ideology. It's more useful to think of it as *mess* media than mass media. Even in those parts of the process where it gets hung up on repeating formulas—the celebrity cover story, for example—there are endless little variations on how it can be put together and how it can be read. So eventually, scholars such as John Hartley twigged to this, and started looking at the virtual dimension of pop media, at the variety of things it *might* mean to a variety of people.[21]

All of which starts to come together in the work of a writer like Catharine Lumby. As I wrote in an earlier chapter, Lumby was part of the Power Institute crowd of the 1980s who explored how quirky and ironic the play of meaning in a text can be. She then became a journalist for the *Sydney Morning Herald*, where most of the editorial control is in the hands of a few men, but most of the actual stories are written by women, and where getting hold of, and hanging on to *female* readers is crucial to the survival of the paper. I suspect that gave her an experience of how subtle the issues of gender, power and control are in the media. In her book *Bad Girls*, Lumby puts it all together in an examination of the complex ways in which popular media work both for and against women in the 1990s.[22] If 'difference' was the catch word of the 1980s, *Bad Girls* sums up a series of investigations of the media through which scholars discovered just how *differently* different culture can actually be.

BEYOND THE FANTASY

I don't think it's an accident that a lot of useful work in getting feminism and cultural studies beyond the fantasy stage happened through studying the media, which is where the people who are the public meet the things that are public concerns. Nor is it an accident that a lot of the pioneering research happened in Australia in the 1980s and early 1990s, when a decade of social democracy enabled thinkers and writers to get on with innovating ways through which Australians might come to know themselves, govern themselves, and become free. And not surprisingly a lot of creative energy went into rethinking feminist media studies and media practice, because it was a time that looked forward, to the postmodern republic, rather than backwards, to the Ming dynasty.

What actual contact with the texts and practices of the media reveals about the state of Australian culture is something like this: minority cultures have sources of power; the 'dominant' culture is itself always plural, and there are plenty of cracks in it. That's not to collapse the whole thing into a happy liberal pluralism. Not everyone is equally entitled. Not all kinds of entitlement are recognised. But I think it's important to get beyond the fantasy of the big bad other, be it patriarchy or political correctness. It might be morally satisfying to be able to polarise the whole space of debate and attribute all the bad stuff to the other side, but I don't think it's a terribly effective cultural politics. The irony is that while I wouldn't deny that there is a little too much 'ideological soundness' in some writing in the humanities, I think they have been remarkably ineffective as instruments of transformation. Where feminism worked, it's more through its coming to power in new institutional forms. Where cultural studies has had some effect, it has likewise been through inventing structures that create new possibilities for cultural dialogue.

Cultural studies does get a bit stuck at each of the steps along the way, particularly when it cuts itself off from the messy, plural way culture can work, as is evident in the media. Sometimes the discovery of cultural difference seemed to be an end in itself. Sometimes the blanket critique of the allegedly dominant culture eclipses all attempts to move the agenda on to positive developments elsewhere. Sometimes the notion of a positive process of creating a diverse culture is too obsessed with cultural policy, looking for administrative ways around the unavoidable need to engage with cultural change where it really happens—through popular culture and the media.[23] In overestimating the power and homogeneity of the 'dominant discourse', cultural studies sometimes treated the big white bloke way of talking as the universal model of public speech at precisely the time when it was no longer quite so.

It's no accident that my first book, *Virtual Geography*, was about how the international impinges on all this; how the global flows of news media interact and intersect with local cultural differences and frictions. It seemed like the right kind of topic for a white bloke to write about, as it seemed more important to me, in the early 1990s, to *listen* to what, for example, Aboriginal people were saying about Australian cultural issues. So I concentrated on how flows of images and stories from one country to another affected people's perceptions of the local and the global.[24] When the PC stuff started to come up, it seemed obvious to me that here was an example of what I had found in those studies. Images and stories that arose out of a specific conflict, transported across national borders, being used to articulate quite other conflicts. It's an odd example of the pervasiveness of the vector, and an ironic one. It's often the people who were so paranoid about American influence in Australia in the 1970s who took up the PC charge with such unquestioning zeal in the 1990s.

Meanwhile, cultural studies continued on its merry way. Asking questions. Finding new ways of creating spaces for people to speak. Working particularly on the most intractable problem in Australian culture—finding ways to have a dialogue with Aboriginal people and to recognise their entitlement to speak *on their own terms*. I can't remember a single major cultural studies conference that didn't put Aboriginal speakers in the plenary. But the small world of the humanities academy is only one of the worlds in which people may find themselves speaking. Not many scholars are all that media-savvy. Nobody took much trouble to explain what was going on. So when someone like David Williamson took a peek at a few frankly pretty second-rate English and American textbooks and crib sheets for undergraduates, alarm bells went off. What was in the main an experiment in creating new, additional ways of speaking was taken to be some Machiavellian plan to design and impose a replacement. Neither Williamson nor anyone else has ever provided much evidence, but nevertheless the fantasy got about.

FREE SPEECH—AND CHEAP TALK

A consequence of the success of the campaign against PC is that it licensed the kinds of resentment and confusion lurking in the remnant bits and pieces of what was once a dominant white discourse that one hears in Pauline Hanson or Graeme Campbell. (I'll spare the reader further discussion of those two, at least until a later chapter.) Cultural studies has been very good on identifying the hidden injuries of race and gender, and finding ways within the academy to articulate those grievances, to have them heard. But it hasn't been so good on the hidden injuries of class. At a time of globalisation and rationalisation and every other top down 'euphemisation' for the reorganisation of Australia to suit the banks and big business, it escaped a lot of people's attention that there were sections of the community who were—and are—really hurting. Working people who find their skills are no longer up to scratch, small businesses squeezed out by the big franchises, farmers watching their credit and their markets dry up quicker than a river in drought.

The attack on PC has been a good thing to the extent that it is a reminder that articulating those cultural differences is not something that can be administered, it is something that can only grow of its own accord. But it won't grow while Australians who are already fearful of losing what little they have are thrown into conflict with each other. The wilder claims about PC in the universities are false. The cultural studies movement, which brought together many of the new strands of thinking in the humanities, didn't get it quite right in the way it went about addressing questions of cultural difference. But the whole idea, as I understood it, was to learn along the way. I'd like to think I'm still a learner; that I don't shut my eyes and chant the mantra.

One thing that cultural studies was dead right about was that in the absence of the invention of a new language for phrasing cultural differences, the door is left open for the irrational expression of resentment and paranoia—for blaming cultural difference for things it doesn't cause, such as the erosion of the life chances and economic opportunities at the bottom end of the class divide. The issue is not that resentful or paranoid people ought not to speak. The issue is rather one of knowing how to rephrase that. Cultural studies was, and remains, a contribution to the practice of free speech. Not least because one of the main things it is about is an ethics of how to choose what kind of phrasings one might append to what kinds of previous statements, such that possibilities for conversation among different people open up further, rather than close down.

For free speech to be an absolute right for any individual to say what they like however they like, we must assume that

THE VIRTUAL REPUBLIC: AERIALS

what any individual actually says has no effect on the ability of others to speak effectively. If that were true, then there would be little point in actually exercising such a right in the first place. What may actually happen, however, is that an individual asserting that absolute right to add a phrase deters others from adding their phrase. This deterrent effect may be achieved by creating an atmosphere of prejudice preventing another phrase from being heard, by shaping the space of conversation such that it precludes the possibility of other points of view being legitimate—or by simply taking up all the available time.

A case in point is the public conversation about free speech itself. Defenders of the concept will frequently present only one side of the issue—the individual's absolute right. They will then roundly denounce anyone who does not support this individual right in its absolute form as politically correct thought-police, closet Stalinists with secret agendas, and so on and so forth. This is then the last word on the topic. No conversation ever follows, or can follow.

To avoid such possibilities, to achieve free speech as the goal of the process as a whole, means that there are limits to the degree to which individual parties to a conversation can exercise their right. The individual right to speak freely has to be recognised, in all cases, but it does not follow that it is absolute. It is limited by its obligation to recognise the reciprocal right of others.

Looking around the classroom at my morning tutorial group as they arrive and settle in, I think about this for a moment. I study the young woman fiddling with her biro. She reminds me of myself when I was a student, sitting in classes in this very same room at Macquarie—thankfully not the one with the bean bags. She's keen, but she talks too much. Must think of a way to cut her off without hurting her feelings. She comes over all confident, but I think that confidence masks some kind of fragility, something that hurts. I look at the two Asian students, lurking in the corner, who never say a word. I think about how I might draw them into this thing, without putting them on the spot. They talk to each other in—what?—Thai, I think. I don't know yet if they can follow what's being said. I don't know if they are just shy or if the whole thing about speaking in public is an alien concept.

Is everyone's right to add a phrase to the conversation here the same? Not in my class. Students who I think know what they are talking about get more time than ones who don't. Students already at ease with the notion of a public conversation have to help me draw the others into it by knowing when to leave space, when to invite others into it. This is not rocket science. It's something harder: the art of conversation—the very basis of the virtual republic.

Over the years, as class sizes increase, it has become harder and harder to run tutorials as one would wish. But this is not the only difficulty. One of the things women's studies courses were about was creating spaces for conversations where women weren't automatically silenced, sidelined and shut up. A similar problem arises now that education is an export industry. There may be quite large numbers of students in classes who come from cultures with completely different ideas about how to have a conversation.

So I don't think it is at all surprising that it is people in education who have been among those most concerned with questions about the protocols of phrasing. Educators are on the front line when it comes to formulating and reformulating ways of making things public. As the composition of the culture changes, new ways of creating zones of indifference within which cultures might meet need to be invented. Zones of indifference where particular kinds of experience and ways of communicating it can hear each other, without giving up their differences, but where they can recognise each other's rights.

The public non-conversation about political correctness did not achieve this, because it was mainly about making excuses for not even giving it a go. What the PC charge did was stigmatise anyone who did not conform to a fantasy about the right ways of speaking as being an enemy of that way of speaking. The paradox of it was that what it stigmatised this mad, bad other for was precisely the thing that the anti-PC campaign itself relied on as its main tactic. It excluded others from speaking by claiming those others exclude people from speaking. It erected a fantasy about the bad other as a danger to 'us' in which what was dangerous about it was its fantasy about us as a bad other. Thus it polarised the whole field of media and culture. But this only prevented, for a time, the coming together of culture and media, in their different tempos and distributions of vectors, as a virtual republic. A place where we talk about those who are different from us, not to exclude them on the basis of their being different, but in order to recognise their right to join a conversation while remaining different. A virtual republic, in other words, is where when we recognise them, we accept them as different, and in so doing, accept them at the same time as belonging with us.

7

Postmodernism meets the attack of the killer Darwinists!

Man is what he believes.

Anton Chekov

Whatever it is, I'm against it!

Groucho Marx

THE PLAGUE

They are a cancer, a danger and a plague. They are multiplying like mice, but they are masters only of the sterile. Theirs is a life hating ideology. They seek the revenge of the uncreative and to discredit all natural genius. Every time civilisation gets rid of this spectre, it turns up with a new hat on. All of which sounds like one of the anti-Semites in Helen Demidenko's novel, talking about the Jews. Actually, all these words were used by Christopher Koch, when he accepted the 1996 Miles Franklin Award. Words he did not use at all about the Jews. He is talking about postmodernists.

'Never listen to a deconstructionist' he warns. He seems at least to be consistent in following his own advice. The account he gives of postmodernism, or deconstruction is—in a word—silly. He commends David Williamson for his 'courage' in standing up to this 'plague', but he heads for the safe high ground and prudently refuses to actually name any living Australian postmodernists. That would open up the awful possibility of exposing Koch's wild claims to some actual public scrutiny.

Koch's accusations are oddly reminiscent of Joe McCarthy waving a bit of paper at the media and claiming that there are 124 Communists in the White House. Or is it 145? We never did see that list, but there were witch-hunts, sackings, suicides. You may think I'm exaggerating, but Koch himself links 'the Calvinist, the fascist, the communist, the deconstructionist, the post-structuralist'. Behind whom stand 'the shadow of totalitarianism'.

If by 'post-structuralist' he means, for example, the late Michel Foucault, perhaps we might mention his hostility to Stalinism. Or if we mean Jean-François Lyotard, perhaps Koch might take a look at his interventions against the revival of anti-Semitism in Europe and revisionist histories of the Holocaust. But those are facts, and we should not let facts get in the way of a good rant.

As with most hate speech, Koch characterises his phantom foes as every extreme—and its opposite. These puritan ideologues are also self-interested careerists, specialising in 'professional anger'. They are masters only of the sterile, yet are 'multiplying like mice'. They are too uncreative, and yet also too experimental. 'Lobby groups' are destroying 'the harmony that nurtures creativity'. Yet 'we're producing talent and achievement in every field'.

When an enemy is identified by a series of contradictory excesses but no-one is actually named, then we are probably dealing with an irrational expression of fear and resentment—a fantasy. An expression of the passions, mediated by rhetoric, untouched by reason. 'They' are doing bad things. 'They' are responsible for it all. But 'they' never seem to get to speak. And of course 'they' are a special interest group, but Koch is above it all, speaking to and for the 'broad mass of intelligent beings'. Only other people have self-interest, not Koch. Koch, who presumably takes his own advice and doesn't listen to 'any critic or pedagogue'—except when they are handing him a prize and a cheque.

Koch's postmodernists are 'abolishing the notion of beauty'. They claim that 'writers don't really produce their work but are blind instruments of social forces'. My postmodernists, the ones I have on my shelf and have actually read, are rather different. I have Roland Barthes' writings on Zola and Proust, Julia

Kristeva's book on Joyce, Gilles Deleuze on Kafka. And of course I have on the same shelves the books these critics loved so much and thought so much about. If Koch really does have such a broad and deep love and grasp of writing, how can he can so hatefully and wilfully malign other writers—particularly ones he has not read? If literature is so civilising, why is Koch so uncivil?

Koch gives voice to widespread resentment of any intellectual training that involves the rigorous questioning of all assumptions. What is beauty? A sceptical mind responds to such a question by reasoning about it. Koch responds by asserting that it is beyond question. Tradition, not experiment. Belief, not free thought. It is not 'postmodernists' he is trying to run off the road here, but the ghost of Socrates. For at the end of the day all that can be said is common to these 'French' thinkers, who in every other way are a remarkably diverse lot, is that they *think*.

If there is a danger at work in Australian cultural life, it is not from the free inquiry into how culture works and what interests may be at work within it. It comes from this rejection of thinking, from this shrill insistence that we all just take it on faith that this is a culture that is a 'byword for good humour and fair play'. Without actually putting it to the test. So we may a have society that asserts a fair go for all—except postmodernists. Which 'lobby group' gets excluded next?

If this was a debate about politics, boardroom wars or sport, the press would have taken great pains to at least get a quote from the other side. When it comes to these evil postmoderns, the standards of balance and factual accuracy need not apply. In the 1990s, Australian newspaper readers heard what novelists, playwrights and journalists thought about the parlous state and evil influence of contemporary philosophy.[1] We heard from rather fewer philosophers. And so the virtual republic was not what it could be, not least because editors chose, in the main, not to open a space where questions of culture and value might find more than one answer. Koch may be a worthy winner of what is now a worthless award, but his acceptance speech is accepting only in one sense—he did not refuse the prize.

When a version of Koch's acceptance speech appeared in the *Australian*, I published a reply. You've just read it pretty much as I filed it. There was some surprise at the *Australian* afterwards that the responses that came in were pretty much in my favour, although not Jonathan Bowden's, whose considered opinion was that I sounded like the 'squeak of a bat'. But my sense of it was that most people, regardless of what views they hold on the matter, felt the pomo-bashing campaign had gone beyond reason.[2] Shortly after I asked which lobby group would be next to get this kind of paranoid treatment, Pauline Hanson popped out of the woodwork with a list.

THE POWER AND THE PASSION

Exactly what kind of 'courage' did it take for David Williamson to make good publicity—and good money—out of vilifying 'postmodernists'? The courage of going against one's finer judgements, perhaps. Koch's published views on the subject are an unrelieved chequerboard of black and white. In between somewhat similar fantasies, Williamson said things that are a lot more interesting, particularly in the very successful play that started it all—*Dead White Males*. I'll come back to the play, after a quick look at two essays Williamson published on the issues raised in the play, one in the *Bulletin*, the other in an anthology edited by Peter Coleman called *Double Take*.[3]

In the *Bulletin* essay, Williamson attacks 'postmodern, poststructuralist gurus who hold the reins of power in most of our proliferating communications and cultural studies courses', who believe 'that there is no such thing as objective evidence or objective reality. That there is no such thing as free will or choice'. Mutant spawn of Nietzsche, these postmoderns teach 'that humans are not inherently rational but have a "will to power"' and that we harness the metaphoric imprecision of language to bend the truth in our own, or in our own tribe's best interests. A statement which cannot be squared with Williamson's next, concerning Nietzsche's 'descendant' Foucault: 'On the possibility of free will and choice, Foucault explicitly tells us they are mere illusions'. Do these phantom postmoderns of Williamson's have the ability to do all these pernicious things because they do have free will, because they have rid themselves of the power of ideology, and can exercise a will to power? Or is it that they are blind victims of an ideology: in other words, is Williamson accepting the 'postmodern' account of things to explain postmoderns?

Most of the people usually named as ringleaders of the dreaded 'postmodernism' such as Foucault, Lyotard, Barthes were very concerned about the state of the modern world and about the way its media and institutions worked. They diagnosed, named, explained and combatted the things that to people like Koch are still just paranoid intuitions. The irony is that their own work gets put through the machinery of culture and turned into examples of the kind of process they were concerned about. So perhaps it's understandable that things are now so confused that they are held to be the actual causes of things they were trying to analyse. It's a classic case of 'shoot the messenger'.

Such scruples aside, good dramatist that he is, Williamson tells us what is at stake: the threat is that 'a generation of our students are being trained in a pernicious nihilism. This not only tells them that human choice is an illusion, but that morality itself, like everything else, is just an arbitrary construct of language'. Williamson tells us that students despair of this vision of a 'bleak, amoral battleground of competing interests'. And yet as Williamson has himself conceded, Nietzsche is 'not totally wrong', that even Foucault 'has a point'. So—do we not have an obligation to teach that point, even if it causes distress? If the goal of teaching is to search for truth, then, as Nietzsche taught, we have to face the hard fact that truth may be painful to us. Is Williamson suggesting students *not* be taught about power?

Are we to teach what is or what *ought* to be? How much science, how much religion; how much unpleasant truth; how much propaganda? Not an easy question, and as Williamson rightly perceives, your answer depends not only on what you think people are, and what they ought to be, but on what they *can* be. Throughout this book I've advanced a view based on the idea of the virtual. We cannot know in advance what the potentials of human nature are. We have no reason to proscribe the limits of what artifice human ingenuity may create. Nor can we know if those potentials are an original natural inheritance, or inheritance long ago made over into second nature, by institutions that extend and channel our passions, and so combine and channel what we may become.

Foucault, let's not forget, warned about the dark side of such a project. Far from being an advocate of this kind of institutional reshaping of the passions of the body, he was sceptical about whether the most basic forms of it—the prison, the school, the factory, the asylum—were quite the unalloyed good that their promoters would have us believe. He pointed to the resistance bodies put up to being made productive by such institutions, and asked whether the principles of ordering and ranking on which they are based did not always install a permanent authority over ordinary people's bodies. Foucault offers a sobering corrective to the institutional fantasies of some of Hume's over-eager followers.[4]

For example, rather than sending everyone who commits a violent crime to prison, courts start to accept medical evidence about the state of mind of the defendant. If they decide that person wasn't mentally competent, they are spared prison and sent to the asylum instead. For who is this a good outcome? It's good for psychiatrists. They have whole new areas of authority now, in the courts, and in the asylums. It's not bad for the lawyers, who have whole new areas of legal judgement to argue about. But is it good for the person caught up in the system? Maybe, maybe not. Prison terms are usually fixed terms; some people get caught in the psychiatric system forever. Asylums not only contain the body, many also use stupefying drugs, depriving inmates of mental liberty as well. One might, in the end, still think that criminal psychiatry is a valuable institution. The value of Foucault's histories of such institutions is to enable us to question that value, by showing that they are forms of organised power.

Both a sceptical optimism about further extensions of the institutions more properly of a cultural kind, kept honest by Foucault's relentless questioning of the way kinds of knowledge mesh with kinds of power, seem to me useful intellectual tools here. Such a view inclines me to agree with Williamson in rejecting these evil post-structuralists who think human nature is a blank tape on which ideology records what it wants. What Foucault calls 'resistance', what Deleuze calls 'desire', what de Certeau calls the 'everyday', what Hume calls the 'passions', what I call the 'virtual'; that which exceeds and escapes naming and classifying, ordering and dominating, always seems to be bubbling away in the margins of any theory or regime that thinks it has everything about us all present and correct.

PASSIONS AND INTERESTS

Williamson's postmodernists 'expended a lot of energy attaining academic power' through the 'propagation' of this 'nihilistic creed'. I am one of them, apparently. For in the same paragraph, Williamson writes, 'The methods by which they deride anyone who is not of their faith are much more questionable. Recently, McKenzie Wark, the *Australian*'s cultural studies commentator, declared that Beatrice Faust, Keith Windschuttle and I were "anti-intellectual" for questioning the basic tenets of the ideology'. What I actually said of these three is that they 'refuse to reason. They mock, they assert, they condemn, but they do not think for themselves. They take received ideas from the past on faith and defend them with the tools of reason's enemies: satire, polemic, insinuation'. In short, we both accuse each other of not playing fair. There's no point in pursuing that line of argument—or non-argument—into name calling.

What's more interesting is that Williamson wants to undermine my position by connecting it to the defence of self-interest, while posing as a representative of everybody's interest. I'm happy to admit that I have interests to defend. Is Williamson? He nowhere speaks of his own interests. In his *Double Take* essay he does say that if he accepted postmodern ideas, he could not continue to write the way he does, that characterisation would no longer work. Williamson's interest in postmodernism being wrong is that it removes a challenge to the aesthetic of his own work. If the aesthetic judgements about his work start to be made on new principles, the work may not stand up. So while Williamson wants to oppose postmodernism on universal moral grounds, he lets slip an interest of his own. Which is no crime. We all have them. Interests: rational expressions of the passions as shaped by particular institutions, regardless of whether the institution in question is criminal psychiatry, the academy, or the theatre.

It's in my interests to try to write books that say something new. My academic readership wants either new research or new concepts. I don't particularly care if that limits the sales of my work. My reputation rests, in part, on novelty, and being paid as a (tenured) teacher cushions the risk. What I might dream in my wildest dreams is that I might write something that changes the way cultural studies is done, and thus be assured a place in the endless series of changes to the way it is done that will constitute its literature, long after I'm gone. In short, one of the strategies the present institutional arrangements incline an ambitious young academic towards is modernity.

Williamson writes in such a way that appeals to conventional taste. It's a reasonable choice for a writer who needs to fill theatres and sell film rights. Too much novelty of form is bad for business. But Williamson, in his wildest dreams, dreams as all writers do—of immortality. To achieve it, *Dead White Males* covers its bets each way with an admixture of classicism. It seeks out eternal forms, verities and values. But no matter how he tries to hedge it, it's a long shot, as it is for any artist. The appeal to conventional taste may sell it now, but date it. Try reading *Don's Party* now as anything but a very funny and finely turned period piece. On the other hand, betting on classicism is a risk because each age has its own idea of good form.

It's not hard to fathom why people who have an institution that requires and rewards their loyalty may be sympathetic to institutional theories of creation, while authors who must get by in the marketplace by branding their own name on their goods are not. If we want to talk about interests, I suggest that both Wark and Williamson have interests, but different ones. I suggest also that in saying this, I present a more honest attempt at understanding than does Williamson, if no less speculative.

THE STORYTELLER

Williamson once defined himself as 'storyteller to his tribe'.[5] Four things need to be spelled out a bit for that expression to mean much. We need to know who the 'tribe' is, what stories Williamson contributes to its sense of identity, what form those stories take, and what makes Williamson an authority to these people. That's a job for a cultural historian, but I'll venture a few guesses, as I want to move on and ask a wider question.

I think I belong to that tribe, or that I used to. I've seen many of his plays on stage, and all of the films. In the audience, particularly at the plays, I see people like me—urban, educated, vaguely left of centre. As for what stories bind such a tribe, high on the list would be memories of the 'days of wine and Whitlam'. But also stories that expose the machinery of power, and how passions contend with each other within institutions, like Williamson's *The Club*. It's no secret that Williamson's male characters are usually better drawn than his women. He brought the working man of the 'legends of the bush' back to town for good, and gave him an education, while allowing his basic larrikinism to persist as some loud show of resistance to becoming too middle class at heart. That these stories took the form of theatre, then film, is perhaps an accident of history. A space where a flow of ideas met a potential audience looking for images against which to define itself—and a flow of public subsidy. Williamson's *legitimacy* as a storyteller is the most interesting part. To his audience, Williamson is perhaps the writer who best expresses the conflicts experienced by the tribe. To his rivals and contemporaries, what matters is the boldness with which he broke from his radical theatre roots in Melbourne and embarked on a popular and professional art. It's a break he has justified and apologised for ever since.

It's tempting to put Williamson's dilemma in the structural boxes of Melbourne as opposed to Sydney culture. He starts his career within the embrace of Melbourne's ideological assertiveness, but ends up justifying his commercial success with the Sydney notion of art as something distinct from mere moralism. This is pretty much what happens to the Melbourne playwright and his publisher wife who move to sin city in Williamson's *Emerald City*. The film version has the particular merit of proposing a version of the Sydney versus Melbourne opposition that rings true for Williamson's own generation: that the difference is between self-conscious, self-lacerating self-indulgence in Melbourne, and the Sydney kind which was more of the order of unconscious, self-serving self-abuse.

If Williamson's tribe is an educated and urban one, then his legitimacy rests in part on his claim not just to present the conflicts of the tribe, but to be able to point towards principles for resolution—if not to the big picture questions, at least to the small ones. In particular the conflicting aspirations of middle class men and women, in love, lust, work and domesticity. It rests also on defending the claim to this legitimacy against rival storytellers—and kinds of storytelling. In his essays around *Dead White Males*, what is striking is the way Williamson reaches for sources of intellectual legitimacy to oppose to the rival authority of the humanities academy. He chooses all of the things he suspects it represses or denigrates, but that still have value to the tribe: the authority of science, literature, and liberal humanism. The difficulty is making these things stick together.

DARWIN'S DANGEROUS IDEA

Williamson offers great slabs of paraphrases from the biological sciences in both the *Bulletin* and *Double Take* essays, all of it very interesting. He seems to be an enthusiast for the popular literature on what the distinguished specialist on the social life of insects E. O. Wilson called 'sociobiology'.[6] I think he rather overstates the case for what scraps of evidence from the sciences can prove, namely that the 'humanistic position was right after all'. It would be just too convenient for the things Williamson thinks the contemporary humanities exclude to work as evidence for each other, and against the humanities.

It's true enough that the humanities tend to ignore work in the biological sciences that takes up what the director of the Centre for Cognitive Studies at Tufts University, Daniel C. Dennett, calls 'Darwin's dangerous idea'.[7] By that, he means the idea of evolution, particularly in the form in which it is understood by the great majority of biological scientists today. One half of this is Darwin's idea of natural selection: the pressure of the environment on both competing species and competing individuals within a species which, over time, selects the fittest among them, resulting in the passing on to their offspring of those traits that have the most survival value. To Darwin's idea biologists add Mendel's discovery of genes as the mechanism of transmission. The form of an individual member of the species is an expression of the way information stored in the genes has been transcribed and turned into the complicated assembly of matter that is the organism.

What is so brilliant about this idea is that while scientists argue about the details of it, most are agreed that it holds together the fundamental findings from the fossil record and from observation of living organisms, from studies of populations and from studies of cellular biology. What is so dangerous about this idea is firstly that it can be turned into a dogma for authorising particularly vile and nasty politics. The 'social Darwinism' of the nineteenth century held that the 'survival of the fittest' applies directly to people. The rich and powerful are rich and powerful because they are fitter members of the species. Giving aid and welfare to the poor or the weak is not only contrary to nature, it might even be harmful, artificially raising them up from the bottom where competition has rightly cast them. In the twentieth century, this doctrine acquired a racist cast. Throughout its sordid history, social Darwinism collapses the artifice of institutions into nature, thereby legitimising the current form of them as necessary. Entitlement gained within those institutions is also given a gloss of inevitability. Williamson seems to me a bit cavalier in his dismissal of the problems of this kind of thinking.[8]

Darwinism is dangerous for Dennett for another reason. Earlier, I described the revolution in life sciences that flowed from the discovery, in the South Pacific, of many new kinds of plant and animal, and the overturning of the old Platonist idea that there is an *ideal* form for each species, and that all species together form an immutable order of being, designed by God. What took its place was the notion that one goes looking for *typical* examples of a species, and by defining the characteristics of each species, one can arrange them in categories.

It's a big step forward—trying to discover the categories nature puts living things in, rather than imposing it from a fanciful idea of the pure forms designed by God. But two things separate the life sciences of the eighteenth-century enlightenment from us in the present, living after the acceptance of Darwin's dangerous idea. The first is that to the enlightenment mind, a species was something immutable, unchanging. The second is that the idea still lingered of an ideal form or essence that was imperfectly expressed in any individual member of a species. Just as a classical Greek statue was understood as a pure form of the human body, to which no actual body measured up, it was assumed there was a pure form for every species, of which any example was always a sort of flawed copy. Like Joseph Banks sailing on the *Endeavour*, Charles Darwin sailing on the *Beagle* brought back from the world's antipodes fresh data for the imperial archive of the natural sciences. Data which challenged the way the archive was ordered and sorted, and which eventually put paid to both these 'ideas'.

Darwin showed how species evolved. The species alive now have not been alive for all time. Species die out and species change and differentiate. He hastened the abandonment of the idea of an ideal form or essence for each species. Rather, we can think of a species as the sum of all the variations on its genetic design that exist, together with all the latent possibilities not presently expressed in a given individual, but stored as a genetic possibility. What this means is that God finally makes his exit from the life sciences. We no longer need him to explain who designed all those remarkable plants and animals. The design results from the struggle within a given environment. What Williamson doesn't quite realise is that humanism also makes its exit. There isn't an ideal form of any species—including humans. There is no human nature of which we are all expressions. Humans are a *population* of organisms like any other, and that population expresses part of the range of potential forms that lurk in the virtual domain of genetic possibility.

Williamson toys with the idea, not only that there is an essentially human nature, but that there are essentially different male and female human natures. To do this, sociobiologists use Darwin's dangerous idea in a dangerous way, by making a bit of plausible yet spurious reasoning. Start with an idea about male and female nature: women nurture; men compete. Claim it is universal. Therefore, if people all over the world do things this way, it must be natural, not merely cultural. Create an explanation for its evolutionary advantage. Men's disposition to be competitive arises from the competition to fuck women and pass on genes. Only successful competitors get to fuck, and their genes are passed on, rather than wimp genes. Women's disposition to be nurturing arises from being the one left with the baby while the men are off fighting and fucking. Only babies carefully nurtured survive, so the genes of nurturing women get passed on rather than those of slack mums who lack a 'maternal instinct'.

The first thing to remember is that this is not science. It's a thought exercise. It might even be an hypothesis, if only there were a reliable way of testing it. But there are difficulties at every step. We can't discount the possibility that there is a cultural factor in men's competitiveness and women's nurturing. Even if these were universal characteristics, that doesn't automatically make it a dead cert that the reason is genetic. It probably just made good sense in the past for men to stick to the running about killing things job, and women to the hanging about the place looking after things job, because the running about is hard to do while very pregnant. No particular gene speaking there. Just humans in widely different circumstances hitting on the same way of instituting things.

The place where human nature resides in this explanation is the genes themselves. The argument runs the risk of attributing to them a will and a purpose that even such a fantastically intricate bit of biology cannot have. God has been smuggled back in to the details, in the form of an ideal form or essence that supposedly permeates all of human genes, or in this case, distinguishes male from female human genes. Rather than seeing men and women as variable populations, each is reduced to an ideal. Here the circular reasoning commences: why do men and women behave the way they do? It's natural, it's in the genes. What is this human nature, encoded in the genes? The ways that men and women behave. It's a short step from there to the argument that how it *is* is the only way it *can* be, and hence the way it *ought* to be. Men are rapists; women are sooks—it's just nature.

Because of such hasty conclusions, many people reject sociobiology, and turn their backs on Darwin and the biological sciences. This is unfortunate, because I think a more thorough understanding of Darwin can cut through these kinds of social Darwinist misunderstandings. The trouble stems from taking existing ideas about the social order and looking for a quick way to prop them up with a bit of the authority of science. Both fans of the free market economy, and people like Williamson who are fans of altruistic and ethical social life, go looking for biological rationales for human behaviour—even though in the end they cancel each other out. Competition can be rationalised as having survival value, but so too can cooperation.

It seems to me that the most one can say at present about the biological basis of 'human nature' is, in Daniel Dennett's words: 'Whereas animals are rigidly controlled by their biology, human behaviour is *largely* determined by culture, a *largely* autonomous system of symbols and values, growing from a biological base, but growing indefinitely away from it. *Able to overpower or escape* biological constraints in most regards, cultures can vary from one another enough so that important portions of variance are thereby explained . . .'.[9]

POSTMODERN DARWINISM

Williamson wants to set up a strong opposition between postmodernists in the humanities who reject any kind of biological determinism because they want to think of human nature as infinitely malleable, and biologists who have proven that the humanist understanding of human nature is really true after all.

Unfortunately, real postmodernists and real Darwinians don't quite line up so neatly. What's distinctive about postmodern feminism, if there is such a thing, is its diversity.

In her recent work, feminist philosopher Elizabeth Grosz takes up these questions by exploring the notions of mind and body. In Williamson's arguments, the alternatives are that the mind is determined by culture, or the mind is determined by nature. Grosz is critical of such a view, in which 'biology is somehow regarded as the subject minus culture, as if this could result in anything but an abstraction or bare universal category'.[10]

Grosz thinks that a more subtle view of culture and nature has first to encompass a more subtle view of the relationship of mind to body. Her own image for this relation is the Möbius strip, a continuum in which body inflects mind, and mind inflects body. The challenge is to create a valid continuum also in our knowledges of mind and body, rather than reducing one to the other: culture to nature, mind to body—or vice versa. Both bodies and minds have sexual differences, but no area of knowledge working on its own can account for how this is, let alone determine whether this is the only way things can be or ought to be. As Grosz laconically puts it: 'the scope and limit of the body's pliability is not yet adequately understood'.

While postmodern feminists such as Grosz are examining neurological and biological science, Darwinians have begun asking questions about the independent role played by culture in the fitness, or otherwise, of human societies. Richard Dawkins started it with a very suggestive idea that if the whole point of nature was that organisms exist to transmit their genes, then perhaps the whole point of culture is that its institutions exist to transmit their 'memes'. Dawkins gives as examples of memes 'tunes, ideas, catch-phrases, clothes fashions, ways of making pots or building arches'—in other words, the subject matter of cultural studies.[11] These reproduce themselves by leaping from mind to mind, not unlike a virus leaping from body to body.

Some arresting ideas pop out of this notion of the meme. If one looks at culture from the meme's point of view, then we can come up with a theory of why some cultural forms seem to persist and some don't. While it would be nice to think that culture stays with us because it is good for us, it seems more plausible to argue that culture stays with us when it does little or no harm. Harmful memes are likely to have a short life, killing off their 'hosts'—that is, people who believe in them. Harmless ones might float around for ages. Particularly if they are ideas that are good at coopting the passions of their host towards replicating the meme.

Religious ideas seem to have this quality. If a person catches the viral meme of religion, the first thing it seems to do is make that person into a preserver and transmitter of that religion. Memes might work in combination. The 'education' meme produces people with minds fitted for colonisation by still other memes, ones that require the environment of the educated mind to propagate. The 'great books' meme helps Shakespeare hop from mind to mind, generation to generation, and vice versa, each helping the other. Memes might repel other memes—the beliefs that afflict Christopher Koch seem to prevent him *understanding*, let alone accepting, dangerous new ideas.

A few things follow from this point of view. One is that, as Dennett says, 'the "independent" mind struggling to protect itself from alien and dangerous memes is a myth'. But also: 'no one meme rules anybody; what makes a person the person he or she is are the coalition of memes that govern'. Far from being a support for Williamson's 'liberal humanism', this extension of Darwinian thinking into the realm of culture is quite the opposite. It's a species of the 'anti-humanism' not unlike those of the detested postmodernists.

Anti-humanism here means opposition to the idea that there is an ideal or essential form of humanity from which everything flows or ought to flow. Darwinian thought is anti-humanist in several respects. It insists that humans are animals, not angels. It denies that there is an essence to any species, including humans. It insists all the same that there are as yet unknown biological bases and parameters upon which culture builds. It denies that individual humans are entirely the authors of themselves.

Memes are not like genes. Genetic inheritance is a slow-moving process. One only inherits attributes from one's parents, not from other members of the species who happen to be around at the same time. The effect of natural selection on the shaping of the virtual pool of genes is very slow. Memes are different. They can jump from one body to another, along whatever vectors of communication are available. They can change and blend and mutate very quickly. Perhaps most important in the present context; memes don't require the existence of sexual difference. Humans come in two sexes, so one of the mechanisms through which evolution works is sexual selection. It matters who breeds with whom, as each member of the next generation inherits characteristics from its parents. It's a messy and complicated way for nature to work, but it makes for an amazing amount of variety, keeping a virtual domain of differences alive from generation to generation, each of which expresses in the way they turn out some small fraction of the possible diversity of the whole species.

But memes don't replicate that way. They work through signs and symbols—through culture. As more and more institutions 'evolve' for making memes, as the vectors of communication along which they can travel and 'infect' people proliferate, it comes as no surprise that people experience a bit of an overload. The memes at work in most people's heads encourage some degree of resistance to being displaced by new ones. But if there are more and more varied memes in circulation because there are more and more vectors for them to travel along, it seems to follow that people would experience a tension between the memes they hold in their head and the new ones looking for a way to get in and displace the old ones. It also seems likely that since memes don't require gender difference to organise their propagation, that many memes will circulate that challenge institutions built on gender difference. There will likely be competition between memes that want to organise bodies in space in gendered patterns, as that is the means through which they propagate, and memes that organise bodies in space according to other dispositions.

HUMEAN NATURE

All this is, of course, just a metaphor, a way of speculating on the patterns in culture by seeing them from one point of view. What's interesting is that while some postmodern feminism is heading towards an encounter with evolutionary biology, the latter is also heading towards an encounter with postmodern cultural theory. There is a striking parallel, and some interesting differences, between Dawkins' idea of a meme, Foucault's idea about the circulation of what he called 'statements', or Lyotard's idea about the language game of 'phrases'.[12] The difficulty at present lies in keeping separate the speculative dimension of such thinking from the temptation to ground it in the *authority* of science or obtuse language of the humanities.

The popular theatre, the life sciences, the humanities—all such institutions have their ways of channelling the passions, creating feelings of corporate interest, asserting an authority over other institutions. That is exactly what is going on in the confrontation between Williamson and the postmodernists, or between sociobiology and the humanities and social sciences that leading sociobiology ideologues want to annex. Such confrontations are a good thing; a lively interaction between different kinds of knowledge enriches the virtual republic. But it is dangerous when one or other institution is able to translate its perspective into a political program that speaks not only to what 'human nature' might be, but which pronounces on what it can and ought to be. So perhaps what we need is a working understanding of the object of common study and thought that doesn't decide everything in advance by eliminating the other side's story about it. Neither nature nor nurture, biology nor culture, genes nor memes—not human nature but a 'Humean' nature. I'll explain why I think the leading figure of the Scottish enlightenment can help us here.

Williamson likes to think he stands for 'the Enlightenment belief that we inhabit an objective and knowable world'. For Immanuel Kant, the first project of the enlightenment was quite the opposite—it was to define the *limits* of what reason can reason about.[13] David Hume also thought otherwise. Like most of the enlightenment he rejected the boundless rationalism of the seventhth century.[14] He saw reason as always existing with an admixture of the passions, of human vanity and interest.

As for 'human nature', Hume observed how widely varied were the determinations of what part of human makeup was nature's doing, and what part culture's. He did not oppose one to the other, but saw cultural institutions as a kind of second nature, extending human qualities in particular directions. Not that people might be raised up into something closer to perfection, closer to God. Rather, merely so that their passions might be made productive, useful to themselves and others. 'And tho' we must endeavour to render all our principles as universal as possible . . . 'tis still certain we cannot go beyond experience; and any hypothesis, that presents to discover the ultimate original qualities of human nature, ought at first to be rejected as presumptuous and chimerical.'

Hume thought there were good reasons to direct our minds elsewhere. 'Those who resolve the sense of morals into original instincts of the human mind, may defend the cause of virtue with sufficient authority; but want the advantage, which those possess, who account for that sense by an extensive sympathy with mankind.' The advantage, namely, that if justice is our second nature, produced out of a capacity of human nature, but not necessarily determined by it, then one can have some confidence also in people's capacity as makers of second nature, as makers of the self. Hume frees us from the depressing prospect of original sin, or the secularised, Hobbesian notion of a human nature necessarily violent and competitive, or the Freudian notion of an ever present unconscious structure of raging id.

Hume does this without making the opposite assumption, that of an angelic human nature of sweetness and light, needing only the removal of the bonds of the evil state or of Reich's imposed 'structures' of character. He does it without assuming much at all, other than that what one can experience of human nature are *examples* of its capacities, made over into second nature. At the same time, human nature probably has other potential capacities and qualities; we cannot yet know what they are. We have evidence all around us that whatever that nature originally was, it is something made and made over again by second nature, by the artifice of institutions. I would add, now also by third nature, by the pervasive vectors of the media—revealing new potentials, good and bad, of what humans can make of themselves.

TREATIES AND TRIBES

Returning to Williamson's *Bulletin* essay: 'The likelihood that we are . . . preprogrammed to put our own interests above others is attested by thousands of years of literature and by the abject failure of Marxism to put into effect its cultural prescriptions of selflessness'. I quite agree about the failure of the Stalinist project to create 'Soviet Man', but then I was always on the side of the Mensheviks. As to whether it is 'preprogrammed', I don't see what this adds to the eighteenth-century scepticism about human improvement. It just seems to raise fresh difficulties. In the first place, if academic postmoderns are power hungry little nihilists running on the latest version of Microsoft Will-To-Power for Windows, why are they trying to social engineer culture to aid the *oppressed*? That doesn't seem to make sense. Surely they would suck up to more powerful people, do what Marxists used to accuse the church of doing, and latter day revolutionaries accuse academics today of doing—peddling opium for the masses on behalf of the *ruling* classes?

More challenging to Williamson's species of biological determinism is that if one takes it as far as he does, then it's his position that ends up looking nihilist. 'There is also a strong suspicion', Williamson doesn't say among whom, 'that tribalism is an innate predisposition; and one of the greatest problems the world faces is that what innate moral capacity we do have seems reserved for members of our own tribe and not for the pack of bastards over the hill.' So we might as well give up trying to do anything about it and party down with the bananas while they last.

Williamson's peroration winds us up on a happy note. 'It is my hope that whatever capacity for choice we do have will be strongly exercised over the next 50 years or so, and that we will choose to think of ourselves as one large human tribe fighting an urgent battle to survive on this planet.' At last! A sentiment, which, even if one does not like the figure of speech, we can all agree on. (And note that 'tribe' has emerged here as what it was all along—a figure of speech.) But no, Williamson won't let those postmodern pack of bastards over the hill join the tribe. 'The task . . . is not going to be made any easier by academics who teach their students that each tribe has nothing in common with any other, that there is no common human nature, no universal moral precepts . . .' and so on and so forth.

For people to negotiate a concept of common interest, they not only need to take on faith that there is a common human nature, but that there are also universal moral precepts. This in spite of the fact that just a few paragraphs ago Williamson acknowledges that 'the sanctions against egocentric behaviour and the direction it is allowed to take vary from culture to culture'. And so we get to the real issue. What are the conditions for peace? Williamson sides with those who think that consensus can only be reached on the basis of a universal, and universally accepted, ethical law. Note that Williamson doesn't even begin to say what that might actually be. From Immanuel

Kant to John Rawls and Jürgen Habermas, there have been many attempts to thrash it out.[15] They are not usually based on pop evolutionary thinking, not least because no matter how interesting, the actual results of experiments that might support such a theory are hardly conclusive.

The alternative is to insist that negotiation has to accept cultural differences as they are. Refusing to accept universal moral precepts does not mean rejecting the possibility of ethical judgement. As I have already argued, a notion of judgement might be more useful than a notion of moral law.

So in the end, apart from vilifying postmodernists, what has Williamson added to the debate? Has he actually advanced our thinking about what universal moral precepts might be, or how to get other people to accept them, or about deciding which of the many different 'tribes' of the world gets to decide? How would we decide *who decides* what is a universal moral precept? It could only be by imposing an arbitrary one to begin with, or by a process of negotiation that acknowledges differences. So we would have to start out postmodernists to get to being universalists. But then if that preliminary negotiation that respects difference actually works, then the requirement for a universal principle does not hold.

In any case, we see in Williamson's few bare sentences about universal reason precisely what the danger is in such a notion. It is always founded on something being excluded. Here, the exclusion starts with what is nearest, with a rival theory. How will such an intolerant practice fare once it gets out among the far more diverse 'tribes' of the world?

DEAD WHITE MALES

Writing a preview for the *Sydney Morning Herald*, Andrew Riemer calls the play 'unsubtle but effective'. He notes that 'Williamson has always chafed against the abuse of power and privilege—it's just that, in the past 25 years or so, the location of power and privilege has shifted on the political and cultural spectrum.'[16] Riemer admits the play 'runs the risk of reducing complex issues to cartoon captions'. He points out that even Williamson's very telling and effective artistic renderings of misogyny, particularly in *The Club*, are always organised *against* something. The exception is *Brilliant Lies*, a play which, like

David Mamet's *Oleana*, manages to create a complex space of miscommunication and deceit.

Likewise, for Robert Macklin, *Dead White Males* is more black and white Williamson. Its issue is simple: 'shall we celebrate the atavism that travels under the euphemism of "patriarchy" in the play; or shall we make a better world in which the pluralism that travels under the pejorative "multi-culturalism" in the play becomes a part of our normal, unexceptional and even pleasurable way of life?'.[17] Perhaps we need to get out of these 'either/or' propositions of the stage drama, and piece together a more subtle view, composed more according to the principle of 'this-and-that'.

Williamson, like many professional writers, is hostile to the view that the reader makes the meaning of the text. According to Brian Kiernan's biography, when Williamson attended the reading of the script with the actors for the Sydney Theatre Company production, directed by Wayne Harrison, he brought with him 'a dozen very closely-typed pages on the background to the ideological issues of the play', and lectured the cast on the right line before the reading began. 'Williamson asked if there were any questions. One was that, if poststructuralists claim that readers bring the meaning to the text, does that mean audiences construct the meaning of plays they are watch-ing—while I'm out there acting my heart out? Well . . . yes, it would seem to follow if you accepted that premise. A beaming Wayne Harrison thanked him for the "tutorial" and the reading began.'[18]

A few things stick out as odd about this scene. If the writer constructs the meaning of the text, why do the cast need to be lectured? Surely the meaning of the play is clear, in and of itself. It doesn't seem as if the cast are to have any interpretive role in relation to the text, as far as Williamson is concerned. He tells them what it means, they do it. And yet one of the things Williamson is so passionate about is that free will, and hence free interpretation, is a core part of human nature, perhaps even innate. Why does the cast, and through the cast the audience, have to be *told* they are free? Williamson's lecture to the cast sounds curiously like the lecture to the audience by Dr Swain, which occurs early on in the play. Swain argues that what we think is the effect of ideological programming. Not a view Williamson readily accepts. What Swain and William-son, the evil postmodernist and the unreconstructed 'liberal humanist', share is an anxiety about their audience, about how they are read.

So let's read Williamson from a few different seats in the theatre, and see how the various memes that teem within its text and performance might meet, mix and mingle with a few of the people who caught the show.

AFTER THE SHOW

Characters

Don HENDERSON: a former school teacher and gardening enthusiast, now running a chain of nurseries specialising in native flora

Harry BLOOM: an ageing English lit. scholar, of a conservative bent

Michelle FOUCAULT: Bloom's daughter, a grad. student in cultural studies

Julie KRISTEVA: Don's second wife, an equal opportunity commissioner for the state government

Setting

The dialogue takes place in the home of Don and Julie in the Sydney suburb of Balmain. The lounge room is spacious, with formerly trendy decor, now looking a bit dated. The walls are hung with old Sydney Theatre Company posters, nicely framed. Large, ceiling-high bookshelves line the room, stacked with books.

HENDERSON: So what did you think?

BLOOM: Well, it certainly took the piss out of postmodernism, but apart from that, it was pretty banal.

FOUCAULT: How can you say it took the piss? As a satire, the Swain character was pretty silly. The only thing convincing about him wasn't anything he said, but his pathetic attempts to get laid. I thought the younger characters were what saved it.

KRISTEVA: Angela was just a foil for the competing father-figures. She goes from Swain to Shakespeare to her father, as if all that defined her was her relations to men.

FOUCAULT: She's a lot more interesting than that. And there's three student characters, don't forget. There's Steve, who's like a lost ocker from one of those old plays of his. Steve's just a bit dim and doesn't get it. There's Melissa, who's the pretty one, who keeps trying to instruct Angela in how to manage herself as a woman, in relation to men. Then there's Angela, who's the real hero of the play. It's about her discovering how to use texts to reflect on herself and remake herself. She takes Swain's lecture and uses it to read Shakespeare, and she takes them both and uses them to read her father, and so on. She becomes a critical reader, because that's what the institution is training her to do.

HENDERSON: There's a simpler and much more scientific theory of what's going on. These are all young adults, sizing each other up as potential mates. Swain is attracted to Melissa's looks and Angela's brains, and tries it on with both of them. That's natural. Men are programmed genetically to go after anything in skirts. Steve is just a few quality chromosomes short of a gene pool.

KRISTEVA: You can't really believe that's all there is to it. If that were so, why would Angela and Melissa behave so differently? Melissa doesn't question the patriarchy, because she benefits from the attention she gets on account of her looks.

FOUCAULT: But as Sharon Stone says, 'you can only fuck your way to the middle'. Bloom, you're the professor, why don't you throw your weight around on this, or can't you compete with Alpha-male Don?

BLOOM: I just don't think it's a work that merits the attention. All bad art is sincere. This play is no exception.

FOUCAULT: You don't think it achieves some kind of irony by appropriating a postmodern device to use against the postmodernists?

HENDERSON: What on *earth* are you talking about?

FOUCAULT: I could have asked you the same thing, with all that mumbo jumbo about gene pools. Everyone has their pet jargon. But in this case it's really quite simple. Appropriating from other works in such an obvious way, as a 'quotation', is a classic pomo device.

HENDERSON: You mean pinching a bit of Shakespeare.

BLOOM: Yes, yes. But rather than absorbing and overcoming postmodern literature, not to mention Shakespeare, Williamson displays all the classic symptoms of *anxiety* over his influences.

He doesn't succeed in breaking with them. Take as an example, Swain shooting Shakespeare right at the start. The author has displaced that onto Angela's rather vivid imagination, but I rather think that Swain is, in this instance, Williamson himself, attempting to blow away the competition he knows he can't live up to.

KRISTEVA: I must say I find it puzzling that Williamson is so dead against the public subsidy and teaching of 'minority' works of art, when he has been such a beneficiary of precisely such a notion. Quite substantial amounts of public money went into subsidising the theatres where his works played, into films he scripted, and at least once directly to the man himself. He gets on his high horse about the need to protect Australian culture against the Yanks, on the grounds that Australians need to have their own stories, so they know who they are. If so, surely the same principle applies to women's culture, or black culture. It's the same difference.

BLOOM: You have to remember that like me, Williamson is getting on a bit, and can't play the young Turk forever—if I'm allowed to say 'young Turk' without offending Turks, or young people.

FOUCAULT: Ow, cut it out dad . . .

BLOOM: I think Williamson wants to earn some small measure of classical status. All writers desire immortality. Only few of them crawl out from under the shadows of the great works, even when they are alive.

FOUCAULT: You think the canon of Great Books stabilises over time, but surely Williamson is evidence of something else. He seems to want to arrest critical taste at a point which might value his own works for posterity. If you bet on classicism, there's nothing worse than having a bunch of avant-garde critics come along and change the protocols according to which works of art are judged.

HENDERSON: Surely the Great Books are the ones that express the biologically based truths of human nature.

KRISTEVA: And what might those be, in the case of this play? That men hunt and women gather? Melissa seems to be the one who does the hunting.

HENDERSON: It's not that simple.

KRISTEVA: Isn't it? Nobody is denying that there's a biological basis to the way people behave. But it's drawing a bloody long bow to think that you can explain particular kinds of behaviour as a direct expression of 'human nature', and even more ludicrous to use it as a standard for judging art, or writing it. Williamson's been trying to put this biology guff into his plays for years, and it never quite works. It makes him a lesser artist, trafficking in everyday clichés, rather than as someone who sees a new way of thinking. It makes him a Vita Sackville-West with a dick, and certainly a lesser man than Virginia Woolf.

HENDERSON: Who are they?

KRISTEVA: Fuck, Don! You prattle on about the biology of gender as if you know it all, but you don't even know the names, let alone the work, of major women writers.

BLOOM: Sackville-West is hardly a major writer. But I take your point about Woolf. Woolf didn't evade the canonic works, except perhaps Joyce. What mars Sackville-West's work is dogmatic adherence to the dogmas of eugenics, an ugly intellectual forerunner of this sociobiology crap that so fascinates Williamson. Perhaps the problem with Williamson is that if he seriously wanted to write a major work along the lines of biology is destiny, it would require a very close reading of Darwin.

FOUCAULT: I think it's ironic that I'm the one who's thinking this, but can't we get back to talking about the *play*. I'm tired of hearing about it as if it were just a prop for some ideology—even Williamson's own. Surely it's also a drama about how characters negotiate a situation. I'm curious about the way Melissa, who has no problem with patriarchy or its ideology, ends up pretending to agree with Swain, and letting him flirt with her, to get good marks.

KRISTEVA: Isn't that typical of the kind of situation women find themselves in? She's clearly positioned herself as the object, of men's attention, of men's desire. Her desire is to be desired, and to see herself reflected back in the man's desire for her. Steve doesn't know how to appear as the master signifier who can fulfil the lack she experiences as herself. But Swain does. The irony is that while Swain thinks he can appear as the master of the signifier, and compel her to experience the lack in herself, and to desire him as the desire that fulfils her desire, she is really only bunging it on. Femininity as masquerade. She has to appear as his object of desire, and she does, and she speaks the lines he gives her, but she experiences herself as divided, as a result.

HENDERSON: What the bloody hell does that mean? Look, it's obvious. Swain has the hots for her.

BLOOM: That sounds like a convincing ideology, but it's hardly an interesting basis for making art. Williamson seems to want to believe at one and the same time in biological determinism, and in a sort of vaguely humanist free will. So he goes looking for some slender evidence that free will is biologically determined.

HENDERSON: Well, it is.

FOUCAULT: How can what is basically a category out of Christian religion be something biologically determined? Seems to me that's taking already existing ideas from very different discourses and using them as props for each other. Where does that get us? Language is just a virus, as William Burroughs says . . .

HENDERSON: I thought that was Richard Dawkins? How strange . . .

KRISTEVA: Who would like coffee?

CURTAIN CLOSES *as they argue into the night* . . .

8

The fall of the magic kingdom

Perhaps all of us need a Moscow—or a New York,
a Rome, or a Paris—to dream about without
risking the danger that we might one day see those
magical places with our own eyes and encounter a
sad, pedestrian reality.

Andrew Riemer

I have come almost to love this monstrous world.

Aleksandr Solzhenitsyn

CONFESSIONS OF A TEENAGE COMMUNIST

By the phone in the party room was a rusty red coin tin and
a little sign, lovingly hand painted by a certain well known
professional sign writer of the Marxist persuasion. The sign
featured a stylised black outline of an ear, and a reminder that
YOU NEVER KNOW WHO'S LISTENING. Communists
tend to be a little paranoid.

Just after I was made branch secretary—a largely symbolic
post created to give me something to do—I performed my first
properly branch-secretarial task. I was to 'lead the discussion'
at the branch meeting on the Soviet invasion of Afghanistan.
Having gathered all the fresh headlines, heard the background
briefing on the radio, studied the latest *Tribune*, I was ready. I
launched my own tremulous attack on the Soviet Union.

Discussion followed questions, then the motion. The Newcastle and Northern Branch of the Communist Party of Australia condemns the Soviet invasion of Afghanistan. Only a retired signwriter abstained.

That was years ago. It all came back to me in 1996 while watching militias of the Taliban party take Kabul, capital of Afghanistan. News pictures via satellite of gun-toting cadres and lynched televisions, hung from trees. The Taliban don't like the media, a western infidelity. The image reminds me of some powerful and ambiguous lines I remember from an essay of Mudrooroo's: 'We are dominated by our TV sets, by our consumerism and are doomed to eat and shit out image after image in that present cutting into the future. Lost, we have only our minds to recast a past, rerun a videotape and watch as we edit its contents until we shiver with the ecstasy of always living a lie'.[1]

It's a common enough feeling, this sensation that all these images and stories somehow lack something essential. From this can flow one of two things. A rejection of all *doxa*, of received ideas, opinion, the endless burble of orthodoxies and hetero-doxies, challenging and contending, the search instead for the one true image, the one that really stands for all that lies beyond . . . Or alternatively, a sceptical acceptance of what it means to live in the city of images, within which one does one's best to contribute to the common understanding of public things.

It's a common enough experience of modern life to feel alienated from what is said in it, in the city, or in the media. From this estrangement form two key ways of living and learning modern life: in the school of the master thinkers and in the forum of the sceptical citizens. The Taliban are 'master thinkers', but they are not the first, and nor is it only some strange perversion of the exotic, despotic 'east'.[2] In 'volume one' of the 'Great Books of the West', Plato offers his own solution for the plural mess of the city, to settle conclusively which stories are true and which are false, and which tellers of tales are good, and which are bad.[3] Plato banished the poets; the Taliban—television.

But here I am, watching a TV picture that proposes that Afghanis no longer have pictures. The Taliban came down from their schools and formed themselves into a party, and made some changes to bring Afghanistan into line with their image of how it ought to be. Perhaps a party, whether it be of citizen sceptics or true believers, only has power when it is 'in the know', when people can only get information, and get it right, through its proper channel. Who needs a branch meeting when satellite vectors bypass the party line? The idea of the party is a creature of second nature, of the organisation of bodies in space, and the passing on of information, neighbourhood by neighbourhood. Who needs a party for that when the news is on TV? I'm not a member of anything anymore. The party is over.

TV pictures of rusty old Stalin Mk III tanks and another civil war in Afghanistan: I wonder what the American state department's best and brightest think now of all the money they spent, destabilising that poor little land-locked country? All that effort, only to see it fall into the hands of a faction answerable neither to Washington nor Moscow, perhaps not even to Islamabad, but with a hotline to God. That sceptical citizen David Hume taught that in politics, whenever a master plan purports to guide action, watch out for unintended consequences. The civil wars, lawlessness, terror, fascism, corruption, crime and incipient fascism across the whole sphere of influence of the former Soviet Union are consequences flowing from the much cheered end of the cold war.

Sometimes I miss the cold war. If one could entertain, just for a moment, the mindset of the nuclear fantasy, it lent even the most everyday things a perishing kind of glamour. I remember . . . Down in Sydney for a party meeting, hearing the news of the Soviet invasion of Afghanistan, while standing by Circular Quay on a diamond day when the light seemed impossibly bright, thinking: this mailbox, that kiosk, this beam in my eye, might all vaporise, instantly, here at ground zero. I don't think I'm the only one who has mad flashes of nostalgia for the cold war's crystalline kind of clarity. But I wouldn't wish it back, not for an instant.

THE GHOST OF MANNING CLARK

Media memories concatenate: it all came back to me while Afghanistan and Manning Clark shared space in the papers, like old ghosts from the past pressing like nightmares on the minds of the living. On Saturday 24 August 1996, the Brisbane

Courier Mail beat up a bit of Les Murray's table talk, a woolly-headed yarn about Clark wearing an Order of Lenin medal to dinner. That Clark might wear a Lenin *badge* to dinner strikes me as in character. I never met him, but people speak of a larrikin streak. That this badge might be the Order of Lenin is of course completely absurd. The *Courier Mail's* judgement against Clark had the same nightmare logic as the Athenian's judgement against Socrates: he does not respect our Gods, therefore he must worship someone else's. Excluded from thought is the possibility that he might think something else again.

Perhaps realising that printing the medal story was a piece of irresponsible character assassination, the *Courier Mail* did its best to confuse the issue by also calling Clark an 'agent of influence' for the Soviet Union. This is a bit of paranoid spy jargon from the height of the cold war. ASIO diverted resources from the serious business of chasing real Soviet agents in Australia in order to subject Australian writers and thinkers to the most tedious type of bureaucratic scrutiny. As a democracy, Australians were not to be trusted to think for themselves until the master thinkers of the secret police had vetted who was to do the public thinking for us.

The *Courier Mail's* 'agent of influence' slander is as silly as the medal slander, but not quite as easy to refute. Both got what they deserved from the *Sydney Morning Herald* the following Monday, under the front page heading: **SPYING CLAIMS AGAINST MANNING CLARK 'DISGUSTING'**. The ABC's media commentator Stuart Littlemore also condemned the story to a merciless death by sarcasm.[4] The *Australian* embarrassed itself with equivocation: 'the medallion at the heart of the controversy over whether Australia's most famous historian, the late Professor Manning Clark, worked for the Soviet Union, cannot be found'.[5] That line does not lead; it misleads.

Given that both the *Courier Mail* and the *Australian* are papers owned by the News Ltd companies of Rupert Murdoch, it was certainly a setback for the theory that there is no harm in that very talented media entrepreneur owning 70 per cent of Australian newspapers as measured by circulation. It seemed uncannily close to a situation where, if *Pravda* has airbrushed some apostate out of history, then *Isvestia* will do the same, and the victim will henceforth become a non-person.

I don't really miss the cold war, but clearly some people do. Needing some polar axis to cling to, in needing to believe someone is still listening, old cold warriors crank up the old drill of the 'present danger'. Only the Reds aren't lining up on the other side any more. So ghostly images of them have to be conjured out of half remembered 'security assessments'. As if the gossip, rumour and spite that ASIO chiselled out of its stoolies is somehow the last word on anyone's intellectual worth. And what does it say about writers, academics and intellectuals that ASIO did *not* consider to be 'agents of influence'? That they were of no influence, and of no consequence. Clark was not a cold warrior, but only in a mind that receives its pictures of the world in black and white rather than full colour does that necessarily make him a Communist. To have stood outside both schools of cold war groupthink in his own most singular way was one of Clark's achievements.

Why does the ghost of Manning Clark still dance about in the cerebellum of the cold war thought commandos? That they can't let him die in peace, that they keep calling him back to the present, is testimony in itself to his 'influence'—on them. Some say Clark's six volume *History of Australia* is an epic work, a song of flawed heroes and histrionic folly.[6] But what the repeated attacks on the memory of Clark prove, if nothing else, is that Clark is a flawed hero in another, larger, epic. His spirit still flows in that larger, broader, shallower channel of the Australian media's song of antipodean culture. During the cold war, Clark appeared a man of the past; now the cold war has passed, Clark is a man of the future.

THE RED TIDE

Whether 'communism' distorted the vision of Manning Clark is an obscure issue. One thing that is clear is that it has distorted the vision of Robert Manne. Manne's attack on Clark's memory in the *Australian's Review of Books* is carefully disguised as a defence of some kind of reasonable middle ground.[7] One could say of Robert Manne what Manning Clark said of another Melbourne conservative, Peter Ryan—'a shrewd judge of how to ride a wave'.[8]

Manne is still inside the tube of the fantasy that Stalinists and cold warriors shared. The mutually assured fantasy that the fate of the world hung between them—this was their guilty little secret. While it would be a long search to find a Stalinist of any consequence still holding up the red antipode in this story, there are still plenty of cold warriors holding up the blue end for the free world. The problem is that without any reds with whom to indulge this fantasy any further, the cold warriors paddle about after fresh baddies—'political correctness', 'postmodern scepticism', 'sentimental multiculturalism'—to get the old thrill. Otherwise they might have to face the possibility that the post cold war world just does not need cold war warriors. We're making ploughshares now.

There is no Communist Party of Australia any more. The party I joined in the late 1970s was the one that broke with Moscow in 1968, when Russian tanks put an abrupt end to the Czechoslovakian experiment in 'socialism with a human face'. Without a Moscow or a Beijing to look to for guidance, all kinds of intellectual currents passed through the party bookshops and on from hand to hand.

The three main genealogies of anti-Stalinist thought that mattered traced their roots back to one time and a place: St Petersburg, 1917—the moment of the Russian Revolution. There were those who thought it was a bad thing because it was too radical. There were those who thought it was a bad thing because it wasn't radical enough. There were those who thought it was a good thing turned bad when Stalin and his henchmen took the helm. The first is good old middle of the road, muddle through social democracy. The second is what was known at the time as 'western Marxism'. The third was the various sects and factions formed to carry on the legacy of Stalin's early victims, in particular Leon Trotsky.[9]

As for social democracy, there wasn't much to think about, but a lot to do. Of the Trotskyites, communists used to say, 'two Trotskyists, three factions'. They were prone to splitting into little sects, like most serious-minded protestants. Still, the more intellectually serious 'Trots' authored more and more damning and refined theories about the Soviet regime that weaned western leftists away from Stalinism in all its guises. Until one day, an even more radical apostate forged these 'critiques' into an intellectual hand grenade. Now, out of shock and embarrassment, nobody speaks his name . . .

Eventually, the intellectual and the practical within the Communist Party would break away from each other, but in the 1970s there still seemed to be reasons for the party to exist. The main reason was that the Labor Party, elected in

1972, self-destructed by 1975. It was, and remains, part of popular leftist folklore that the CIA was behind the fall of Whitlam, but even if one believed such a fantasy, it didn't make the hurt of Labor's loss feel any better.[10] Strange to say, the Howard coalition government's performance since its election in 1996 has made me nostalgic about the coalition government Malcolm Fraser subsequently led from 1975 until 1983. There was always a certain dignity about the man, and in his commitment to Australian multiculturalism—principle. But at the time it didn't appear quite so jolly, not with the 'razor gang' making cuts to people's entitlements, all in the name of budget cutting, but aimed at Labor's traditional constituencies.

My modest contribution as a party activist was in the campaign against the imposition of fees for tertiary education—a policy the next Labor government would succeed in implementing where the Liberals so miserably failed. I remember acting in an even more minor capacity for other issues of the early 1980s. Besides **EDUCATION CUTS DON'T HEAL**, we chanted to **FREE EAST TIMOR** from Indonesian colonialism and **FREE NELSON MANDELA** from his South African jail, and for **ROCK AGAINST RACISM**. Mainly, there was the peace movement. **WE DON'T NEED NO FASCIST GROOVE THANG**, as the song of the time said. These were the days when Ronald Reagan and Margaret Thatcher wanted to put first strike weapons in Europe and arm the skies with 'Star Wars' satellite weapons; popular opposition to this thermo-nuclear chastisement was intense.[11]

The funny thing is, I'm not really a political person at all. I've seen real operators up close—the hard man of the Liberals in student union politics was for a time Peter Costello, who went on to become Treasurer in the Howard government. I have too much respect for the real thing ever to pretend to be 'political', and I have very little patience with academics who think that whatever it is they happen to write about is 'political'. Politics means immersing oneself in the turbulent time of events and working to affect their course by working with, and working on, other people. When Bugs Bunny persuades Elmer Fudd into changing his hunting policy by declaring it to be duck season, not rabbit season—now that's politics. So it seemed to me once upon a time. I saw cartoons on television in the afternoon, then watched the police duck-hunt demonstrators against the war in Vietnam, against the Spring-bok tour, against bulldozing the bush. Excellent lessons for the latent sceptic in the politics of folly and the folly of politics.

The Communist Party was also good training. I still know how to run *efficient* meetings. As for kowtowing to Moscow or Beijing—that was somebody else's fantasy. In the oral history of the party I absorbed, the heroes were people expelled or repelled by the party in 1956, for opposing the invasion of Hungary, like Bernard Smith. Or a character like the Push regular Jim Staples, who quietly printed copies of Krushchev's 'secret speech' about Stalin's crimes and slipped them into the party paper *Tribune*.[12] All of which may seem a bit unorthodox, but then they were unorthodox times. Times in which the thread of the cold war fable was already unravelling from both ends. Even the older comrades, like the signwriter, who couldn't quite bring themselves to renounce their old love for Moscow, preserved it as a bittersweet nostalgia for a love betrayed.

No-one I ever came across in the party spoke at all fondly of Manning Clark. Of the many things that comrades put in my hands to read, even on Australian history, his books were not among them.[13] It's hard to think of him as a 'fellow traveller' when he was always wandering off on his own. As Humphrey McQueen puts it in a defence of his old teacher, 'the progress of pilgrims appealed more to Clark than that of industry'.[14] It is only after the Soviet Union's collapse that it's possible to appreciate Clark's peregrinations around the problem of belief.

HIGH NOON

'One of these things is not like the other ones', as they say on *Sesame Street*. Robert Manne thinks that 'from a human point of view, 1917 was more easily linked with 1933 than with 1789', that is, with the Nazi seizure of power rather than the French Revolution. For the cold warriors, both Lenin and Hitler founded totalitarian states that developed into something more than common or garden variety tyrannies. They planned and executed a new type of industrialised mass control over the whole space of social life that could perpetually crush internal opposition. This theory always appeared to be more right than left, but all the same I think it is more right than wrong.

What was wrong, then and now, with this cold war theory of totalitarianism is that it does not go far enough. As André Glucksmann writes, it 'shows a tiresome tendency to boil down always to a critique of totalitarianism *elsewhere* . . . Totalitarianism means the others'.[15] It's a fantasy where *all* the bad things can be pushed to the other end of the polar opposition. But 'there is no point in running off to the antipodes to sniff exotic events', says Glucksmann. Empires closer to home, including the British and the American, used the same techniques of Panoptic power, vectoral power, and at times plain terror that together make totalitarianism so total. As Glucksmann says, 'The massacre of the New World began with its discovery, as is testified by Montaigne, an already horrified witness'. The words 'terror' and 'territory' have the same root, meaning roughly the line drawn in the sand at which point strangers are to be scared off. What all empires have in common is that they reserve the right to draw that line wherever they choose.

The only way terror and violence in Europe, east or west, can be made somehow more significant than terror and violence in Africa, Asia, Australia and the Americas is either by insisting that there are differences in quality, quantity, or through plain racism. It's true enough there are differences in the mix of technique. The Polish journalist Ryszard Kapuściński makes a great joke out of the sheer quantity of barbed wire that the Soviet Union coiled around all its labour camps, military zones, its borders both internal and external. No wonder 'one can buy neither a hoe nor a hammer, never mind a knife or a spoon'.[16] By contrast, the British or American form of total power rests more on the vectoral, on the ability to dispatch the gunboats or the bombers. Over the years, improvements in technique made terror and violence possible with greater scale, speed and efficiency. There are improvements along all three axes between the British bombing of Iraq in the 1930s and the American bombing sixty years later. There are great differences in the size of the populations marked out for forced labour, forced removal, or extermination. But it seems monstrous to make a moral distinction somewhere along that gradient and award ourselves the white hat. The cold warriors were right—the west is best. But their defence rests in the end on moral relativism.

For Glucksmann, the master thinkers are at work anywhere an elite decides it must wield power on behalf of a people, and in the name of a people, so that the people might be free. Looking across the territory it has at its disposal, the master thinker sees only a mess of artifice, where there should be the clear outline of the pure and the true. Being in possession of the knowledge of the pure and the true, the master thinker sets about implementing it. Territory becomes a theatre of operations for a plan. Plans work best on a 'greenfields' site, where people relinquish any claim to know or govern themselves. What the master thinker desires is *terra nullius*, and there are more or less easy ways to obtain it: gunboats, gulags, or as general Curtis Lemay said of Vietnam, 'bomb them back into the stone age'. So this is the plan: Eradicate doubt. Mobilise knowledge. Educate elites. Raze territories. Pacify populations. Persuade the people that the destruction of their way of life will set them free. Persuade them that it is better than the alternative, and that it is the *only* alternative: the absolute state or the absolute market.

An objection at this point might be that clearly a place like postwar Australia was objectively a more free country than, say, postwar Czechoslovakia. Glucksmann's response is to insist that the same techniques of power pervade the modern world. What varies are the institutional possibilities of opposing it, such as 'the very concrete possibilities of communicating one's opinion, of going on strike, of demonstrating, of examining the records of the powerful, of stopping a colonial or imperial war, or of preventing its secret commencement. No general staff granted these liberties: here and there they were seized'.

But Glucksmann does not argue this in order to award the white hat to the peoples of the free world rather than its states. The point of his rephrasing of the theory of totalitarianism is to argue that the imaginary polarisation of the good and true versus the evil and false is actually part of the problem. Hence the cold war mentality is *itself* an instance of incipient totalitarianism. Whereas if one takes account of this complexity, this plurality of power, 'it becomes impossible to imagine a single, ultimate revolution, wherein good and bad face each other in a decisive battle'. Or ultimate counter-revolution, for that matter.

The fantasy of the showdown at the OK Corral between the black hats and the white hats expresses the fantasy of the master thinkers. It's a step towards totalitarianism. If the bad guys have gunslingers, then we better get some too. Bring on

The Magnificent Seven. Or perhaps an old warrior like John Wayne in *The Searchers.* He must not only hunt down the Indian chief who stole and defiled our woman, he has to kill the woman for becoming an Indian. Compare the best westerns, those of John Ford, to the best Russian films, such as those of Sergei Eisenstein, and you see that they are part of the same genre.[17] Like Wagner's operas, they are the political unconscious of empire. So too are the Hollywood action and horror movies of today. It's hard to tell whether film makers are borrowing plots from old cold warriors or vice versa. In both it's the same bad guys, from Islamic fundamentalists to the psychic powers of television, only Hollywood plays with people's fear with a lot more irony, as it knows that people play with Hollywood's images with make-believe fear.

There is a pessimism in Glucksmann that reminds me of John Anderson. Both see the messy, plural nature of social conflict as a defence against tyranny, as a sort of mutual deterrence in which each institution holds the other in check. Personally I prefer to let a little virtual light into such a dismal room. There is a certain irony about the way institutions work. Even an institution created long ago, as a way of productively channelling certain conflicts long forgotten, can have quite another life. The English common law, for example, from which come the Mabo and Wik decisions that recognised 'native title' to land. It's better to be Eddie Mabo and have institutional spaces within which to negotiate for one's liberty, than to be Ivan Denisovitch and have only the tiniest cracks of everyday life.

I mention all this because Glucksmann, like Manning Clark, was a person who wound up on some weird diagonal to the antipodes of the cold war. An ultra-leftist troublemaker in the grand French style, Glucksmann spent the 1960s and early 1970s idolising Mao Zedong and third world guerrilla movements—exactly the kind of romantic radicalism that Robert Manne once so accurately criticised.[18] But Glucksmann seemed to swing hard right out of repugnance for what he read in Solzhenitsyn's prison essay concerning what went on behind all that Soviet-made barbed wire.[19] And so he wrote *The Master Thinkers,* from which I have been quoting. It's the essay that made him a poisonous apostate to the left, and no more digestible to the right. It made him, instead, a media star. I first read about him in *Time* magazine.

Many on the left tried to limit the charges against Stalinism to Stalin himself, or to some sort of 'bureaucratic deformation' of the socialist project. What made Hannah Arendt's essays on totalitarianism matter was that they brooked no such equivocation.[20] Both 1917 and 1933 mark the beginnings of regimes that mobilised people against 'enemies', that seized power in the name of the people only to subordinate the people to power. The public life that for Arendt guards against tyranny was squashed flat by force of arms. Everyone agrees about Berlin in 1933, but many on the left stubbornly held on to a fantasy about 1917, often simply *because* the right insisted that Stalinism had its roots there and then, in the storming of the Winter Palace, the original Communist coup. Everyone needs a story, about a place and a time, through which to make sense of the seemingly senseless events of this place, this time.

What made Glucksmann interesting is his radical rewriting of this virtual geography of the western political imagination. He agreed with the right about 1917, and went one better and extended the critique of totalitarian power to Paris, 1879—to the glorious liberal revolution, and beyond. To him it didn't matter whether the slogan was **LIBERTY, EQUALITY AND FRATERNITY**, or **LAND, BREAD AND PEACE**, or **REICH, VOLK, FÜHRER**, we are talking about moments when the 'master thinkers' stop writing books about remaking the world and start writing on the world to remake it along the lines of their books. Whether it's the Kristallnacht or the Gulag, the Terror or the Taliban, the parties of the master thinkers 'collected author's royalties from their subjects, paid in human flesh', Glucksmann says.

It doesn't matter, in the end, if the book was any good. Literary criticism is beside the point here.[21] Hitler's *Mein Kampf*, and Lenin's *What is to be Done?*, were meant not for citizens to read and debate but for subjects to read and obey. They are not to be studied, but *implemented*. Jean-Jacques Rousseau once noted the paradox: the new book of the law announces itself in the name of the people, but the people did not write it, they read in it of the freedom that will be granted them, in their own name.[22] Meanwhile the Jacobins built their state and their power with Rousseau in their pockets. Perhaps we can all be thankful that it was such a confused and confusing blueprint.

Was the English-speaking world ever all that different, with

216

its bibles and battleships? Sure, there is progress. From gaining power over poor countries by blasting them from gunboats, to gaining power over poor countries by lending them money. Once the colonies got divisions of redcoats and instruction in the Great Works of English literature. Now it's epigones of Adam Smith and bankers in a uniform of grey. The English had their own species of master thinkers. That incorrigible radical William Hazlitt, in an essay on Bentham, observed that he 'turns wooden utensils on a lathe for exercise, and fancies he can turn men in the same manner'.[23] These days, the lathe would be automated—programmed in Indiana, but turning in Indonesia.

This is Glucksmann's provocation: to think of the machinery of instrumental power without restricting oneself to previous centuries, as Michel Foucault had done, or restricting one's criticism of it to the east, as the cold warriors did and still do. Rather, to cut into the appearances of the world another way. If you go down to the woods today, beware of a nasty surprise. You may find some people organised around the desire to make the world over according to their image of it. Folks who divide the world into good and bad, where the bad is to be confronted and the true order built on its ashes. You have found the total idea of power. With any luck, you found them in some backwood. If you are unlucky—you found Tudjman or Milosovic, and their teddy bear's picnic is running the joint.

THE TRUE UNBELIEVER

Manning Clark wanted to believe in that final, decisive battle, that judgement day, but couldn't. It's the spectre haunting his work. Glucksmann wanted to escape from that spectre, and thought he had at least traced it to its intellectual source: the party of the master thinkers in all their forms and guises. For Glucksmann their prototype is Plato and his airbrushed portrait of Socrates. Plato makes doubt merely the clearing of the throat before the unfolding of an ideal order. Freed from doubt, with the weapon of certainty in their hands, the party of the master thinkers will seek other weapons, until they have the power to expel the false and the bad from the world and make it over in its true image. Glucksmann was not the first to offer this pessimistic critique of the roots of the fantasy of power in the thought of the west, but he said it loudest and clearest. He found the one good use for the structure of feeling of intellectual paranoia—exposing the use of paranoia as an instrument of power.

The master thinkers of an age now passing dreamed of the true world of the state. Those of the age to come dream of the true order of the free market. Others, like the Taliban, of orders more divine. In each case, the combination of reason, passion and power works to eliminate the complexity of the world as it appears to us in everyday life. Glucksmann's interests centred on the connection between reason and power, and he proposes a counter-reason. It's no accident that Socrates, the Greek sceptics and Montaigne are cited approvingly. Glucksmann's Socrates is the one the young Kierkegaard found under the Platonic gloss, the Socrates of irony and doubt. Like Ern Malley, this Socrates is a figure who is all the more useful for having never quite existed.

Clark's interests were more to do with the connection between the passions and power, and so he has less to offer by way of another mode of reasoning. Once we take the cold war blinkers off, what we can see through Clark's eyes, when he visited the Soviet Union, are his experiences of what becomes of the structure of feeling when the complexity of culture has been flattened out and subordinated to a grid of power. He also had an image or two in his head of a time and a place where the master thinkers did not rule. But in the main, I think his interest in going to the Soviet Union was to check out a culture which, though very different from Australia, was also trying to consciously remake itself. Clark wanted Australian culture to get out of the structure of feeling of the empire, so I don't think he was ever likely to want to get into another one.

Robert Manne truthfully reports that in *Meeting Soviet Man* Clark 'did not deny the crimes of Stalin'.[24] He might have added, but doesn't, that Clark also mentions the new inequalities, low standard of living, religious persecution. Clark is also alive to the evidence of corruption, bribery, chicanery and greed. Manne has no understanding of Clark's perception of Stalin. Manne is trapped in the cold war battle plan—Clark was not. Clark seems only half persuaded by 'a case for Stalin as a 20th century version of the Grand Inquisitor, as a man who believed that the Revolution could only be preserved by terrible cruelty, lies and murder . . .'. But above all, Clark takes Carlyle's advice: 'pity them all'.[25] If Carlyle could pity Robespierre, and from that starting point begin to learn from contemplating him, then what might one begin to learn about Stalin if one could get that close to him? For what is Stalin if not Robespierre plus the telegraph, Bentham with barbed wire? Clark doesn't really attempt it. Stalin is a figure for another storyteller, perhaps for a time not yet come. But already he is indicating a path beyond the way of writing about Stalin of the cold warriors. They think that having arrived at the right moral fable in relation to his crimes they have ended the conversation, but they have not even begun to tell the story.

'Nothing inhuman is alien to me', Glucksmann quips, inverting a famous line from the Roman writer Terence.[26] In other words, like Clark, like Baudelaire, like the Rolling Stones, Glucksmann had sympathy for the devil. His most stunning declaration of this principle came at the Frankfurt Book Fair in 1989, when he accepted the Frankfurt Peace Prize on behalf of Vaclav Havel.[27] At the time, Havel was still a Czech writer and dissident. He was not yet the first president of a new Czech republic. The Berlin Wall still stood. 'Hitler c'est moi!' Glucksmann declared, to this crowd of German booksellers. Their reaction is not recorded.

What Glucksmann, whose parents were both Jewish, and both worked in the underground against the Nazis, meant by that remark is that one has to recognise one's own capacity for becoming a monster. It is not enough to point to the monster and say: 'Look! Monster!' after the fact. Clark wrote in his Russia book that Australians had 'stopped taking Soviet Man seriously'—and hence had lost their ability to understand the Soviet Union. Clark, unlike Manne, puts the faculty of understanding ahead of that of judging. Clark wasn't afraid to go meet the monster, in Russia, or in himself. Nor was he afraid of what others might say about him as a consequence.

One thing I find curiously revealing about the cold war mentality is how often it is assumed that Stalinism is seductive, attractive, something to stay away from lest one give in to the siren song. But attractive to whom? To cold warriors more than to people like Clark. To intellectuals like Glucksmann who had fantasies of power, but unlike him have not confronted them fully. What cold warriors and Communists had in common was a bent for intellectual certainty in the service of power. No wonder so many cold warriors in the west were former Communists, gone over to the 'other side', where you could get cocktails with the head of security and a better rate of pay. Clark found no home in the Soviet Union for people like himself, spiritual exiles who 'felt strangers in this world'. He was contemptuous of all that. Clark gets closer to Soviet culture that he might get to love it less; closer so that it might further estrange him from his own culture, so that he might return and explore it with fresh eyes.

'Why did Lenin—a man who seems to have been Christlike, at least in his compassion—have to die, and this other one take over from him?' Humphrey McQueen explains away this notorious line of Clark's, perhaps just a little too well. Clark was clearly fascinated by the image of Lenin, which when Clark was in Russia would have been emblazoned across surfaces great and small, like a Communist saint. Clark seems to me fascinated by his own fascination with this image and its story. To my knowledge neither Clark's defenders nor denigrators have ventured to read it in terms of what it might say of Clark's feelings for Jesus, rather than his feelings for Lenin. Jesus was an ambiguous figure for Clark, particularly the Jesus of: 'I come not to bring peace but the sword' and 'let the dead bury the dead'. Pasolini gives a riveting portrait of this Jesus in his film *The Gospel According to St Matthew*.[28] The Jesus who had become an emblematic front man for a plan to remake the world, as Dostoyevsky feared. It's interesting how, as the various leftist factions split off from the Stalinist church fathers, they always appealed to the true image of Lenin. A genuflection from which Glucksmann, for all his faults, was free.

MASTER PLANS FOR THE MODERN WORLD

Clark consistently referred to Communists as 'the spiritual popes of the twentieth century'.[29] Hiding in this typically Clarkian term is, I think, a quite particular understanding of the genesis of Soviet ideology. Like so much in Clark, one of the things coursing through it is Dostoyevsky. This time, the Dostoyevsky of the *Writer's Diary*, which Clark read while in Europe in the 1930s.[30]

Dostoyevsky thought that three ideas contended for the leadership of civilisation: the Catholic, the Protestant and the

Slavic. His sympathies, like Solzhenitsyn's, were with the last. He thought that only if Russia's intellectuals were true to the culture of their own people could they form a common bond with them strong enough to forge a force in the world. Only through realising its specific values could Russia join, and perhaps even lead, the civilised world in the quest for peace and universal brotherhood. The striking boldness and confidence of Dostoyevsky's prose when he declaims these sentiments, clearly and directly in the *Diary* more than anywhere else, can be quite affecting. Both the style of thinking and the style of writing clearly made an impression on Clark.

In Clark's use of the term 'spiritual popery' lurks Dostoyevsky. It was not the Slavic idea that won in Russia but what Dostoyevsky thought of as the 'Catholic idea'. Which might at first sight seem like a strange proposition, but I think it is a key, both to how Clark thought of the Soviet Union, and how he later developed the theme of the ideas transplanted to, and contending for, the soul of Australia. France was, for Dostoyevsky, 'the most complete incarnation of the Catholic idea'. Even after the revolution of 1789, France developed her own peculiar socialism, 'the pacification and organisation of human society without Christ and outside of Christ, as Catholicism tried but was unable to organise it in Christ'. Even the slogan **LIBERTY, EQUALITY AND FRATERNITY** is for Dostoyevsky, in 'the actual style and spirit of a pope of the middle ages'. So while French socialism appears on one level to be nothing but the overthrow of the Catholic church, it is also the usurper and conserver of one aspect of its idea. 'For French socialism is nothing other than the compulsory union of humanity, an idea that derived from Ancient Rome and that was subsequently preserved completely in Catholicism.' In other words, Dostoyevsky could smell the master thinkers at work in the various doctrines exported from France since the revolution.

When Lenin enumerates the constituent parts making up Marx's view of the world, he cites three ideas: the German Idealist philosophy that culminates in G. W. F. Hegel, English liberal political economy descended from Adam Smith, and the French utopian socialists. A list to which Lenin could add his own handiwork—the 'democratic centralist' organisation of the party as an elite, in possession of this true synthesis of the knowledge of power, to be wielded in the name of the people, and against them if necessary. This scheme, like Dostoyevsky's, is no doubt quite arbitrary. What is interesting is the positing of a passive people, active elites, and contending master plans for achieving power. What Lenin saw in Marxism was a synthesis of the master plans of the age. Clark does not say so, but by the time he arrived in Russia, the Stalinists had liquidated the political economists and the philosophers within the party—all that was left were its thugs and priests. 'Soviet Man is dedicated to . . . that belief in reason, in progress, in perfection, which Dostoyevsky had predicted would end in murder and degradation.' Clark's views on the Soviet Union are only optimistic when measured against the benchmark Clark himself would have used—Dostoyevsky.

Clark's tour of Moscow and Leningrad convinced him of one thing, at least, that these cities fulfil 'most of what Dostoyevsky had prophesied. The age of the human ant heap has arrived: they have not been able to agree on the distribution of wealth, and have resorted to terror; they have created the life of men without God . . .'. Or rather, the life of people without institutions independent of the state, such as the church, a space of indifference where other things might flourish besides fear and calculation. What marks Clark as clearly not contemporary is his attachment to his sense of loss, not for such institutions, but for some substantive value in which to believe.

THE SOVIET CULTURE INDUSTRY

Meeting Soviet Man is a serious critique of practically every institution for the manufacture and propagation of Soviet culture. Clark framed his tour of Soviet institutions in terms that one would now recognise as modernity—a term which has proved a useful way out of the impasse of cold war rhetorics. As the Soviet Union experiences its forced modernity, 'The world of gadgetry and creature comforts' threatens to erase cultural differences. 'In this brave new world everyone will look at, participate in, big pleasures in a little way—the world of constant titillation.' Clark was deeply worried that this 'technology would make of us all . . . as those men Tocqueville talked of, those men who touch but do not feel'.[31] And so, by way of an experiment: 'I wanted then to find out whether

Soviet Man in this mass environment was any different from mass man in a capitalist environment'.

Manne makes a vain effort to present Clark as yet another muddled leftist seduced by the grand tour of the USSR. But what is striking about Clark's book is that even from such a cursory trip he made some very acute insights. He limits himself to the cultural institutions: 'We had come as a writer's delegation to meet their writers and see their culture'. So that is exactly what he writes about. Clark inquires into what kind of culture such institutions might, or might not, engineer.

Clark finds the flaw in each of the mighty undertakings of the Soviets to fill the void with culture. He sketches a series of distinct cultural institutions in terms of the values they propagate, and what they fail to propagate. Stalinists and anti-Communists alike tended to see all institutions of Soviet society as imbued with the same essence, which was then coloured good or evil according to their chosen moral fable. Clark considers each institution separately, in terms of how its structure of feeling limits its particular functioning.

He wants to hope that cultural institutions might even be a force that could keep alive the positive, 'enlightening' values of the revolution through the dark times of Stalin. Here he thinks like an historian of culture, looking for the distinctive temporality and residual strength of formations from the past. Perhaps he even hoped that cultural institutions might be bases of resistance: the priests against the commandants. He is no doubt aware that this is to make the best case for Soviet culture. What completely eludes Manne is that, even with this concession of treating culture distinctly, making the best case for it, Clark still finds fault with it. What Clark wrote is really an exemplary bit of cultural studies. One that merits rereading now, after the cold war, when it might tell us something about modernity.

BIG PARADES

Those big parades, they scare me—even if it's just old newsreel. Humans machined into perfect shape and good working order, stamped with the outer mark of modernity, ranked and rolling between the tanks and the tractors. Clark was a witness to the big parade for the forty-first anniversary of the October

Revolution. He notes the muted applause for the post Stalin
leadership. He remarks with a heavy irony about a speech by
the Minister of Defence that 'it was a good three quarter time
speech by a coach to a team which, despite great handicaps,
had just taken the lead . . .'.

If Clark believed anything, it is that culture is an intractable, resistant, erratic pulse that can't be made to march in
time. 'Here on this Red square one could only see people who
seemed to believe in getting there, and were proud and confident in their power to do so.' Clark is sceptical about the doxa
of deferral, of the damage it does to one's reflection on the
richness of the present. The massing of bodies, the disciplining
of their movements, the celebration of production quotas. But
you have to give the police their due, Solzhenitsyn says, 'in an
age when public speeches, the plays in our theatres, and
women's fashions all seem to come off the assembly lines,
arrests can be of the most varied kind'.[32] That is the exception
in this relentless form of modernity as calculation, where only
the output matters. The present marching into a future that is
just like the present, only more. To this idea of time as the
march of progress, Clark will sometimes try to juxtapose what
Walter Benjamin called messianic time. 'No one can say what
it will be like when the dead awaken.'

THE ARCHIVE

In Moscow, the Museum of the Revolution causes him to
comment on the airbrushed photos of all the revolutionaries—
'all except the ones dispatched in the purges'. Clark sees this
as a faulty relation to have to the past. 'Here, in fact, is a
people part of whose doxology is the proposition that the past
weighs on the brain of the living, yet who allow only a doctored
version of the past to appear . . .' For Clark, here is the first
lapse from the 'high ideals' of the enlightenment that the party
otherwise claims to uphold. The nightmare of a past *prevented*
from weighing on the minds of the living. Clark will return to
Australia and go on to write a polyphonic history, in which
figures from old photographs strive against each other, making
history discord, but progress by virtue of it.

In the Lenin library, Clark observes all the foreign publications on open display, and concludes that the party operates

on 'the Pauline principle that the strong in faith can handle the arguments of the unbelievers better than the weak'. Such is the optimism of spiritual popery. It expects, merely by the enunciation of its truth, always to prevail. Clark spares us from much of a moral sermon, but in these two anecdotes is a story still worth pondering: a regime that trusts its people so little with their own history but trusts its own trusties so much with news from afar. A cultural machine stripped to a minimum of simple gears, yet supposed to explain a great stream of data. Culture reduced to an operation of the state.

What could explain this? Clark doesn't explain it, but the story still says enough. Only a singular reliance on terror could strip the party of intellectual leadership of the very means with which to lead, yet leave it with the pious belief in its own adequacy to interpret the channels of the world. No wonder that to Clark it is a culture that only appears confident, but with an obvious 'thirst for approval' by outsiders, who come from where all that stuff in the Lenin library comes. I think about this, 40 years later, as I watch a news report whisk across the lone and level sands of global satellite news, reporting on the Lenin library now, its building decaying, its collection dissembling into chaos, its librarians in despair.

HIGH CULTURE

At a performance of *Swan Lake*, he marvels at an apparently confident high culture that does not fear the reaction of 'philistines' to its 'imposing highbrow performances on everyone'. And yet Clark wonders how long a culture can make do with revivals, with 'picking over the creations of the past'. A question for all 'new' cultures: when does an unrenewed past run out?

Clark makes the place of famous Russian authors a touchstone for the breadth of cultural life. Especially Dostoyevsky: 'he had seen himself as a tortured, anguished pilgrim, wanting to believe but finding that the stronger became his desire or his need to believe the more powerful became the arguments for unbelief'. An attitude, incidentally, which was just as much Clark's, and explains his remarks about Stalin. I don't think Clark really even wanted to believe that the revolutionary ends—happiness—justified Stalin's crimes, but the point is his sensitivity to those who could entertain such a fantasy.

Visiting Tolstoy's home, turned into a museum, Clark recites the bog-Marxist explanation for the class basis of what Count Tolstoy wrote, but points out that there isn't in that an answer as to *why* he wrote. 'For without class they become like men suddenly struck blind—they grope.' Even Manne will admit, apropos contemporary Stalinist historian Eric Hobsbawm, that 'Marxism is undeniably a powerful analytical tool'.[33] But neither Manne nor the guide Clark meets at the Tolstoy museum quite grasp the larger question that haunted Clark throughout his life—the problem of the absolute singularity of the artist. 'All historians are parasites feeding on the food of genuine artists.'[34]

The Moscow Art Theatre even made Chekhov into an optimist, which surprised Clark and caused him to reflect. Manne does not quite understand Clark's feelings about the optimism of Soviet culture. He writes that 'Clark experienced everywhere in the Soviet Union great "uplift". In the West one felt nothing but "cynicism, madness and despair"; in the Soviet Union, purpose and optimism, "common faith, common hope". After a visit to the Tolstoy Museum . . . he was finally sure. He knew now he was in a country that was "recapturing its bearing and the ideas of 1917"'. Of course, anyone who knows Clark's writings would know that he was never sure of anything. The enthusiasm passes. The Tolstoy chapter is perhaps the most elusive, and concludes with a long quotation from Lenin, on Tolstoy. I suspect that what Clark responds to here is not a Leninist version of Tolstoy, but the Tolstoyan strain in Lenin. Like those nested Russian dolls, inside Stalinist cultural machinery is Lenin, and inside Lenin—Tolstoy.

There is a solemn side to this story that might make us pause. Now, after the demise of the Soviet system, if there is nothing in Clark's hope that nested in the shell of Soviet Man is a little of Tolstoy; if nothing survived in the institutions, or in the practices of everyday life, if totalitarianism really did work as advertised . . . then the future for Russia is absolutely hopeless. It matters that we entertain the possibility that something survived in those institutions, and that new ones can be made out of the broken shells of the old. If not, then Russia's future is just guns and money.

POPULAR CULTURE

Clark visits a factory club that 'had all the sanctions to enforce conformity'. He discovers that the Soviet answer to the alien-ation experienced by workers whose free time is utterly divorced from their work time is to regiment and organise their free time as well. Clark also sees it at work in the policing of the behaviour of youth subcultures, a Soviet equivalent to the teds, mods and rockers that so exercised the imagination of English cultural studies in the 1960s as well.[35] Clark observed that they were brought into line with a 'boy-scout bourgeois code'.

For Clark the enlightenment meant the rational reform of social conditions, which would remove the forces deforming human culture, and begin its raising up, its perfecting, the release of its potential. What he finds is quite the reverse; human culture rationalised and machined to fit an industrial order that perfects nothing, that releases nothing. That Clark finds optimism in every cultural institution he trips through looks to the cold war mentality to be a propaganda point, but to Clark, it's an indictment. And the premise for one of his great, sly, ironic lines: 'for the lunch, as ever, had been so gargantuan that one felt perhaps a day would come when human beings would not want to hurt each other'.

The irony is telling. Clark reacts strongly against what Theodor Adorno called 'extorted reconciliation'.[36] Having ground everyday life down into fragments, to be organised and reorganised at the will and whim of a mobilised knowledge, modern culture will, when left to its own devices, express frustration, bewilderment, alienation. Unless that culture is organised, not to express experience, but as a representation of the happy ending, as fragmentation reconciled. This is why the surfaces of 'happy-happy, joy-joy' in Soviet life are for Clark in the end so unappealing. It suppresses the virtual multiplicity of culture by administrative order.

RUSSIAN INTELLECTUALS

Given his dismissive views on 'professional Red baiters', it is really no surprise that Clark suspected professional Reds as well. As he wrote elsewhere of the communist journalist Egon Kisch: 'He had a long experience in not telling people in power things they wanted to know'.[37] The intellectual apparatchiks Clark meets are 'men of faith, or seemed to be . . .', and '. . . like all people living in an age of faith they sounded simple, even naive'. Clark is grappling with, but not quite grasping, a problem that exercised those philosophers among his contemporaries who would later be canonised as the beginning of the postmodern turn. What if enlightenment itself became an ideology, a faith? What if reason itself were applied to the practice of repression?

Clark turns back toward faiths he cannot have, looking back from modernity, not without a little nostalgia. But he anticipates another turn, that of postmodern thought, which pits the rationality of enlightened thinking against the institutional products of just such a rationality. The enlightenment as a way of thinking, and a way of life, arose in the first place as institutions and ways of self making that opposed themselves to inherited, unthinking ways, wrapped in the mysticism of church and crown. Continuing in that tradition cannot be like continuing in any other. It is a tradition that can only be inherited by subjecting it to the very same caustic scrutiny that it inflicted on its own past. The enlightenment is confident only in the moment of fresh doubt.

One of the first irksome signs Clark notes in the whole book is a certain overweening confidence of the Soviet structure of feeling. Soviet culture administers itself to stop itself knowing, and in particular to stop knowing what it does not know. Clark could not accept pronouncements against a writer like Pasternak made in the name of the 'Soviet people'.[38] Such edicts he found 'almost as damning of their civilisation as murder, because it uncovered the spiritual blindness, arrogance, obtuseness, in which cruelty, even bestiality, could grow unopposed'. If the party 'insisted on such spiritual popery, then Soviet Russia desperately needed its Martin Luther, the one led astray by private judgement'. Led astray, as Clark always hoped he was.

AUSTRALIAN STORYTELLER

Let me tell you a story. Once upon a time, a king fought a savage battle, and lost his kingdom. The victors made the king stand by the window and watch as they looted everything and took away all that was his. His queen, his throne, his wealth—all passed by him in the triumph. He did not blink or flinch. One by one, everything of value in his kingdom, from the first to the last, passed by. Still he did not blink or flinch. His herds and flocks, his sheets and towels, everything passed by. Still he did not blink or flinch. At last, bringing up the rear, a wrinkled old retainer who had served him for years, shuffled by in the parade. And this is when the former king broke down and wept. What can such a story mean?

Clark's ideas about the stories he wrote have a turbulence about them, as if several currents blew against each other. The sixth and final volume of his *History* winds up with a peroration: 'It is the task of the historian and the myth maker to tell the story of how the world came to be as it is. It is the task of the prophet to tell the story of what might be. The historian presents the choice: history is a book of wisdom for those making the choice'. There's something ambiguous about that. Is the historian also the prophet? Or is the historian presenting the choice to the reader between history and its other? In the end, Clark's reputation will come to rest, not on his facts or his judgements, and certainly not his prophecy, but on his ability to tell a story. The wisdom is not in what Clark thinks it is in, but it is in Clark, nevertheless.

In his essay 'The Storyteller', Walter Benjamin claims that 'the art of storytelling is coming to an end' because 'experience has fallen in value', particularly for the generation who experienced the first war, those damaged, modern souls, for whom 'nothing remained unchanged but the clouds'.[39] And what does Benjamin mean by a story? 'It contains, openly or covertly, something useful.' But it is no longer possible for the storyteller to communicate some practical or ethical wisdom, for experience itself, the medium of the story, is a devalued currency. The 'epic side of truth' is dying out.

The novel contributes to the decline of storytelling, for it is tied too intimately to the form of the book. Unlike the tale, the legend, perhaps even the essay, it has few links to or from oral culture. The storyteller takes from, and contributes back to, speaking and listening, weaving knowledge into everyday life. The novelist is by contrast someone apart from the process. The novel shifts the locus of wisdom from experience to literature. The instrument of the newspaper also devalues storytelling. News is about information that has currency, can be verified, and appears to explain itself—has 'news value'. With news the stories are nearly always the same few simple plots, just with new names and places—the 'information'—filled in. The historians of fact, analysis and judgement also displace the story, by seeking in history the typical and the tendency, and thus eliminating the singular—the very thing upon which the story thrives.

Storytelling is different. Benjamin writes a story from Herodotus—a writer who fascinated both Benjamin and Hannah Arendt as the original ancestor of historical storytelling.[40] The story he chose is the one about the king I just recounted above. Benjamin gives the gloss on it offered by Montaigne, before giving his own explanation. But the point is that the explanations are external to the story. 'The value of information does not survive the moment in which it was new. It lives only at that moment; it has to surrender to it completely and explain itself to it without losing any time. A story is different. It does not expend itself. It preserves and concentrates its strength and is capable of releasing it even after a long time.' Montaigne and Benjamin attempt different explanations for why the king finally broke. I'd like to know how the Queen felt about the whole thing. There is a virtual side to the story, in that a good story can contain all this, and more, waiting for the right time to appear to the storyteller's listeners.

Benjamin was interested in the problem of a writer's relation to the past, and he thought the solution lay in rethinking the role of the storyteller's tales. 'By basing their historical tales on a divine plan—an inscrutable one—they have from the very start lifted the burden of demonstrable explanation from their own shoulders.' There is a place for histories that get the facts right. It is always useful to have information. But Benjamin was interested in using the past another way. Not as something to dig up to find certainty, but as a reservoir of instances of the way people acted in the face of events, particularly those about which they could have no reliable information. How are we to think and act in the *absence* of information? Stories preserve past actions. Not ones that were the same as a present predicament, but ones that are useful because, like our present circumstances, they speak of singular conjunctions.

Both Benjamin and Clark sometimes put their stories up against a messianic time, a time in which all the singular fragments of time might be brought back together, not to extort from them a reconciliation, but so that they illuminate each other in their very singularity. This messianic time is perhaps time's irony. It's a way of telling stories other than in order to prove what happened or to conjecture why. This is not the 'science of history' of which Hume dreamed along with Marx. The purpose of that, even in Hume, was to guide the plans of the master thinkers. As Manne so clearly puts it, that history is a 'powerful analytic tool'. The purpose of the story, on the other hand, is to guide the citizen.

I think both Benjamin and Clark return to the art of the storyteller in their writings. Given how singular both these writers were, where they went from that point could not be more different. But both see the problem of the relation to the past as at once aesthetic and ethical. That is to say, they ask at one and the same time for a proper relation to the past, but one that respects the singularity of the one who asks. Both are impatient with moral fables. Neither bends to conform to anybody's groupthink. But here in Benjamin's words is an epitaph for both of them: 'his gift is the ability to relate his entire life; his distinction, to be able to tell his entire life. The storyteller: he is the man who could let the wick of his entire life be consumed completely by the gentle flame of his story . . . The storyteller is the figure in which the righteous man encounters himself.'

Benjamin himself became one of those ruined fragments of the past blasted by the present, waiting for another time. Clark saw the Nazi terror that consumed Benjamin's life first-hand— he arrived in Berlin the day after Kristallnacht. The extraordinary thing is that unlike Benjamin, Clark had reason to hope, and to write. Or perhaps he was just naive, as Manne claims. But then it was a naivete that saved him, that made him an epic writer. The wisdom of the epic is transmitted by fools who know nothing—but who *know* they know nothing. (Even if, as in Clark's case, they are too vain to admit it.) Only fools have aerials tuned to enough channels at once to avoid flattening time out in a moral fable.

ON THE BEACH

Clark 'has been left behind' writes Bill Cope, summing up the most common objection to Clark from the left. 'There are now

separate histories of Aborigines, women, immigrants and workers, because their experience is different.'[41] But in producing
those separate stories, questions fall by the wayside. How do
separate and singular experiences come into dialogue with each
other, in the living, turbulent time that becomes history, and
how ought they to come together, here and now? This is where
Clark's epic history still has some relevance, as a story of how
differences did meet, so that we may contemplate for ourselves
how they ought to meet.

A certain irony always folds Clark's representations back
over on themselves, so that, when it works, Clark gets close
and yet distances himself, bringing the reader in close and then
pushing the reader away, so that the past becomes not a clear
channel but a self-conscious citation in which voices come to
call past each other—a murmur that might become a virtual
republic, where differences meet, tell their stories, make judgements, and finally, come to act, as a sovereign will. Paul Carter
is close to the mark when he calls this an 'imperial history'.[42]
Clark stages Australia as a modern epic, one that begins with
Aeneas in chains, cast up on Botany Bay. Others, including
Aboriginal people, are drawn into that modernity, into the
whirlwind of it. And yet they struggle to find a place to speak
and act in it.

Conservatives are most vocal in their distaste for what their
heroes become in Clark's ironising hands. On Menzies, for
example, Clark writes that he was a 'magnificent showman'.
'Nature had played a trick on him. He wanted to be number
one, to be first rather than last . . . but chance and circum-
stance have developed in him a taste for inflicting pain on
those with lesser ability.' 'But so clamorous were his passions
for good food, good wine, the approval of the high and mighty
and the honours the British conferred on their gifted loyal
subjects in Australia, that his judgement was warped and his
conscience stifled.' He is of course famously more sympathetic
to Labor heroes: 'if Ben Chifley were God he would forgive
everyone'. And on H. V. Evatt: 'All those who looked to the
day when Australia had overcome the giant of British philistin-
ism, suburban smugness and grovelling to the English welcomed
him as their leader'. These are character sketches like the ones
Plutarch wrote about the 'great' Roman leaders.[43] He also took
sides. It's not hard to see how much conservative harrumphing
about Clark is just jealousy. They wanted their stories told with

some style too. What they got was Geoffrey Blainey's lovingly detailed histories of various mining companies.

The irony of the attacks on Clark by Manne, like those of Peter Ryan and others before him, is that they make Clark himself a character out of one of his own stories. In the attack by his former publisher Ryan, the portrait is fauvist—a riot of colourful extremes.[44] Manne seems to think he can tone Clark down. But they are way behind Clark once again. As he wrote in the conclusion to the final volume of his *History of Australia*, what is distinctive about contemporary Australia is that 'accounts of the past became part of the struggle for power in Australia'. A sure sign of the postmodern turn, when the suspicion spreads beyond a few fey aesthetes that the past and the present are always made together. In the last volume, Clark's style anticipates this, by becoming more self-consciously ironic, staging itself, but knowingly so.

Everyone needs a time and a place as a reference point for living in the modern topsy-turvy. How strange that the place and time that anchors official Australian culture should be a beach in Turkey. For David Williamson, in the film he scripted for Peter Weir, *Gallipoli* is about the everyday practices of mateship, caught up in a global network of vectors, modern and machine-like and relentless, and entirely out of Australian control. For John Anderson, it was on the contrary not a story to tell for the tribe, but one to oppose. Through a renunciation of the mythic power of a founding story, one stays free of the servility implied by the embrace of pointless sacrifice. Clark's view is interesting for what those two polar views lack—irony. 'Australians now had a faith, but what that faith was no one could say.'

When he writes in that mood, Clark is an essayist, and good training in scepticism. Anderson's famous and controversial attack on war memorials was not a broadside on the notion of the institution. On the contrary it was a part of the creation of another one—Andersonianism. I'm not sure he had the wit to see it that way at the time. This is scepticism gone wrong. Anderson casts doubt on a fantasy and an institution, not in the manner of Socrates, but that of Plato—in order to clear away the rubble for another one. Williamson is also caught up in a story about the other. The structural grid he plays on pits British officers against Australian cannon fodder. But this antipodal reading of history turns the facts into 'canon' fodder, to feed a fantasy, rather than unravel the complexities of actions.

Or to give another example of an attempt to redirect the passions connected to an institution, think of Paul Keating's attempt, inspired by Don Watson, to channel the focus from Gallipoli and the first war to the Kokoda Trail and the second. This didn't quite come off, and for a number of reasons. The news images of the Prime Minister, bum up, pucker down, kissing the dirt on the spot where Australian troops stopped the Japanese advance through Papua New Guinea was not the sort of thing that inspires. Questions of whether the surviving locals and their descendants were to get anything for their troubles were too insistent a reminder of Australia's neo-colonial relation with its former protectorate. But perhaps the real problem is that to the extent this image played to an Australian audience, it is the audience that, directly or indirectly, imbibed its Australian history via Clark. An audience trained to take such an image as an expression of national sentiment, but also to take it as cause to distance oneself, just a little, from the whole idea of national sentiment. Still, I don't blame Watson and Keating for trying. Intervening in cultural institutions is always complicated, and plagued by unforeseen outcomes. The real significance of this and other Keating era institutional tinkerings lie not in what the press made of them the next day, but of how they bed down and inflect culture over time. I predict an interesting future for the memory of Paul Keating.

Writing a premature epitaph, Clark concludes: 'In the second half of the twentieth century Australians lived in a country where neither the historians, the prophets, the poets nor the priests had drawn the maps'. Perhaps it's overstating the case to suggest that there are any maps at all, save those drawn by the vectors of movement and media. If there is a criticism one has, in the end, to make of Clark, it is not about his limitations as a storyteller but about his insistence on interpreting the stories as well. What is great about his *Meeting Soviet Man* is that the stories stand a little more naked, a little less in the fashion of the day. In Clark's *History of Australia*, the stories have to be peeled out of their shells.

Still, in this otherwise pretentious, oracular pronouncement, there is something to heed: 'The people broke the Tablets of the Law. The people killed their gods. The people turned to worship the Golden Calf'. It's not so much the loss of old institutions, but the shallowness of the new ones that seems to me cause for concern. One of the last things Clark notes in the history is that on 23 January 1935 a Qantas Empire Airways plane landed at Darwin after a flight of 14 days from Paris. The vectors are closing in. Politicians start addressing the nation via radio, while new cultural trends seep in along new vectors from America. Clark's history stops short of the full integration of Australia into the third nature of global media culture and events. By the time Clark finished it, Clark himself was fully a part of that media landscape.

Clark seems to me to have been aware of himself as a character playing in third nature, where his authority rested on both the past he recounted and his own past, rooted in things that could be made to appear prior to, and untouched by, the flickering image of the Golden Calf show on TV. Clark fashioned *himself* into an institution for the times. He always appeared in costume, from the broad, big buckled belt to the even broader bushman's hat. Looking, for all the world, as if he were waiting to be cast in a musical. I think of Clark and Williamson, receiving honorary doctorates together at the University of Sydney in the Bicentennial year.[45] What might they have said to each other?

Both men have their critics. That's the easy part. The difficult part is in thinking how to continue to create ways of articulating culture and media in Australia, such that there are stories through which a people can know itself, but not believe too much in itself—so that there might be a virtual republic, and not a paranoid and reactive nationalism, quick to exclude, quick to reduce the potentials of cultural difference to the polarities of fear. 'Are we doomed to rely on a humane conservatism?', Clark asks in a letter to Kathleen Fitzpatrick. What is always worth recalling about Clark is that even during the cold war, he could see a play of forces, rather than two opposing sides. He was neither cold warrior nor Communist, true believer nor thorough sceptic, neither Melbourne nor Sydney, always hovering in some indeterminate Canberra of the mind. He is the yardstick against which to measure a writer like Williamson—or Manne—and their freely confessed anxieties.

SATELLITE OF LOVE

'This world-soul, dominating the entire world from horseback'— that's what Hegel called Napoleon, the revolutionary general,

spreading enlightenment across Europe. 'This world-soul, dominating the entire world via comsat' is how I think of Rupert
Murdoch, traversing the globe with satellites—a good step up
in vectoral power from horses. And as Hegel says of Napoleon,
riding by, 'it is impossible not to admire him'. Like Napoleon,
Murdoch rose from relative obscurity and conquered the world
by knowing the lines along which it was available, at that point
in time, to be conquered. Napoleon started out in artillery;
Murdoch, in newspapers. Murdoch kept a bust of Lenin in his
rooms at Oxford.[46] In an earlier time, he might as well have
had a bust of Napoleon, for they were once popular with
bourgeois souls with dreams of power, just as Lenin was to
Murdoch's generation. I wonder someday if young masters will
grow up around busts of that wily Scots-Australian Rupert
Murdoch.

I mention all this because I've just read, on the front page
of the *New York Times*, a headline that runs: **DEAL BY
MURDOCH FOR SATELLITE TV STARTLES INDUSTRY**.[47]
Murdoch's News Corporation intends to do for America what
it did for Asia with Star TV and Europe with Sky TV—beam
on down with a vector from the sky. Like Napoleon, Murdoch
is a man with a plan and a vector, in search of territory. Will
this be his Russian campaign? I sincerely hope not. New vectors
mean new possibilities, new spaces for the virtual. I'd rather
those new spaces were carved out of third nature than out of
the second nature where we all have to live and work. In the
same week, I read a story about a New York based Russian
mobster called Tarzan Fainberg who struck a deal with the old
New York Mafia and Columbian cocaine interests for a plan
that involved buying a submarine from the former Soviet
Union.[48] The story is probably a beat-up, worthy of one of
Murdoch's colourful tabloids. What is interesting is that it is
possible. Is *this* the magic kingdom the cold warriors wanted?

One of the more curious mutations of the cold war fantasy
is the one that makes, not postmodernists or political correctness the bad guy in the black hat, but the media itself. This
seems to be where Robert Manne is concentrating his energies.
I've used Manne as a foil throughout this essay because of the
quality of his writing. It embodies the most extreme modera-
tion, the most aggressive calmness, the most unbounded
restraint. At least until it came time to write about why we
need more censorship of the media.

There are intimations of this in his book about Demidenko. 'Deep in my heart I believed that in a truly civilised culture a book like this would not have been published.' But this is not a civilised culture, but a culture of forgetting, in which 'no utterance seemed impossible'; one that is making Manne feel a 'sense of cultural destabilisation'.[49] It is shortly after this that he embarks on a series of newspaper columns about why Australians need more censorship. A Taliban policy—but a very moderate one.

The old cold war structure of feeling gets a new lease of life. The bad guys in the black hats are evil video nasties. They seduce the minds of the young and the vulnerable—the people who cannot think for themselves. They come from without, from that Kremlin of the image known as Hollywood. What is to be done? A new administrative order, in which people give up *just a little more* of their freedom to the censors, who will vet what is appropriate and not appropriate for Australian public life. And why not? Security officers and customs officers have done such a fine job in the past of protecting poor-bugger-me Australians from such filth as James Joyce's *Ulysses*, there's no reason they can't be trusted with sparing us from thinking about the films of, say, David Cronenberg and Wes Craven.

It's obvious to anyone who grew up on media culture and understands it that the texts most frequently targeted as a threat to 'civility' are those that call into question that very civility. The 'civil' is the culture of the city, in which citizens shout and argue and piss each other off, then have a drink together and forget about it. Crucial to this term ever since Adam Ferguson coined it is the idea of self-government. A civilised culture can stare its own lapses in civility square in the face, and treat them as suitable matters for discussion rather than as suitable cases for treatment, to be walled off out of sight. Civitas means trust one's own judgement and that of others, but keeping always in mind the fallibility of judgement. Those master's apprentice minds who thought they needed to protect us from James Joyce have their parallels today who feel they need to protect us from David Cronenberg, and are just as likely just as wrong. As Tina Turner sings, in *Mad Max III*, 'we don't need another hero' to save us from thinking for ourselves. Rupert Murdoch is not going to come and get us in the dark.

So when someone points to a book like *The Hand That Signed the Paper* or the *Child's Play* movies, and says 'Look!

Monster!', that is an invitation to discuss what the civilised might be, what the monstrous might be—and nothing more. If one really wants to point at monsters, why not choose strong-men like Tudjman or Milosovic, who came to power precisely by saying, 'Look! Monster!'. To the Serbs, the monsters included the Croats, and to the Croats, Serbs. The monsters came to power by getting people to relinquish their autonomy to think and act, and entrusting it to the monsters who would protect them from monsters.

Andrew Riemer put it too strongly and too simply when he accused Robert Manne of 'totalitarianism'.[50] The cold warriors are not monsters. It's a teddy bear's picnic. And yet all they offer is the *same policy* as the monsters. They do not look for the little bit of monster in themselves, and in my book, therefore, they cannot be trusted. Citizens need trust no-one but themselves, acting as citizens. There is no higher authority than one's own fragile powers of feeling and thinking. There is no certainty other than in the distrust of those who hold out certainty on price of relinquishing freedom. Australians are not all doomed, as Clark feared, to a 'humane conservatism'. All that is required is a little acceptance of the happy fact that citizens are condemned to be free.

9

Fair go, Pauline

Our attachment to one division, or to one sect, seems often to derive much of its force from an animosity conceived to an opposite one . . .

Adam Ferguson

No one is free from uttering stupidities. The harm lies in doing it meticulously.

Michel de Montaigne

MATESHIP AND MERITOCRACY

There was something slightly incongruous about a freshly elected Prime Minister John Howard appearing on the TV news in a casual shirt, casual pants and bush hat. Even more odd—he held a stubbie of Victoria Bitter in his hand, high enough so you could see it even in the close-up. While a reporter questioned him, Howard raised the bottle, yes the *bottle*, to his lips for a swig.

Whatever Howard actually said in this interview about renegade Queensland member of parliament Pauline Hanson, and it wasn't much, matters far less than the image. It looked a little too carefully staged to be anything but a pitch for Hanson's 'forgotten people'. Howard posing as a bloke who would give his mates a fair go, in anticipation of the inevitable *60 Minutes* feature on Hanson, in which she looked perfectly

cast as the fish lady from up the street. The show attracted
2.5 million viewers, and was the most watched edition of the
year.[1]

Hanson is no longer just the battling divorcee and fish shop
proprietor, or even just another independent member of parliament. She has become a political and media legend. An AGB
McNair poll claimed 81 per cent awareness of her maiden
speech in parliament. On 10 September 1996 the Independent
member for Oxley stood in the chamber and called for with-
drawal from the United Nations, an end to foreign aid, the
abolition of the Aboriginal and Torres Strait Islander Commission, as well as any welfare benefits that are specifically aimed
at Aboriginal people, compulsory national service, and an end
to immigration. She also called for large scale public works, the
raising of protective tariffs and Australian ownership of key
industries. While John Howard took to dressing down, Hanson
appeared in a neat blue suit and gold brooch, although in her
cover picture for the *Bulletin*, she posed behind a pie and chips
meal—complete with a bottle of Victoria Bitter.[2]

'I consider myself just an ordinary Australian', she said in
her maiden speech, one who 'wants to keep this great country
strong and independent and my greatest desire is to see all
Australians treat each other as equals as we travel together
towards the new century.' This idea of a 'fair go' is supposed
to be the defining idea of a distinctly Australian structure of
feeling. Meanwhile, two competing ideas about what's fair and
who gets a go of it battled it out from one public issue, and
public image, to the next.

The old idea of a fair go comes from what historian Russel
Ward called the 'Australian legend'.[3] Ward thought he saw its
roots in the cooperative cultural practices of bush workmen,
but it is clear that the formulation and presentation of just
such an ethic in a series of media forms, from popular songs
and periodicals, up to and including Ward's book itself, played
a significant role in propagating it. The basis of bush ethics is:
everyone looks out for his mates, and everyone who is a mate
deserves a go. Becoming a mate involves an initiation, proving
that you are 'one of us'—that you share the values of mateship.
It's a mildly levelling ethic, which takes a dim view of inherited
wealth and privilege, sneers at the over-educated and is dis-
respectful of authority—mostly behind its back. It was also an
assimilationist ethos. Writing in the 1950s, Vance Palmer

remarked that 'it cannot be said that before the gold era there was sufficient immigration from countries outside the British Isles to affect the general character of the population. Yet it was greater than is often admitted, and one reason why it attracted so little notice is that the people it brought were so quickly absorbed. This was particularly the case with the small Scandinavian groups that came to the country. The very likeness of their surnames to English ones helped them to become merged into the community. Most of the Hansens, Petersens, Andersens, and Larsens changed the spelling of their names slightly and within a generation became Australian . . .'.[4]

Since the Labor government of Gough Whitlam (1972–1975), Australia charted an unsteady course away from the culture of mateship towards a quite different idea of a fair go—the meritocratic society. If democracy is a way of life in which entitlement is shared equally among the members of the tribes (demes), then meritocracy is one in which merit is its governing principle of allocation. In principle, if not exactly in practice, meritocracy means everyone competes for their fair share, and everyone gets what's coming to them according to supposedly objective measures of performance. Anyone can compete for the glittering prizes, regardless of age, gender, ethnicity or sexual preference. It's a hierarchical ethos, just as opposed to inherited wealth and privilege as mateship, although there the similarity ends. Meritocracy values formal education and honours the authority of high achievers. It is a view of the fair distribution of rewards that is opposed to inherited wealth and privilege, on the grounds, as Chamfort once put it, that 'rank without merit earns deference without respect'.[5]

Equal opportunity law, expanded higher education and multiculturalism were three central planks of the meritocratic society. Anyone should be able to compete for qualifications, compete with those qualifications for work, and earn the right through hard work to enter any area of social life. Yet many Australians harbour suspicions about becoming a society where rewards are handed out purely on the basis of measurable merit. Are the measures of merit really fair? Not everyone feels they can make a claim to entitlement to a fair go in the kinds of language in which such issues are administered and reported. Other doubts go further, and question the whole basis of the meritocratic society. As successful meritocrats scramble aboard that part of the Australian economy that can keep afloat on

THE VIRTUAL REPUBLIC: AERIALS

the new global economic tides, mates find they are no longer reserved a berth at birth.

THE GLASS HOUSE

The master of the prestigious Ormond College at the University of Melbourne makes improper sexual advances to two young women resident at the college, or at least that's what the two women claim. They seek a hearing for their complaint against the master within the college. They take up their complaint within the university. This gets them nowhere. Not finding a remedy within the institution, they go to the police, file a complaint, and take him to court. The novelist and screenwriter Helen Garner wrote a book length essay on this, the 'Ormond College affair', called *The First Stone*. I'd like to consider it in the light of these kinds of scepticism about meritocracy. Most critics took up what it had to say about feminism.[6] That's fair enough, but I don't see why it should only be regarded as speaking to and for and about feminism.

To writers such as Cassandra Pybus and Virginia Trioli, it was only fair and proper that the two women took their complaint against the master to the cops. The master controls the bursary fund at the college on which students such as these depend. He has a professional responsibility towards all the students of the college. To introduce a sexual element in his relations with particular students breaches his responsibilities towards them as part of the college body. How could he allocate resources based solely on criteria of merit if he is involved with any of them on more than a professional level? While it would have been preferable for the college to find a way of settling the complaint internally, failing that, the students were entitled to seek a remedy through other institutions.

I think that's a strong argument. What it doesn't quite solve are the nagging little doubts that Garner raised about how these formal procedures of merit, entitlement and justice actually work out in practice. This is the side of her account which, whatever its flaws, is worth rereading. The rules of meritocratic entitlement are supposed to be applied in a formal way. Like the law, meritocracy is supposed to be 'blind' to any qualities of those it judges, other than according to the criteria before it. The popularity of Garner's book rests, I think, on the glimpse it provides for its readers into the workings of these kinds of procedure. More and more people come up against a vastly expanded world of procedures for measuring merit, from 'performance assessments' to 'benchmarking' to the now seemingly endless credentialing offered by higher education. It is of wider and wider concern that all this dense drift of paperwork is really fair, but it is transparently obvious that it never *quite* works as it ought.

Garner wrote about the singular little details of the interactions between the parties, of how a middle-aged man might react, at a party, to the kind of self-display of a sexually active, attractive and confident young woman. I wouldn't want to exonerate the master. What's more interesting is getting to the little frictions and frissons of everyday life that happen when the grid of meritocracy is superimposed on the flux of everyday interaction. Garner wrote about what practically everyone has experienced—that the singular qualities of people never quite fit in the grid of merit.

It matters that biases in the allocation of entitlement not be systematically skewed. That's why things like equal opportunity law are important. But it matters also that popular scepticism about procedures of a far more subtle kind be frankly acknowledged. Mateship dealt with differences among people on a far more finely grained basis, but was unable to extend itself across a wide range of differences. Meritocracy adopts the acceptance of a wide range of differences as its administrative object, but at the price of dealing with differences, not as singularities, but as types. The expansion of meritocracy in the 1970s and 1980s answered political objections to the pervasiveness of the culture of mateship and its exclusions. I don't think it's terribly surprising that meritocracy also gives rise to resentments, or that these might also take a political form. In the absence of a politics of advancing or refining meritocracy, or even of just acknowledging its imperfections, some of that reaction to it took the form of a sentimental appeal to the days when mateship ruled.

There are two kinds of resentment to meritocracy. One is resentment 'from below', from people who have very little except mateship to protect their interests and identity, and see it slipping away. The other kind of resentment is 'from above', from that most rarefied and least talked about kind of 'mateship' that organised the interests and identities of those who populate the private clubs, the boardrooms, the peak bodies of politics, administration, the professions—and Ormond College. In the long run meritocracy is even more of a threat to the old boys than to blue collar mates.

THE POLITICS OF ENTITLEMENT

The former Rhodes scholar R.J.L. Hawke, known as Bob to his mates, appealed electorally to the culture of mateship, and as Labor Prime Minister (1983–1991), he kept the country on course towards meritocracy. Then Paul Keating, the boy from Bankstown, pure product of NSW Labor's mateship machine, deposed Hawke, assumed the Prime Minister's post, created his own style of appearances, and quickly found himself typecast as a meritocrat. His kitchen cabinet was a meritocrat's wet dream. Figures like the economist Don Russell and historian Don Watson embodied the best and the worst of meritocratic culture: educated, articulate and confident—but also a bit abstract and aloof.

What struck me about meritocracy Keating-style is that it appealed to the aspirations of otherwise disparate wings of the middle class. Meritocracy mixes well with an emerging ethos of the business world, the let 'er rip, no holds barred celebration of competition as the decider of talent and divider of the spoils. It also fits in with Labor's real 'heartland', the white collar public sector who are David Williamson's 'tribe'. Despite their antagonisms towards each other, these meritocratic cultures are in some ways quite complementary. Public sector meritocracy is about getting everyone to the starting gate without a handicap. Welfare, education, equal opportunity and multiculturalism are meant to make the race fair. Private sector meritocracy is about the race results, performance and its rewards.

Meritocracy is not without its faults. It values formal credentials over personal experience. It takes a somewhat abstract view of what counts as valid knowledge. Its 'benchmarks' of what's fair may only appear to be objective. These alone are reasons enough for the persistent half-heard murmur against its principles and practices that punctuate the air like talkback from a badly tuned radio. In the attacks on Asian immigration, on arts funding guidelines, on political correctness, on the intellectual fashions of higher education, on Aboriginal reconciliation, it's a widespread assumption that rather than removing the handicaps suffered by minorities in getting to the starting gate, these policies were putting lead in the saddlebags of a silent majority of mates.

The ugly side of the ethos of mateship is that it is only egalitarian once one has been accepted as 'one of the fellas'. In popular imagination, the culture of early post-war migration was about making migrants into mates—a procedure National Party MP Bob Katter once described as 'dewogging'. On the other hand, more recent migrants are perceived as dangerously enthusiastic about meritocracy, particularly through higher education.

It took the Liberal Party a while to figure out how to capitalise on this discontent and find a leader who could embody it. John Hewson led the party to defeat against Keating in the 1993 election. Once described by David Williamson as the 'plastic Baptist', Hewson embodied the meritocratic ethos a little too fully—his Fightback plan was a classic meritocrat document: abstract, top down, put together by the top specialists using the latest research.[7] Next to that even Paul Keating looked like everybody's mate. Hewson's hapless successor, Alexander Downer, failed because he smacked of old boy privilege, the one thing mates and meritocrats both detest.

It's a tribute to John Howard's political skills that he could tap the resentment and reaction brewing in the land of mateship purely by means of hand signals. But Howard's victory comes at a price—Pauline Hanson. In a fine essay on the prehistory to matey Anglo populism, historian Peter Cochrane says, 'Hanson has sensed a soul mate in the Prime Minister because she sees that he is helping her to mobilise the unwelcome possibilities in people'.[8] Howard's problem is that he profited electorally from what Phillip Adams calls 'the diagonal nod' he allowed himself in the 1996 federal election that encouraged disenfranchised mates to vent their frustrations with meritocracy by supporting the Liberals.[9] That put both major parties in the predicament of having to uphold their commitment to a meritocratic society plugged into a global economy, while casting around for ways of keeping on board sections of the electorate who felt they have more to lose than gain from such a course.

PHRASING RESENTMENT

Meritocracy works, but it doesn't work for everybody. Meritocracy as a pattern of belief only appears legitimate if one expects to get a fair go by it. In the media coverage of the tribulations of meritocracy, issues of race and gender predominate. Feminism and multiculturalism have indeed had some success in becoming part of the administrative language of setting fair rules of merit. What Pauline Hanson articulated is the hidden injuries, not of race and gender, but of class. She articulates those elements of traditional blue collar workers and the self-employed who feel they have lost ground.

According to Queensland historian Ross Fitzgerald, Hanson's Ipswich is a provincial centre suffering from extensive structural unemployment, partly as a result of the decline of the region's two key industries—coal mining and the railways. Ipswich has seen an influx of Aboriginal people and displaced rural folk, coming in from the west in search of jobs or to get closer to services. The federal seat of Oxley, which is centred on Ipswich, was once one of the safest Labor seats in the country. It was held for many years by a former treasurer and leader of the Labor party, Bill Hayden. How could Labor have lost such a prize? It doesn't help that, as Fitzgerald says, the Labor Party in Queensland 'is seen throughout Australia as the epitome of destructive factionalism and irresponsible machine politics'.[10] That is probably more the view from inside the party than inside the electorate, but it does shed light on how the party managed to lose the confidence of its once firm supporters in its ability to deliver, either through the practices of mateship or meritocracy, a fair go.

As Cochrane writes: 'Hanson's potency rests not only on racism but on a powerful sense of cultural loss—of displacement from the centre of things—which has been worked readily into a mythology of victimisation'.[11] Cochrane draws attention to a series of cultural and media milestones leading up to the explosion of Hanson onto the front pages: poet Les Murray's 1976 attack on the 'new ascendancy' in *Quadrant*, historian Geoffrey Blainey's 1984 speech in a Wollongong RSL, and radio host Ron Casey's 1989 *Confessions of a Larrikin*. Of these, Murray's essay is the most interesting, and I'll come back to it.

For Hanson's 'battlers', not only is the meritocratic idea

losing its legitimacy, it is coming to be the very thing to blame. In discarding central planks from the policies of both major parties, populists cast around in the lumber room of political memory for alternatives, and sometimes come up with as odd a laminate as Liberal and Labor legends R. G. Menzies and A. A. Calwell. There is an element of nostalgia for a lost master plan. A common theme is betrayal. Australian elites sold out Australian interests to the 'multinationals'. They take away the entitlements of the circle of mates and flog them off to foreign interests. Meanwhile they let migrants in and give them jobs on the basis of merit that mates are entitled to by birthright. Since this plot involves the steady erosion of institutions that hold a matey social solidarity together in the interests of the market, the lost master plan to which populists appeal usually involves a strengthening of social solidarity through the state. Hence Campbell and Hanson talk freely of public works schemes and conscription—mechanisms by which the state takes over the responsibility of securing the economic conditions for the maintenance of mateship that the market threatens to erode.

In short, expanding market liberalism erodes the social organisations, the unions and communities through which people organise and express their interests and identities. This pushes some of those people who feel most threatened by this to embrace the notion of a strong state that might reverse it.[12] Not a meritocratic state interested in offering fair access to work in the local branch plants of a global economy; probably more of an authoritarian state that restricts entitlement to resources, both cultural and economic, to mates. That the meritocratic society actually works, that it does entitle a wide strata of Australians to economic and cultural participation is I think the reason that populist backlash in Australia has been retarded for so long. Social democrats and genuine conservatives more or less agree that the stability and equity afforded by the institutions of a meritocracy sponsored by government but maintained at arms length is well worth the price. It remains to be seen whether flat earth economic rationalism will cut all of that away, or if wiser heads will prevail.

'She is just plain wrong, and wrong in a way that can lead to great evil.' In saying this of Hanson on *60 Minutes*, Malcolm Fraser, Prime Minister from 1975–1983, provided a timely reminder of how a Liberal statesman is required to behave. But it is not enough. Cochrane is right in saying that 'Her limits only enhance the aura of exclusion on which her appeal is based . . . Her emphasis on exclusion is a cover for a refusal to share, a nostalgia for a culture of the enchanted glass, for a time that was narrow, conformist, exclusive and intolerant—the heyday of the simple white folk. Is that the future we want to go back to?'. The prospect is that until the language of the meritocratic society phrases the fair go in a way that articulates the hopes and fears of its forgotten mates, its legitimacy will continue to weaken.

Jerzy Zubrzycki, author of the groundbreaking 1977 essay 'Towards a Multicultural Society in Australia', goes as far as to ask whether 'the continued use of the term multiculturalism is not a deterrent to the acceptance of an ideology that seeks the pursuit of justice, fairness, civility and decency for all Australians . . .'.[13] Multiculturalism was a brilliant bit of institutional artifice, but one in need of renovation. Not least because in its original formulation, influenced by Zubrzycki and implemented by the Fraser government, it was an essentially conservative doctrine, aimed at preserving viable ethnic communities. Under Labor, multiculturalism edged closer to a complex of institutional arrangements with a basis in ideas about social justice. But in both cases, the complexity of the interactions that might take place between people of widely varying ethnic self-identity, both using and defying multicultural formulations, was not quite yet something that could be foreseen. Multiculturalism sometimes masks a mere biculturalism, in which the fantasy dividing line is Anglo/non-Anglo, and passions are organised at either extreme against the antipode of the other.

VIRTUAL MULTICULTURALISM

When a seemingly autobiographical short story called 'Other Places' appeared in 1995, authored by one Helen Demidenko, the main interest in it centred on its remarkable similarities to a story by Brian Matthews, who at the time ran the Menzies Centre for Australian Studies in London.[14] Now that the plagiarism issue has been aired, I want to take another look at the contrast between the Matthews and Demidenko stories, and use them to assay some complexities of ethnicity and race in everyday life.

The Matthews story, 'Pioneering', is an autobiographical yarn about how a school teacher became a distinguished scholar. The Demidenko story shifts the action from the 1960s to the 1980s, and from the point of view of the teacher to that of a student. Here is the Matthews version: 'During the day, I taught Leaving English and History and Form Two French at a raw, new, outer-suburban high school—one of those 1960s bulldozer-blitzed sites criss-crossed with duckboards over the yellow mud in winter and ballooning with dust like a nuclear cloud in summer.'

And here is the Demidenko: 'It's summer of 1985 and I'm a year nine student at Kawawatha High, a raw, new outer-sub-urban school—one of those 70s bulldozer blitzed sites criss-crossed with duckboards over the yellow mud in winter and ballooning with dust like a nuclear cloud in summer.'

It would seem, over the decades, across the country from Melbourne to Brisbane, that nothing much has changed. Darville, writing as her Demidenko persona, tells the same stories as Brian Matthews and lifts a good many of his words. It's either a piece of schoolgirl cheek or lunatic piracy, or both. Why not both? Of course she plagiarised. This is the girl who, as the story goes, won the Westpac Bank maths prize with a 100 per cent score, prompting the bank manager to say 'She must have cheated'.

Demidenko's story is about 'losers'. The author returns to her old school to talk to the English class, who like her are losers. They all know they are losers, but think the author has escaped from all that. But she has written a book 'about losers. About death'. Even as the author of a controversial book, she is still a loser. 'She's fulla shit' one of the kids says about a review of the book that says 'after reading the Kovalenko's story, I still don't know why . . . none of them suffered remorse'. Young Vitaly provides the reply: 'She's never been kicked while she's down . . . I'd join the SS. Better than the fuckin' dole'.

Matthews' story is about his own ascendancy. Teaching was just a day job along the way. He loved the kids he taught, but he had a way out. Did they? Not in the Demidenko version. Only death, depression and the 'steel motel'. Cut from their context and placed in one of Demidenko's making, Matthews' words reveal another side—or appear to. The story is no more real, it's just a story. But it's a nice reversal—the successful academic who beavers away writing stories and a thesis while teaching suburban brats becomes the suburban brat who succeeds by writing about losers and is herself still a loser at heart. Either she cheated on her maths test or she failed to persuade the local authorities that her talent's genuine, and is thereby still a loser. That both the identity of the author of this story and some of its content are not what they seem is singularly apt.

Matthews engages in a project of his own self making, 'pioneering' not only Australian literary history, but a sense of self as an Australian writer, concerned with Australian issues. Demidenko neatly reverses this, by portraying what Matthews left behind—young people for whom that project of self making isn't even a realistic option for the gifted young alumnus who writes. What they have is neither the personal self creation of a Matthews, nor the official nationalist self creation of the 'Celebration of a Nation' banner that the teacher buys for the school, and that the students set on fire. Rather, there is the everyday practice of alliance and conflict, always shifting along different lines.

In another story, 'Pieces of the Puzzle', which also gives Demidenko as its author, a fight breaks out among a mob of school kids.[15] 'The fight takes up and spreads. Everybody yells.' The fight is about history, about what these kids' parents did, to each other, in the past. 'People take sides. The half-dozen skips in the crowd look bewildered.' One of the 'skips'—short for Skippy the bush kangaroo, or Anglo-Australian—tries to intervene: 'This is Australia, for fuck's sake. Stop it!'. Only to be told 'This is a wog fight, so skips stay out!'.

The story is of course no more 'naturalistic' than David Williamson's ocker comedies. It is probably not even terribly plausible. But I think the significance of these stories has something to do with telling the story of the conflicting pasts that must remain an insoluble trace within the multicultural project. When the 'overworked history teacher' Mr Glover confronts one of his kids and asks him if his parents tell him anything about their past, the kid replies, 'It's not what you remember, sir. It's what you've forgotten. What you've got to forget. What you go on forgetting all your life'.

That for migrant people, the process of forgetting is still an active one, and hence a zone of intensity in Australian culture, is perhaps one of the things troubling the kind of Anglo rump of 'skippies' to whom Pauline Hanson appeals. People who, by contrast, are far more likely to have forgotten what they have forgotten. People whose account of themselves is as shaky as mine. Multiculturalism is so often presented as a goal for the future that one tends to forget what it implies about the past. Namely, that the potential pasts that can be remembered and made the material for amending identity in the present is rendered almost incalculably vast by migration. Migrations run along vectors from almost everywhere, and thereafter continue to point back to pasts elsewhere and everywhere.

This is what makes the virtual republic in Australia such a rich and complicated project. To the extent that it has a shared past from which to tell stories that might illuminate the present, that past is world history. Only we do not know how to articulate the past of everywhere to the present of this place in particular. The unfinished project of Australian multiculturalism is not just one of those enlightenment projects for the future that both stirred and disturbed Manning Clark. It is also a project to do with the unrealised potential of the pasts Australia has acquired, but cannot articulate.

Look what happens when one young Queensland writer tries to find a form for it, a way of creating not only a story, but a storyteller, and all literary hell breaks loose. In a flash, public debate is alive once again, but one has to be either for or against Demidenko, just as one has to be for or against Manning Clark or Helen Garner. What slips away in the clamour to put the white hat or the black hat on the characters who animate these stories is a grasp of the contradictions that make their story available for such summary judgement in the first place. The machinery of meritocracy has, in the end, to decide yes or no, and as impartially as is possible. But the conversation of the virtual republic need not be such a summary judgement.

AUSTRALIAN STORIES

In relation to this enormous expansion of a virtual past, one can juxtapose these remarks by Jane Hyde, writing in *Quadrant*: 'Non-ethnic Australians suffer from nostalgia, from an insidious and unspoken sense of loss for the days when we used to know who we were by virtue of a dream from whose awakening we resile in dismay'.[16] That dream connected one people to one past, which ran back through the pioneering of the land to English origins, along one vector: the dream of a lost world of coherent identity. Les Murray takes credit for expanding this category from 'Anglo-Saxon' to 'Anglo-Celtic'. Which might be progress, of a sort, but it seems to me to expand the circle of complexity within which we can understand the roots of Australian culture only a little, and not far enough.

I sketched my own personal version of just such a story early on in this book. There was a time when the Wark story might have been held up as some kind of ideal exemplar of just such a dream. Not-quite-but-almost-Anglo immigrants made good. There was a time when it might have appeared typical. It would be the kind of thing alongside which one could classify minor variations, the inheritors of which might be encouraged to assimilate to the main stem of family stories. Now it appears, to me if not to Jane Hyde, as just singular. Everyone has a story, where place names and proper names connect through the verb of events. These stories never quite fit types.

The difficulty, and Hanson's stirring tapped into this, is that Aboriginal Australians and non-English migrant Australians were obliged to construct stories for themselves in opposition to an assumed main type, and did so with considerable cultural vigour. Meanwhile Anglo-Australian cultural tradition, once inflated to the proportions of a national ideal, then contracting to the slightly less exalted dominance of the major type, found itself in considerable difficulty adapting to the notion of stories being all more or less singular, different, and in principle equally resonant in the threads they might draw between the past and present.

Perhaps this is all a story about a culture pushing against the limits of identities that only work because of their antipodal relation to a source of otherness within the national culture. Aboriginality often played this role of being the other term, in B. Wongar's novels, for example. The 'new Australian' who arrives in John O'Grady's *They're A Weird Mob* fulfils the same role.[17] A 'mainstream' culture produces the habit of saying 'we' against the background of this other term, which in principle is in a process of being 'assimilated' into the mainstream, and yet which plays this contradictory role of defining where the boundary of mainstream lies. By these acts of ventriloquism, the mainstream speaks itself by speaking of what it is not.

Take this structure of feeling, then give it a good shake and set it down again. What you have now is what replaces it: a cocktail of cultural identities that are just a little more mixed, and just a little more frothy at the edges. A culture part of the way to becoming something else, but not quite yet. That other culture might be one in which forms of cultural identity don't rely always on this fantasy of the other in order to speak of 'we'. It's not an easy transition to make. Perhaps the heightened cultural attention to external points of reference—to an economic future with Asia, to a colonial past with Britain—perhaps these are ways of finding a fulcrum of otherness at a time when the internal ones seem so difficult to deploy.

DOMINANT CULTURE

So many things lurk beneath the bland assurance that there even is such a thing as a 'dominant' culture. Without for one minute wanting to deny that there are persistent inequalities in access to cultural resources, and in the presentation of cultural difference in the media, it helps to unpack that notion of a dominant culture long enough to see how the tensions within it mix and intersect with the kinds of differences recognised as multicultural.

For example, it is not as if the tension between the 'sterling' and the 'currency' ever really went away. The idea of Australian culture as a continuum and continuation of Britishness, and the idea of it as a break—a new beginning—have always had a class resonance. The cultural project of national independence overlaps with that of the creation of a state that protects worker's rights. While traditionally an idea with connections to the Labor Party and labour movement, in Graeme Campbell it also shows its rightward drift. Campbell was the Labor member for the vast outback seat of Kalgoorlie in Western Australia. Expelled from the party after addressing a meeting of the right-wing organisation the League of Rights, Campbell held the seat at the 1996 election as an independent.

Peter Cochrane argues that the coming of industrial modernity to Australia took place within the context of a continued dependence on Britain rather than a break from it.[18] Economic and cultural dependence ran together, at least until the out-break of war with Japan. The concurrent links between Australian culture and industry with those of its dominant centre of capital and strategic interests has from then on an interesting history. Defenders of the cultural link to Britain preserve half of this legacy, while the other has gone 'all the way with LBJ' at the height of American dominance of the region, and has since courted an economic 'Asianisation' that raised difficult questions of what form the flows of cultural exchange along such a new pattern of trade dependence ought to take. Grass roots labour movement populism has always been hostile to the foreign 'money power', and developed a resistant cultural nationalism partly in reaction to it. It is only when transferred from fear of British, then American, to Japanese imperial power that this particular aspect of reactive national-ism appears in a specifically racialist form. What would have appeared as 'left-wing' anti-American sentiment in the 1970s turned up as 'right-wing' anti-Japanese sentiment in the 1980s.

This is not to deny the persistent racism of labour move-ment culture, particularly connected to notions of unfair competition and the protection of living standards for local workers. What is striking is that the boundaries of who is included as a mate in the protective embrace of resistance to outsiders is quite moveable. Older waves of migrants can be articulated to the cause in opposition to newer ones. In his book *Australia Betrayed*, Graeme Campbell makes a point of talking about 'old Australians', as a cultural category, the dreamers of Jane Hyde's dream, the Anglo core of Australian culture that in *his* dream is to be preserved.[19] To this category he adds 'new Australians', a now obsolete terms from the days of assimilationist policies, by which he means the mostly European migrants of the 1950s and 1960s. Campbell courts his 'new Australians' for the purposes of a protective economic and political alliance, but does not really accept them on equal terms culturally. Both groups are meant to oppose multicultural-ism, perceived as a policy that undermines not just the cultural sovereignty of Anglo-Australians, but the prospect of an eco-nomic and political fair go for 'old' and 'new' Australians alike.

There is more—and perhaps this is what is most remarkable: the volatility with which the passions can align, for or against those of others, when organised by appeals that cut any which way across the plurality of identities. It is not as if Hanson merely represented some kind of generic racism, and her detractors were all pure of heart and tolerant all the way to their tippy toes. Anti-racism, even though its effects may be far preferable to racism, often seems to take exactly the same form. Where racists see some group, identified by some marker of appearance or culture, as either deficient or excessive in some scary way; anti-racists often do exactly the same thing, only nominating *racists* as the problem category.

This kind of anti-racism does not grasp the way far more subtle and pervasive forms of discrimination come to work across the plural world of cultural differences of multiculturalism itself.[20] The challenge is not just to oppose racism with anti-racism, but to find ways of organising the passions that play across the differences of multiculturalism itself, so that every type of identity it recognises can articulate itself in a productive way, both to other types of identity and to the very matrix of cultural identity. Both racism and anti-racism identify a 'problem group' and make it an other, relieving its adherents of responsibility. I don't mean in saying this to make these things ethically equivalent. They are not. I merely want to point out that some of the unintended consequences of anti-racist campaigns might stem from reliance on this fantasy structure. Hanson has clearly learned a certain method and style of speaking *from multiculturalism*, and turned it back against its source.

WELCOME TO THE CULTURE WARS

Speaking of plagiarists: by an odd coincidence, bits of rhetoric used by the Prime Minister, John Howard, are the same as those employed by Graeme Campbell. Both deride the 'McCarthyist' and 'politically correct' policies of the previous Labor government. Both have referred dismissively to the 'Aboriginal Industry'. Howard's remarks about education sound remarkably like Campbell on the 'white guilt view of history'. Campbell's book, *Australia Betrayed*, ends with the idea that 'our major concern should be providing jobs for our own people'.[21] Excise the coy reference to 'our own' and you have Howard's post-Hanson publicity effort on employment. Even Howard's response to Pauline Hanson contained a sideways glance to this shared rhetoric of right-wing populism. Borrowing the same line as Graeme Campbell, John Howard used the opportunity of what was supposed to be his answer in parliament to Pauline Hanson to decry the 'sort of McCarthyism that was creeping into Australian politics under the former prime minister'.[22]

Of course there is a great deal of difference between Howard and Campbell, but even after Hanson exposed the Liberal Party's quiet appeals to the disenchanted, Howard still tailored his public rhetoric towards the rising tide of reactive populism. Rather than denouncing reaction in the unambiguous terms of Liberal elder statesman Malcolm Fraser, Howard pitches woo. Rather than coopting the emotional force of accumulated resentments that lie behind the rising visibility of populist mouthpieces, he legitimised their language.

For a government harbouring strong desires for an accelerated modernising of the economy, the consequences are stifling. What Campbell and his ilk perceived more clearly than most is that economic rationalism, the level playing field, competition in all things, the search for Asian markets—all this was all very compatible with the kind of 'social rationalism' of equal opportunity legislation, expansion of higher education, the administration of art and culture according to multicultural principles. All this provided the social and cultural glue for an Australia that in principle rewards nothing but merit and according to no other measure but efficiency. All of the administered cultural and social policies, which on the face of it look quite the opposite, are really just about getting disadvantaged groups up to the starting line on an equal footing, so that no potential talent is wasted. No athlete of the calibre of Cathy Freeman will go untrained and unrewarded, whether by the Institute of Sport or corporate sponsors.

The overall effect of immigration policy, when thought of at the level of sustainable communities rather than individuals, is to maintain pools of educated, talented recruits for a high skill, high wage economy where barriers to the social entry into its rewards would be progressively removed. Since the days of the Fraser government, the organisation of Australian life has moved in fits and starts, and with no end of political bargaining and trade-offs, towards a combination of economic and social rationalisation designed to keep Australia afloat on the stormy waters of a global economy. Economic rationalisation is usually perceived as a product of the right, and social rationalisation as of the left, but this is misleading. Whatever their origins, both fitted in pretty well to their respective branches of administration. For all their anti-government petulance, free marketeers and social radicals make pretty good public servants. Under Hawke and Keating, both got their own train sets to play with.

Howard's 1996 election victory put together a very awkward coalition of economic modernisers who felt that this process was not going far enough and popular resentment of the fact that modernisation of any kind had got this far at all. Campbell and Hanson articulated not only grievances about social modernisation—their attacks on immigration and political correctness, for example. They also stood for that sizeable chunk of the electorate who saw no improvement in their life chances after more than a decade of economic change. As Mudrooroo put it, 'my friends, liberty, equality and fraternity may have universal appeal; but do they have particular appeal without the necessary capital?'.[23]

By playing, with the odd wink and hint, to the social reaction behind these populist personalities, Howard unwittingly strengthened popular resistance to the government's economic agenda. The attack on 'political correctness', aimed at the social rationalisers of the arts and culture, equal opportunity and higher education, was borrowed by Howard, Campbell and many others from the 'culture wars' in the United States. As I've outlined in an earlier chapter, far-right foundations poured money into well publicised attacks on what they perceived as 'liberal' social institutions and agendas. But the American context is quite different. The institutions attacked were hardly agencies of social rationalisation. Those that were attacked in Australia mostly are. They are the necessary and unavoidable social overhead of rapid economic change.

The campaign against 'political correctness' effectively scotched the possibility of a populist movement from the left leaping in to fill the breach. Phil Cleary, the left wing populist independent who won Bob Hawke's former seat of Wills in a by-election, remains an isolated case. The more likely possibility is the persistence of a populism of the right as a national irritant.

Having undone the always uneasy alliance of economic and social rationalisation at the heart of Australian politics, Howard replaced it with odd rhetorical bedfellows. Australia's economic participation in Asia means Asian participation in Australia, through migration, higher education, purchase of real estate and businesses. After he attended the November 1996 Asia–Pacific Economic Co-operation forum in the Philippines, Howard said that 'one of the things I am certainly going to do as a result of this meeting is to step up the explanation to the Australian public and step up the communication to the Australian public of the benefits of trade liberalisation and the benefits of globalisation, because there are great benefits'.[24] Good news for Australians who expect direct or indirect benefits, provided they are prepared to accept some modest changes to the administration of cultural and social life. Bad news for those who don't see how their life chances will improve. The problem that arises is finding a positive way of bringing these disenfranchised groups back into the economic bargain. All Howard achieved with his 1996 election win was to acknowledge their refusal of the social bargain that goes with it. But without something more substantial than window-dressing on jobs, the disenfranchised and the disenchanted drift further and further from the common wealth.

PRODUCING FREE SPEECH

To the extent that Hanson affirmed the democratic and secular nature of ethical thought and practice in Australia, fine. Only as we've seen, it's not quite so simple. It would be nice if some of the feverish campaigners against PC had got off their bums and become equally agitated in reply to the kind of free speech they've encouraged to come out of the woodwork. Where were they once they had provided the covering fire for Pauline Hanson? Or for Port Lincoln Mayor Peter Davis, who thinks, and feels confident stating publicly, that 'if you are a child of a mixed race, particularly, if you will, Asian-Caucasian or Aboriginal-white, you are a mongrel and that's what happens when you cross dogs or whatever'.[25] I am of course quite happy to defend Peter Davis' right to call people mongrels, and feel free to exercise my right to call Peter Davis an asshole.

When talkback radio personality Stan Zemanek appeared on ABC TV's *Lateline*, arguing against academic Mary Kalantzis and judge Pat O'Shane, he did his level best, as one might expect, to control the show. Zemanek claims to give his listeners what they want, as if that were just something 'out there'. His detractors claim that he manipulates opinion, as if he were entirely the cause. Given that talkback is a key media in the circulation of resentment—of the attribution of dangerous kinds of lack or excess to all kinds of types of people—it is worth looking at its role here. Phillip Adams provides a very acute diagnosis of the talkback radio phenomena. It's worth pausing to consider it as an example of the difficulties of even framing the question of free speech, when the way speech is produced in public is itself a channelling of passions, rather than a mere expression of a repressed, 'natural' energy.

Recalling remarks made by John Howard about Asian immigration on the John Laws radio program in 1988, Adams says that on his own show, which followed Laws', he could see the callers banking up on his screen, ready to have a go at Asians. Most of the callers, he says, are regulars. 'Some call because they're angry. Others because they're lonely. Others because they want to win things . . . Talkback is a feedback loop, with presenters training the callers to perform. The more aggressive the better.'[26] Adams' own strategy was to talk them around the other way: interestingly, by persuading callers that Dr Victor Chang, the famous heart surgeon, must be a 'good bloke'; and Dr John Yu, the paediatrician. By engaging callers' sympathies with particular people, he was trying to engage them in the wider artifice of sympathy and recognition of entitlement.

Perhaps Adams overestimates the degree to which the host controls the direction in which desire flows in such dialogues. I wonder how much talk show hosts are directed *by* their audiences? Adams relates a conversation at radio station 2UE in which one producer proposed getting a 'maddie' to host a time slot, the context being that the station was losing ratings in that slot to another station with a well known bigot. So perhaps it's more the production of a mutual passion between hosts and callers, in which everything is always displaced onto the other. In place of a passion to produce something, singly or collectively, out of the mixed resources one has, a desire forms that is about resenting the other—particularly, in Australian talkback, Asians. For example, 2KY's Ron Casey articulating a fear that Cambodian boat people will 'descend on the nation' bringing 'all sorts of diseases'.[27]

I had first-hand experience of the effects of this back in 1984 when historian Geoffrey Blainey called into question levels of immigration, the numbers of Asian migrants and the policy of multiculturalism.[28] At the time I was in love with a fourth generation Chinese-Australian woman, and we would often walk down King Street in Newtown, Sydney, hand in hand, as people do. But after Blainey's remarks were televised, we were spat on, insulted, threatened with violence. I would strongly defend Blainey's right to speak his mind, and I am not accusing him of racism, or of personal responsibility for what might result from what he said. The problem has more to do with the persistence of a structure of feeling in which when 'leaders' speak, people *mobilise*. From world wars to cold wars, this culture remained, and has yet to be seriously dismantled in the realms of education and public life.

At a time when the way people interact with each other in second nature is in flux, third nature provides a space for fantasy about the anxieties generated by those changes. Fears about conduct and power in the workplace, on the streets, at home, become the impetus for the use of the virtual geography of available media vectors for something other than a virtual republic. In other words, the potentials of the technical space of media vectors aren't used to develop the full range of potentials for constructing forms of productive, self-defining, self-changing passion. Not that radio, for example, is as monolithic as it is sometimes made to sound. Have a listen to Wendy Harmer, Helen Razer, Mikey Robbins, or Phillip Adams himself, and you hear quite another structure of feeling used as the basis for popular media. Still, I can't shake the sense that in Pauline Hanson, the anonymous radio talkback caller finally found a face and a full name.

FREEING PRODUCTIVE SPEECH

At the moment 'Anglo-Celtic' culture is caught in a dilemma. One horn of which is to identify itself with multiculturalism. Not as a particular culture within it, but to identify itself with the whole of multiculturalism, as author, overseer and central presence within it. It's the paradox of a culture attempting to retain its dominance by publicly disavowing it. The other horn of the dilemma is to react against multiculturalism as a whole.

Hanson lacked the wit to see the power of this—but not Graeme Campbell. This is to take a step back from petty racism and reject the whole system according to which cultural difference is ordered. A good deal of the debate Hanson sparked hinges on these incompatible alternatives.

What was not on the agenda, but perhaps should be, is something quite different from the organising of cultural identity into the types of multiculturalism where Anglo culture still presides; nor yet the fantasy of a return to the dream of an ideal Anglo community, with only one history, one culture, one relation to itself and others. Perhaps the really challenging thing is to conceive of what went into 'Anglo' culture as singular and specific culture in their own right.

The distinction between 'Anglo' and 'Non-English Speaking Background', or 'Nesbian', has value as a distinction for trying to assure a fair distribution of resources, to overcome disadvantage, to work for social justice. But it also has limitations, in that it treats as homogenous things that are not. It is widely recognised that 'Nesbian' is a bureaucratic invention, but not so widely perceived that 'Anglo' is also something that did not construct itself, but was made in that image by the process of rendering multicultural principles into a typology for naming and dealing with constituencies.

No wonder 'Anglos' do not know themselves, and react either by identifying with the whole structure as its author, or sometimes react against it. 'Anglos', as such, don't exist. Look at the sheer amount of rhetorical violence Hanson had to deploy against her overly-industrious Asians and overly-indolent Aboriginals to keep her Anglo fantasy afloat. So I think it's time to break down the Anglo type, and create in its place more singular stories of places, events, institutions, kinds of descent. What one finds, on such an inspection, is just how much those 'Anglos' have been strapped to the wheel of a modernity that they may have been the agents of inflicting on others, but could hardly be said to control.

By telling stories about the institutions of modernity, it seems to me possible to shift the issue from the acceptance or refusal of guilt in history to the acceptance or refusal of responsibility. I think that stories framed in terms of the guilt of a people, no matter how true such stories are, don't produce anything except resentment. But stories that trace the trajectories of institutions that shape lives both for those that dominate and are dominated by the institution; such stories call for a different kind of judgement, a judgement of responsibility. What is a citizen's responsibility in the virtual republic? To 'respond', to contribute to improvising new institutions and new conversations that recognise wide and varying kinds of entitlement to a fair go.

ENTITLED TO HER OPINIONS

'This country cannot live on fish and chips alone!' This was the battle cry of 'Filipina-born' Rose Hancock-Porteous, as reported in *Woman's Day*.[29] Porteous first claimed public attention as the wife of West Australian tycoon Lang Hancock. She has since remarried, and is now a celebrity in her own right. The story arose out of a clash between Hanson and Porteous on the Foxtel TV talk show, *Beauty and the Beast*. I mention it because the popular, 'down-market' media were stigmatised by some participants in the debate as liable to beat up the racism story in the clamour for audiences. Jerzy Zubrzycki said as much on ABC TV's *Lateline*. So let's look at an instance of the pop media response to Hanson.

The story runs between pictures of Porteous and Hanson. The latter appears, just as she did on the cover of the *Bulletin*, eating a pie and chips, head canted, with a bottle of VB. Porteous appears, in a fabulous yellow double-breasted dress, holding a mixing bowl and looking directly at the camera. 'I would like to cook for Pauline Hanson. I'd invite her for dinner and cook her Asian food that she'd never tasted before and I bet she'll crave it.'

On being informed that Hanson will appear with her on *Beauty and the Beast*, Porteous says: 'I'm going to treat her with dignity. Just like any other human being, she's entitled to her opinions'. But Hanson's reference to 'you Asians', angered Porteous, and she walked off the show. 'I came here, I scrubbed floors. I didn't go on the dole', Porteous says. 'I have experienced racism—that's why I'm qualified to talk about it. I was the wife of Lang Hancock. He had money, yet I experienced things the hard way. How much more do other Asians suffer?'

Compare this to the way the *Bulletin* phrased it on its *second* cover story about Hanson: **POLL SHOCK. 'AT LEAST SEVEN SEATS'. PAULINE'S PARTY: A NEW FORCE.** It's been a long time since anyone would confidently describe the *Bulletin* as 'quality journalism', but I'm sure Jerzy Zubrzycki would still be a bit surprised by the contrast with the even more 'down-market' *Woman's Day*. The latter seems to me to have approached the Hanson issue in the spirit of the virtual republic. The first thing it gets right is contained in the quote from Porteous about dignity. Hanson is *entitled* to her views—even though there was no shortage of commentators who wanted to take that entitlement away from her. How does it sound to anyone who runs a shop or has a job in one to hear the master thinkers say that the fish lady is not entitled to her opinions?

Putting Porteous in the limelight also strikes me as inspired. What qualifies her to speak is not that she is the talking head for some organisation, or wrote a report on racism, but that she *experienced* it. When the 'quality' media drag in some 'experience' off the street, usually it is in the form of the 'vox pop'—literally just a random sample of 'typical' voices. Porteous is not 'typical', she is absolutely singular, a character in her own right, with her own story and her own entitlement to tell it. Where talking heads in the up-market media usually represent an organised interest, celebrities in pop media don't represent anyone except themselves. They are not authorities speaking for a type of interest, they are particular instances of a kind of universal singularity. In principle, nothing distinguishes a celebrity from an ordinary person except their celebrity. A celebrity may have talents, just as ordinary people have talents, but it isn't necessary. Celebrities are instances of the virtual, in that anyone could become an image for a time, for no particularly good reason, and simply by being there express the passions of many people to whom that image appears. The wit of *Woman's Day* lies in rephrasing Hanson, not as a political representative, but as a celebrity, gently nudging her sideways into the realm of third nature, where anyone can appear at any time talking about anything.

Then of course, there is food, and on that subject, there is no argument.

In short, *Woman's Day* seems to me to know what responsible reporting is, while 'the Bully' does not. The *Woman's Day* story speaks the language of what Les Murray calls the vernacular republic. Turn the pages and you'll find diet tips, celebrity gossip, Fergie, working mums, Hollywood, more Fergie. All in all, a range of images, mostly of women, that express a wide range of feelings and perceptions about living with modernity. This is a flourishing branch of the 'public sphere'. Contrary to the alarums sounded to the right and left about its decline, it is alive and well in the form of a conversation conducted by, for and about women, through the popular magazines.

'It's crucial, of course, to speak back to Hanson. But there's a difference between speaking back and speaking down'.[30] So writes Catharine Lumby in the *Sydney Morning Herald*, putting into practice some of the postmodern experience of the media vector that I spoke about in an earlier chapter. Where *Woman's Day* just instinctively speaks back, and the quality press just as instinctively speaks down, Lumby reflects on what it means for Hanson to speak and for others to speak back. 'Hanson is a potent sign to politicians on both sides of the House that the barbarians are no longer at the gates—they're inside the castle, redecorating', Lumby quips. She is a 'double sign—as someone who wants to return us to an old social order, but whose very existence suggests that it's already at an end'. Hence the difficulties pundits and politicians alike found in responding to her. 'Ironically . . . Hanson is herself proof that traditional social hierarchies no longer apply'. What's curious is the way she has constructed a speaking position for herself in the media, just as other minority voices have, as excluded from elite culture. 'Perversely, Hanson's ability to make herself heard is premised on the breakdown of everything she wants to reinstate'.

What I think is interesting, and contemporary, about these remarks of Lumby's is the way they combine a savvy grasp of mainstream media and cultural practices with an attentive ear for difference. 'If democracy has any meaning, we need to listen to speech we don't like'. And in this era of third nature, we are going to hear speech not previously heard, carried via media vectors, from one part of the culture to another, and brought to us by some very singular personalities. We are going to hear Pauline Hanson and Helen Demidenko, David Williamson and Catharine Lumby, Noel Pearson and John Howard, Baz Luhrmann and Les A. Murray. What constitutes the value of a public figure is their unique challenge to our ability to find a way to hear them that moves us closer to the differences they articulate, without losing our grasp on our own experience and judgement. The virtual republic is a citadel built on vernaculars, not a Babel destroyed by them.

THE VERNACULAR REPUBLIC

A helicopter cuts a straight line through the sky. Cameras poke out of it, grabbing pictures of the countryside on a heading west of Taree in northern New South Wales. The pictures are for the TV news. Only there is no flood, no fire, no greenies clinging to the trees. The news value of these pictures concerns poetry. Les Murray, the 'poet lorikeet of the Country Party', has just won the T. S. Eliot prize, perhaps the most prestigious gong that the English administer for poetry. 'Murray has attitude in a distinctly Australian shade—touchy, argumentative, egalitarian—but his cascading verse buries the cultural cringe in a flood of generous and moving ideas and images.' So chirps Boyd Tonkin in London's *Independent* newspaper.[31] I wonder how Murray feels about being an Englishman's idea of an Australian.

My introduction to Murray's verse came in high school. I was enthusiastic about poetry then, and fortunate enough to be in Newcastle, where there was a lively Hunter Valley poetry scene. In the WEA meeting rooms, poets of the calibre of Roland Robertson and Peter Kocan would offer their advice, and on a lucky night, read work of their own. I met Les Murray at a weekend poetry retreat in the valley once, at Morpeth, I think. An honour.

But it's not Murray's verse I want to conclude with, but his essay on 'The Australian Republic'.[32] Two phrases of Murray's have already percolated through this book. The first is 'the Ascendancy', which I restricted to 'the Whitlam Ascendancy', a more limited notion than Murray's of an intellectual cohort that found its niche in the cultural world in the mid-1970s, when Murray wrote his 'Republic' essay. The second phrase is the 'vernacular republic', which is what Murray counterposes to the Ascendancy as a more positive cultural formation. Murray acknowledges that there is more than one vernacular, although I don't know if he would accept my use of the term for the kind of conversation that happens in women's magazines. The bottom line is that whenever anyone tries to draw a line through Australian culture, whether it be mateship/meritocracy or skip/wog or Melbourne/Sydney or Ascendancy/vernacular or whatever, we are dealing with a fantasy. Like the line a helicopter describes through the air, first it's there, then as soon as it's drawn, it disappears in the turbulence.

A key point Murray makes in his 'Republic' essay is that the various squabbling factions of the Ascendancy will never admit that they all belong to the same class. Each claims to speak for the public interest, and each tries to exclude other claims to articulate the common world. My only dissent is that I think we need to include Murray himself as well, even though he would like to appear as the 'peasant mandarin' somehow outside that social class of talking heads who populate the world of appearances. That a writer appears to articulate the interests of a social class doesn't make the writer necessarily a member of that class. The act of writing seriously makes one a thing apart. I learned that from Murray himself, actually. Long ago, at the Morpeth poetry retreat. I learned it not so much from anything he said as from his very demeanour, at once open and detached. A man apart from the worlds he embraces.

Public life tends to be punctuated by more or less eventful moments in which more or less professional talking heads try to articulate the common good and exclude other claims to speak for it. While it's rare that writers play this role, I've concentrated on some weird moments when writers have stepped into the breach. Perhaps, I suggest, a sign of uncertainty among the professionals of certainty, particularly the political talking heads.

When writers have their fifteen minutes of media fame, they usually perform one of two roles for the public. Sometimes they add lustre of authority to the prevailing fantasy when doubts about it emerge. Sometimes, something more useful— opening up the resources of the past to reveal the virtual at work within it, to ease the anxiety over the contingencies of history as it presses its indelible stamp on the structure of feeling modern life. This is that writing Shelley called the poetic, which 'awakens and enlarges the mind itself by rendering it the receptacle of a thousand unapprehended combinations of thought'.[33]

Writers who open a door to the virtual, even inadvertently, run the risk of being run out of business. That's why I've taken sides in favour of Helen Demidenko, Manning Clark, the postmodernists and even the phantom armies of the politically correct. When a fantasy comes into existence that seeks to exclude challenging points of view in the name of the public interest, then I think the ethical thing to do is to counter that fantasy, even if it means being typecast in fantasy's relentless logic of otherness. Perhaps there's no escape—I certainly operate within fantasies of my own. To give just one instance, the fantasy of the cold warriors, whom I would like to see demobilised now that their war is over. What I was attempting—and every essay is merely the record of an attempt—was to keep open the plurality of the virtual republic, to keep an open mind on those writers and writings whose works challenge the very categories of judgement about what writing, or culture, or memory, is or can be.

I even think it worth trying to extend the generosity of understanding to the minds of monsters, fools, ghosts and one-hit-wonders. It disturbs me when talk shifts so easily from denying that what Pauline Hanson says is true to denying her entitlement to speak. I think the entitlement has to be recognised on principle, even when one strongly disagrees with what that entitlement is used for. If the lucky country's run of luck holds up just a bit longer, then I think even the dangers of right-wing populism will pass, when people talk and think about it—the sceptical cast of the virtual republic will cast that lot to the winds. The trick is always to find a way to phrase even the most monstrous statement such that something is revealed that tells us how such statements are possible.

Everyone has their own republic. It is such a fertile meme. There's the captive republic, the reluctant republic, the vernacular republic, the muddle-headed republic, the minimal republic, the postmodern republic and, of course, the virtual republic. I'd like to think that what makes the last of these different is that it is meant as an image of the inexpressible reservoir of images from which came all of the other, and all possible ideas of the public thing. It is not a sum or a synthesis of republics, it is the practice of generating actual instances of public things as an ongoing conversation. 'Waiting for the republic is like waiting for the other shoe to drop', says Murray. I think of it less as a story to be completed than as the art of storytelling itself, within which one shoe, then another, then a third, fourth, fifth . . . might drop from the lips of citizens speaking about their experience, of shoes and signs and ships and many other things.

Murray describes the vernacular republic with quite a different kind of metaphor to any I would use. It is the 'subsoil of our common life', he says, and 'the bush' is its traditional reservoir. This vernacular republic underlies any possible formal or juridical one. While Murray clearly thinks of it as a kind of practice of everyday life, a structure of feeling, he also thinks it can work as a form of criticism. 'A republican critique would by no means be antipathetic to all innovation or cultural borrowing; quality, in particular, would always be able to get past its guard. It would stress the native traditions and the "set" of the national mind as the touchstones by which innovations should be judged.'

To some extent these are sympathies that a lot of people can share—so long as you don't try to define too much actual content in a metaphor like 'subsoil', 'tradition' or the 'set' of the mind. There's a point in Murray's writing where the mind sets in concrete, and it's usually when he defines what it is in Australian culture that the vernacular republic defines itself against. It is no longer really credible to set the authentic spirit of the people against the fantasy other of women, blacks or Asians. That only worked so long as those groups had few entitlements upon which to stake their claim to join the conversation. It no longer works to set one's mind against the communists—they no longer exist. Setting the mind against the imperial might of Britain, America or Japan is more promising, as it does them no harm, even if it does the 'us' it defines no good, and simply makes Australians feel like a powerless antipodes to the scene of the action, always elsewhere. Making 'the media' the other is suitably abstract, but is really the intellectual equivalent of sticking your head in the sand. It is those aspects of the media that reveal most about living with contemporary media that are first in line for the censors' snip. Compared to these alternatives, Murray offered a fantasy over 20 years ago with much more purchase on the problem of knowing oneself by hating somebody else. He named the bad other the Ascendancy, and in one form or another it's turned up ever since, mutating into postmodernists or the politically correct or the multiculturalists.

Among the fog of words that describe the Ascendancy, Murray offers the 'cultivated critics', the 'mandarin branch of the establishment', the 'new class', the 'educated caste', the 'left', the 'trendies', the 'epigone', the 'radical intelligentsia', the 'bohemians', or best of all the 'subsidised martyrs'. Murray prefers the notion of Ascendancy, as 'this at least connotes both the foreign derived oppressiveness of the new class and its arriviste, first generation flavour'. The basis of its power is tertiary education, which becomes the system of entitlement that replaces land ownership—the currency of entitlement in previous ascendancies. This new one has 'captured most of education, much of the arts, and much of fashion in Australia'. These arrivistes arrived under the Whitlam Labor government of 1972–1975. Murray was writing after the defeat of Labor in 1975, but seems to have a similar attitude to 'Reascendancy' of the Hawke and Keating years, 1983–1996.

The stronghold of the Ascendancy is higher education, which 'as in any other colonial territory, are systems of foreign ideas imposed from above, whose usual effect is to estrange people from their own culture and injure their rapport with their own people'. Murray himself found it prudent to 'use and resist' Sydney University. 'All I knew was that if ever I snubbed or denied my fellow country people, those who hadn't had the education I was getting, I would be lost.'

What I find striking is how Murray can so confidently claim to stand outside of all this by making the whole of the formal cultural apparatus into an antipode to the sweetness and light of the rural vernacular. Everything, once again, is pushed onto the other pole. When Murray says that country people are being excluded from the conversation, that's something I think it's important to hear. But I can't accept the idea of any component of the conversation, ignored or not, having a monopoly on the reservoir of the common culture. Nor am I happy with the neat division Murray draws between the vernacular, which equals the local, and the Ascendancy, which equals the foreign. What most people discuss over the back fence or on the bus includes whatever was on television last night as much as it includes any residues of deep cultural mud sticking to those country boots treading that country 'subsoil'. Third nature cut its vectors across the city/country division long ago, and while city and country people may tend to make different things of media culture, it is still part of vernacular culture, from one side of the continent to the other.

A republican criticism that lets nought but *quality* cultural imports past its guard also seems to me to be a curious fantasy. Migration makes the distinction between what is foreign and what is not, particularly in terms of cultural genealogies, a hard line to draw. I've not hesitated in this book to connect the

ideas that pop out of local Australian events to ideas that pop
out of no less local events that happened elsewhere. In any
case, what is an acceptable borrowing to one person is an
insidious foreign monstrosity to another. No culture is an
island, least of all this island culture, product of the global
vector of British naval power, now redefining a collective life
for itself out of vectors made of media and money, weaving us
into yet another version of the modern world.

Writing in a later essay on 'The Trade in Images', published
in the year of the Bicentenary, we find Murray in a different
mood, distancing himself from 'those often tartly hectoring
sociocultural studies of our country'. He has also partly repu-
diated his former enthusiasm for the republic, I suspect partly
because of its embrace by the dreaded Ascendancy. 'I sometimes
grow apprehensive, as I know many other people quietly do,
as to what sort of an ideological whited sepulchre a fully
realised Australian republic might be.'

I read that before I started writing this book. It is what set
me off in the direction of thinking of the republic, not as any
particular cultural symbol, but as a practice and a process with
no necessary content. What there is in that subsoil of the
practice of everyday life is to me no particular essence, but the
memory of past improvisations, in the face of events, as
recorded in stories. What there is in that virtual republic is a
conversation, not about any thing in particular, but about what
the conversation itself decides is the public thing, the thing
that matters. It is not for me to decide what the culture is, or
what the republic is. It's in the conversation the republic has
about the things that appear to it, as read through the stories
people inherit or acquire.

Murray put it quite well, the problem of the virtual: 'You
can't make an image of any large reality. You can't make an
image of Australia and do justice to all its aspects'. One can
never render complete justice, it's always an unfinished, ongoing task, but in the practice of making a republic, justice can
be done to one aspect, after another, after another, provided
those who feel responsible for aspects of the culture are all
entitled, one way or another, to join in. 'The whole can't be
described; it can only be invoked.' Murray will invoke even
this image of invoking in a Catholic, theological vein. For me
the virtual is something far more practical. It is what an essayist
does: relating one thing to another, such that one sees through

particular things so related, to the practice of relating. The practice through which we make the world, and make this habit of saying 'we' that can have a conversation about the natures of the world it makes.

PART THREE

NOTES

I've tried to keep the clutter of notes to a minimum and to use them mainly to show both the roots back to certain literatures and the routes forward from this text to others one might wish to pursue. An essay is always just a relay between other essays, traversing the same ground but in different ways, so I encourage the reader to deviate from my path on to those of other writers I have relied on, wherever and whenever the inclination strikes.

Notes

INTRODUCING THE VIRTUAL REPUBLIC

1 Friedrich Hugo, *Montaigne*, University of California Press, Berkeley, 1991, p. 347. On the essay as a contemporary way of writing, Reda Bensmaïa, *The Barthes Effect: The Essay as Reflective Text*, University of Minnesota Press, Minneapolis, 1987.

2 Charles Baudelaire, *Intimate Journals*, Picador, London, 1989, p. 4. The most useful work I have found on the collective labours through which English cultures shaped English words is Raymond Williams, *Keywords: A Vocabulary of Culture and Society*, Oxford University Press, New York, 1985.

3 See Wayne Hudson and David Carter (eds), *The Republicanism Debate*, UNSW Press, Sydney, 1993; Malcolm Turnbull, *The Reluctant Republic*, William Heinemann, Port Melbourne, 1993; Thomas Keneally, *Our Republic*, William Heinemann, Port Melbourne, 1993; John Hirst, *A Republican Manifesto*, Oxford University Press, Melbourne, 1994; and for the prehistory to contemporary republicanism, Mark McKenna, *The Captive Republic*, Cambridge University Press, Melbourne, 1996; Helen Irving, *To Constitute a Nation: A Cultural History of Australia's Constitution*, Cambridge University Press, Melbourne, 1997.

4 Noel Pearson, 'Open our hearts, and minds' *Australian*, 22 Nov. 1996.

5 Helen Irving, 'Home is where the republic is' *Australian*, 27 Jan. 1997.

6 Immanuel Kant, 'Perpetual peace: a philosophical sketch' in *Political Writings*, Cambridge University Press, Cambridge, 1991; David Hume, 'Of public credit', in *Political Essays*, Cambridge University Press, Cambridge, 1994.

7 Jeanette Hoorn and David Goodman, *Vox Republicae: Feminism and the Republic*, La Trobe University Press, Bundoora, Vic., 1995.

8 Howard Rheingold, *Virtual Reality*, Mandarin, London, 1992; *Virtual Community*, Addison Wesley, Reading, Mass., 1993.

9 A particularly readable account of the life of this key republican thinker is Sebastian de Grazia, *Machiavelli in Hell*, Princeton, NJ, 1989.

10 I may appear to be unduly neglecting the vectoral revolution of the nineteenth century, the railway, on which see Wolfgang Schivelbusch, *The Railway Journey: The Industrialisation of Time and Space in the Nineteenth Century*, University of California Press, Berkeley, 1986. Given that the decision by the states to build railways on different gauges inhibited rather than helped spatial integration, I've passed over Australia's railway journey.

11 It seems ironic that the internet should spawn a vast literature in book form, but it has. Two particularly interesting works are Allucquére Roseanne Stone, *The War of Desire and Technology at the Close of the Mechanical Age*, MIT Press, Cambridge, Mass., 1995, ch. 3; William J. Mitchell, *City of Bits: Space, Place and the Infobahn*, MIT Press, Cambridge, Mass., 1996. For an Australian guide to just exactly what people and institutions are bringing to, and putting up on, the internet, see Jon Casimir, *Postcards from the Net: An Australian's Guide to the Wired World*, Allen & Unwin, Sydney, 1996.

12 Edmund Burke, *Reflections on the Revolution in France*, Penguin Books, Harmondsworth, 1986. While I have never been much of a fan of Burke's politics, one can only admire his style, on which see Christopher Reid, *Edmund Burke and the Practice of Political Writing*, Gill & Macmillan, Dublin, 1985.

13 Michel de Montaigne, *The Complete Essays*, trans. by M. A. Screech, Penguin Books, Harmondsworth, 1991, p. 908, p. 909. The Screech translation is the most widely available now, but I still prefer *The Complete Essays*, trans. Donald Frame, Stanford University Press, Stanford, Conn., 1992, p. 611. Among the secondary literature on Montaigne, I recommend Jean Starobinski, *Montaigne in Motion*, Chicago University Press, Chicago, 1985; Hugo Friedrich, *Montaigne*, University of California Press, Berkeley, 1991; Ermanno Benciavenga, *The Discipline of Subjectivity: An Essay on Montaigne*, Princeton University Press, New Jersey, 1990.

14 That the literature on postmodernism is so vast and contradictory might be taken to be the first symptom of the 'postmodern condition'. Jean-François Lyotard, *The Postmodern Condition*, University of Minnesota Press, Minneapolis, 1984, is the classic text on the postmodern as a particular kind of thought. Hal Foster (ed), *The Anti-Aesthetic: Essays on Postmodern Culture*, Bay Press,

Port Townsend, Wash., 1983, was an early and influential collection of texts. Andreas Huyssen, *After the Great Divide: Modernism, Mass Culture, Postmodernism*, Indiana University Press, Bloomington, Ind., 1986 contains a thoughtful exposition of the main lines of postmodern thinking in France and Germany, as expressed in the kind of essays selected by Foster. An equally useful account, with more on English language literature, is John Frow, *What Was Postmodernism?*, Local Consumption Occasional Papers, Sydney, 1991.

15 McKenzie Wark, *Virtual Geography: Living With Global Media Events*, Indiana University Press, Bloomington, Ind., 1994. In that earlier book I was concerned with essaying the way global news media like CNN contribute to the creation of a media landscape in which otherwise distant places and cultures can get threaded together in weird global media events such as the Gulf War, the fall of the Berlin Wall, the Tiananmen Square 'massacre' and the Black Monday Wall Street crash of 1987. The picture of global media and their effects on local cultural forms that I arrived at in that book is the background against which, in *Virtual Republic*, I take up questions of how a small country might get along in such an environment.

16 Michel de Montaigne, *The Complete Essays*, trans. Donald Frame, Stanford University Press, Stanford, Conn., 1992, p. 455.

17 'There is nothing outside the text', as the actress said to the bishop. An idea widely misunderstood. See Niall Lucy, *Debating Derrida*, Melbourne University Press, Melbourne, 1995.

WHEN I HEAR THE WORD 'CULTURE'

1 Henry David Thoreau, *Walden and Civil Disobedience*, Penguin Books, New York, 1986, p. 50. What's great about *Walden* is the way Thoreau sets about building second nature for himself, and inquiring along the way about what kind of relation to nature second nature could be. It's about the virtual dimension of creating the nature–second nature relation. Likewise, I would like to propose an inquiry into the virtual dimension of the second nature–third nature relation.

2 Richard White, *Inventing Australia*, Allen & Unwin, Sydney, 1981; Paul James, *Nation Formation: Towards a Theory of Abstract Community*, Sage, London, 1996.

3 Kevin Kelly, *Out of Control*, Addison-Wesley, Reading, Mass., 1994, pp. 5–28. This book seems like an unconscious parody of Bernard Mandeville's *Fable of the Bees*, Penguin, Harmondsworth, 1970, first published in 1714. I'll return to the problem of

'nature' and its figures of speech, as applied to the social world, in Chapter 7.

4 See Jon Katz, *Virtuous Reality*, Random House, New York, 1997.

5 On the artifice of the market and the conditions under which historically it arose, see Lewis Mumford, *The City in History*, Secker & Warburg, London, 1961. I've also been influenced by Karl Polanyi's study of economic history, *The Great Transformation*, Beacon Press, Boston, 1971.

6 Graeme Turner, *Making It National: Nationalism and Australian Popular Culture*, Allen & Unwin, Sydney, 1994, p. 157.

7 Richard Bolton (ed), *Culture Wars*, New Press, New York, 1992.

8 Eva Cox, *A Truly Civil Society*, ABC Books, Sydney, 1995.

9 Eric Schlosser, 'America busted' *New Yorker*, 24 Feb. 1997, p. 49.

10 Lawrence Grossberg, *We Gotta Get Out of This Place*, Routledge, New York, 1992.

11 David Hume, *A Treatise of Human Nature*, Penguin Books, Harmondsworth, 1985, p. 533, p. 535, p. 537. My reading of Hume has been particularly influenced by that of Gilles Deleuze in *Empiricism and Subjectivity: An Essay on Hume's Theory of Human Nature*, Columbia University Press, New York, 1991; see also John Mackie, *Hume's Moral Theory*, Routledge, London, 1995; John Passmore, *Hume's Intentions*, Duckworth, London, 1980.

12 Adam Smith, *The Wealth of Nations, Books I–III*, Penguin Books, Harmondsworth, 1986, pp. 118–119, and p. 122, p. 110 for the later quotes. The Penguin edition is the most widely available one, but it has been especially mutilated in order to preserve the ignorance of the economics student about Smith's political thought. The edition published by Everyman, London, 1991 is complete. See also Donald Winch, *Adam Smith's Politics*, Cambridge University Press, Cambridge, 1978. The anecdote about Smith at Oxford comes from Robert L. Heilbroner's useful introductory book on the classical economists, *The Worldly Philosophers*, Simon & Schuster, New York, 1967, p. 42.

13 Les A. Murray, 'The bonnie disproportion', in *Persistence in Folly*, Angus & Robertson, Sydney, 1978. All of the Murray essays I've cited are also reprinted in Les A. Murray, *A Working Forest: Selected Prose*, Duffy & Snellgrove, Sydney, 1997.

14 Both liberal and Marxist interpreters of the Scottish enlightenment separate Smith from his contemporaries and then separate the economic doctrines from the rest of Smith—in short they are precisely the kinds of narrow folk Ferguson warned against. Hence the necessity to read them in other contexts—no less specialised—such as philosophy or the history of ideas. See J. G. A. Pocock, *The Machiavellian Moment*, Princeton University Press, New Jersey,

1975, pp. 462–505; Duncan Forbes, *Hume's Philosophical Politics*, Cambridge University Press, Cambridge, 1976.

15 Adam Ferguson, *An Essay on the History of Civil Society*, Cambridge University Press, Cambridge, 1995, p. 242.

16 Karl Marx, *Capital*, vol. 1, Penguin Books, Harmondsworth, 1979. Like most classic works, it's much better read in the original than in the numerous cribs. It helps to read Chapters 14 and 15, on the division of labour and on heavy machinery, before tackling the rather abstract first chapter.

17 R. W. Connell, *Ruling Class, Ruling Culture*, Cambridge University Press, London, 1977, pp. 190 ff.

18 See for example, Alan Wood, 'Where the budget missed its mark' *Weekend Australian*, 24 Aug. 1996; 'Social cohesion's real enemy' *Australian*, 10 Sept. 1996.

19 Patrick Dodson, 'A decent job, a decent school and decent treatment' *Australian Options*, Nov. 1996, p. 14.

20 Michael Oakeshott, *The Politics of Faith and the Politics of Scepticism*, Yale University Press, New Haven, 1996.

21 Georg Simmel, 'The metropolis and mental life' in *The Sociology of Georg Simmel*, Free Press, New York, 1950.

22 Raymond Williams, *The Long Revolution*, Hogarth Press, London, 1992, p. 41 ff. The best introduction to Williams is Williams himself, starting with his early, classic work, *Culture and Society*, Columbia University Press, New York, 1983. For Williams' subsequent influence, see Graeme Turner, *British Cultural Studies: An Introduction*, Routledge, New York, 1996.

23 Henri Lefebvre, *Critique of Everyday Life*, Verso, London, 1991. See also his *Introduction to Modernity: 12 Preludes*, Verso, London, 1995.

24 Karl Marx, *The Revolutions of 1848*, Penguin Books, Harmondsworth, 1973, pp. 70–71. On Marx as a prophet of modernity, see Marshall Berman's *All that is Solid Melts into Air: The Experience of Modernity*, Verso, London, 1982, ch. 2.

25 The Scottish enlightenment pass into European consciousness through their influence on German thinking—it was from Ferguson that we derive the idea of 'civil society' that runs from Hegel to Habermas. See Jürgen Habermas, *The Structural Transformation of the Public Sphere*, Polity, Cambridge, 1989.

26 Guy Debord, *The Society of the Spectacle*, Zone Books, New York, 1994, p. 23. By far the most entertaining account of Debord's life, art, politics and the radical tradition to which he belongs is in Greil Marcus, *Lipstick Traces: A Secret History of the Twentieth Century*, Harvard University Press, Cambridge, Mass., 1986.

27 Michel de Certeau, *The Practice of Everyday Life*, University of California Press, Berkeley, 1988. See also the essays in Michel de Certeau, *Heterologies: Discourse of the Other*, University of Minnesota

Press, Minneapolis, 1986; Jeremy Ahearne, *Michel de Certeau: Interpretation and its Other*, Stanford University Press, Stanford, Conn., 1995.

28 Matthew Arnold, *Selected Prose*, Penguin, Harmondsworth, 1987. To put Arnold in the context of the functions English literature was meant to serve, see Chris Baldick, *The Social Mission of English Criticism*, Clarendon Press, Oxford, 1983.

29 Tim Flannery, *The Future Eaters*, Reed Books, Port Melbourne, 1994; Eric Rolls, *From Forest To Sea*, University of Queensland Press, St Lucia, Qld, 1993.

30 Bruce Chatwin, *Songlines*, Picador, London, 1988.

31 Barry Jones, *Sleepers Wake!: Technology and the Future of Work*, Oxford University Press, Melbourne 1995, p. 13.

32 Paul Virilio, *Pure War*, Semiotext(e), New York, 1983; *Speed and Politics*, Semiotext(e), New York, 1986. See also McKenzie Wark, 'On technological time: cruising Virilio's over-exposed city' *Arena*, no. 83, 1987.

33 Mudrooroo, 'World bolong tok-tok' in *The Mudrooroo/Müller Project: A Theatrical Casebook*, ed. Gerhard Fischer, University of New South Wales Press, Sydney, 1993, p. 140. On the question of whether Mudrooroo is or is not an 'Aboriginal writer', I've chosen to remain silent. See Lucy Frost, 'Year of passing' in *Australian Humanities Review*, March 1997.

34 Harold Innis, *The Bias of Communication*, University of Toronto Press, 1991; *Empire and Communication*, Clarendon Press, Oxford, 1950.

35 James Carey, 'Technology and ideology: the case of the telegraph' in *Communication as Culture: Essays on Media and Society*, Unwin Hyman, Boston, 1989.

36 Geoffrey Blainey, *The Tyranny of Distance*, Macmillan, Melbourne, 1987. For historical material on the development of communication vectors in and to Australia, see: Ann Moyal, *Clear Across Australia: A History of Telecommunications*, Nelson, Melbourne, 1984; Edgar Harcourt, *Taming the Tyrant: The First Hundred Years of Australia's International Communication Services*, Allen & Unwin, Sydney, 1987; Graeme Osborne, *Communication Traditions in Twentieth-Century Australia*, Oxford University Press, Melbourne, 1995.

37 David Marc, *Comic Visions: Television Comedy and American Culture*, Unwin Hyman, Boston, 1990.

38 Joshua Meyrowitz, *No Sense of Place*, Oxford University Press, New York, 1985; Lyn Spigel, *Make Room For TV: Television and the Family Ideal in Postwar America*, University of Chicago Press, Chicago, 1992.

MAPPING THE ANTIPODES

1 Besides Vincent Scully, *Frank Lloyd Wright*, George Brazilier, New York, 1960, the book I first knew Wright from was Peter Blake, *The Master Builders*, Norton, New York, 1966, a title that seems ironic to me now. My modernist fantasies about grand architecture in the Le Corbusier fashion were punctured by Robert Hughes' television program *The Shock of the New*, also published as a book by the BBC, London, 1980.

2 Geoffrey Blainey, *The Tyranny of Distance*, Macmillan, Melbourne, 1981, p. 215.

3 See Denis Wood, *The Power of Maps*, Guilford Press, New York, 1992.

4 On animated cartoons, see Norman Klein, *7 Minutes*, Verso, London, 1993.

5 See McKenzie Wark, 'Third nature', *Cultural Studies* vol. 8, no. 1, Jan. 1994, pp. 115–132.

6 On this idea of the 'modern', see Marshall Berman, *All that is Solid Melts into Air*, Verso, London, 1984.

7 I'm thinking of Poe's story, 'The cask of Amontillado' in Edgar Allan Poe, *Tales of Mystery and Imagination*, Everyman, London, 1993.

8 Geoffrey Bolton, *The Oxford History of Australia Volume 5: The Middle Way 1942–1995*, Oxford University Press, Melbourne, 1996, p. 91.

9 On Ultimo: Deidre Macken, 'Asia's southern suburb' *Sydney Morning Herald*, 6 Sept. 1996; Leonie Lamont, 'Life in a fish bowl can sure beat suburbia' *Sydney Morning Herald*, 13 July 1996; Peter Lalor, 'There goes the neighbourhood' *Daily Telegraph*, 21 Sept. 1996; and on the east versus the west of Sydney: Deidre Macken, 'A city divided' *Sydney Morning Herald*, 5 October, 1996.

10 Manuel Castells, *The Informational City*, Basil Blackwell, Cambridge, 1989.

11 Karl Marx, *Capital*, vol. 1, Penguin Books, Harmondsworth, 1976, p. 895.

12 John Prebble, *The Highland Clearances*, Penguin Books, Harmondsworth, 1969, p. 304. Other books in his series of narrative 'histories from below' of key events in modern Scottish history are: *Culloden*, Penguin Books, Harmondsworth, 1967; *The Darien Disaster*, Mainstream Publishing, Edinburgh, 1968; *Glencoe: Story of the Massacre*, Penguin Books, Harmondsworth, 1968. His autobiography is *Landscapes and Memories*, HarperCollins, London, 1994.

13 G. W. F. Hegel, *The Philosophy of History*, Prometheus Books, Buffalo, New York, 1991, p. 90. The best work I know on this supremely difficult thinker is Charles Taylor, *Hegel*, Cambridge

University Press, Cambridge, 1975, which begins with an excellent essay on the enlightenment and romanticism, the two things Hegel tried to synthesise.

14 See McKenzie Wark, *Virtual Geography: Living With Global Media Events*, Indiana University Press, Bloomington, Ind., 1994, pp. 11–14.

15 William Gibson, *Neuromancer*, Ace Books, New York, 1984; *Count Zero*, Gollancz, London, 1988; *Mona Lisa Overdrive*, Bantam, New York, 1988. See also Scott Bukatman, *Terminal Identity: The Virtual Subject in Postmodern Science Fiction*, Duke Univesity Press, Durham, NC, 1993; Mark Dery, *Escape Velocity Cyberculture at the End of the Century*, Grove Books, New York, 1996.

16 Don Watson, *Caledonia Australis: Scottish Highlanders on the Frontiers of Australia*, Collins, Sydney, 1984; Les Murray, 'The bonnie disproportion' in *Persistence in Folly*, Angus & Robertson, Sydney, 1984. I hope both will forgive me for placing them in the same paragraph.

17 Not professing any competence as a reader of her poetry, I'll restrict myself to citing Wright's prose and essays: *Preoccupations in Australian Poetry*, Oxford University Press, Melbourne, 1965; *The Generations of Men*, Oxford University Press, Melbourne, 1959; *The Cry for the Dead*, Oxford University Press, Melbourne, 1981; *Born of the Conquerors: Selected Essays*, Aboriginal Studies Press, Canberra, 1991.

18 Karl Kraus, *Half Truths and One and a Half Truths: Selected Aphorisms*, University of Chicago Press, Chicago, 1990.

19 Michel Foucault, 'Nietzsche, genealogy, history', in *Language, Counter-Memory, Practice*, Cornell University Press, Ithaca, 1977, p. 139, p. 144 for the following quote; see also Michel Foucault, *The Archaeology of Knowledge*, Tavistock, London, 1977. On the Panopticon, see Michel Foucault, *Discipline and Punish*, Penguin Books, Harmondsworth, 1977. Among the many studies of Foucault, see Clare O'Farrell, *Foucault: Historian or Philosopher?*, St Martins Press, New York, 1989.

20 See Jeremy Bentham, *The Panopticon Writings*, Verso, London, 1988.

21 Robert Hughes, *The Fatal Shore*, Collins Harvill, London, 1987, p. 123.

22 Paul Foss, 'Theatrum nondum cogitorum' in *The Foreign Bodies Papers*, Local Consumption Series 1, Sydney, 1981.

23 The most readable account of Harrison's work is Dava Sobel's delightful little book *Longitude*, Fourth Estate, London, 1996.

24 McKenzie Wark, 'The logistics of perception', *Meanjin* vol. 49, no. 1, Autumn 1990.

25 See Gilles Deleuze's essay, 'Plato and the simulacrum', in his book

The Logic of Sense, Columbia University Press, New York, 1994 for a very useful exposition of the classical conception of the ideal form and its worldly copies.

26 Michel de Montaigne, *The Complete Essays*, trans. Donald Frame, Stanford University Press, Stanford, Conn., 1992, p. 116.

27 Bernard Smith, *European Vision and the South Pacific*, Oxford University Press, Oxford, 1989. See also Peter Beilharz, *Imagining the Antipodes: Culture, Theory and the Visual in the Work of Bernard Smith*, Cambridge University Press, Cambridge, 1997.

28 Thomas Richards, *The Imperial Archive: Knowledge and the Fantasy of Empire*, Verso, London, 1993.

29 See Paul Carter, *The Road to Botany Bay*, Knopf, New York, 1988. On the relationship between land and landscape, see also his *Lie of the Land*, Faber, London, 1996.

30 Meaghan Morris, 'Panorama: the live, the dead and the living' in *Island in the Stream: Myths of Place in Australian Culture*, ed. Paul Foss, Pluto Press, Sydney, 1988.

31 Robert McNamara with Brian VanDeMark, *In Retrospect: The Tragedy and the Lessons of Vietnam*, Time Books, New York, 1995; Samuel Huntington, *The Clash of Civilisations and the Remaking of World Order*, Simon & Schuster, New York, 1996.

32 Theodor Adorno and Max Horkheimer, *Dialectic of Enlightenment*, Verso, London, 1979.

33 On the idea of ethics as responsibility to the other, see Sean Hand (ed.), *The Emmanuel Levinas Reader*, Blackwell, Oxford, 1989.

34 Chris Healy, *From the Ruins of Colonialism: History as Social Memory*, Cambridge University Press, Cambridge, 1997.

35 Peter Carey, *The Unusual Life of Tristan Smith*, Vintage, New York, 1996. On the relationship of the Eficans to the Voorstanders, or perhaps of the Australians and the Americans, see Philip Bell and Roger Bell, *Implicated: the United States in Australia*, Oxford University Press, Melbourne, 1993.

36 Oscar Wilde, *The Wit and Humor of Oscar Wilde*, Dover, New York, 1959, p. 49.

37 Gerhard Fischer (ed.), *The Mudrooroo/Müller Project: A Theatrical Casebook*, University of New South Wales Press, Sydney, 1993; the Müller play is also available as 'The task', in *Hamletmachine and Other Texts for the Stage*, PAJ, New York, 1984. Mudrooroo's perspective on writing is *Writing from the Fringe*, Hyland House, Melbourne, 1990.

38 Martin Heidegger, 'The age of the world picture', in *The Question Concerning Technology and Other Essays*, Harper, New York, 1977. For a good introduction to this difficult thinker, see George Steiner, *Martin Heidegger*, University of Chicago Press, Chicago,

1989. I pursue this more fully in *Virtual Geography*, Indiana University Press, Bloomington, Ind., 1994, pp. 158–164.

39 The best place to start on the rather strange collaborative writings of Gilles Deleuze and Felix Guattari is perhaps the occasional interviews collected in Gilles Deleuze, *Negotiations*, Columbia University Press, New York, 1995; Felix Guattari, *Soft Subversions*, Semiotext(e), New York, 1996; *Chaosophy*, Semiotext(e), New York, 1995, before tackling their main works together *Anti-Oedipus: Capital and Schizophrenia: vol. 1*, Athlone Press, London, 1984; *A Thousand Plateaus: Capitalism and Schizophrenia vol. 2*, University of Minnesota Press, Minneapolis, 1988; *What is Philosophy?*, Verso, London, 1994. For Guattari's critique of Heidegger, see *Chaosmosis*, Power Publications, Sydney, 1992.

40 See for example, Bob Hodge and Vijay Mishra, *Dark Side of the Dream: Australian Literature and the Postcolonial Mind*, Allen & Unwin, Sydney, 1991, pp. 216–219.

41 For a place to start in on the literature of postcolonial criticism, try Bill Ashcroft, Gareth Griffiths and Helen Tiffin, *The Postcolonial Studies Reader*, Routledge, London, 1995. A good critical history of it is Robert Young, *White Mythologies: Writing History and the West*, Routledge, London, 1990. The critic most associated with the subtle business of finding the cracks in colonial identity is Homi Bhabha, *The Location of Culture*, Routledge, London, 1994.

42 See Ross Gibson's essays, especially his reading of Mad Max in *South of the West*, Indiana University Press, Bloomington, Ind., 1992.

43 Roland Robertson, *Globalisation: Social Theory and Global Culture*, Sage Books, London, 1992.

44 The local and the global in Australian broadcasting was first explored by Tom O'Regan, 'Towards a high communications policy' *Continuum*, vol. 2, no. 1, 1988; see also Tom O'Regan, *Australian Television Culture*, Allen & Unwin, Sydney, 1993; Toby Miller and Stuart Cunningham, *Contemporary Australian Television*, UNSW Press, Sydney, 1995; Stuart Cunningham and Elizabeth Jacka, *Australian Television and International Mediascapes*, Cambridge University Press, Cambridge, 1996; John Sinclair, Stuart Cunningham and Elizabeth Jacka (eds), *New Patterns in Global Television*, Oxford University Press, New York, 1996.

45 This particular moment of conflict between trade and cultural imperatives is taken up by Stuart Cunningham, *Framing Culture: Criticism and Policy in Australia*, Allen & Uniwn, Sydney, 1992; Toby Miller, *The Well-Tempered Self*, Johns Hopkins University Press, Baltimore, 1994.

46 Gilles Deleuze and Felix Guattari, *Anti-Oedipus: Capitalism and Schizophrenia vol. 1*, Athlone Press, London, 1984, p. 321.

47 McKenzie Wark, *Virtual Geography*, Indiana University Press, Bloomington, Ind., 1994, p. 64.

THE LIBERTARIAN LINE

1 For selections of the classic texts of structuralism, see Michael Lane (ed.), *Structuralism: A Reader*, Basic Books, New York, 1970; John Sturrock, *Structuralism and Since*, Oxford University Press, New York, 1979; or Robert A. Segal, *Structuralism in Myth*, Garland Press, New York, 1996.

2 Germaine Greer, *London Observer*, 1 Aug. 1982, quoted from Stephen Murray-Smith, *Dictionary of Australian Quotations*, Mandarin, Port Melbourne, 1992, G148.

3 Donald Horne, *The Lucky Country: Australia in the 1960s*, rev. edn, Penguin Australia, Ringwood, 1964, p. 238; see also John Docker, *Australia's Cultural Elites*, Angus & Robertson, Sydney, 1974.

4 Judith White, 'The push for freedom' *Sun Herald*, 2 June 1996; see also Humphrey McQueen, 'Pushing it uphill' *Sydney Morning Herald*, 8 June 1996; John Tranter, 'The rebels in the public bar' *Weekend Australian*, 15 June 1996.

5 Anne Coombs, *Sex and Anarchy: The Life and Death of the Sydney Push*, Viking Penguin, 1996. For the Jim Staples quote, p. 93; Anderson as remorseless, p. 51; the fantastical way of life, p. 33, p. 170; Push heroines, pp. 69–70; *Tharunka*, pp. 243–4; Jenny Coopes, p. 274; Brian Kennedy, *A passion to Oppose*, Melbourne University Press, Melbourne, 1996. Anderson on idealism and capitalism, p. 65; Judy Ogilvy, *The Push: An Impressionist Memoir*, Primavera Press, Sydney, 1995; on Push women, p. 80; on Push sexuality, pp. 112–13.

6 See Michel Foucault, *The Use of Pleasure: The History of Sexuality vol. 2*, Pantheon, New York, 1990. A useful critique of Foucault's work on sexuality is the work of the sociologist R. W. Connell, *Masculinities*, Allen & Unwin, Sydney, 1995.

7 Heraclitus, *Fragments: A Text and Translation* (with commentary by T. M. Robinson), University of Toronto Press, Toronto, 1987, fragments 12 and 49a.

8 For more than usually engaging accounts of contemporary realism, see Edward Pols, *Radical Realism: Direct Knowing in Science and Philosophy*, Cornell University Press, Ithaca, 1992; James Robert Brown, *Smoke and Mirrors: How Science Reflects Reality*, Routledge, London, 1994.

9 John Anderson, 'Empiricism' in *Studies in Empirical Philosophy*, Angus & Robertson, Sydney, 1962.

10 Jim Baker, *Australian Realism*, Cambridge University Press, Cam-

bridge, 1986. For a particularly clear statement of realism, see David Armstrong, *Perception and the Physical World*, Humanities Press, New York, 1961.

11 John Anderson, 'Art and morality' in *Art & Reality: John Anderson on Literature and Aesthetics*, Hale & Iremonger, Sydney, 1982, p. 87; on 'refusal to serve', p. 88.

12 John Anderson, 'Realism and some of its critics' in *Studies in Empirical Philosophy*, p. 53.

13 Ermanno Benciavenga, *The Discipline of Subjectivity: An Essay on Montaigne*, Princeton University Press, New Jersey, 1990, p. 23. The famous line from Montaigne is in *The Complete Essays*, trans. Donald Frame, Stanford University Press, Stanford, Conn., 1992, p. 611.

14 Donald Horne, *The Education of Young Donald*, Penguin Books, Ringwood, 1975, p. 205.

15 quoted in Coombs, p. 13.

16 Nietzsche returns to Sydney more than once, and always very differently. Norman Lindsay was at one time an enthusiast. See Peter Kirkpatrick, *The Seacoast of Bohemia*, University of Queensland Press, St Lucia, Qld, 1992. He was much read again in the 1980s. See Paul Patton (ed.), *Nietzsche, Feminism and Political Theory*, Allen & Unwin, Sydney, 1993.

17 Guy Debord, *Panegyric*, Verso, London, 1991, p. 34.

18 Wilhelm Reich, *The Mass Psychology of Fascism*, Penguin Books, Harmondsworth, 1975.

19 See Jean Starobinski, *Jean-Jacques Rousseau: Transparency and Obstruction*, University of Chicago Press, 1988. I'm not much of a fan of Rousseau, but the *Confessions*, Penguin, London, 1994, are interesting both as a descendant of Montaigne's *Essays* and for their S & M flavour.

20 Manning Clark, *The Quest for Grace*, p. 194–5.

21 Frank Moorhouse, *Futility and Other Animals*, Picador, Sydney, 1996, first published in 1969. Interesting to reread now alongside *Grand Days*, Picador, Sydney, 1993.

22 For selected documents, see Frank Moorhouse, *Days of Wine and Rage*, Penguin, Ringwood, Vic., 1980. See also Dennis Altman's memoir, *Defying Gravity*, Allen & Unwin, Sydney, 1997, p. 69 ff.

23 The Situationists have lately enjoyed a publishing revival. See in particular, Guy Debord, *The Society of the Spectacle*, Zone Books, New York, 1994; Elizabeth Sussman (ed.), *On the Passage of a few People Through a Rather Brief Moment in Time: The Situationist International 1957–1972*, MIT Press, Cambridge, Mass., 1989.

24 Tim Rowse, 'The pluralism of Frank Moorhouse' in Susan Dermody, et al. (eds), *Nellie Melba, Ginger Meggs and Friends: Essays*

in Australian Cultural History, Kibble Books, Malmsbury, Vic., 1982.

25 Humphrey McQueen, *Australia's Media Monopolies*, Widescope, Camberwell, Vic., 1977.

26 Beatrice Faust, 'My friend Germs' in Richard Walsh (ed.), *Ferretabilia: Life and Times of Nation Review*, University of Queensland Press, St Lucia, Qld, 1993, pp. 80–81.

27 Virginia Woolf, 'Montaigne' in *Collected Essays*, Hogarth Press, London, 1967, vol. 3.

28 Germaine Greer, *The Female Eunuch*, Harper Collins, London, 1981; on carnal knowledge, p. 78; psychoanalysis, p. 104; extended family, p. 249; pleasure principle, p. 366; women becoming outcasts, p. 367.

29 Kathy Bail (ed.), *DIY Feminism*, Allen & Unwin, Sydney, 1996.

30 Liz Fell and Carolin Wenzel (eds) *The Coming Out Show: Twenty Years of Feminist ABC Radio*, ABC Books, Sydney, 1995.

31 S. A. Grave, *A History of Philosophy in Australia*, University of Queensland Press, St Lucia, Qld, 1984, pp. 213–217. Jean Curthoys takes a very different view of the legacy of the Libertarian and liberationist roots of feminism in *Feminist Amnesia: The Wake of Women's Liberation*, Routledge, London, 1997.

32 Paul Feyerabend, 'Marxist fairytales from Australia' in *Science in a Free Society*, Verso, London, 1978, p. 155.

33 For a selection of key texts, see Graeme Turner, *Nation, Culture, Text: Australian Cultural and Media Studies*, Routledge, London, 1993.

34 Quoted in Helen Wilson, 'Afterword', in Helen Wilson (ed.), *Australian Communications and the Public Sphere: Essays in Memory of Bill Bonney*, Macmillan, Melbourne, 1989.

35 Bill Bonney and Helen Wilson, *Australia's Commercial Media*, Macmillan, Melbourne, 1993, p. 77.

36 Ross Poole, 'Public spheres' in Helen Wilson (ed.), *Australian Communication and the Public Sphere*, Macmillan, South Melbourne, Vic., 1989, p. 7.

37 This is clearest in their interviews. See Michel Foucault, *Power/Knowledge*, Pantheon, New York, 1980; Gilles Deleuze, *Negotiations*, Columbia University Press, New York, 1995.

38 Socrates explains his method in the 'Apology': Plato, *Last Days of Socrates*, Penguin Books, Harmondsworth, 1979, pp. 42–76. Anderson's 'Socratic' inquiry into the fetish for war memorials is recounted in Brian Kennedy, *A Passion to Oppose*, Melbourne University Press, Melbourne, 1995, pp. 95–104. For instances of contemporary critical inquiry, starting likewise from common experience, see Meaghan Morris, *The Pirate's Fiancée*, Verso, London, 1988; *Ecstasy and Economics*, EmPress, Sydney, 1992;

White Panic: History in Action Cinema, Verso, London, forthcoming. I look at Morris' essay writing in more detail in McKenzie Wark, 'Speaking trajectories: Meaghan Morris, antipodean theory and Australian cultural studies' *Cultural Studies*, vol. 6, no. 3, Oct. 1992, pp. 433–448.

39 See Geoffrey Dutton, *The Innovators*, Macmillan, Melbourne, 1986, p137ff; Tim Rowse, *Australian Liberalism and National Character*, Kibble Books, Melbourne, 1978, p. 214 ff.

40 D. M. Armstrong, *Perception and the Physical World*, Humanities Press, New York, 1961, p. 191.

A SECRET HISTORY

1 Some of the essential texts for thinking about the peculiarities of Australian postmodernism are collected in E. A. Grosz, et al. (eds), *Futur*fall: Excursions into Post-Modernity*, Power Publications, Sydney 1986; Pamela Hansford (ed.), *Wit's End*, Museum of Contemporary Art, Sydney, 1993; John Frow and Meaghan Morris (eds), *Australian Cultural Studies: A Reader*, Allen & Unwin, Sydney, 1993. The latter is particularly useful for demonstrating why postmodernism and cultural studies are not the same thing. Rex Butler (ed.), *What Is Appropriation?*, Power Publications, Sydney, 1997, and Rex Butler, *An Uncertain Smile*, Artspace, Sydney, 1996 are useful if somewhat reductive reconstructions of the 1980s aesthetic.

2 Don Watson, 'A toast to the postmodern republic' *Island*, no. 55, Winter 1993.

3 For the context of the 'lucky country' and the 'cultural cringe', see John Docker, *Australian Cultural Elites*, Angus & Robertson, Sydney, 1974; Tim Rowse, *Australian Liberalism and National Character*, Kibble Books, Melbourne, 1978.

4 Jean-Luc Nancy, 'The Deleuzian fold of thought' in *Deleuze: A Critical Reader*, ed. Paul Patton, Blackwell, Oxford, 1996, p. 107.

5 Greil Marcus, *Lipstick Traces: A Secret History of the Twentieth Century*, Harvard University Press, Cambridge, 1989, pp. 1–11. Also recommended are his books *Mystery Train*, Penguin, New York, 1990; *In the Fascist Bathroom: Writings on Punk*, Penguin, London, 1994; *The Dustbin of History*, Picador, London, 1996. My essay in appreciation of Marcus is in *World Art*, no. 1, 1997.

6 Vivien Johnson, *Radio Birdman*, Sheldon Booth, Melbourne, 1990; see also Philip Hayward (ed.), *From Pop to Punk to Postmodernism*, Allen & Unwin, Sydney, 1992; John Potts and McKenzie Wark, 'Play that funky music white boy', *Communal/Plural*, no. 4, Sydney, 1995.

7 Michael Heyward, *The Ern Malley Affair*, Faber, London, 1993, p. 235.

8 Jean-François Lyotard, *The Postmodern Condition*, University of Minneapolis Press, Minnesota, 1984, p. 81; *Just Gaming*, University of Minneapolis Press, Minnesota, 1985, p. 8.

9 Søren Kierkegaard, *The Concept of Irony*, Princeton University Press, New Jersey, 1989, p. 270–271.

10 Peter Handke, *The Weight of the World: A Journal*, Macmillan, New York, 1990, p. 46.

11 See Michel Sanouillet and Elmer Peterson, *Marchand Du Sel: The Essential Writings of Marcel Duchamp*, Thames & Hudson, London, 1975; Thierry De Duve (ed.), *The Definitely Unfinished Duchamp*, MIT Press, Cambridge, Mass., 1991; Thierry De Duve, *Kant After Duchamp*, MIT Press, Cambridge, Mass., 1996.

12 See the introduction to Arthur C. Danto, *Beyond the Brillo Box*, Farrar, Strauss and Giroux, New York, 1992, for a good, succinct summary of the import of early Warhol. Writing about irony in art tends to be a somewhat turgid and unironic affair. Warhol's own books escape that trap: Andy Warhol and Pat Hackett, *Popism: The Warhol 60s*, Harper & Row, New York, 1980; Andy Warhol, *From A To B and Back Again*, Picador, London, 1976.

13 Hear for example, Dave Graney and the Coral Snakes, 'Rock'n'roll is where I hide', on *The Soft'n'Sexy Sound*, Mercury Records, 1995. The scripts for *Frontline* are published by Viking Penguin, Ringwood, Vic., 1995, and several episodes are available on video from the ABC.

14 Catharine Lumby, 'Smiling saboteurs', in *Wit's End*, Pamela Hansford (ed.), Museum of Contemporary Art, Sydney, 1993, p. 107–8.

15 McKenzie Wark, *Virtual Geography: Living With Global Media Events*, Indiana University Press, Bloomington, Ind., 1994, p. 225.

16 Catharine Lumby, 'Media culpa', *21*C*, no. 2, 1996, p. 20; See Michael Rogin, *Ronald Reagan: The Movie*, University of California Press, Berkeley, 1987.

17 Eric Michaels, *Bad Aboriginal Art*, Allen & Unwin, Sydney, 1994, p. 180; originally 'My essay on postmodernism', *Art & Text*, no. 25, 1987.

18 The media carried on a somewhat one-sided debate against postmodernism in 1995–96. See Beatrice Faust. 'Unthrifty Writers', *Australian Rationalist*, No. 38, 1995; McKenzie Wark, 'The new mysticism', *Australian Rationalist*, no. 39, 1995; David Williamson, 'Universal moral soldier' *Bulletin*, 2 April 1996. See also David Williamson, *Dead White Males*, Currency Press, Sydney, 1995, which includes Keith Windschuttle's favourable review.

19 Catharine Lumby, 'Videodrome: the aesthetics of surrender' *Frogger*, no. 19, Nov. 1985.

20 Ted Colless and David Kelly, 'The lost world 3' *Art & Text*, no. 12/13, Summer 1983, p. 88; reprinted in Edward Colless, *The Error of My Ways*, IMA, Brisbane, 1996.

21 Paul Taylor, 'A culture of temporary culture' *Art & Text*, no. 17, Summer 1994, pp. 94–106.

22 Two influential books by Jean Baudrillard, *Simulation*, Semiotext(e), New York, 1983 and *In the Shadow of the Silent Majorities*, Semiotext(e), New York, 1983, made their presence felt around the time Taylor was writing. For a more recent collection, see Paul Foss and Julian Pefanis, *The Revenge of the Crystal*, Pluto Power Publications, Sydney, 1990. For the context to the writings of this particularly perverse French essayist, see Julian Pefanis, *Heterology and the Postmodern: Bataille, Baudrillard*, Duke University Press, Durham, NC, 1991.

23 . . . and collected in Paul Taylor, *After Andy: Soho in the Eighties*, Schwartz City, Melbourne, 1995.

24 Richard Ellmann (ed.) *The Artist as Critic: Critical Writings of Oscar Wilde*, Chicago University Press, Chicago, 1982. There is also a strong connection between irony, postmodernism and camp—the connecting thread between Wilde, Warhol and Taylor, and part of the reason for the violent distaste for all three displayed so consistently by their more muscular critics. See Susan Sontag, 'Notes on camp' in *Against Interpretation*, Anchor Books, New York, 1986.

25 Meaghan Morris, 'Politics now', in *The Pirate's Fiancée*, Verso, London, 1988, p. 178; originally published in *Intervention*, no. 20, 1985, the issue which includes my extended reply to it, 'The last post'.

26 I'm thinking of the Walter Pater of the famous suppressed 'aestheticist' afterword to *The Renaissance*, University of Chicago Press, Chicago, 1994.

27 'Folly' in *The Error of My Ways*, p. 20.

28 See Ross Gibson's brilliant essay on the essay, Montaigne, and the essay-films of Chris Marker, in *South of the West*, Indiana University Press, Bloomington, 1992.

29 John Docker, *Postmodernism and Popular Culture*, Cambridge University Press, Melbourne, 1994; Peter Goodall *High Culture, Popular Culture: The Long Debate*, Allen & Unwin, Sydney, 1995.

30 Peter Wilmoth, *Glad All Over: The Countdown Years 1974–1987*, McPhee Gribble, Ringwood, Vic., 1993.

31 *On the Beach* (1959), directed by Stanley Kramer, based on the novel by Neville Shute. *Mad Max* (1979), *Mad Max 2* (1981) and *Mad Max: Beyond Thunderdome* (1985) were all directed by Dr George Miller.

32 Ross Gibson, 'Yondering: a reading of *Mad Max Beyond*

Thunderdome' Art & Text, no. 19, Oct. 1985, pp. 24–33; reprinted in Ross Gibson, *South of the West*, Indiana University Press, Bloomington, Ind., 1992.

33 Krim Benterrak, Stephen Muecke and Paddy Roe, *Reading the Country: Introduction to Nomadology*, Fremantle Arts Centre Press, Fremantle, 1984; see also Stephen Muecke, *Textual Space: Aboriginality and Cultural Studies*, UNSW Press, Sydney, 1992. For Mudrooroo's criticisms, see Mudrooroo Narogin, *Writing from the Fringe: A Study of Modern Aboriginal Literature*, Hyland House, Melbourne, 1990, p. 151.

34 Gilles Deleuze and Felix Guattari. *A Thousand Plateaus*, University of Minnesota Press, Minneapolis, 1987. See also Brian Massumi, *A User's Guide to Capitalism and Schizophrenia*, MIT Press, Cambridge, Mass., 1992.

35 Here I follow the various accounts given by Eric Michaels. His key works are: 'Constraints on knowledge in an economy of oral information' *Current Anthropology*, vol. 26, pp. 505–510; *Aboriginal Invention of Television*, Australian Institute for Aboriginal Studies, Canberra, 1986; *For A Cultural Future*, Artspace, Sydney, 1987; *UnBecoming*, EmPress, Sydney, 1991, *Bad Aboriginal Art*, Allen & Unwin, Sydney 1994. See also Tom O'Regan (ed.), 'Communication and tradition: essays after Eric Michaels' *Continuum*, vol. 3, no. 2, 1990.

36 Stuart Cunningham, *Featuring Australia: The Cinema of Charles Chauvel*, Allen & Unwin, Sydney, 1990.

37 Stephen Muecke, 'Australia, for example' in *Columbus' Blindness and Other Essays*, ed. Cassandra Pybus, University of Queensland Press, St Lucia, Qld, 1994, p. 16. This essay subsequently became the concluding chapter of Muecke's book *No Road*, Fremantle Arts Centre Press, Fremantle, WA, 1997.

38 See Bernard Cohen, *Tourism*, Picador, Sydney, 1991; Sabrina Achilles, *Waste*, Local Consumption, Sydney, 1995; Justine Ettler, *The River Ophelia*, Picador, Sydney, 1995; *Marilyn's Almost Terminal New York Adventure*, Picador, Sydney, 1996; Bernard Cohen, *The Blindman's Hat*, Allen & Unwin, Sydney, 1997. The lines I've quoted from *Blindman's* are on pp. 52–3 and from *Ophelia*, pp. 299–300. I would not like to give the impression that the UTS writers' program produces writers all of one stamp. To the range of styles and concerns of these three authors, one could add the very different work of Beth Yahp, Gillian Mears and Jane Messer, all of whom also passed through the program.

39 Interview with the author, quoted in McKenzie Wark, 'The courses of true fiction', *Australian*, 5 Oct. 1994.

40 John Docker, *Postmodernism and Popular Culture*, Cambridge University Press, Melbourne, 1994. The conference was Manuf(r)acturing

Australia. Papers from it by Adrian Martin, Ross Harley, Catharine Lumby and McKenzie Wark appear in *On the Beach*, no. 10, 1986.

41 Catharine Lumby, 'Speech impediments' *On the Beach*, no. 10, 1986.

42 John Anderson, *Art & Reality*, Hale & Iremonger, Sydney, 1982; A. J. Baker, *Anderson's Social Philosophy*, Angus & Robertson, Sydney, 1979.

43 See Adrian Martin, 'No Flowers For the Cinephile' in *Islands in the Stream*, ed. Paul Foss, Pluto Press, Sydney, 1988.

44 Catharine Lumby, *Bad Girls: The Media, Sex and Feminism in the 1990s*, Allen & Unwin, Sydney, 1996. Lumby also draws on a contemporaneous style of feminist writing, but that's another story, and would require another essay to tell it.

45 Mark Mordue, 'A postmodern rose' *Cinema Papers*, no. 114, 1997.

46 See for example, Christopher Chapman, *1996 Adelaide Biennial of Australian Art*, AGSA, Adelaide, 1996.

47 Peter Callas, 'Some liminal aspects of the technology trade' *Mediamatic*, vol. 5, no. 3, 1990; The Jean Baudrillard work is *America*, Verso, London, 1988, p. 32. See also Peter Callas, 'Structure without substance', *Artlink*, vol. 4, no. 3, 1987.

48 See special issues of *Art Network*, Spring 1984; *Tension*, Aug. 1990; *Art & Text*, Sept. 1991 and *Zones of Love: Contemporary Art From Japan*, Museum of Contemporary Art, Sydney, 1991; and the book *Higher than Heaven, Japan, War and Everything*, PGI, Sydney, 1995, by Tony Barrell and Rick Tanaka, formerly the producers of the 2JJJ radio program *Nippi Rock Shop*.

THE DEMIDENKO EFFECT

1 On news value, see Herbert J. Gans, *Deciding What's News*, Vintage Books, Random House, 1980; John Hartley, *Understanding News*, London, Methuen, 1982.

2 Michael Oakeshott, *The Politics of Faith and the Politics of Scepticism*, Yale University Press, New Haven, 1996.

3 Michael Pusey, *Economic Rationalism in Canberra*, Cambridge University Press, Melbourne, 1992. See also Chris James, et al. (eds), *A Defence of Economic Rationalism*, Allen & Unwin, Sydney, 1993; Donald Horne (ed,), *The Trouble with Economic Rationalism*, Scribe, Newham, Vic., 1992.

4 See Helen Daniel (ed.), 'Symposium on authenticity', *Australian Book Review*, no. 187, Dec. 1996.

5 David Bentley, 'Questions posed on author's past' *Courier Mail*, 19 Aug. 1995, reprinted in John Jost, Gianna Totaro and Christine Tyshing, *The Demidenko File*, Penguin Books, Ringwood, 1996, pp. 98–99.

6 McKenzie Wark, 'A welcome at the back door' *Australian*, 31 Jan. 1996.

7 Ghassan Hage, quoted in John Jost, et al., p. 149.

8 Karl Marx, 'The eighteenth brumaire of Louis Bonaparte', *Surveys From Exile*, Penguin, Harmondsworth, 1973, p. 147.

9 Andrew Riemer, *America With Subtitles*, Reed Books, Port Melbourne, 1995; *The Demidenko Debate*, Allen & Unwin, Sydney, 1996.

10 Robert Manne, *The Culture of Forgetting: Helen Demidenko and the Holocaust*, Text, Melbourne, 1996.

11 On the theme that the university system is to blame, see *Quadrant* magazine's coverage from September to December 1995.

12 Hannah Arendt, *The Origins of Totalitarianism*, Harcourt, Brace, Jovanovich, New York, 1973, p. 356.

13 Susan Moore, 'Home truths' *Quadrant*, Oct. 1995, p. 13.

14 Arendt, 'Thinking moral considerations' in *Social Research*, vol. 38, 1971, pp. 417–446, at p. 420.

15 For an introduction to Arendt on judgement, see M. W. Jackson, 'The responsibility of judgement and the judgement of responsibility' in Gisela T. Kaplan and Clive S. Kessler, *Hannah Arendt: Thinking, Judging, Freedom*, Allen & Unwin, Sydney, 1989.

16 David Hume, *A Treatise of Human Nature*, Penguin Books, London, 1985, p. 522.

17 Hannah Arendt, *The Human Condition*, Doubleday, New York, 1959, p. 50.

18 Arendt, *The Human Condition*, p. 57.

19 For a useful discussion of the 'virtual' in the philosophers Henri Bergson and Gilles Deleuze, see Michael Hardt, *Gilles Deleuze: An Apprenticeship In Philosophy*, University of Minnesota Press, Minneapolis, 1993, pp. 13–25.

20 I'm compressing to very bare statements the ideas about how language actually works in the world offered by Michel Foucault and Jean-François Lyotard, respectively. For an introduction to their work see Meaghan Morris, *The Pirate's Fiancée*, Verso, London, 1988, Chapters 2 and 11.

21 Sophie Knox, 'Sydney Jewish Museum', in *Sydney Inside Out*, eds Jenny Andersen, et al. Intervention Publications, no. 24, Sydney, 1996.

22 William Gass, *The Tunnel*, Knopf, New York, 1995; Daniel Goldhagen, *Hitler's Willing Executioners*, Little, Brown, New York, 1996. On the latter, see Adam Shatz, 'Browning's version', *Lingua Franca*, vol. 7, no. 2, Feb. 1997.

23 Romona Koval, 'A conversation with William Gass on the tunnel' *Quadrant*, July 1996.

24 Jean-François Lyotard develops this idea through a number of his

works, particularly in *The Postmodern Condition*, University of Minnesota Press, Minneapolis, 1984; *Just Gaming*, University of Minnesota Press, Minneapolis, 1985, and most fully in *The Differend: Phrases in Dispute*, University of Minnesota Press, Minneapolis, 1988. A helpful secondary text is Bill Readings, *Introducing Lyotard: Art and Politics*, Routledge, New York, 1991.

25 McKenzie Wark, 'Revamp the culture club', *Australian*, 13 Sept. 1995; 'A Welcome At the Back Door', 31 Jan. 1996. Raymond Gaita responded in *Eureka St*, August 1996. Meaghan Morris and myself replied in *Eureka St*, September 1996, Gaita again in October 1996. I continued the debate in *Meanjin*, no. 3, 1996. More 'ripostes' followed in *Meanjin*, no. 1, 1997. There, Guy Rundle gives a very poor account of my argument and parrots charges originally made by Gaita. Christopher Cordner subjects my arguments to a far more professional bout of logic-chopping, but does not grasp that my charge against the 'theological' character of Gaita's moral philosophy is a Nietzschean one. Much contemporay philosophy still has the character of the theological even in the absence of the deity. God is dead, but Gaita still occupies his universe. The irony is that by the simple act of choosing to reply, both Rundle and Cordner affirm, by their actions, my main point: that ethics is a practice of public conversation about a common object or event.

26 John Hughes, 'An essay on forgetting', *Heat*, no. 1, 1996.

27 For exemplary readings of writing as a transgression of its own form, see Maurice Blonchot, *The Work of Fire*, Stanford University Press, Stanford, 1995; Gilles Deleuze and Felix Guattari, *Kafka: Towards a Minor Literature*, University of Minnesota Press, Minneapolis, 1986.

28 Hannah Arendt, *The Origins of Totalitarianism*, Harcourt Brace, 1975, p. 56 ff; Lucy Dawidowicz, *The War Against the Jews 1933–45*, Penguin Books, Harmondsworth, 1975, pp. 215–46, p. 410ff.

29 Hannah Arendt, *Eichmann in Jerusalem*, Penguin Books, London, 1992, p. 252.

30 Arendt, *Origins*, p. 356. See also M. Bittman, 'Totalitarianism: career of a concept' in Gisela Kaplan, et al. (eds), *Hannah Arendt: Thinking, Judging, Freedom*, Allen & Unwin, Sydney, 1989.

31 Walter Benjamin, 'The storyteller', *Illuminations*, Shocken Books, New York, p. 87. On Benjamin, see Momme Brodersen, *Walter Benjamin: A Biography*, Verso, London, 1996.

32 Primo Levi, *Survival in Auschwitz*, Collier Books, New York, 1993. On Levi, see Mirna Cicioni, *Primo Levi: Bridges of Knowledge*, Berg, Washington, DC, 1995.

33 Theodor Adorno, *Prisms*, MIT Press, Cambridge, Mass., p. 34. For an intellectual history that puts Adorno in the context of the

'Frankfurt School', see Martin Jay, *The Dialectical Imagination*, Little Brown, Boston, 1973.

34 Andrew Riemer, *The Demidenko Debate*, Allen & Unwin, Sydney, 1996.

35 Edmond Jabès, *The Book of Margins*, University of Chicago Press, Chicago, 1993, p. x. See also Eric Gould (ed.) *The Sin of the Book: Edmond Jabès*, University of Nebraska Press, Lincoln, 1985.

36 Theodor Adorno and Max Horkheimer, *Dialectic of Enlightenment*, Verso, London, 1979.

37 Robert Manne, *The Culture of Forgetting*, Text Publishing Co., Melbourne, 1996, p. 191.

38 ibid. p. 2, p. 167.

39 As quoted in Jean-François Lyotard, *The Differend: Phrases in Dispute*, University of Minnesota Press, Minneapolis, 1988, p. 2.

40 William Schaffer, 'The book that evaded the question', *Southerly*, Spring 1995; Bernard Cohen, 'The quality of anti-semitism in *The Hand That Signed the Paper*', *Southerly*, 1996.

41 See Michel Foucault's essay on Bataille, 'A preface to transgression', in *Language, Counter-Memory, Practice*, Cornell University Press, Ithaca, 1977.

42 The two key essays here being Roland Barthes, 'The death of the author' in *The Rustle of Language*, University of California Press, Berkeley, 1989 and Michel Foucault, 'What is an author?' in *The Foucault Reader*, Penguin, London, 1991.

43 Raimond Gaita, *Good and Evil: An Absolute Conception*, Macmillan, London, 1991, p. 7.

44 Raimond Gaita, 'Taboos and corruptions' *Quadrant*, no. 264, Mar. 1990, p. 46, for this and the following quotes.

45 The classic text for the sceptical method is Sextus Empiricus, *Outline of Scepticism*, translated by Julia Annas and Jonathan Barnes, Cambridge University Press, Cambridge, 1994. See also Richard H. Popkin, *The History of Scepticism from Erasmus to Spinoza*, University of California Press, Berkeley, 1979.

46 Robert Manne, *The Shadow of 1917*, Text Publishing, 1994, pp. 17–19.

47 McKenzie Wark, *Virtual Geography: Living With Global Media Events*, Indiana University Press, Bloomington, Ind., 1994, p. 49 ff.

POLITICAL CORRECTNESS

1 The three essays by David Williamson addressed in this chapter are: 'Truce in the identity wars' *Weekend Australian*, 11 May 1996; 'Men, women and human nature' in *Double Take: Six Incorrect Essays*, ed. Peter Coleman, Reed Books, Port Melbourne, 1996; and 'Universal moral soldier' *Bulletin*, 2 April 1996.

2 Marlene Goldsmith, *Political Incorrectness: Defying the Thought Police*, Hodder & Stoughton, Rydalmere, 1996, p. 140. There is a quote from Professor Stephen Knight, on p. 144. She does not link Knight with PC, and what she makes of the sentence is too risible to mention. See also Marlene Goldsmith, 'The politics of correctness', *Sydney Morning Herald*, 3 June 1996, with a reply by Andrew Jakubowicz. Phillip Adams (ed.), *The Retreat from Tolerance*, ABC Books, Sydney, 1997 contains a number of useful essays on PC in Australia, and an earlier version of this chapter.

3 Allan Boom, *The Closing of the American Mind*, New York, Simon & Schuster, 1987; Dinesh D'Souza, *An Illiberal Education: The Politics of Race and Sex on Campus*, New York, Vintage Books, 1992. See also Lawrence Levine's spirited reply to both books, *The Opening of the American Mind*, Beacon Press, Boston, 1996. Also of interest: Russell Jacoby, *The Last Intellectuals: American Culture in the Age of Academe*, Basic Books, New York, 1987; Tod Gitlin, *The Sixties: Years of Hope, Days of Rage*, Bantam Books, New York, 1987; Tod Gitlin, *The Twilight of Common Dreams: Why America is Wracked By Culture Wars*, Metropolitan Books, New York, 1995; Andrew Ross, *No Respect: Intellectuals and Popular Culture*, Routledge, New York,1989.

4 Richard Hofstadter, *The Paranoid Style in American Politics, and Other Essays*, Knopf, New York, 1965. For a more recent work, both influenced by and critical of Hofstadter, see Sara Diamond, *Roads to Dominion: Right Wing Movements and Political Power in the US*, Guilford Press, New York, 1995. I take up some of these issues further in McKenzie Wark, 'The anti-public sphere', *21C*, no. 2, 1995.

5 See for example, Victor Navasky, *Naming Names*, John Caldor, London, 1982. The story of E. H. Norman is told in John W. Dower's poignant introduction to E. H. Norman, *Origins of the Modern Japanese State*, Pantheon, Random House, New York, 1975. The story of just how damaging the McCarthyite witch-hunt among Asian studies scholars was to America's ability to think through its foreign policy in Asia, especially in Vietnam is told in David Halberstam, *The Best and the Brightest*, Penguin Books, Harmondsworth, 1972, pp. 128–50.

6 David McKnight. *Australia's Spies and Their Secrets*, Allen & Unwin, Sydney, 1994, Part II; Fiona Capp, *Writers Defiled*, McPhee Gribble, Melbourne, 1993; John McLaren, *Writing in Hope and Fear: Literature as Politics in Postwar Australia*, Cambridge University Press, Cambridge, 1996.

7 Robert Hughes, *Culture of Complaint: The Fraying of America*, Oxford University Press, New York, 1993, p. 30; for another view see Nadine Strossen, *Defending Pornography: Free Speech, Sex, and the*

Fight for Women's Rights, New York, Scribner, 1995; and the person heard from least in the mainstream reporting of this one—Stumhoffer herself: 'Goya's *Naked Maja* and the classroom climate' *Democratic Culture*, Spring 1994.

8 Wendy Steiner, *The Scandal of Pleasure: Art in the Age of Fundamentalism*, Chicago University Press, Chicago, 1995.

9 The information for the following few paragraphs can be found in John K. Wilson, *The Myth of Political Correctness: The Conservative Attack on Higher Education*, Duke University Press, Durham, 1995. Also of interest is Michael Bérubé, *Public Access: Literary Theory and American Cultural Politics*, Verso, New York, 1994; Jeffrey Williams (ed.), *PC Wars*, Routledge, New York, 1995; Paul Berman, *Debating PC: The Controversy Over Political Correctness on College Campuses*, Dell, New York, 1992.

10 David Mamet, *Oleana*, Pantheon Books, New York, 1992.

11 The film is supposedly based on the Orr case, a considerably more interesting and reliable account of which can be found in Cassandra Pybus, *Seduction and Consent: A Case of Gross Moral Turpitude*, Reed Books, Port Melbourne, Vic., 1994.

12 Helen Garner, *The First Stone*, Picador, Sydney, 1995; David Williamson, *Dead White Males*, Currency Press, Sydney, 1995.

13 For views on Garner's book by younger women, see Virginia Trioli, *Generation F*, Reed Books, Melbourne, 1996; Kathy Bail (ed.), *DIY Feminism*, Allen & Unwin, Sydney, 1996. On the generational divide in public life more generally, see Mark Davis, *Gangland*, Allen & Unwin, Sydney 1997. For other interesting views on Garner's book see Anne Summers, 'Shockwaves at the revolution' *Good Weekend Magazine*, 18 March, 1995; Cassandra Pybus' review in *Australian Book Review*, May 1995, pp. 6–8 and the interview with Pybus and Garner by Romana Koral pp. 9–12; Helen Garner, 'The fate of the first stone', and Jenna Mead, 'Feminism and non-fiction', both in *Sydney Papers*, Spring 1995 and Ann Curthoys, 'Discussion' in *Australian Feminist Studies*, Autumn 1995.

14 Research published as: Vivien Johnson, *The Last Resort: A Women's Refuge*, Penguin, Ringwood, Vic., 1981; Rosemary Pringle, *Secretaries Talk: Sexuality, Power and Work*, Allen & Unwin, Sydney, 1989; Judith Allen, *Sex and Secrets: Crimes Involving Australian Women Since 1880*, Oxford Univesity Press, Melbourne, 1990.

15 Slavoj Zizek, *Tarrying With the Negative*, Duke Univesity Press, Durham, 1993, p. 200 ff. See also Slavoj Zizek, *The Sublime Object of Ideology*, Verso, London, 1991.

16 For collections of Australian cultural studies material, see John Frow and Meaghan Morris, *Australian Cultural Studies: A Reader*, Allen & Unwin, Sydney, 1993; Graeme Turner (ed.), *Nation,*

Culture, Text: Australian Culture and Media Studies, London, Routledge, 1993.

17 Meaghan Morris and Stephen Muecke, 'Editorial' *UTS Review*, vol. 1, no. 1, Aug. 1995.

18 More thoughtful feminist thinkers have moved beyond the closed world of the Lacanian drag of psychoanalytic theory. See for example: Liz Grosz, *Volatile Bodies*, Allen & Unwin, Sydney, 1994; Elspeth Probyn, *Outside Belongings*, Routledge, New York, 1996 and Moira Gatens, *Imaginary Bodies*, Routledge, London, 1996.

19 For book-length documentation of the existence of a postmodern, pop feminism, see Kathy Bail (ed.) *DIY Feminism*, Allen & Unwin, Sydney, 1996, particularly the essay by Sherryn George, former editor of *Women's Forum* magazine; Virginia Trioli, *Generation F*, ibid. Trioli is a journalist for *The Age* newspaper in Melbourne; Helen Razer, *In Pursuit of Hygiene*, Random House, Sydney, 1996. Razer is a popular breakfast announcer on JJJ radio; Kaz Cooke, *Get a Grip*, Penguin, Ringwood, Vic., 1996. Cooke is a columnist for the *Sydney Morning Herald,* and a popular cartoonist, creater of Hermione the Modern Girl.

20 See for example, Ien Ang, *Watching Dallas*, Methuen, London, 1985; *Desperately Seeking the Audience*, Routledge, London, 1991; *Living Room Wars*, Routledge, London, 1995.

21 See in particular the work of John Hartley, *Tele-ology*, Routledge, London, 1991; *Politics of Pictures*, Routledge, London, 1992; *Popular Reality*, Edward Arnold, London, 1996.

22 Catharine Lumby, *Bad Girls*, Allen & Unwin, Sydney, 1997.

23 Central to the debate on cultural policy studies, and embodying both its strengths and weaknesses, is Stuart Cunningham, *Framing Culture*, Allen & Unwin, Sydney, 1992. See also McKenzie Wark, 'After literature: culture, policy, theory and beyond', *Meanjin*, vol. 51, no. 4, Summer 1992. That issue of *Meanjin* contains a lively debate on cultural policy studies.

24 McKenzie Wark, *Virtual Geography*, Indiana University Press, Bloomington, Ind., 1994, pp. 18–23.

POSTMODERNISM

1 For example: Keith Windschuttle, *The Killing of History*, Macleay Press, 1995; Beatrice Faust, *Australian Rationalist*, no. 38, 1995.

2 The coverage in the *Australian* pursued other issues. The headlines pretty much sum it up: Christopher Koch, 'Academics put the con in deconstruction', *Australian*, 14 June 1996; McKenzie Wark, 'A cry from the postmodernists', *Australian*, 17 June 1996; Jonathan Bowden, 'Academe's shrill assault on art', *Australian*, 24 June

1996; Luke Slattery and Evan McHugh, 'Fact vs fiction' *Weekend Australian*, 6 July 1996; Christopher Koch, 'Author strikes back' *Weekend Australian*, 13 July, 1996.

3 David Williamson, 'Men, women and human nature' in *Double Take: Six Incorrect Essays*, ed. Peter Coleman, Reed Books, Port Melbourne, 1996; 'Universal moral soldier', *Bulletin*, 2 April 1996.

4 Michel Foucault, *Discipline and Punish*, Penguin, Harmondsworth, 1977.

5 Jim Davidson, 'Interview: David Williamson' *Meanjin*, vol. 38, no. 2, July 1979, p. 186.

6 The first significant statements on sociobiology are: E. O. Wilson, *Sociobiology: The New Synthesis*, Harvard University Press, Cambridge, 1975; and Richard Dawkins, *The Selfish Gene*, Oxford University Press, 1976, rev. edn 1989. E. O. Wilson extended sociobiological thinking from social insects and animals to humans in *On Human Nature*, Penguin, Harmondsworth, 1995. Critical reactions against sociobiology are Steven Rose, R. C. Lewontin and Leon Kamin, *Not In Our Genes*, Penguin, Harmondsworth, 1990; Stephen Jay Gould, *An Urchin in the Storm*, Penguin, Harmondsworth, 1990. On the two-way traffic between social and biological metaphors, see Andrew Ross, *Strange Weather: Culture, Science, and Technology in the Age of Limits*, Verso, New York, 1991; Andrew Ross, *The Chicago Gangster Theory of Life: Nature's Debt to Society*, Verso, New York, 1994. Williamson doesn't refer directly to E.O. Wilson and may draw his ideas on sociobiology from writers other than its founder. But he does name one James G. Wilson, a conservative political scientist and author of *On Character*, American Enterprise Institute, Washington DC, 1995; *The Moral Sense*, Free Press, New York, 1993. A juxtaposition so wildly unlikely that it seems—what else?—postmodern.

7 Daniel C. Dennett, *Darwin's Dangerous Idea*, Penguin Books, London, 1995. See also Bo Dahlbom (ed.) *Dennett and His Critics*, Blackwell, Oxford, 1995.

8 See Marek Kohn, *The Race Gallery: The Return of Racial Science*, Vintage, London, 1996.

9 Dennett, *Darwin's Dangerous Idea*, p. 491. Italics in the original.

10 E. L. Grosz, *Volatile Bodies*, Allen & Unwin, Sydney, 1994, p. 191.

11 Richard Dawkins, *The Selfish Gene*, Oxford University Press, Oxford, 1989, p. 192. Dawkins appears to have derived the idea of language as a new and divergent form of memory in the evolution of life on earth from François Jacob, *The Logic of Life*, Penguin, Harmondsworth, 1982.

12 Michel Foucault, *The Archaeology of Knowledge*, Tavistock, London, 1977; Jean-François Lyotard, *The Differend*, University of Minnesota Press, Minneapolis, 1988.

13 On Kant in relation to the German enlightenment, see James Schmidt (ed.), *What is Enlightenment?*, University of California Press, Berkeley, 1996.

14 For a history of the eighteenth century enlightenment in social and historical context, see Peter Gay, *The Enlightenment: The Science of Freedom*, Norton, New York, 1977.

15 See Kimberly Hutchings, *Kant, Critique and Politics*, Routledge, London, 1996.

16 Andrew Riemer, 'The long path towards the dead right male' *Sydney Morning Herald*, 15 Mar. 1996.

17 Robert Macklin, 'A hectoring tone that ill befits Williamson' *Canberra Times*, 23 Aug. 1995.

18 Brian Kiernan, *David Williamson: A Writer's Career*, William Heinemann, Sydney, 1996, p. 288–289.

THE FALL OF THE MAGIC KINGDOM

1 Mudrooroo, 'The Aboriginalising of Heiner Müller', in Gerhard Fischer (ed.) *The Mudrooroo/Müller Project: A Theatrical Casebook*, University of NSW Press, Sydney, 1993, p. 19.

2 The classic study of the west's fantasies about the East is Edward Said, *Orientalism*, Routledge, Penguin Books, London, 1995.

3 Plato on the poets can be found in *The Republic*, Penguin Books, Harmondsworth, 1983, pp. 436–9. Some people draw a contrast between Socrates and Plato, even though we know the former mostly from the latter's writings. See Cornelius Castoriadis, *Philosophy, Politics, Autonomy*, Oxford University Press, New York, 1991, pp. 5–7. In the dialogues collected in Plato, *Early Socratic Dialogues*, Penguin Books, Harmondsworth, 1987, I think we are closer to the 'historical' Socrates, if there is such a person, than in some of the 'later' works, like *The Republic*, in which he becomes a character espousing Plato's rather different philosophy.

4 For Littlemore's own account of his role in the virtual republic, see Stuart Littlemore, *The Media and Me*, ABC Books, Sydney, 1996.

5 Jill Rowbotham, 'Family rejects medallion claim' *Australian*, Monday 26 Aug. 1996.

6 See Carl Bridge, *Manning Clark: Essays on His Place in History*, Melbourne University Press, Melbourne, 1994, for a range of views. For Clark in context, see Stephen Holt, *Manning Clark and Australian History*, University of Queensland Press, St Lucia, Qld, 1982; Rob Pascoe, *The Manufacture of Australian History*, Oxford University Press, 1979.

7 Robert Manne, 'The whole bloody muddle' in *The Australian's Review of Books*, Oct. 1996.

8 Susan Davies (ed.) *Dear Kathleen, Dear Manning: The Correspondence of Manning Clark and Kathleen Fitzpatrick*, Melbourne University Press, Melbourne, 1996, p. 49.

9 *New Left Review*'s collection, Gareth Steadman Jones, et al. *Western Marxism: A Critical Reader*, New Left Books, 1979, was my starting point on that topic. One can follow its fate through Perry Anderson's essays: *Considerations on Western Marxism*, Verso, London, 1979; *Arguments Within English Marxism*, Verso, London, 1980; *In the Tracks of Historical Materialism*, Verso, London, 1984. Anderson wanted to revive a European radical tradition, but E. P. Thompson wanted to root a renewed left in the more English soil of the 'Liberty Tree'. See E. P. Thompson, *The Making of the English Working Class*, Vintage Books, New York, 1966; *The Poverty of Theory and Other Essays*, Monthly Review Press, New York, 1978. The best expression of the social democratic alternative I'm aware of is Gosta Esping-Andersen, *Politics Against Markets: The Social Democratic Road to Power*, Princeton University Press, Princeton, N.J., 1985; *The Three Worlds of Welfare Capitalism*, Princeton University Press, Princeton, N.J., 1990.

10 John Pilger, *A Secret Country*, Vintage, London, 1990, pp. 179–232.

11 See E. P. Thompson (ed.) *Exterminism and Cold War*, Verso, London, 1982.

12 Anne Coombs, *Sex and Anarchy: The Life and Death of the Sydney Push*, Penguin, Ringwood, Vic., 1996, pp. 96–7.

13 Communists were much more inclined to read political economy: Ken Buckley and E. L. Wheelwright, *No Paradise For Workers: Capitalism and the Common People in Australia 1788–1914*, Oxford University Press, Melbourne, 1988; E. L. Wheelwright and Abraham David, *The Third Wave: Australia and Asian Capitalism*, Left Book Club Co-operative, Sydney, 1989.

14 Humphrey McQueen, 'Unusual suspects' *Australian Book Review*, Nov. 1996, p. 39. See also John Larkin, 'When hysteria becomes history' *Sydney Morning Herald*, 31 May, 1997, 9s. McQueen and Manne slug it out in Humphrey McQueen, *Suspect History: Manning Clark and the future of Australia's Past*, Wakefield Press, Adelaide, 1997 and Robert Manne, 'Battle for history's high ground' *Weekend Australian*, 7 June, 1997. A plague on both their old, cold houses.

15 André Glucksmann, *The Master Thinkers*, Harper & Row, New York, 1980. I'm quoting first from the concluding essay, 'The finishing of history', p. 267 ff; then paraphrasing 'The impossible Mr Socrates', p. 66 ff.

16 Ryszard Kapuściński, *Imperium*, Knopf, New York, 1994, p. 86.

17 On John Ford, see Andrew Sarris, *John Ford: Movie Mystery*, Indiana University Press, Bloomington, 1975; on Sergei Eisenstein, Ion Barna, *Eisenstein*, Little Brown, Boston, 1973.

18 Robert Manne,*The Shadow of 1917*, Text Publishing, Melbourne, 1994.

19 Aleksandr Solzhenitsyn's most famous work is *The Gulag Archipelago, 1918–1956: An Experiment in Literary Investigation vol. 1*, Collins & Harvill, London, 1978; see also *A Day in th Life of Ivan Denisovitch*, Penguin, Harmondsworth, 1971; *A Nobel Lecture on Literature*, Harper & Row, New York, 1972.

20 Hannah Arendt, *The Origins of Totalitarianism*, Harcourt, Brace Jovanovich, New York, 1973.

21 For an interesting reading of *Mein Kampf*, see J. G. Ballard, *A User's Guide to the Millennium: Essays and Reviews*, Picador, New York, 1996.

22 Jean-Jacques Rousseau, *The Social Contract*, Dent, London, 1973, pp. 193 ff.

23 William Hazlitt, a remarkable radical essayist, against whom one can only say two things: that he was quite racist towards the Scots, and late in life wrote an extraordinary hagiography of Napoleon, all in sentences of the most beautiful cadence. See his *Selected Writings*, Penguin, Harmondsworth, 1989.

24 Manning Clark, *Meeting Soviet Man*, Angus & Robertson, Sydney, 1962.

25 Manning Clark, *A Historian's Apprenticeship*, Melbourne University Press, 1992, p. 21.

26 Glucksmann is quoted in Adam Gopnik, 'Cinéma disputé' *New Yorker*, 5 February, 1996, p. 37. He is inverting a line from Terence, from *The Self-Tormentor*, Act 1, Scene 1.

27 Vaclav Havel at his best is, I think, the *Letters to Olga*, Faber, London, 1988.

28 Perhaps the most relevant writings of Pier Paolo Pasolini to cite in this context are the *Lutheran Letters*, Carcanet Press, Manchester, 1983; and *Heretical Empiricism*, Indiana University Press, Bloomington, 1988.

29 C. M. H. Clark, *A History of Australia*, vol. VI, Melbourne University Press, 1987, p. 489. All the following quotes are also from this volume.

30 Fyodor Dostoyevsky, 'Three ideas', in *A Writer's Diary, Volume II 1877–1881*, Quartet Books, London, 1994, pp. 811–16

31 Alexis de Tocqville was the author of the famous *Democracy in America*, 2 vols. Vintage Books, New York, 1990. Clark studied Tocqueville while in Europe.

32 Aleksandr Solzhenitsyn, *The Gulag Archipelago*, vol. 1, HarperCollins, New York, 1991, p. 10.

33 Eric Hobsbawm's narrative histories of the modern period are: *The Age of Revolution 1789–1848*, Vintage, New York, 1996; *The Age of Capital 1848–1875*, Vintage, New York, 1996; *The Age of Empire 1875–1914*, Vintage, New York, 1996; *The Age of Extremes 1914–1991*, Vintage, New York, 1996.

34 Manning Clark, *The Quest for Grace*, Penguin Books, Ringwood, Vic., 1990, p. 122.

35 The key work here is Stanley Cohen, *Folk Devils and Moral Panics*, McGibbon & Kee, London, 1972.

36 See Theodor Adorno, *The Culture Industry: Selected Essays on Mass Culture*, Routledge, London, 1990; *Minima Moralia*, New Left Books, London, 1979.

37 *A History of Australia*, vol. 6, p. 464. Egon Kisch was the author of, among other things, *Tales From Seven Ghettoes*, R. Anscombe, London, 1948.

38 Boris Pasternak was the author of *Doctor Zhivago*, Pantheon, New York, 1958, and see also *An Essay in Autobiography*, Collins & Harvill, London, 1956.

39 Walter Benjamin, 'The storyteller' in *Illuminations*, Shocken Books, New York, p. 83 ff.

40 I'm (mis)quoting this story from Walter Benjamin, ibid., pp. 89–90, who got it from Michel de Montaigne, *The Complete Essays*, Stanford University Press, Stanford, Cal., 1992, p. 6, who, in turn, got it from Herodotus, *The Histories*, Penguin Books, London, 1996, pp. 154–60.

41 *Labour History*, no. 55, 1988, pp. 92 ff.

42 Paul Carter, *The Road To Botany Bay*, Knopf, New York, 1987, Introduction.

43 Plutarch's essays and 'lives' were an influence on both Montaigne and Shakespeare. *Makers of Rome*, Penguin Books, London, 1991; *Fall of the Roman Republic*, Penguin Books, London, 1991.

44 Peter Ryan, 'Manning Clark' *Quadrant*, vol. 37, no. 9, 1993. Robert Manne was editor of *Quadrant* at the time. For an excellent account of the 'Ryan Affair', see Peter Craven's essay in Carl Bridge, *Manning Clark: Essays on his Place in History*, Melbourne University Press, Melbourne, 1994.

45 Brian Kiernan, *David Williamson: A Writer's Career*, William Heinemann, Sydney, 1996, p. 237.

46 Hegel's letter concerning Napoleon is quoted in Shlomo Avineri, *Hegel's Theory of the Modern State*, Cambridge University Press, Cambridge, 1972, p. 63; Murdoch's youthful admiration for Lenin is recounted in William Shawcross, *Murdoch*, Simon & Schuster, New York, 1993.

47 Mark Lander, 'Deal by Murdoch for satellite TV startles industry' *New York Times*, 26 Feb. 1996.

48 Jennifer Gould, 'The Russian mob's submarine scheme' *Village Voice*, 4 Mar. 1997, p. 32.

49 Robert Manne, *The Culture of Forgetting*, Text Publishing, Melbourne, 1996, p. 2, p. 191, p. 105. The following headlines for columns by Manne and myself sum up the war of opinion on 'video nasties': Robert Manne 'Liberals deny video link' *Australian*, 6 January 1997; McKenzie Wark, 'Video link is a distorted view' *Australian*, 8 January 1997; Robert Manne 'Evidence demands a tenacious stand on censorship' *Australian* 13 January 1997; and McKenzie Wark, 'Danger in culture of silence' *Australian*, 22 January, 1997.

50 Andrew Riemer, *The Demidenko Debate*, Allen & Unwin, Sydney, 1996, pp. 83, 170.

FAIR GO, PAULINE

1 According to Scott Ellis, 'Pauline's 60 Minutes of fame' *Daily Telegraph*, 22 Oct. 1996.

2 A selection from the great mass of Hanson coverage: Michael Millett and Mike Seccombe, 'The power of Pauline Hanson' *Sydney Morning Herald*, 12 Oct. 1996; David Leser, 'Inside the mind of Pauline Hanson *Good Weekend*, 30 Nov. 1996; Judith Brett, 'The politics of grievance' *Australian's Review of Books*, May 1997; David Marr, 'Beyond the pale with Pauline' *Sydney Morning Herald*, 12 May 1997; and Nicholas Rothwell, 'Pauline's people' *Weekend Australian* 17 May 1997.

3 Russel Ward, *The Australian Legend*, Oxford University Press, Melbourne, 1958.

4 Vance Palmer, *The Legend of the Nineties*, Currey O'Neil, Melbourne, n.d., p. 24.

5 W. S. Merwin (ed.), *Products of the Perfected Civilisation: Selected Writings of Chamfort*, Macmillan, Toronto, 1969, p. 121.

6 Helen Garner, *The First Stone*, Picador, Sydney, 1995. See also Virginia Trioli, *Generation F*, Reed Books, Melbourne, 1995 and Cassandra Pybus, *Seduction and Consent: A Case of Gross Moral Turpitude*, Reed Books, Port Melbourne, 1994.

7 The Williamson remark is quoted from Brian Kiernan, *David Williamson: A Writer's Career*, William Heinemann, Sydney, 1996, p. 279.

8 Peter Cochrane, 'An Anglo Celtic echo' *The Australian's Review of Books*, Nov. 1996.

9 Phillip Adams, 'Our bigotry has never been silenced' *Weekend Australian*, 12 Oct. 1996.

10 On Ipswich, Ross Fitzgerald, 'The voice of the underclass' *Bulletin*,

22 Oct. 1996, pp. 20–21; on party factionalism, Ross Fitzgerald and Harold Thornton, *Labor in Queensland*, University of Queensland Press, St Lucia, Qld, 1989, p. 357.

11 Peter Cochrane, 'Voices of the past in anglo primal scream' *Australian*, 10 Oct. 1996.

12 For a succinct version of this argument, see Maurice Glasman, *Unnecessary Suffering: Managing Market Utopia*, Verso, London, 1996.

13 Jerzy Zubrzycki, 'Cynics woo the ethnic vote' *Australian*, 15 Oct. 1996; the earlier essay refered to is in M. Bowen (ed.) *Australia 2000: The Ethnic Impact*, University of New England, Armidale, 1977.

14 Helen Demidenko, 'Other places' *RePublica*, no. 3 1995, pp. 93–97; Brian Matthews, 'Pioneering' in *Toads*, ed. Andrew Sant, Allen & Unwin, Sydney, 1992.

15 Helen Demidenko, 'Pieces of the puzzle' *Meanjin*, no. 3, 1995, pp. 430–437.

16 *Quadrant*, Nov. 1995.

17 See any of the novels Sreten Bozic wrote under the pen name B. Wongar, and John O'Grady's *They're a Weird Mob*, Ure Smith, Sydney, 1963, which he wrote under the name Nino Culotta.

18 Peter Cochrane, *Industrialisation and Dependence: Australia's Road to Economic Development 1870–1939*, University of Queensland Press, St Lucia, Qld, 1980.

19 Graeme Campbell and Mark Uhlmann, *Australia Betrayed*, Foundation Press, Carlisle, WA, 1995. On the racist legacy of the labour movement, see Humphrey McQueen's classic account, *A New Britannia*, Penguin Australia, Ringwood, Vic., 1986.

20 On 'multi-racism', see the introductory essay in Ellie Vasta and Stephen Castle (ed.), *The Teeth Are Smiling: The Persistence of Racism in Multicultural Australia*, Allen & Unwin, Sydney, 1996.

21 Campbell and Uhlmann, *Australia Betrayed*, p. 201.

22 John Howard, 'Tolerance a part of policy', *Australian*, 9 Oct. 1996; compare to Graeme Campbell and Mark Uhlmann, *Australia Betrayed*, p. 178.

23 Mudrooroo, 'The Aboriginalising of Heiner Müller', in Gerhard Fischer, *The Mudrooroo/Müller Project: A Theatrical Casebook*, University of NSW Press, Sydney, 1993, p. 21.

24 Quoted in Greg Sheridan, 'APEC: mission accomplished in Subic Bay' *Australian*, 27 Nov. 1996.

25 Peter Davis, 'Mayor's mongrels claim leaves him in a council of one' *Australian*, 23 Oct. 1996.

26 Phillip Adams, 'Extreme exposure' *Weekend Australian*, 16 Nov. 1996.

27 Andrew Jakubowicz, *Racism, Ethnicity and the Media*, Allen & Unwin, Sydney, 1994, p. 71.

28 Geoffrey Blainey, *All For Australia*, Methuen, North Ryde, NSW, 1984.

29 Karen Lateo, 'The chips are down' *Woman's Day*, 2 Dec. 1996.

30 Catharine Lumby, 'Racial assumptions skin-deep' *Sydney Morning Herald*, 6 June, 1997.

31 Quoted in Brain Woodly, 'A cry from the bush' *Weekend Australian*, 18 January 1997. See also Nicholas Rothwell, 'Poetic justice' *Australian Magazine*, 10 May, 1997. Murray won the T.S. Eliot Prize with *Subhuman Redneck Poems*, Duffy & Snellgrove, Sydney, 1996. On Hunter poetry and Murray's connection with it, see Ross Bennett (ed.), *This Place: Poetry of the Hunter Valley*, Nimrod Publications, Newcastle, 1980, pp. 78–90, 152.

32 Les A. Murray, 'The Australian republic'. Also discussed here is 'The trade in images'. Both essays are in Les A. Murray, *A Working Forest: Selected Prose*, Duffy & Snellgrove, Sydney, 1997.

33 Percy Bysshe Shelley, 'A defence of poetry', in David Lee Clark (ed.), *Shelley's Prose*, 4th Estate, London, 1988, p. 282.

Acknowledgements

The first bunch of people I have to thank are the reviewers of my last book, *Virtual Geography*. Thanks for taking the trouble to read it, think about it, and offer some leads for corrections, revisions and developments of its lines of thought: R. Cathcart, John Conomos, Simon Cooper, David Cox, John Docker, Simon During, Mark Gibson, Ben Goldsmith, Noel Gough, Liz Jacka, Alan McKee, David Marshall, Ade Peace, Sally Singer, Mark Sinker, Gerald Toal, and Darren Tofts.

The Virtual Republic started life in the virtual republic of the press, so thanks first of all to Jane Richardson, who edits the *Higher Education Supplement* of the *Australian*, and Helen Trinca, who edits the *Opinion* page. Both have allowed me to contribute passing thoughts to the discussion of all of the 'public things' of this book. Thanks to Ashley Crawford and Ray Edgar: the pages of *World Art* and *21C* magazines have offered me space for longer essays, particularly on the media. Thanks to the editors of *Arena* magazine for challenging me to write something about culture. Thanks to Christina Thompson, editor of *Meanjin*, John McLaren at *Overland* and Morag Fraser at *Eureka St* for making space for me in their respective journals. The chapter on political correctness happened at the prompting of Susan Morris-Yates at ABC Books.

Two fine scholarly journals, *Media International Australia* and *Continuum* published parts of this material and gave me access to scrutiny from my academic peers. Everything has been rewritten and rewritten again since it first appeared—writing is not a thing, it's a process. I'm thankful to all of my editors for enabling me to write my drafts in public and benefit from their feedback and that of their respective readerships.

The producers of programs on ABC Radio National and on the regional and metro stations also provided me with valuable opportunities for talking about these issues. The talkback shows have been particularly enlightening. A special thanks to the hosts and producers of *Meridian*, *Late Night Live* and *Arts Today*, and a cheerio call to Mikey on the JJJ breakfast show.

Thanks to my agent Gaby Nahor at Hickson Associates, the proposal for *Virtual Republic* found its way to Sophie Cunningham, who was brave enough to put it in her trade list. Whatever the fate of this book, let's hope there's a future for the kind of serious Australian non-fiction of the kind that Sophie has been publishing at Allen & Unwin. Thanks to Emma Cotter for her editorial supervision and Margaret Falk for her very useful comments.

My students in media studies at Macquarie University have always been great people with whom to work out ideas. I'm particularly indebted to the MAS 201 and 301 print media classes of 1995 and 1996 and to fellow staff members Chris Chesher and Maria Stukoff. Together we made two books, *Media in the New Millennium* and *Sydney Inside Out*—I learned a lot about print media through teaching it. Students in the Masters in Media Technology and Law, and in the Masters in International Communication gave me the benefit of their wide experience in seminars on the public sphere and culture, at home and abroad. Thanks also to my colleagues in media studies, particularly former head of department Philip Bell. I learned a great deal from Philip, one of the pioneers of critical media studies in Australia.

A small grant from the Australian Research Council enabled me to get some of the research done. Thanks to Colin Hood for his always resourceful assistance with that. A Macquarie University Research Grant provided the one thing researchers in the humanities really need—time off. The Commonwealth Fund and the Literature Board of the Australia Council both chose not to support this project. Thanks all the same to my referees and assessors for all of my applications.

This book was finished while I was a visiting professor in American Studies at New York University. Thanks to Andrew Ross for making that possible. Sometimes writing requires a change of scene and a home away from home. Thanks to

ACKNOWLEDGEMENTS

Christen Clifford for making me at home in Brooklyn, New York. (*There are lines for you, not to follow but to feel, coming from within; not to speak but to sense, connecting in with out; not to dream but to be, becoming beauty of the virtual.*) Sometimes writing requires just leaving writing alone and hiding out for a while. Special thanks to Kaye Shumack and the sun on the water at Bondi. Thanks to Kathy Acker, who reminded me, and just when I needed it, what a writing life is and why it matters. And to my best mate, sparring partner, comrade, colleague, confidante and co-conspirator, Catharine Lumby, who always keeps me on my toes—*words fail me*.

The Virtual Republic is dedicated to my father, Ross Kenneth Wark. I designed it with you most in mind.

Kenneth McKenzie Wark
Brooklyn, New York
April 1997

Index